From Political to Economic Awakening in the Arab World

The Path of Economic Integration

MENA DEVELOPMENT REPORT

From Political to Economic Awakening in the Arab World

The Path of Economic Integration

A Trade and Foreign Direct Investment Report
for the Deauville Partnership

Jean-Pierre Chauffour

THE WORLD BANK
Washington, D.C.

Library of Congress Cataloging-in-Publication Data

From political to economic awakening in the Arab world : the path of economic integration.
        p. cm. — (MENA development reports)
    "A Trade and Foreign Direct Investment Report for the Deauville Partnership."
    Includes bibliographical references and index.
    ISBN 978-0-8213-9669-8 (alk. paper) — ISBN 978-0-8213-9670-4 (alk. paper)
    1. Arab countries—Foreign economic relations.   2. Arab countries—Commercial policy.   3. Arab countries—Commerce.   4. Investments, Foreign—Arab countries.   5. Middle East—Economic integration.   6. Middle East—Economic policy.   I. World Bank.
    HF1610.F76 2012
    337.1'174927—dc23

2012035605

Contents

Acknowledgments		**xiii**
About the Main Author		**xv**
Abbreviations		**xvii**
Overview		**1**
1	**Introduction**	**13**
2	**Adapting to a Changing Trade and FDI Landscape**	**37**
	A New International Context	38
	The Trade and FDI Landscape in Partnership Countries	43
	Notes	61
	References	62
3	**Improving Market Access and Regulations**	**65**
	Agriculture	66
	Manufacturing	79
	Services	98
	Energy	114
	Labor Mobility	122
	Regulatory Convergence	141
	Notes	154
	References	155
4	**Fostering Competitiveness and Diversification**	**163**
	The FDI Regime	164
	The Business Climate	180
	Economic Governance	195
	The Knowledge Economy	213
	Notes	225
	References	226

5   Facilitating Trade, Access to Trade Finance, and Remittances   231

Trade Facilitation   232
Trade Finance   248
Diaspora Engagement   262
Notes   275
References   277

6   Promoting Inclusiveness, Equity, and Sustainability   281

Social Policies   282
Regional Policies   289
Societal Policies   293
Notes   306
References   306

Appendix A   Potential for Diversification into More Sophisticated Products in Partnership Countries   311

Additional Sources Consulted   317

Boxes

1.1   How Does the Trade and FDI Engine Work?   18
1.2   The EU-Turkey Customs Union: A Model for Future
        Euro-Med Integration?   31
2.1   PTAs Involving the Arab World   46
2.2   Have the Export Baskets of the Partnership Countries
        Diversified Toward Higher-Value-Added Goods?   52
2.3   Trade and Investment Promotion, a Cornerstone of
        Partnership Countries' Action Plans   60
3.1   Improving the New Regional Convention on Pan-Euro-
        Mediterranean Rules of Origin   82
3.2   Measuring Nontariff Barriers   87
3.3   Services Trade Provisions in Partnership Country Trade
        Agreements   108
3.4   The Right Mix of Unilateral, Regional, and Multilateral
        Reforms to Further Integrate Partnership Countries into
        Regional and Global Services Markets   111
3.5   Comparative Advantage, Integration, and Technology:
        Solar Power from the Deserts of the MENA Region   118
3.6   The Migration Landscape around the Mediterranean Basin   124
3.7   The Resurgence of Old Migration Tools in the Euro-Med
        Context   134
3.8   Elements of Best Practice in Circular Migration Schemes
        in Canada and New Zealand   136

3.9   Bottlenecks and Areas of Progress in Implementation of the
      French-Tunisian Agreement   138
4.1   Jordan's Record in Privatization and Public-Private
      Partnerships   169
4.2   Competition Laws and Competition Agencies in
      Partnership Countries   185
5.1   The Logistics Performance Index   235
5.2   Trade Infrastructure in Partnership Countries   239
5.3   Status of Customs Reforms in Partnership Countries   241
5.4   Dealing with Increased Political Risks: MIGA's MENA
      Initiative   255
5.5   Islamic Development Bank Recommendations to Improve
      the Executive Program for Enhancing Intra-OIC Trade   257
5.6   The Scope for Developing Islamic Trade Finance
      Instruments   259
5.7   Reverse Factoring: The Case of NAFIN, Mexico's
      Development Bank   260
5.8   Defining Diasporas   263
5.9   Evidence on the Poverty Reduction Effects of the Diaspora
      in Partnership Countries   268
5.10 The Indian Diaspora and Development of the Indian
      IT Industry   274
6.1   An Overview of Social Policies in Partnership Countries   286
6.2   Jordan: Responding to a Sweatshop Scandal through
      Capacity Building and Monitoring   303

Figures

1.1   GDP per Capita Growth in Deauville Partnership Countries,
      1981–2010   20
1.2   Manufactures Exports as Share of Merchandise Exports in
      Deauville Partnership Countries, 1981–2010   20
1.3   FDI Inflows as Share of GDP in Deauville Partnership
      Countries, 1996–2010   21
1.4   Concentration Index of Merchandise Exports in Deauville
      Partnership Countries and Selected Comparators,
      1995–2011   22
1.5   Poverty Headcount Ratio at $1.25 per Day in Deauville
      Partnership Countries, 1991–2008   22
1.6   Gini Index in Deauville Partnership Countries, 1991–2008   23
1.7   Unemployment as Share of the Labor Force in Egypt,
      Morocco, and Tunisia, 1999–2008   23

1.8   Share of Unemployed with Tertiary Education in Morocco
      and Tunisia, 1995–2005   24
1.9   World Bank Governance Indicators for Deauville
      Partnership Countries, 1996–2010   24
1.10 GDP per Capita in Deauville Partnership Countries and
      Turkey, 1980–2010   26
2.1   Increase in Trade Integration, 1985–2010, and South–South
      Trade, 1990–2009   39
2.2   Evolution of Regional Shares of Global Exports, 1988–2008   43
2.3   Growth of Non-Oil Merchandise Exports in Value Terms
      by Types of Margin, Selected World Regions, 1998–2008   44
2.4   Export Share by Destination (Excluding Oil) for Maghreb
      and Mashreq Countries, 2000 and 2007   45
2.5   Distribution of MENA Trade by Region, 1998 and 2008   48
2.6   Export Coverage of Imports and Share of Exports in Total
      Trade of Deauville Partnership Countries, 1996–2010   50
2.7   Non-Oil Export Performance Relative to Potential,
      MENA Countries and Selected Comparators, 1998–2007   51
2.8   Index of Export Market Penetration in Tunisia, Morocco,
      and Selected Comparators, 1999 and 2008   53
2.9   FDI in MENA Countries, 1990–2010   54
2.10 Growth in Oil Prices and FDI Inflows to MENA,
      1992–2010   55
2.11 FDI Inflows and FDI-Related Jobs in MENA, by Sector,
      2003–11   56
2.12 Greenfield FDI Inflows to Deauville Partnership Countries
      as Shares of Total, 2003–11   57
2.13 FDI-Related Jobs in MENA Countries, 2003–11   58
B2.1.1 The Network of MENA Regional Agreements   47
B2.2.1 Productivity Content of Exports (EXPY) from Deauville
      Partnership Countries and East Asian Comparators,
      1980–2008   52
3.1   Market Access Overall Trade Restrictiveness Index, by
      Exporters and Markets, 2008–09   83
3.2   Changes in Tariffs by Region on Total Trade, Agriculture,
      and Manufacturing, 2008–09   84
3.3   Tariff-Only Trade Restrictiveness Index, by Region, 2008   84
3.4   NTM Frequency and Coverage Ratios in Tunisia, Morocco,
      and Selected Comparators   88
3.5   Cost of Morocco's Import Subsidies as Share of GDP and
      Current Expenditure   88
3.6   Frequency Ratios for Core NTMs in Selected MENA
      Countries, 2001 and 2010   89

3.7   Average Number of NTMs Imposed per Product in
        Selected MENA Countries and the European Union   90
3.8   NTM Incidence by Type of Trade (Intra-Regional vs.
        Total Trade)   91
3.9   Overall Trade Restrictiveness Index for Deauville
        Partnership Countries and Selected Regions, 2008   92
3.10 Services Trade Restrictiveness Index, by Region, 2008–11 103
3.11 Services Trade Restrictiveness Index, by Region and Sector,
        2008–11   103
3.12 Existing Commitments, Doha Offers, and Actual Policy, by
        Region   104
3.13 Trade in Services as a Share of GDP, Deauville Partnership
        Countries, 2002–10   105
3.14 Trade in Services Net Surplus, Deauville Partnership
        Countries and Lebanon, 2010   106
3.15 Travel and Transport Services as Shares of Total Services
        Exports, Deauville Partnership Countries and Selected
        Comparators, 2010   107
3.16 Insurance/Financial and Communications Services as Shares
        of Total Services Exports, Deauville Partnership Countries
        and Selected Comparators, 2010   107
3.17 Projected Change in Labor Force, 2005–50, by Country
        and Age Group, EU and MENA   125
3.18 Projected Change in Labor Force, 2005–50, by Age Group
        and Education Level, EU and MENA   126
3.19 Total Job Openings in the EU Due to Replacement and
        Expansion Demand, 2006–15   127
3.20 Employment Trends by Industry in the EU25, 2006 and
        2015   128
3.21 Levels and Growth of Employment by Occupation in the
        EU, 2006–15   128
3.22 Share of Unemployed Adults Who Hold a Tertiary
        Degree, Selected MENA and European Countries,
        2000 and 2010   129
4.1   Estimated Welfare Benefits of Trade Reforms in Tunisia
        and Morocco under Restrictive and Flexible Labor
        Markets   182
4.2   Investment Response to Policy Reforms in Selected Regions 186
4.3   Average Entry Density for Selected Emerging Economies,
        2004–09   187
4.4   Trends and Composition of Private Investment   190
4.5   Global Competitiveness Report Ratings for Deauville
        Partnership Countries, 2011–12   191

4.6   Integrated Index for Educational Access, Equity, Efficiency, and Quality in Selected MENA Countries   192

4.7   SME Loans as Share of Total Loans in Selected MENA Countries, 2009   193

4.8   Control of Corruption and per Capita Income, Selected Countries, 2009   198

4.9   Transparency International Corruption Perceptions Index for MENA Countries and Selected Comparators, 2011   199

4.10 Perceptions of Corruption in World Bank Enterprise Surveys, by Region   199

4.11 Ratings for MENA Countries and Comparator Countries on Global Integrity's Rule of Law Indicator   201

4.12 Ratings for MENA Countries and Comparators in Global Integrity's Executive Accountability Rankings, 2010   202

4.13 Ratings for Deauville Partnership Countries and Comparators on Economist Intelligence Unit's Democracy Index, 2011   203

4.14 Voice and Accountability vs. Competitiveness around the World   204

4.15 The Firm and Its Investment Climate: Rules and Policies and the Institutions That Implement Them   207

4.16 Performance of Deauville Partnership Countries and Comparators on the Knowledge Economy Index, by Component, 2011   216

5.1   Trade Costs for Industrial vs. Agricultural Goods Traded between Selected Maghreb and European Countries, 2007   234

5.2   LPI Scores for MENA Compared to Other Regions   236

5.3   LPI Scores for Deauville Partnership Countries Compared to MENA and the United Arab Emirates   237

5.4   LPI Component Scores for Deauville Partnership Countries Compared to MENA and the United Arab Emirates   237

5.5   Global Trade Finance Arrangements by Market Share, 2008   249

5.6   Constraints on Bank-Intermediated Trade Finance, by Country, 2010   252

5.7   Effect of the Recent Turmoil in MENA on Investment Plans in the Region, 2011   254

5.8   Effect of the Recent Turmoil in MENA on Perceptions of Political Risk in the Region, by Type of Risk, 2011   254

5.9   The International Remittances Agenda   270

6.1   Share of Firms Offering Formal Training in Egypt, Morocco, and Selected Comparators   287

6.2   Labor Force Participation Rates by Gender in the MENA
        Region, 2010 or Latest Data   294
6.3   Public Sector Employment as a Share of Total
        Employment, by Gender, in the MENA Region   295
A.1   Egypt: Product Space, 2007–09   312
A.2   Jordan: Product Space, 2007–09   313
A.3   Libya: Product Space, 2007–09   314
A.4   Morocco: Product Space, 2007–09   315
A.5   Tunisia: Product Space, 2007–09   316

Tables

2.1   Direction of Trade: Deauville Partnership Countries'
        Exports to and Imports from Selected Countries, 2000
        and 2008   49
2.2   Growth of Goods and Services Trade in Deauville
        Partnership Countries, 1996–2010   50
2.3   Top Investors in Deauville Partnership Countries   58
3.1   Role of the Agricultural Sector in Selected MENA
        Countries, 2010   68
3.2   Urban and Rural Poverty Rates in Egypt, Jordan, and
        Morocco, 2005–08   69
3.3   Measures of Food Import Dependence in Selected MENA
        Countries, 2010   75
3.4   Agricultural Land Resources in Selected MENA Countries,
        2009   77
3.5   Comparison of Selected WTO and PTA Liberalization
        Commitments   110
3.6   Share of Natural Gas in Total Primary Energy Supply of
        Deauville Partnership Countries, 1980–2008   120
3.7   Competition and Efficiency in the Food and Textile
        Industries in Deauville Partnership Countries, 2007 or
        Latest Available Data   144
3.8   PTAs with MENA Countries Containing Government
        Procurement Provisions   148
4.1   Inward FDI Flows to Deauville Partnership Countries,
        2004–10   166
4.2   Inward FDI Potential Index, Deauville Partnership
        Countries, 1990–2009   167
4.3   Inward FDI Performance Index, Selected Countries,
        1990–2010   171
4.4   Doing Business Rankings for Deauville Partnership
        Countries, 2011   188

4.5   Averages and Dispersion (Coefficients of Variation) of
      Firms' Days Waiting for Regulatory Services in Jordan,
      Morocco, and Selected Comparators   189
4.6   Leading Constraints, by Country, from the World Bank's
      Investment Climate Survey (ICS) and the World
      Economic Forum's Global Competitiveness Report (GCR)
      Executive Opinion Survey   194
B4.2.1 Competition Laws and Agencies in Deauville Partnership
      Countries   185
5.1   Costs of Bilateral Trade in Industrial Products between
      Selected Trade Partners in the Mediterranean Region,
      2007   234
5.2   Shipping Connectivity (LSCI) and Logistics Performance
      (LPI) in Selected MENA and European Countries,
      2010 and 2012   238
5.3   Ease of Trading across Borders, MENA Countries, 2012   238
5.4   Moody's Credit Ratings for Deauville Partnership Countries,
      2007, 2010, and 2011   252
5.5   Top Destinations of Migrants from Deauville Partnership
      Countries, 2010   264
5.6   Total Remittances to Deauville Partnership Countries,
      2010   265
5.7   Top Sources of Remittances to Deauville Partnership
      Countries, 2010   267
5.8   Costs of Sending Remittances to Deauville Partnership
      Countries, Third Quarter 2011   269
6.1   Rate of Long-Term Unemployment among the
      Unemployed, by Education and Gender, in Jordan,
      the Arab Republic of Egypt, and Tunisia   296
6.2   Legal Restrictions on Women in MENA Countries   297
6.3   Examples of Human Rights in Preferential Trade Agreements:
      Comparing the European Free Trade Association, the
      European Union, the United States, and Canada   305
A.1   Egypt: RCA for Selected Products with Highest Export
      Share, 2000–02 and 2007–09   312
A.2   Jordan: RCA for Selected Products with Highest Export
      Share, 2000–02 and 2007–09   313
A.3   Libya: RCA for Selected Products with Highest Export
      Share, 2000–02 and 2007–09   314
A.4   Morocco: RCA for Selected Products with Highest Export
      Share, 2000–02 and 2007–09   315
A.5   Tunisia: RCA for Selected Products with Highest Export
      Share, 2000–02 and 2007–09   316

Acknowledgments

The main author of this book is Jean-Pierre Chauffour. The core team of authors includes Elena Ianchovichina and Bob Rijkers (trade and FDI landscape), Nicholas Minot and Julian Lampietti (agriculture), Olivier Cadot and Mariem Malouche (manufacturing), Husam Mohamed Beides and Hayat Taleb Al-Harazi (energy), Olivier Cattaneo (services), Manjula Luthria and Yann Pouget (labor mobility), Khalid Sekkat (regulatory convergence), Joseph Battat (FDI regime), Andrew Stone (business climate), Fabian Seiderer (economic governance), Zeine Ould Zeidane and Jean Eric Aubert (knowledge economy), Jean-François Arvis (trade facilitation), Frederic Trahin (customs), Rami Abdelkafi and Salim Refas (trade finance), and Sonia Plaza and Dilip Ratha (remittances), under the supervision of Manuela Ferro and Bernard Funck.

Other contributors who provided inputs to the various chapters or research assistance include Patricia Augier and Julien Gourdon (nontariff measures), Abdelmoula Ghzala (trade facilitation), Guenter Heidenhof (governance), Nicholas Jones (regulatory convergence), Hiau Looi Kee (trade indicators), William Peter Mako (business climate), Paul Barbour (political risks), Marc Tobias Schiffbauer and Hania Sahnoun (product space analysis), and Thomas Walker (gender issues). Hania Sahnoun and Talajeh Livani provided the overall research assistance and data analysis, Muna Abeid Salim was in charge of professional administrative support, and Catherine Sunshine edited the book.

The book was coordinated by the Center for Mediterranean Integration (CMI), drawing on the expertise of the World Bank and in partnership with the Islamic Development Bank and other specialized institutions, including the World Customs Organization and the International Food Policy Research Institute.

The book benefited from the overall guidance of Inger Andersen, vice president of the World Bank's Middle East and North Africa (MENA) Region, as well as Caroline Freund, Mats Karlsson, and Jonathan Walters. An Advisory Committee, including Rami Abdelkafi (Islamic Devel-

opment Bank), Patricia Augier (Université de la Méditerranée), Uri Da-
dush (Carnegie Endowment for International Peace), Ahmed Ghoneim
(Economic Research Forum and Cairo University), Pierre Jacquet
(Agence Française de Développement), Cécile Jolly (Méditerranée 2030
Prospective Group), Riad al Kouri (Erbil University), Pedro de Lima
(European Investment Bank), Jean-Louis Reiffers (Femise), Raed Safadi
(OECD), Sübidey Togan (Bilkent University), and Frédéric Trahin
(World Customs Organization), provided guidance at the concept stage
and comments on the final draft.

The book benefited from comments from peer reviewers Bernard
Hoekman and Jeff Lewis, as well as from other reviewers including Carlos
Alberto Braga, Kevin Carey, Ndiame Diop, Caroline Freund, Steen Lau
Jorgensen, Julia Nielson, Mustapha Rouis, Fabian Seiderer, and Jonathan
Walters.

The book was prepared in consultation with the authorities of the
Deauville Partnership and other public and private stakeholders who provided input into its production, including in the course of consultations
in Abu Dhabi, Amman, Ankara, Brussels, Cairo, Marseille, Paris, Rabat,
Riyadh, Tunis, and Washington, DC.

Stephen McGroarty, Paola Scalabrin, Rick Ludwick, and Nora Ridol-
phin of the World Bank's Office of the Publisher managed typesetting
and production.

The team would like to thank all of those who contributed and participated in the various stages of production of this book, including those
whose names may have been inadvertently omitted.

About the Main Author

Jean-Pierre Chauffour is lead economist and regional trade coordinator in the World Bank's Middle East and North Africa Region, where he works on regionalism, competitiveness, and economic integration issues. Prior to joining the World Bank in 2007, he spent 15 years at the International Monetary Fund, where he held various positions, including mission chief in the African Department and representative to the World Trade Organization and United Nations in Geneva. Mr. Chauffour has extensive economic policy experience and has worked in many areas of the developing world, most extensively in Africa, the Middle East, and Eastern Europe. He holds master's degrees in Economics and Money, Banking, and Finance from the Panthéon-Sorbonne University in Paris. He is the author of *The Power of Freedom: Uniting Human Rights and Development* (Cato Institute, 2009) and has recently co-edited two books: *Preferential Trade Agreement Policies for Development: a Handbook* (World Bank, 2011) and *Trade Finance during the Great Trade Collapse* (World Bank, 2011).

Abbreviations

ACAA	Agreement on Conformity Assessment and Acceptance of Industrial Products
AML/CFT	Anti-money laundering/combating the financing of terrorism
AMU	Arab Maghreb Union
ANETI	Agence Nationale pour l'Emploi et le Travail Indépendant (Tunisia)
ASEAN	Association of Southeast Asian Nations
ASYCUDA	Automated Systems for Customs Data (UNCTAD)
BIT	Bilateral investment treaty
BoP	Balance of payments
BPO	Business process outsourcing
BRIC	Brazil, Russia, India, and China
CEE	Central and Eastern Europe
COMESA	Common Market for Eastern and Southern Africa
Comtrade	Commodity Trade Statistics Database (United Nations)
CSP	Concentrated solar power
CUD	EU-Turkey Customs Union Decision
DCFTA	Deep and Comprehensive Free Trade Area
DTT	Double taxation treaty
ECI	Eight-Country Interconnection
EFTA	European Free Trade Association
EIU	Economist Intelligence Unit
EPA	Export promotion agency
EU	European Union
EXPY	Productivity content of exports
FDI	Foreign direct investment
FTA	Free trade agreement

G8	Group of Eight (Canada, France, Germany, Italy, Japan, Russia, United Kingdom, United States)
GAM	Global Approach to Migration
GATS	General Agreement on Trade in Services
GCC	Gulf Cooperation Council
GCR	Global Competitiveness Report
GDP	Gross domestic product
GPA	Government Procurement Agreement (WTO)
GVC	Global value chain
HRSDC	Human Resources and Skills Development Canada
HS	Harmonized System (WCO)
IAB	Investing Across Borders (World Bank)
ICS	Investment Climate Survey (World Bank)
ICT	Information and communication technology
IT	Information technology
IEMP	Index of export market penetration
IFC	International Finance Corporation
ILO	International Labour Organization
IPA	Investment promotion agency
ISO	International Organization for Standardization
IT	Information technology
KE	Knowledge economy
KPO	Knowledge process outsourcing
LDC	Less developed countries
LFPR	Labor force participation rates
LNG	Liquefied natural gas
LPI	Logistics Performance Index (World Bank)
LSCI	Liner Shipping Connectivity Index (UNCTAD)
M&E	Monitoring and evaluation
MA-OTRI	Market Access Overall Trade Restrictiveness Index
MAST	Multi-Agency Support Team
MENA	Middle East and North Africa Region (World Bank)
MENA TIP	Middle East/North Africa Trade and Investment Partnership
MFN	Most favored nation
MIGA	Multilateral Investment Guarantee Agency
MMBtu	Million metric British thermal units
MRA	Mutual recognition agreement
MSME	Micro, small, and medium enterprise
NAFIN	Nacional Financiera (Mexico)
NAFTA	North American Free Trade Agreement
n.e.s.	Not elsewhere specified
NTM	Nontariff measure

OECD	Organisation for Economic Co-operation and Development
OIC	Organisation of Islamic Cooperation
OFII	Office for Immigration and Integration (France)
OTRI	Overall Trade Restrictiveness Index
PAFTA	Pan-Arab Free Trade Area
PISA	Programme for International Student Assessment
PPP	Purchasing power parity
PTA	Preferential trade agreement
R&D	Research and development
RCA	Revealed comparative advantage
RIA	Regulatory impact assessment
SAR	Special administrative region
SAWP	Seasonal Agricultural Workers Program (Canada)
SME	Small and medium enterprise
SPS	Sanitary and phytosanitary
SSA	Sub-Saharan Africa
STRI	Services Trade Restrictiveness Index
TFP	Total factor productivity
TIMSS	Trends in International Mathematics and Science Study
TIR	International Road Transport (Transports Internationaux Routiers)
TRI	Trade Restrictiveness Index
TTRI	Tariff-only Trade Restrictiveness Index
UNCTAD	United Nations Conference on Trade and Development
USAID	United States Agency for International Development
WCO	World Customs Organization
WEF	World Economic Forum
WTO	World Trade Organization

Note: All dollar amounts are U.S. dollars unless otherwise stated.

Overview

The forces unleashed by the Arab political awakening have the power to be transformational. One critical parameter of success will be whether the Arab political awakening is accompanied by a concurrent economic awakening. Such an economic awakening would need to generate quality employment for the millions of young men and women who are looking for jobs and a decent life. In most Arab countries, it has become evident that the development paradigm of the past can not achieve the qualitative and inclusive growth expected by the population. The Deauville Partnership launched by the Group of 8 (G8) Heads of State in Deauville, France, in May 2011 to support the historic political and economic transformation under way in the Middle East and North Africa (MENA) region is thus strategic and timely. The "Deauville partners" include Canada, France, Germany, Italy, Japan, Kuwait, Qatar, Russia, Saudi Arabia, Turkey, the United Arab Emirates, the United Kingdom, the United States, and nine associated international and regional financial institutions. All have expressed their commitment to support the "Partnership countries" currently engaged in political and economic transformation: the Arab Republic of Egypt, Jordan, Libya, Morocco, and Tunisia.

Economic integration through increased trade and foreign direct investment (FDI) is one key means available to policy makers in the short to medium term to put the Partnership countries on a higher path of sustainable economic growth and in a position to decisively tackle the problem of unemployment, especially youth unemployment. In Jordan, for instance, more than 70 percent of the unemployed are under 29 years old. Economic integration, both unilateral and in a regional cooperation context, has proven to be a key ingredient of development in many emerging economies. High-performing countries, that is, countries that have grown at an average rate of 7 percent or more a year for 25 years or longer since 1950, used the global economy to increase productivity through trade, FDI, technology flows, and migration. All engaged in and tried to make the most of the global economy, not to push the technological frontier but to catch up with existing technology and knowledge—a much more manageable task. In choosing such a development path, including a reform process of regulatory convergence with the European Union (EU), Turkey has been able to create more than 3 million new jobs since the mid-2000s. Through trade and investment, Deauville partners can therefore help newly democratizing Arab countries embark on inclusive export-led growth and achieve their objectives in two main ways: by effectively expanding market opportunities and by supporting the public policy and regulatory reforms that would be necessary to reap the benefits of greater integration into global markets.

To be sure, skepticism abounds in the region over the merits of trade, FDI, and the integrity of the private sector in light of "crony capitalism," where the benefits of past policies are perceived to have accrued to only a well-connected few. There are legitimate concerns over income and wealth inequalities. Many areas within the MENA region are lagging behind. Unemployment rates, especially for youth and women, are skyrocketing. New leaders are understandably preoccupied with pressing domestic political and institutional matters. There is the urgency of economic stabilization in a very difficult global economic environment. The eurozone crisis is hitting oil importers in the region hard. Managing expectations and the political economy of reforms in this transition period appears more daunting than ever before. The dominant concern in the region at the moment, therefore, is not economic integration—even if a new momentum for increased intra-Arab integration is perceptible. Yet greater integration of MENA's economies, and of the countries undergoing transition, will need to be part of any sustainable and inclusive economic recovery. An absolute priority for the Deauville Partnership is to help all stakeholders maintain the long view and to do no harm.

One implication of the emergence of global value chains as well as the experience of Partnership countries with past reforms is that the trade and investment policy agenda increasingly goes beyond the traditional domain of trade ministries to include many domestic behind-the-border policies and regulations. A corollary is that this new agenda spans a wide range of public policy areas that are the responsibility of other parts of government, including a variety of regulatory agencies. When an economic opening is not accompanied by domestic reforms to promote competition and transparency in the domestic market, by the reallocation of factors through market flexibility, and by the adjustment of relative prices, the effect is often to displace rents rather than reduce them. Under such circumstances, the gains from economic liberalization can be captured by a well-connected few. In the same vein, the benefits of economic opening cannot be fully reaped if the design and governance of public policies, including sectoral policies, distort economic decisions and stifle competition. A new integration strategy through trade and FDI should therefore show a clear break from the past. Such a strategy will need to confront political and political economy challenges, both from vested interests that benefit from markets not open to greater competition and from groups that have an instinctive resistance to inward FDI and greater imports. It should only support public policies that are designed and governed to foster growth and welfare.

Leadership is needed in both Partnership countries and Deauville partners to provide a credible long-term vision and explain the mutual benefits of economic integration. One such powerful vision could be the pursuit of a partnership aimed at gradually promoting four key freedoms in the Mediterranean and beyond: the free movement of goods, services, capital, and eventually persons. Trade and migration in the economic space encompassing the European Union, Turkey, the Balkans, the Maghreb, the Mashreq, and the Arabic peninsula has been happening for millennia. Now is the time to recognize these links across the Mediterranean and build bridges aimed at forging a common destiny. The vision of a common Mediterranean economic space, if offered, could provide both the framework and motivation for implementing difficult policy reforms in Partnership countries. In the current uncertain global economic environment, the ability of leaders to offer a transcendent, outward-oriented vision is certainly constrained; yet it will determine the chances for growth and prosperity in the Mediterranean region. The benefits could go beyond the immediate economic returns, serving to promote common human values, peace, and stability.

Deauville partners share with Partnership countries the responsibility for offering a clear, understandable, and ambitious vision for the Arab people as they pursue their democratic transition. The vision would be to help integrate the Partnership countries into the world economy, including through the creation of a common economic space spanning the two rims of the Mediterranean and embracing the Gulf Cooperation Council (GCC) countries as well. While each partner or group of partners will naturally continue to pursue detailed trade and investment discussions on a bilateral basis, the Deauville Partnership could be an instrument of increased synergy and coherence to help expand market access, lower barriers to trade and investment, and promote increased integration among partners.

- The European Union could deepen its trade relationships with the Arab Republic of Egypt, Jordan, Morocco, and Tunisia, developed under the Association Agreements and the European Neighbourhood Policy, with the effective implementation of the proposed Deep and Comprehensive Free Trade Areas (DCFTAs). DCFTAs will be comprehensive agreements on trade and economic relations covering a full range of regulatory areas of mutual interest, such as trade facilitation, technical barriers to trade, sanitary and phytosanitary measures, investment protection, public procurement, and competition policy.

- In a coordinated and coherent approach, and on the basis of both its process of accession to the EU and its growing political and economic influence in the region, Turkey could similarly deepen its existing Association Agreements with each Partnership country to foster trade and investment in the agricultural and services sectors and promote labor mobility. This could build on Turkey's recently signed memorandums of understanding with Tunisia and Libya.

- The GCC could strengthen its relationship with Egypt and Tunisia in the framework of a deepened cooperation with the Agadir Agreement (Jordan and Morocco have already been officially invited to join the GCC). This would allow citizens of member countries to enjoy equal rights and privileges, including the rights to move, settle, and work; receive social protection, retirement, health, education, and social services; and engage in various economic activities and services. This greater integration between the GCC and Partnership countries would need to be coordinated with the ongoing negotiations on a EU-GCC free trade agreement (FTA) covering all areas of trade relations, notably fisheries and industrial and agricultural goods.

- Consistent and in coordination with initiatives being undertaken by the EU and other Deauville partners, the United States could (a) increase the value of its existing agreements with Jordan and Morocco, and (b) invite Tunisia and, once the appropriate circumstances are in place, Egypt and Libya to enter into free trade agreements as well. These actions would be part of the proposed Middle East/North Africa Trade and Investment Partnership (MENA TIP), which will include a broad set of arrangements designed to increase job creation, trade, and investment between and among the United States and countries in the region.

- Other G8 members could contribute in a similar manner. Canada's completed FTA with Jordan and parallel agreements on the environment and labor cooperation could enter into force, and the FTA negotiations with Morocco could be completed as soon as feasible. Canada could also launch similar negotiations with Tunisia and, once the conditions are in place, with Egypt and Libya. The Russia-Arab Cooperation Forum and bilateral intergovernmental commissions could be further leveraged to strengthen relations between Russia and Arab countries in the economic, financial, and investment sectors. Similarly,

Japan could further strengthen the Japan-Arab Economic Forum and Japan's investment agreements with Partnership countries.

- Deauville partners could also help promote intra-Arab regional integration and integration of Partnership countries into global markets. The Agadir Agreement between Egypt, Jordan, Morocco, and Tunisia could be deepened, and Libya could receive the necessary support to join the World Trade Organization (WTO).

To signal their determination to pursue a coherent, ambitious, and credible vision in support of the political and economic transition of Partnership countries, the main Deauville partners could join forces to announce commitments in six areas with high immediate job-creating potential. Those six areas and the various recommendations of the report, including their prioritization and sequencing, were identified following a consultation process with most of the countries and partners concerned.

- Agriculture. Improve Partnership countries' access to the agricultural, processed agricultural, and fisheries markets of Deauville partners, particularly for fruits, vegetables, and olive oil. Steps would include the progressive abolition of quotas, reference prices, seasonal restrictions, domestic and export subsidies, and other nontariff barriers to agricultural trade.

- Manufacturing. Negotiate mutual recognition agreements, such as Agreements on Conformity Assessment and Acceptance of Industrial Products, between Partnership countries and Deauville partners to reduce the market fragmentation effect of technical barriers to trade. This is especially relevant in priority sectors that account for a large part of Partnerships countries' exports and employment, such as mechanical and electric industries and construction materials.

- Services. Negotiate between Partnership countries and Deauville partners specific sectoral commitments on labor mobility, especially for skilled workers, as part of Mode 4 on the movement of persons in future deep and high-quality trade agreements with Deauville partners.

- Energy. Negotiate a multilateral agreement on solar energy imports from the Middle East and North Africa that will govern how the parties share the burden of paying for the incremental cost of solar imports. (European subsidies for renewable energy could be made available for imports, with appropriate adjustments.) The agreement could be concluded initially between Morocco and interested EU member states, such as Germany, Spain, France, Italy, and perhaps others. Other Partnership countries could also be invited to join the agreement, depending on how fast they move with concentrated solar power projects.

- Migration. Launch labor Mobility Partnerships or similar mobility schemes between Partnership countries and Deauville partners, including visa facilitation for some categories of workers, readmission, concerted border management, and easier access to the job market of the Deauville partners, especially for less-skilled workers from Partnership countries.

- Intra-Arab integration. Adopt and implement simpler and more liberal rules of origin in preferential trade agreements between Partnership countries and Deauville partners, including an improved EU regional convention on preferential Pan-Euro-Mediterranean rules of origin.

The implementation of far-reaching domestic reforms in Partnership countries would be critical to effectively reap the growth and employment opportunities offered by greater economic integration and regulatory convergence with the most advanced economies. In facing and adapting to a rapidly changing trade and investment landscape, Partnership countries have all recognized and emphasized the importance of taking a new comprehensive approach to trade and investment in their competitiveness and development strategies. Trade and investment were at the core of the countries' action plans submitted at the G8 Finance Ministers' Meeting in Marseille in September 2011 to boost inclusive growth, employment, and productivity. To further enhance trade and FDI and to achieve the vision of an Arab world more integrated into global markets, the trade and commerce pillar of the Deauville Partnership could therefore focus on four overarching priority areas of reforms and support: (a) improve market access opportunities and market regulations; (b) foster competitiveness, diversification, and employment; (c) facilitate trade and mobilize trade finance and diaspora resources; and (d) promote the inclusiveness, equity, and sustainability of the structural transformation brought about by the process of integration. These are discussed briefly below.

Market Access Opportunities and Market Regulations

The ability of the Partnership countries to use trade and FDI to advance their development objectives depends in part on the market access conditions that confront their exports and on the policies affecting their imports of goods and services. On both fronts, the Deauville Partnership could help lower trade and investment costs, spur economic growth and employment, and promote the economic integration of Partnership countries—with each other, with regional partners, and with the G8 countries. Rules and discipline are key to market access opportunities that are predictable, transparent, and nondiscriminatory. There are six priorities for the Deauville Partnership in this area:

- Improve market access for agricultural products and encourage investment to upgrade sanitary and phytosanitary standards, promote agricultural research and extension, and deliver efficient irrigation services. As a significant first step, Morocco could expect to export an additional 58,700 tons of tomatoes and 13,600 tons of olive oil per year once the agriculture agreement recently signed with the EU enters into force.

- Reduce tariffs on manufactured goods; streamline unnecessary nontariff measures to reduce trade compliance costs, red tape, and discretion; adopt liberal rules of origin; and upgrade industrial norms and standards, testing, and certification procedures. There is much scope for expanding trade in goods in the region. Excluding petroleum exports, the MENA region, with over 400 million people, exports roughly the same amount as Switzerland.

- Enable services trade to move up the value chain by fostering services liberalization and regulatory reforms, improving regional connectivity and cooperation, and supporting the presence of global services providers. A study conducted in India estimated that a one-standard-deviation increase in the aggregate index of services liberalization resulted in a productivity increase of 11.7 percent for domestic firms and 13.2 percent for foreign enterprises.

- Promote solar energy exports, including through a multilateral agreement concluded in the near term between interested EU and MENA countries and providing for nondiscriminatory market access for concentrated solar power exported from MENA to those EU countries. Over the medium term, expand transmission infrastructure, synchronize power grids, and open up predictable access to transmission systems. Based on solar exports to Europe, manufacturing of concentrated solar power equipment in the Partnership countries could eventually create more than 80,000 jobs and demonstrate the impact of market access, technology transfer, and diversification.

- Formulate comprehensive labor mobility strategies and open a sensible dialogue on ways to achieve a mutually beneficial increase in labor mobility through new mobility schemes (South-North but also North-South), especially for less-skilled workers, based on an incentive-compatible design under the principle of shared responsibility. Nothing separates an individual from the benefits of development so much as the lack of a work visa. Canada's Seasonal Agricultural Workers

Program builds on bilateral agreements to bring about 20,000 workers from Mexico, Central America, and the Caribbean annually to do seasonal work on Canadian farms for up to eight months.

- Promote the process of regulatory convergence of norms and standards and other behind-the-border regulations related to competition policy, government procurement, and other trade- and FDI-enhancing aspects of the regulatory environment. For an average developing country like Morocco, where government spends about 15 percent of its national income on goods and services, a 10 percent saving on procurement contracts is equivalent to 1.5 percent of gross domestic product (GDP)—an amount that often exceeds the total amount of aid received. Partnership countries can benefit from the experience of countries that have adopted, in part or in full, the rules and legislation governing the EU Single Market. These include Turkey's experience in developing the EU-Turkey Customs Union and the creation by Central and Eastern European countries of dedicated institutional mechanisms to drive regulatory harmonization.

Competitiveness, Diversification, and Employment

An important reason that Partnership countries have not been able to save and invest in the future as much as the more successful emerging economies is an overall lack of competitiveness and diversification. Competitiveness is central to harnessing private sector growth for sustainable employment, poverty reduction, and, ultimately, wealth creation. Firms, especially small- and medium-size ones, serving export and domestic markets in all sectors cannot exploit opportunities if they are burdened by costs outside their control that make them uncompetitive. Increasing the number and value of products produced, the number of markets served, and the survival rate of firms is conditional on lowering such costs. And Partnership countries need investment now. This requires economy-wide policies and regulations aimed at creating the proper business environment and investment climate, including trade policy (restrictions on imports and FDI); trade in services as a new means to access international best practices and expand exports; and the design and implementation of specific actions to address market and information failures. There are four priorities for the Deauville Partnership in this area, including absolute priority for the recommendations aimed at attracting FDI and fostering domestic investment:

- Strengthen the FDI regime by phasing out de jure and de facto restrictions on foreign equity participation in most economic sectors; by simplifying and rationalizing investment regimes; easing access to production factors (industrial land, foreign exchange, and expatriate workers); by completing privatization programs; and by launching negotiations with Deauville partners on investment. For example, privatization and other reforms in the telecommunications sector in Jordan in the mid-2000s generated 25,000 additional jobs.

- Improve the domestic business climate by fostering competition and limiting opportunities for rent seeking; by building strong rule-bound market institutions to reduce discretion and opacity; and by promoting new institutional dialogue among stakeholders on the design, implementation, and evaluation of policies. Barriers to the process of "creative destruction" in Partnership countries are enormous. The average age of firms in the MENA region is almost 10 years older than the average for firms in East Asia or Eastern Europe. Croatia's working-age population is comparable in size to Jordan's, but the average number of newly registered firms in Croatia was almost five times higher in 2004–09.

- Address structural economic governance issues by fighting corruption, discretion, and the uneven implementation of policies; by restoring voice, accountability, and checks and balances; by strengthening the rule of law and the level playing field; and by promoting transparency through freedom of information. Jordan is the first MENA country that is a member of the Open Government Partnership, which includes 55 countries around the world. The other Deauville Partnership countries should seek to meet the eligibility criteria of fiscal transparency, access to information, assets disclosure, and citizen engagement as soon as possible.

- Foster the four pillars of a knowledge economy aimed in the first instance at catch-up growth (i.e., imitation) by harnessing more technological spillovers from existing and future FDI; by launching a major overhaul of education systems, including effective vocational training programs; by developing comprehensive knowledge and innovation strategies; and by further diffusing information and communication technologies. Romania, which competes with Morocco in offshoring, has nine times the international bandwidth capacity per capita.

Trade Facilitation, Trade Finance, and Remittances

Tackling costs associated with inefficient trade facilitation and logistics and weak access to trade finance and remittances is central to further integration of Partnership countries, both regionally and globally. The

costs of "connectivity" are often fixed, and as a result they disproportionately affect small firms, farmers, and the poor, severely limiting
their participation in trade and investment. Reducing the costs associated with moving goods along international supply chains, whether
these costs are measured in terms of time, money, or reliability, is a core
element of a trade and FDI agenda. Such costs are also partly determined by access to and pricing of trade finance and associated export
credit insurance products. This factor has become more important for
Partnership countries' exporters, especially small and medium enterprises (SMEs), since the recent crisis, as higher financing costs are expected to prevail in the medium term. There are three Deauville Partnership priorities in this area:

- Modernize trade facilitation services by enhancing the performance of
  trade corridors, whether air, sea, or land, and network infrastructure
  for energy and telecommunications; by improving markets for logistics services; by increasing the efficiency of border management, including customs; and by facilitating the cross-border movement of
  service suppliers. Container dwell times in Morocco or Tunisia are
  about a week, compared to four days in Malaysia and two and a half
  days in Shanghai. Trade logistics costs can be as high as 26 percent of
  the product price for Jordanian potatoes and 15 percent for Egyptian
  garments.

- Improve access to affordable trade finance and related insurance and
  guarantee products for SMEs, including Islamic finance; build the
  technical capacity of both SMEs and financial institutions in the management of trade finance at all transaction stages; and develop new
  interfirm finance products, such as factoring. Only 20 percent of SMEs
  in MENA have a loan or line of credit, a significantly lower share than
  in all other regions except Sub-Saharan Africa.

- Harness the remittances, technology and skills transfer, and investment of workers abroad by strengthening engagement with the
  diasporas, using government institutions such as embassies and consulates; by mobilizing diaspora savings through the issuance of
  targeted financial instruments, such as diaspora bonds; and by establishing more dedicated diaspora programs to promote development
  in the origin countries. The intra-regional movement of people
  dwarfs the movement of goods in the Arab world. Diaspora remittances sent to Jordan and Egypt from other Arab countries are 40 to
  190 percent higher than trade revenues between these and other
  Arab countries.

Inclusiveness, Equity, and Sustainability

The process of integration—like the process of change brought about by technological progress—benefits society at large, but it also generates winners and losers. To be sustainable, the political economy of trade and FDI requires that the benefits of integration, which are often concentrated in the large cities and among the more privileged sectors of the population, be shared as widely as possible across regions and people. Addressing and dealing effectively with the short-run distribution effects of opening up and technological upgrading will probably be the most critical social challenge facing Partnership countries in the coming years. Trade and FDI are more than simple exchanges of material goods and services: they have to do with people and their expectations, norms, and values. Trade partners need to recognize the possible tensions between those norms, as they relate for instance to women's rights, labor rights, or other human rights, and find ways to ease these tensions over time. There are three priorities for the Deauville Partnership in this area:

- Target social policies to help the most vulnerable people manage trade- and FDI-related shocks, address the needs of the unemployed during transition periods, and retrain workers in sectors that lose as a result of integration. In Partnership countries, the rich tend to receive a larger share of consumption subsidies in absolute terms than the poor, especially gas and water subsidies. In Jordan, the poor receive only about 11 percent of total subsidies.

- Develop regional policies to connect lagging and remote areas to urban centers, promote internal trade, and help poor people in these areas connect to the places where opportunities are concentrated. In Morocco and Tunisia, only about 40 percent of the population lives within two kilometers of an all-weather road.

- Promote common societal policies in trade and investment rules, including in the areas of women's rights, labor rights, and other human rights. Female labor force participation rates in Egypt, Jordan, and Morocco are about half that of Indonesia.

Conclusion

In each of these four priority areas—market access, competitiveness, trade facilitation, and inclusiveness—the attached report recommends a number of steps that Partnership countries could consider implementing

in the short and medium term with the support of their Deauville partners. While the report focuses on the challenges that are largely common
to all five Partnership countries, it does not propose a single blueprint.
Heterogeneity across countries and industries implies that there is no
one-size-fits-all approach and that all partners need to be willing to learn
and adapt to the local social and political processes most conducive to
their long-term objectives. While the recommended policy actions are
prioritized and sequenced in each of the four priority areas, the areas
themselves are essentially complementary in their effects and so offer few
opportunities for trade-offs. Governments need to tackle the formidable
list of policies that would need to accompany greater openness, often with
limited administrative capacities. The onus is on the G8 and other Deauville partners—notably the international and financial institutions involved—to provide the necessary technical assistance, capacity building,
and financial resources to support the Partnership countries individually
and as a group in their own reform efforts.

The comprehensiveness of the proposed integration strategy is also
designed to facilitate its political feasibility and acceptance. Although any
single efficiency-enhancing reform may hurt a particular group or individual, once it is part of a broad and comprehensive reform agenda, the
potential negative effects of reform tend to cancel out each other, making
everyone a winner. A focus of the Deauville Partnership should therefore
be to support the establishment of credible domestic public-private consultative mechanisms to identify the difficulties faced by exporters, investors, and other economic actors in the expansion of their activities and
propose broad and comprehensive solutions to these difficulties. The
building of strong and influential pro-reform constituencies that can ad-
vocate change, including by promoting jobs and inclusion, will be a critical determinant of the Arab economic awakening. The Deauville Partnership itself could become a supranational mechanism to coordinate
integration initiatives, help deal with possible negative externalities, and
promote regional public goods and the commons. This may also be a way
to unify the three pillars of the partnership: the trade and commerce pillar
would converge with the governance and finance pillars to support the
democratic transition and homegrown strategies for sustainable growth
and employment.

CHAPTER 1

Introduction

The forces unleashed by the Arab political awakening have the power to be transformational. In a number of countries, formerly disfranchised citizens have started to reclaim their basic rights and dignity and have voiced their demand for a new social contract, underpinned by the principles of freedom and open governance and by a more inclusive socioeconomic development strategy. Whether the Arab Spring will give birth to vibrant, long-lasting democracies that promote peace, security, and all fundamental freedoms remains to be seen. The result will not be known for years, perhaps even decades. The revolutions in Tunisia and the Arab Republic of Egypt exposed the structural deficiencies in the countries' governance structures and highlighted the weaknesses of the previous development model, which was unable to provide economic opportunities to all citizens, in particular jobs for educated youth.

One critical parameter of success will be whether the Arab political awakening is accompanied by a concurrent economic awakening. Economic conditions in the fragile nascent democracies, perhaps more than any other factor, will determine the fate of the Arab Spring. Freeing the entrepreneurial spirit, moving from privileges to merit, and establishing fair and transparent rules of the game are preconditions for unlocking private sector–led growth and employment. In the aftermath of the Arab Spring, countries in the Middle East and North Africa (MENA) region have an unprecedented window of opportunity in which to transform their governance structures and development strategies by implementing comprehensive institutional reforms, both economic and political.

In most Arab countries, it has become evident that the development paradigm of the past cannot achieve the qualitative and inclusive growth expected by the population. A singular failure of the Arab world is that it has been unsuccessful in developing a strong private sector that is connected with global markets, survives without state assistance, and generates productive employment for young people (Malik and Awadallah

2011). Although the state–business relationship varies tremendously across the region, it is usually a personalized rather than an institutionalized relationship. Businessmen and rulers are often connected through overlapping networks, which makes their engagement with the state informal, exclusive, and short-term (Luciani and Hertog 2010). Public expenditure—increasingly constrained—and a bloated civil service can no longer compensate for the failure of these policies to create economic opportunities and jobs. The Arab countries that have traditionally preserved their social order through a combination of repression and redistribution need a fundamental rethinking of their social contract. It is now widely recognized that sustainable economic growth and job creation can only be achieved by fully unlocking private initiatives, innovation, and investments, both domestic and foreign, maximizing the benefits of an increasingly integrated world. The newly democratic Arab nations therefore need economic opportunities, far-reaching reforms, and multi-pronged support. Above all, they need a vision that Arab people can trust to channel their energy toward high-quality, sustainable, and inclusive growth.

The Deauville Partnership

The partnership launched by the Group of Eight (G8) in Deauville, France, in May 2011 is thus strategic and timely. It provides a platform to support the historic political and economic transformation under way in some countries in the MENA region. Recognizing that the private sector must be the engine of growth and job creation, the Deauville Partnership aims to promote trade and investment, enhance support to private sector development, and coordinate support from international and regional financial institutions for homegrown economic and governance reforms. The Deauville "partners" include Canada, France, the Federal Republic of Germany, Italy, Japan, Kuwait, Qatar, Russia, Saudi Arabia, Turkey, the United Arab Emirates, the United Kingdom, the United States, and nine associated international and regional financial institutions.[1] All have expressed their commitment to support the "Partnership countries" currently engaged in political and economic transformation: the Arab Republic of Egypt, Jordan, Libya, Morocco, and Tunisia. Building on the country programs, the partners will help the Partnership countries achieve macroeconomic stability, social cohesion, and more equitable growth. Given the increasing fragility of the macroeconomic fundamentals in the region and the Partnership's focus on regional integration, it was decided to organize the Deauville Partnership around three pillars: governance, finance, and trade and commerce.

At the Deauville Partnership Finance Ministers' Meeting in Marseille, France, in September 2011, ministers launched the finance pillar of this Partnership. In Marseille, the finance ministers affirmed that regional and global integration is key to the economic development of the Partnership countries. Noting that increased integration would require action both within the region and with external partners, they expressed their commitment to advance and complement their respective bilateral and multilateral initiatives, including by removing barriers to trade and investment. They supported the acceleration of ongoing trade negotiations and efforts for better regional and global integration of the Partnership countries, notably through gradual integration in areas of mutual interest with the G8 countries and progress in the work toward an Arab Customs Union.[2] At a subsequent Deauville Partnership meeting in New York later in September 2011, the foreign affairs ministers emphasized the importance of regional integration for the Partnership and expressed their willingness to enhance existing initiatives by providing broader mutual market access opportunities and reducing barriers to trade and investment.[3]

In order to provide an appropriate framework in which to enhance trade and foreign direct investment (FDI), the Deauville Partnership requested the Marseille Center for Mediterranean Integration, drawing on the expertise of the World Bank and in partnership with the Islamic Development Bank, to coordinate an analytical report to be completed in 2012.[4] This report is the response to the Deauville Partnership request. The thrust of the report is that economic integration through increased trade and FDI is one key means to put the Partnership countries on a higher path of sustainable economic growth and in a position to decisively tackle the problem of unemployment, especially youth unemployment. Moreover, trade and investment is a means available to policy makers of the Deauville Partnership to show results in the not too distant future. The G8 countries, Turkey, the Gulf states, and other Deauville partners can help the new Arab democracies achieve their objectives in two main ways: by effectively expanding market opportunities and by supporting domestic regulatory reforms.

Why Trade and FDI?

To be sure, the quest for long-term, inclusive, and sustainable growth remains as elusive as ever. The prescription—if there is a prescription—for achieving and sustaining high rates of economic growth and job creation seems to require myriad ingredients in uncertain dosages adapted to local economic and political realities. Above all, determining and prioritizing the key drivers of growth and employment is an enormous challenge that confronts all developing and developed countries alike, including those united in the Deauville Partnership. In all sectors—health, education, energy, and so on—institutions, policies, and practices need improvement, but it is often unclear which ones deserve priority attention. Policy makers may be tempted to retreat from a long-term strategic vision in order to address more immediate, but less consequential, issues of the day. Well-intentioned policies with a short-term focus often have adverse unintended consequences in the long run. The Deauville Partnership therefore should be seen as an opportunity to develop a shared vision for the long-term prosperity and stability of the Mediterranean region.

Even so, the successful emerging economies of the last 60 years have had striking points of resemblance. The Commission on Growth and Development (2008) found that the economic success of these countries involved five key ingredients. They had committed, credible, and capable governments; they maintained macroeconomic stability; they fully engaged in and made the most of the world economy; they let markets allocate resources; and they mustered high rates of saving and investment.[5] The high-growth economies typically built their prosperity on sturdy political foundations. In fast-growing economies, policy makers understood that successful development entails a decades-long commitment and a fundamental bargain between the present and the future. Even at very high growth rates of 7–10 percent, it takes decades for a country to make the leap from low to relatively high incomes. During this long transition period, citizens must forgo consumption today in return for higher standards of living tomorrow. This bargain will be accepted only if the country's policy makers convey a credible vision of the future and a strategy for getting there. They must be trusted as stewards of the economy, and their promises of future rewards must be believed. Then, and only then, can policies aimed at maintaining macroeconomic stability, opening up to regional and international trade and investment, and fostering market forces produce their full benefits. That is the central premise of this book.

Trade and FDI as Vehicles for Inclusive Growth

Economic integration has proven to be a key ingredient of development. High-performing countries, that is, countries that have grown at an average rate of 7 percent or more per year for 25 years or longer since 1950, used the global economy to increase productivity through trade, FDI, technology flows, and migration. All engaged in and tried to make the most of the global economy, not to push the technological frontier but to catch up with existing technology and knowledge—a much more manageable task. These high-growth countries benefited from integration in two ways. First, they imported ideas, technology, and know-how from the rest of the world. Second, they exploited global demand, which provided a deep, elastic market for their goods. The inflow of knowledge dramatically increased the economy's productive potential; the global market provided the demand necessary to fulfill it. As simply put by the Commission on Growth and Development (2008), "They imported what the rest of the world knew, and exported what it wanted."

Successful economies also demonstrate that integration can take different institutional forms. There can be different ways to achieve sustainable, positive outcomes in terms of economic transformation, growth and employment, standard of living, and other social objectives. There is no single prescription, and the degree as well as the kind of integration is likely to depend on political economy factors that may not be economically optimal. Economic integration may take a variety of forms: unilateral liberalization; a free trade area, where tariffs are eliminated between member countries; a customs union, where member states establish a common external tariff; a common market, where not only trade restrictions but also restrictions on factor movements are eliminated; an economic union, where, in addition to the free circulation of products and factors of production, member states undertake some degree of harmonization of national economic policies; and, finally, complete economic integration, which involves the unification of monetary, fiscal, social, and countercyclical policies and the setting up of a supranational authority whose decisions are binding for the member states (Balassa 1961).

For these successful emerging economies, economic integration through trade and FDI was not an end in itself but a means to promote long-term economic growth and employment. Trade and investment could be seen as two main engines to help promote sustainable economic growth and job creation—one of the top concerns of the Partnership countries but also of all countries in the Mediterranean region (box 1.1). At a broader level, freedom of exchange is not merely a means to spur economic growth, create jobs, and reduce poverty; it is also a way to advance human liberties, bring people together in peaceful and mutually beneficial exchanges, and promote peace and stability. The massive popular uprisings in Tunisia, Egypt, Libya, the Syrian Arab Republic, and other parts of the Arab world are the most recent reminder of this universal quest for freedom.

Trade and FDI as a Means to Create Jobs

The five Deauville Partnership countries display some significant commonalities in their past economic performance. Weak private sector per-

BOX 1.1

How Does the Trade and FDI Engine Work?

Trade and investment raise productivity through more efficient allocation of resources, economies of scale, increased competition, faster rates of capital accumulation and technical progress, and increased flows of ideas, knowledge, and innovation from abroad. Trade and investment not only promote faster economic growth and job creation; they also help countries move up the global value chain, diversify, and improve their resilience to external shocks. Conversely, government action to restrict access to trade and investment reduces commercial opportunities, increases cost of inputs, and limits job opportunities. It also limits consumers' choices, thereby reducing their well-being, and can give rise to a variety of rents and rent-seeking behaviors. These threats typically are not limited to the freedom to trade in goods and services but also encompass restrictions on the free flow of capital, technological knowledge, and ideas more generally.

Empirical evidence generally supports a positive link between openness and economic growth. Levine and Renelt (1992) found a positive correlation between trade and investment and suggest that the effects of trade liberalization may operate through resource accumulation. Using a larger sample of developing countries, Edwards (1992) and Dollar (1992) found that trade liberalization improves growth performance. On the other hand, Rodriguez and Rodrik (1999) questioned the robustness of the positive impact of openness on growth. The main reason for their doubt is that the indicators of openness used in the literature are generally of poor quality and may themselves be endogenous. Frankel and Romer (1999) conducted a detailed analysis of the causal impact of trade on growth that takes into account potential endogeneity of trade indicators. They found a significant and important causal impact of trade on growth.

The link between openness and equity is more ambiguous. Dollar and Kraay (2002), among others, have shown that macroeconomic growth translates one-for-one into growth in income of the poor. While these findings seem robust to different concepts of poverty, a set of other factors can inhibit such beneficial effects. First, some evidence shows that the link between growth and poverty is fragile. Lopez (2004), examining the impact of various policies on inequality, found that while improvements in education and infrastructure could contribute to reducing income inequality, financial development, trade openness, and decreases in the size of the government might have the opposite effect, that is, to increase inequality. Their calculations suggest that, at least in the short run, the negative impact of these policies might offset the positive impact on inequality. Second, the empirical findings suggest that, for both developed countries (Dewatripont, Sapir, and Sekkat 1999) and developing countries (Lee and Vivarelli 2006), trade is not the main cause of labor market problems, such as unemployment or the wage gap. The impact of trade liberalization on the labor market is largely context-specific and tends to vary from one country to another. In addition to trade liberalization, one should take account of the macroeconomic cycle, labor market institutions, and technological capabilities.

formance in the MENA region has deep historical roots (Kuran 2004). Traders and investors were politically powerless under the Ottomans, and Arab socialism of the twentieth century reinforced this tendency. However, starting in the early 1990s, growth accelerated in all Partnership countries, driven by an opening up of their economies. There was a surge in trade and FDI, but little economic diversification. This led to a reduction of poverty, but not of inequality. Importantly, this improved economic performance made only a small dent in the high unemployment rate, especially among youth, educated people, and women. Meanwhile, the quality of institutions was deteriorating, and regional integration attempts were largely unsuccessful. Neither the pan-Arab integration agreements nor those linking the Partnership countries with the United States, the European Union (EU), or Turkey succeeded in generating exports and jobs. The perception is that these agreements have, more often than not, been associated with dislocations and that the benefits have been captured by a few individuals belonging to the first circle of politically connected. Any new vision would need to show a clear break from this past.

A closer look at the economic developments of the past two decades in Partnership countries reveals the following:

- The adoption of more pro-market economic strategies in the Partnership countries in the mid-1980s and early 1990s resulted in significantly higher economic growth rates. Over the period 1996–2010, the per capita real growth rates in Egypt, Jordan, Morocco, and Tunisia were markedly higher than during the preceding periods.[6] These countries also performed better than the average for the MENA region, although still not as well as countries in East Asia and Pacific (figure 1.1).

- Since the mid-1980s, manufactured exports increased markedly in all Partnership countries except Egypt and, because of the dominance of oil in the economy, Libya. Over the period 1996–2010, manufactured exports as a percentage of merchandise exports were much higher than during the preceding period, except in Egypt and Libya (figure 1.2). In Jordan, Morocco, and Tunisia, the ratio increased markedly. In Jordan and Tunisia, it greatly exceeded the average for MENA, reaching a level comparable to the world average. Egypt's performance, however, remained weak.

- FDI inflows increased significantly. Over the period 2006–10, FDI inflows as a percentage of gross domestic product (GDP) increased in the four countries, and particularly in Egypt and Jordan (figure 1.3).

- Manufactured exports did not diversify. While the share of manufactures in total exports has increased, diversification is still an issue in the

FIGURE 1.1

GDP per Capita Growth in Deauville Partnership Countries, 1981–2010

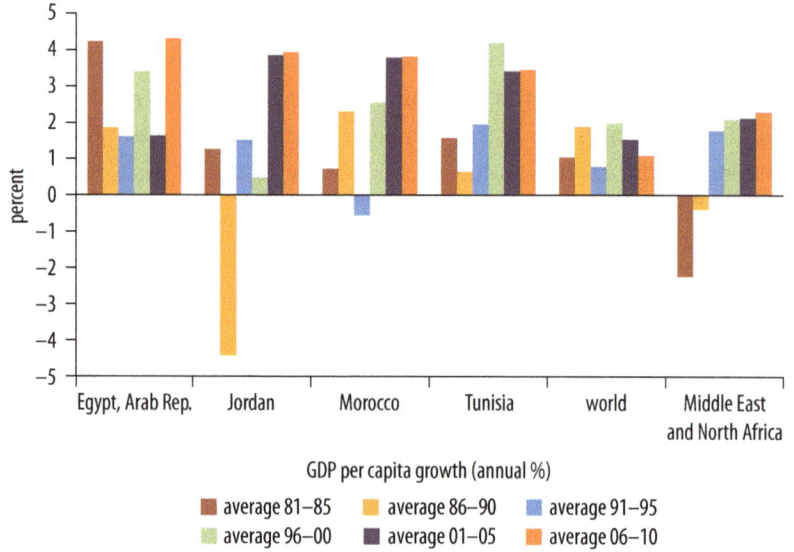

GDP per capita growth (annual %)

- average 81–85
- average 86–90
- average 91–95
- average 96–00
- average 01–05
- average 06–10

Source: World Bank, World Development Indicators 2011.

FIGURE 1.2

Manufactures Exports as Share of Merchandise Exports in Deauville Partnership Countries, 1981–2010

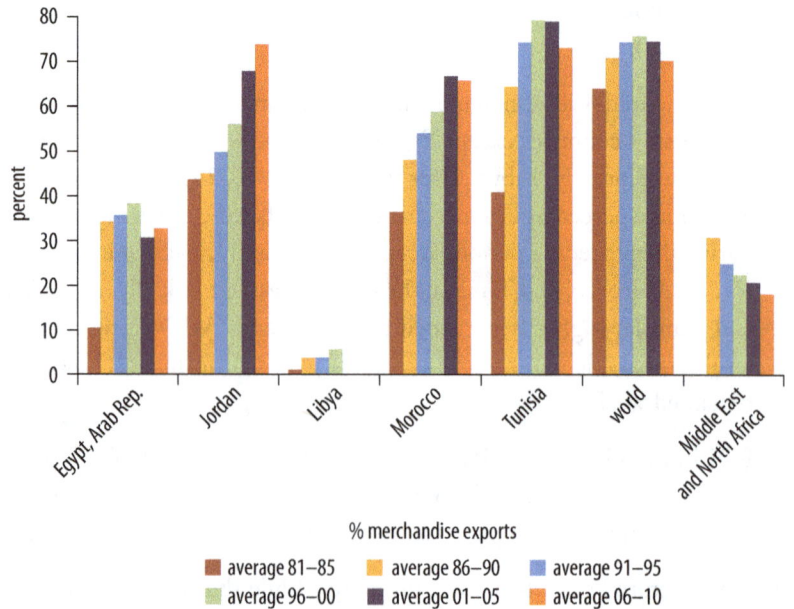

% merchandise exports

- average 81–85
- average 86–90
- average 91–95
- average 96–00
- average 01–05
- average 06–10

Source: World Bank, World Development Indicators 2011.

FIGURE 1.3

FDI Inflows as Share of GDP in Deauville Partnership Countries, 1996–2010

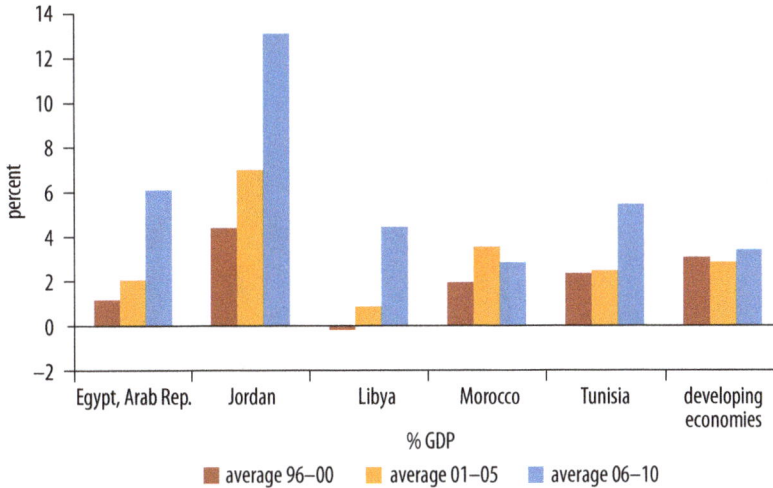

Source: United Nations Conference on Trade and Development, UNCTADstat. 2011.

four countries. Arguments similar to those advanced against dependence on natural resources apply to their exports specialization pattern. The Concentration Index of merchandise exports shows that the Deauville Partnership countries have a much higher degree of specialization in their exports than do the emerging economies. Since 1995, their situation has not improved significantly, especially compared to countries like Turkey (figure 1.4).

- The share of poor people in the total population decreased. Extreme poverty—that is, the share of the population below $1.25 purchasing power parity (PPP) per day—declined significantly, but at different rates across the countries (figure 1.5). In Morocco and Tunisia, the share of the poor population increased between 1991 and 1996 and decreased afterward to the level of the early 1990s.

- While poverty has declined, income inequality has not improved and has even worsened slightly in Jordan and Morocco. Inequality is lowest in Egypt and highest in Tunisia (figure 1.6). In Morocco, income inequality by 2008 was somewhat higher than in the early 1990s.

- The unemployment situation remained a serious concern throughout the period. While unemployment in the Partnership countries was on a declining path prior to the global economic crisis, in 2008 it remained much higher than the average in Latin America or in East Asia and Pacific (figure 1.7).

FIGURE 1.4

Concentration Index of Merchandise Exports in Deauville Partnership Countries and Selected Comparators, 1995–2011

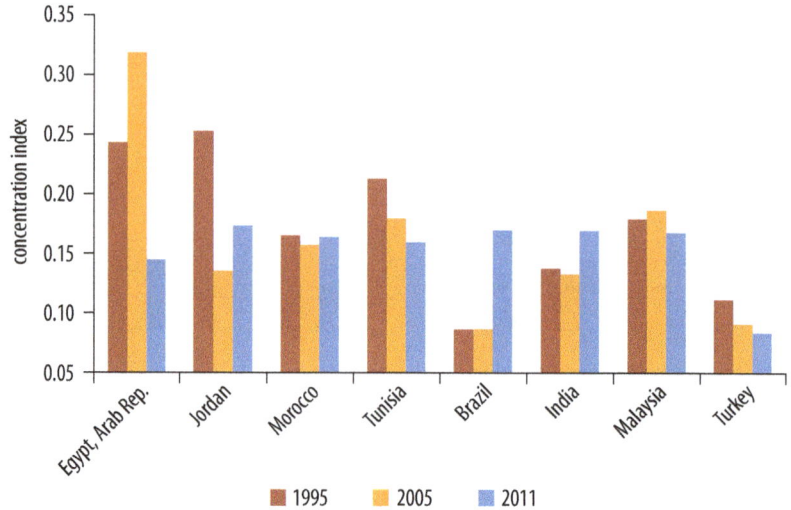

Source: United Nations Conference on Trade and Development, UNCTADstat. 2011.

FIGURE 1.5

Poverty Headcount Ratio at $1.25 per Day in Deauville Partnership Countries, 1991–2008

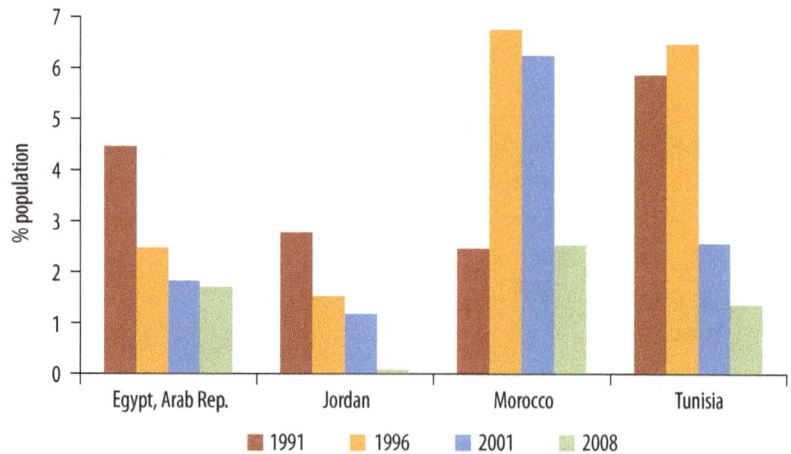

Source: World Bank, World Development Indicators 2011.
Note: The dates of observation differ between countries due to data availability.

- Unemployment was particularly high among graduates. In Morocco, unemployed workers holding a tertiary education degree represented more than 20 percent of total unemployment in 2008, and the trend was upward (figure 1.8). While the corresponding rate in Tunisia was

FIGURE 1.6

Gini Index in Deauville Partnership Countries, 1991–2008

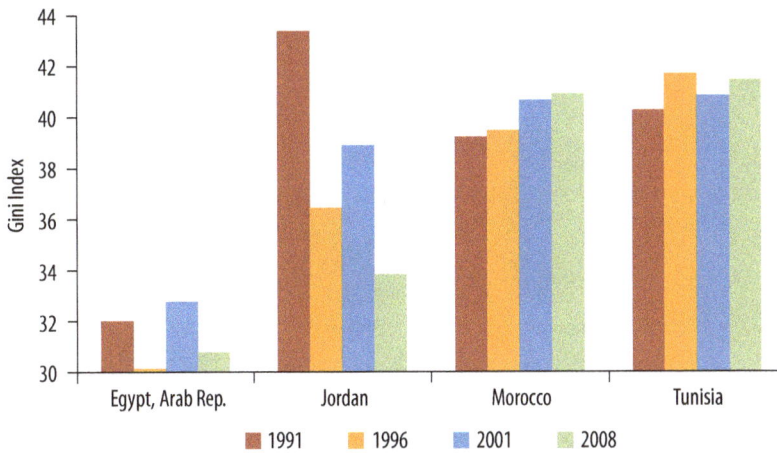

Source: World Bank, World Development Indicators 2011.
Note: The dates of observation differ between countries due to data availability.

FIGURE 1.7

Unemployment as Share of the Labor Force in Egypt, Morocco, and Tunisia, 1999–2008

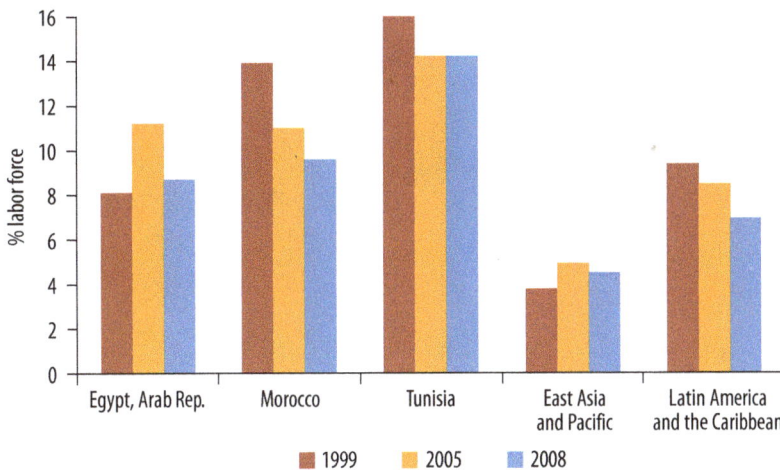

Source: World Bank, World Development Indicators 2011.

around 14 percent, there was a similar rising trend. These rates are even higher than the Latin American average.

- The quality of institutions has deteriorated. As measured by a simple average of the World Bank governance indicators, the quality of market-friendly institutions was worse in 2010 than in 2006. The deterioration was steady in all countries except Morocco, where a dra-

FIGURE 1.8

Share of Unemployment with Tertiary Education in Morocco and Tunisia, 1995–2005

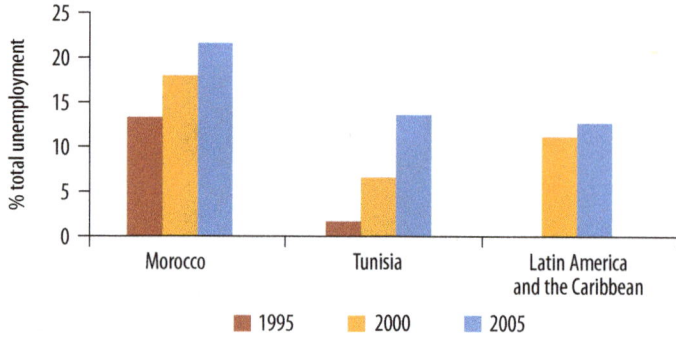

Source: World Bank, World Development Indicators 2011.
Note: 1995 data are not available for Latin America and Caribbean.

FIGURE 1.9

World Bank Governance Indicators for Deauville Partnership Countries, 1996–2010

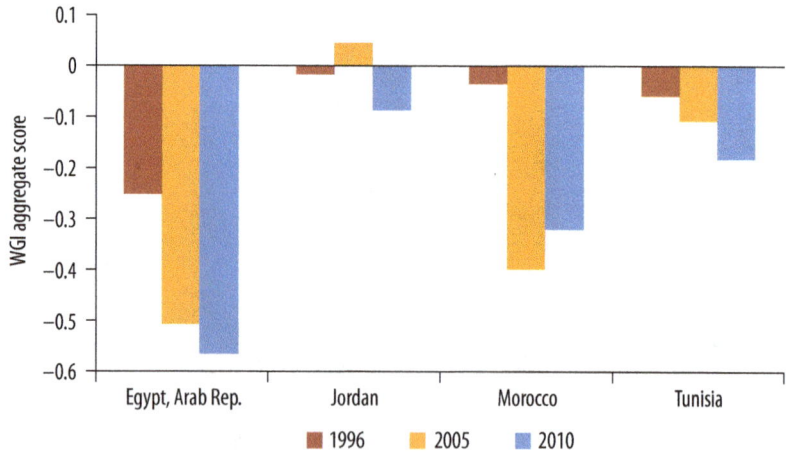

Source: World Bank, World Development Indicators 2011.
Note: Each score is an average of six aggregate indicators in the areas of voice and accountability, political stability and absence of violence, government effectiveness, regulatory quality, rule of law, and control of corruption.

matic decline after 1996 gave way to a slightly improving trend after 2005 (figure 1.9).

Given that employment and job creation are the most urgent economic concerns in Partnership countries, an integration agenda necessarily constitutes an important element of a strategic policy response. Under the right circumstances, integration through trade and investment can promote lasting, high-value-added employment. Reducing barriers to FDI in services in particular has been found to increase demand for more highly skilled labor. Integration can also promote labor market participation, especially among women. In comparison to education and other long-term growth-enhancing policies—which of course are beneficial in their own right—trade and investment can have more rapid effects on growth and employment creation (OECD 2011). Yet such effects of integration (and globalization more broadly) on jobs, wages, and job security are not necessarily immediate. There is evidence that the short-run impact of trade liberalization can be a temporary increase in the unemployment rate due to a job creation time lag and the displacement of workers from previously sheltered import-competing industries (Dutt and Traca 2005). Moreover, the reforms that help expand trade should be part of more comprehensive programs aimed at improving competitiveness and economic efficiency, and these may also entail adjustment costs. On balance, however, in the medium term, expansion of trade and FDI holds promise for substantial dividends in terms of job creation, job quality, and income growth.

In a number of countries that successfully integrated into global markets, export-led growth eventually brought large employment dividends. In many cases—most notably Eastern Europe, Turkey, China, India, and some other Asian countries—globalization's promise in terms of employment has been fulfilled. For example, Turkey has been able to accelerate economic growth and create more than 3 million new jobs since it opened up and entered into a process of regulatory convergence with the EU in the mid-2000s (figure 1.10). High-productivity employment opportunities have expanded, and structural change has contributed to overall growth. Turkey's recent economic performance offers a natural experiment in economic integration and sustained reforms that could be particularly relevant for the new Arab democracies. The expansion beyond national markets of production in developing countries, especially in labor-intensive manufacturing such as textiles and clothing, footwear, and food processing, eventually spurs demand for labor and boosts workers' earnings. Because of weak economic governance and lack of complementary structural transformation, MENA countries (and also until recently in Latin America and Sub-Saharan Africa) have found it difficult to make trade a driver of employment creation and growth (World Bank 2003). Evidence suggests that trade openness has contributed less to overall employment creation in manufacturing in MENA than in other developing regions. In a number of instances, because of an inadequate economic environment, globalization appears not to have fostered the desirable kind of structural change; instead, labor has moved from more productive to less productive activities, including, most notably, the informal economy.

FIGURE 1.10

GDP per Capita in Deauville Partnership Countries and Turkey, 1980–2010

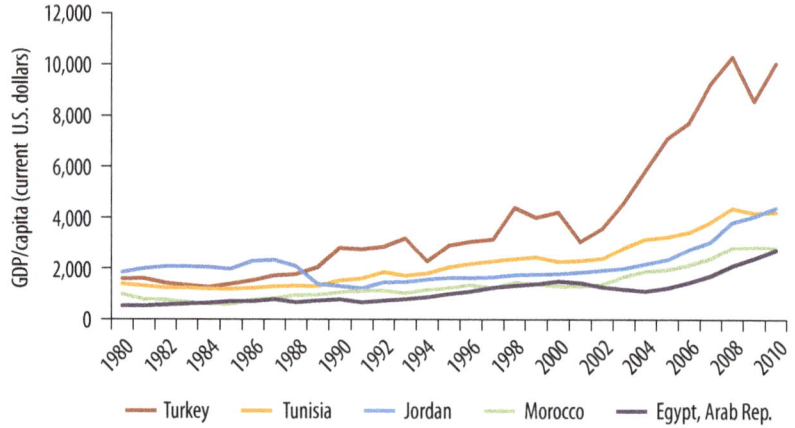

Source: World Bank, World Development Indicators 2011.

Until now, except for the oil sector, the MENA region has remained one of the least integrated regions, in terms of both intra-regional integration and integration into the world economy. It has suffered from relatively high trade and investment barriers, poor trade facilitation and logistics, lack of services trade integration, and weak rules and discipline for trade and investment, including for intra-regional trade agreements such as the Pan-Arab Free Trade Area (PAFTA). This creates an opportunity, in that steps to address these deficiencies could yield large beneficial results in a relatively short period of time. Looking forward, economic integration through greater trade and investment is an overarching development strategy that can do for the MENA region what it did before for Central and Eastern Europe, East Asia, and other emerging trade partners that are now sustainable growth poles (Chauffour 2011). Greater economic integration would be particularly effective in addressing Partnership countries' underperformance in intra-industry trade and investment.

Leadership for a Trade and FDI Vision

Leadership is needed in both Partnership countries and Deauville partners to provide a credible long-term vision and explain the mutual benefits of economic integration. One powerful vision could be the pursuit of a partnership aimed at gradually promoting four key freedoms in the Mediterranean: the free movement of goods, services, capital, and persons. Trade and migration in the economic space encompassing the EU, Turkey, the Balkans, the Maghreb, and the Mashreq has been happening for millennia (Abulafia 2011; Braudel 1949). Now is the time to recognize these links across the Mediterranean and build bridges aimed at forging a common destiny (Niblett and Spencer 2012). The vision of a common Mediterranean economic space, if offered, could provide a motivation for difficult policy reforms in Partnership countries. In this bleak global economic environment, the ability of leaders to offer a transcendent, outward-oriented vision will determine the chances for growth and prosperity. The benefits would go beyond the immediate economic benefits, serving to promote common human values, peace, and stability.

The historical circumstances may also be ripe for Partnership countries to take the lead and make a strong push toward greater Arab intraregional integration. As an overarching purpose, the Deauville Partnership could help current and future Partnership countries and the Arab world more generally invent their own model of integration. To date, intra-Arab integration has been largely a failure. Although Arab countries embarked on economic cooperation earlier than many other developing regions (the Arab Economic Unity Agreement dates back to 1957), and they have signed the highest number of regional integration agreements (more than 20), almost none of these agreements has been implemented effectively. Even some land borders remain closed between Arab countries, such as between Algeria and Morocco. Moreover, in spite of a limited number of "open" intra-Arab wars since the end of World War II, political tensions in Arab countries have been omnipresent. Hence, the Arab region has witnessed a vicious cycle of lack of integration and high political tensions between states. In particular, political considerations have hampered efforts to set up effective institutional arrangements. In principle, the gains from integration should provide an incentive to policy makers to foster regional integration. However, they do not seem to be enough to counterbalance political considerations that act against deeper integration of markets in the MENA region (Fawzy 2003). Unlike the European countries, which have put in place a set of supranational institutions that are responsible for pushing integration, Arab countries have always resorted to an intergovernmental approach that reflects, to a large extent, the reluctance of their leaders to transfer sovereignty to supranational bodies (Hoekman and Sekkat 2010).

Yet regional integration has been a significant driver of better overall performance for countries in Central Europe and Eastern Europe, Southeast Asia, and other regions of the world. The Arab political awakening for greater voice and representation, economic opportunities, and openness could create the circumstances for a genuine new beginning. The Arab world's approach to regional integration should be anchored in the region's evolving realities and circumstances. There are several considerations to take into account in advancing regional integration.

First, such a vision could help the Arab world take better advantage of a shared heritage and common identity. There are in fact several Mediterranean and Arab "worlds," or subregions, each with its own characteristics and prospects. The Maghreb countries are economically oriented toward the EU, while the Mashreq countries have a more diverse reach. The third group, the countries of the Gulf Cooperation Council (GCC), is more globally integrated, although overwhelmingly through oil and gas. The larger Arab world is also somewhat more integrated in terms of investment flows (from the GCC) and labor flows (into the GCC, but also other destinations) than in terms of trade. With respect to subregional integration, the three subregions are at different stages of economic convergence. While the GCC countries are moving from a customs union to developing a common market, with a possible monetary union on the horizon, the other two subregions remain internally divided, with long-standing political disputes and/or conflicts. In each subregion, countries are also at various stages of progress toward establishing liberal democracies and open market economies. Yet Arab peoples have more in common in terms of culture, identity, and sense of belonging than do the populations of many other regional trading blocs.

Second, the Arab world needs stronger regional engines to power cooperation. Generally speaking, the development of regional cooperative institutions that are efficient and effective appears to be fundamentally driven by the initiative and interests of major regional powers. France and Germany were critical in the early stages of the EU; Japan nurtured the "flying geese" model of development in East Asia and took lead in fostering regional cooperation; the United States drove the North American Free Trade Agreement (NAFTA); Russian and Chinese interests may drive the regional integration of Central Asia. However, as in many other regions of the world, it is not yet clear which power or powers in the Arab world could lead and drive regional cooperation. There is no one natural hub or anchor country, as there is in North America. Nor is there a clearly defined subset of equally large countries that have an interest in cooperation, as was the case with EU regionalism (Hoekman and Messerlin 2002). Yet most Arab countries understand that they are now part of a regional architecture and that they have an interest in promoting healthy, dynamic, flexible regional institutions for finance, trade, the movement of ideas and people, and environmental protection, among other functions.

A third factor is that the emergence of a new, fast-evolving multipolar world economy could help trigger the exceptional conditions that are often required for regional integration. The examples of East Asia and Eastern and Central Europe illustrate the kinds of historical conditions that can unleash the integration process, in this case the collapse of Japan after World War II and the discrediting of a political system in Eastern Europe. In the absence of such historical conditions, regional integration tends to be an extremely protracted political process. The current political transformation in the MENA region, coinciding in time with the rebalancing of the world economy, offers unique opportunities for the Arab world. The political transformation could help ease tensions between Arab countries and pave the way for a virtuous circle of political cooperation and economic integration. The move toward multiple poles of growth is accelerating as middle classes grow in developing countries, billions of people join the world economy, and new patterns of integration combine regional intensification with global openness. For the Arab world, the rise of China, India, and the Association of Southeast Asian Nations (ASEAN) offers great opportunities that go beyond the expansion of energy markets (Pigato 2009). Arab countries are an important source of capital for the rest of the world and increasingly a business-service hub linking East and South Asia with Europe and Africa. The Maghreb could soon be part of a reinforced Euro-Med integration system linked to both the Middle East and Africa. The prospects of a Union for the Mediterranean encompassing 43 countries from Europe and the Mediterranean basin could also become more favorable with the democratic transitions in North Africa, the Middle East, and the Balkans.

The historic changes under way in the Arab world have the potential to open the door to the kind of economic transformation that occurred in the Northern Mediterranean, Central and Eastern Europe, South Asia, Latin America, and other world regions in recent decades. As in other historical episodes of liberation, the aspirations of the Partnership countries' peoples for freedom, human rights, democracy, job opportunities, empowerment, and dignity have led them to take control of their own destinies. However, making use of these newly acquired freedoms could be as daunting as the fight and sacrifice to achieve them. The lack of proper democratic institutions and practices, as well as the need to develop appropriate checks and balances in the exercise of government power, means that the original liberation momentum will be difficult to sustain, setbacks will inevitably occur, and some expectations will remain unmet.

The transitions in the Northern Mediterranean (e.g., in Greece, Portugal, Spain, and Turkey) could provide some useful lessons. First, the process was not homogenous: different countries took different courses, with varying degrees of success. Second, the transitions did not prove to be linear; there were ups and downs. Every country in the Northern Mediterranean went through at least one major economic crisis—hence the importance of keeping a long-term view. Third, the sequencing of reforms was important. Success was often rooted in a clear road map based on consensus and consistency in the approach and implementation. Fourth, transparency and accountability provided the overarching reform umbrella for both governments and the private sector. Fifth, the existence of an external anchor (i.e., the EU) was key to the success of the transitions. Finally, the transitions in those countries involved rethinking the role of the state and the military. The subsidy culture had to be changed and replaced by a pro-market culture. While this rethinking took a variety of forms reflecting the local political economies, the success of the transition everywhere involved the promotion of an enabling state as opposed to a controlling state. Turkey's recent economic performance offers a natural experiment in economic integration that could be particularly relevant for the new Arab democracies (box 1.2).

To be sure, the lessons from history can only be partial. The initial conditions in Partnership countries differ from those that prevailed in Greece, Portugal, Spain, or Turkey during their transitions in at least two key respects: the average level of education and the commitment to market reforms. The initial conditions in partner countries also differ. The relationship between the G8 countries and the Arab world prior to the Arab Spring contrasted sharply with the relationship between the Western world and the former European dictatorships at the time of the Cold War. Another critical difference is the state of the world economy, which has suffered since 2007 from food, fuel, and financial crises and is currently affected by the sovereign debt crisis in European and other developed nations.

A Trade and FDI Agenda

To start implementing the vision of an integrated economic space in the Mediterranean basin, the Deauville Partnership could focus on five priority areas. These are to help Partnership countries (a) adapt to a fast-changing trade, FDI, and jobs landscape; (b) improve market access opportunities and market regulations; (c) foster competitiveness, diversification, and employment; (d) facilitate trade and mobilize trade finance and diaspora resources; and (e) promote the inclusiveness, equity, and sustainability of the structural transformation brought about by the process of integration. These five areas have emerged as the key priorities from the consultation process with the Partnership countries and the various Deauville partners under the guidance of an Advisory Committee established for the purpose of this report. They are outlined briefly below and discussed in more detail in chapters 2 through 6 of this book.

BOX 1.2

The EU-Turkey Customs Union: A Model for Future Euro-Med Integration?

The 1995 EU-Turkey Customs Union has been a major instrument of integration of the Turkish economy into the European Union and global markets, offering powerful tools for Turkish economic reform. Under the terms of the union, Turkish producers of industrial goods are protected by tariffs from external competition only to the extent that EU producers are, and they face competition from duty-free imports of industrial goods from world-class European firms. In return, Turkish industrial producers have duty-free market access to the European Economic Area. Trade liberalization achieved through the customs union has helped move the Turkish economy from a government-controlled regime to a market-based one, and the remarkable performance of Turkish industrial producers is evidence of its success.

Turkish producers' access to EU markets is determined not only by tariffs, but also by standards, conformity assessment procedures, competition policy, industrial property rights, contingent protectionism measures, and rules of origin. Therefore, to increase its market access, Turkey has had to adopt and implement effectively the EU rules and regulations with respect to each of these. The customs union has contributed enormously toward increasing the competitiveness of Turkish products by offering Turkey opportunities to establish the required new institutions and to modernize and upgrade its rules and disciplines required for the elimination of technical barriers to trade and the implementation of EU's competition, industrial property rights, and contingent protectionism policies. Besides increasing Turkey's market access, these policies, together with the reform of the customs regime, have brought about a more efficient functioning of the Turkish internal market.

Source: Togan 2012.

- *Adapt to a fast-changing trade, FDI, and jobs landscape.* The global trade and FDI environment has changed beyond recognition over the last two decades; one does not trade and invest in the same way today as 20 or even 10 years ago. The emergence of production networks, global value chains, and trade in tasks (as opposed to goods or services) is shaping this new environment, changing the skills and competencies required for employment. The "trade-investment-service nexus" is at the heart of today's international commerce (Baldwin 2011). The Deauville Partnership could foster the development of production networks in Partnership countries and eventually the emergence of an Arab Factory system (equivalent to Factory Asia) as a means to accelerate growth, create jobs, including for women, and reduce poverty.

- *Improve market access and regulations.* The Deauville Partnership could offer more opportunities to trade and invest across borders cheaply, securely, and predictably. This could be done by increasing market access, especially in areas where Partnership countries have comparative advantages, such as in concentrated solar power; by allowing freer labor mobility; and by increasing support to the process of regulatory convergence of norms, standards, and other behind-the-border regulations, such as those dealing with competition policy and government procurement.

- *Foster competitiveness, diversification, and employment.* The Deauville Partnership could support Partnership countries in the implementation of complementary domestic reforms of their business environment, investment climate, and governance structure. The objective is to develop more knowledge- and innovation-oriented economies that are capable of breaking into new markets, reaping the benefits of globalization, and creating high-value jobs.

- *Facilitate trade and mobilize trade finance and diaspora resources.* To support trade and FDI, especially for the development of small and medium-size enterprises, the Deauville Partnership could play a critical role in modernizing trade logistics, customs, and other border agencies, and in mobilizing trade finance and diaspora resources.

- *Promote inclusiveness, equity, and sustainability.* The Deauville Partnership could help make the gains from economic integration more inclusive across populations, equitable across regions, and sustainable over time. These are all critical political economy dimensions that can promote ownership and sustain the reform momentum.

All neighboring partner countries—the EU members, Turkey, and the GCC countries—as well as the United States share with the Partnership countries the responsibility for offering a clear, understandable, and ambitious vision for the Arab people as they pursue their democratic transition. The vision would be to help integrate the Partnership countries into the world economy, including through the creation of a common economic space spanning the two rims of the Mediterranean and, in the long run, embracing the GCC as well. This could include steps such as the following:

- The *EU* could deepen its trade relationships with Egypt, Jordan, Morocco, and Tunisia developed under the Association Agreements and

the European Neighbourhood Policy with the effective implementation of the proposed Deep and Comprehensive Free Trade Areas
(DCFTAs). DCFTAs will be comprehensive agreements on trade and
economic relations covering a full range of regulatory areas of mutual
interest, such as trade facilitation, technical barriers to trade, sanitary
and phytosanitary measures, investment protection, public procurement, and competition policy.

- In a coordinated approach, and on the basis of both its process of accession to the EU and its growing political and economic influence in
the region, *Turkey* could similarly deepen its existing arrangements
with each Partnership country to foster trade and investment in the
agricultural and services sectors and promote labor mobility. This
could build on Turkey's recently signed memorandums of understanding with Tunisia and Libya.

- The *GCC* could strengthen its relationship with Egypt and Tunisia in
the framework of a deepened cooperation with the Agadir Agreement
(Jordan and Morocco have already been officially invited to join the
GCC). This would allow citizens of member countries to enjoy equal
rights and privileges, including the rights to move, settle, and work;
receive social protection, retirement, health, education, and social services; and engage in various economic activities and services. This
greater integration between the GCC and Partnership countries
would need to be coordinated with the ongoing negotiations on an
EU-GCC free trade agreement (FTA) covering all areas of trade relations, notably industrial, fisheries, and agricultural goods.

- Consistent and in coordination with initiatives being undertaken by the
EU and other Deauville partners, the *United States* could (a) increase
the value of its existing agreements with Jordan and Morocco, and (b)
invite Tunisia and, once the appropriate circumstances are in place,
Egypt and Libya to enter into FTAs as well. These actions would be
part of the proposed Middle East/North Africa Trade and Investment
Partnership (MENA TIP), which will include a broad set of arrangements designed to increase job creation, trade, and investment between
and among the United States and countries in the region.

- Other G8 members could contribute in a similar manner. *Canada's*
completed FTA with Jordan and parallel agreements on the environment and labor cooperation could enter into force, and the FTA negotiations with Morocco could be completed as soon as feasible. Canada could also launch similar negotiations with Tunisia and, once the
conditions are in place, with Egypt and Libya. The Russia-Arab Co-

operation Forum and bilateral intergovernmental commissions could be further leveraged to strengthen relations between Russia and Arab countries in the economic, financial, and investment sectors. Similarly, *Japan* could further strengthen the Japan-Arab Economic Forum and Japan's investment agreements with Partnership countries.

- *Deauville partners* could also help promote intra-Arab regional integration and integration of Partnership countries into global markets. The Agadir Agreement between Egypt, Jordan, Morocco, and Tunisia could be deepened, and Libya could receive the necessary support to join the World Trade Organization.

- Last but not least, the implementation of far-reaching domestic reforms in *Partnership countries* would be critical to effectively reap the growth and employment opportunities offered by greater economic integration and regulatory convergence with the most advanced economies.

People in Partnership countries need to see "what is in it for them" in a trade and FDI reform agenda. Many people in the region perceive that the opening that was implemented by governments in the past decade did not generate the benefits advertised. Previous attempts to strengthen private businesses through privatization and deregulation often failed when the reforms were implemented halfheartedly and the benefits were largely captured by a well-connected few. External liberalization was not accompanied by domestic reforms to improve governance, increase transparency, and create a level playing field so the benefits of liberalization could extend to workers and consumers. Rather than creating a legitimate private sector constituency, then, past reforms tended simply to strengthen existing patronage networks and businesses that were "embedded with those in power" (Malik and Awadallah 2011). To avoid repeating the mistakes of the past, the political economy of the Deauville Partnership will be critical. People in the Partnership countries need to own the process of integration and its overall direction. They need to be aware of the changing global trade and FDI environment and see improved infrastructure for trade and investment. They need to perceive greater economic opportunities for themselves and their children and feel that reform efforts are bearing fruit. Finally, they need convincing evidence that all social groups are benefiting from the process and will continue to do so over time.

Notes

1. African Development Bank, Arab Fund for Economic and Social Development, Arab Monetary Fund, European Bank for Reconstruction and Development, European Investment Bank, Islamic Development Bank Group, Inter-

national Monetary Fund, Organization of the Petroleum Exporting Countries (OPEC) Fund for International Development, and World Bank Group. There are several other organizations that have been supportive of the Deauville Partnership, including the Arab League, the Organization for Economic Cooperation and Development, and the United Nations organizations.

2. Deauville Partnership Finance Ministers' Meeting Communiqué, Marseille, September 10, 2011, para. 13.

3. Deauville Partnership Foreign Affairs Ministers' Meeting Communiqué, New York, September 20, 2011, para. 23.

4. Deauville Partnership Finance Ministers' Meeting Communiqué, Marseille, September 10, 2011, para. 14.

5. Throughout the report, the performance of the Deauville Partnership countries (Egypt, Jordan, Libya, Morocco, and Tunisia) will be compared with their main competitors as well as with the 13 economies identified by the Commission on Growth and Development (2008) as having grown at an average rate of 7 percent or more per year for 25 years or longer since 1950: Botswana; Brazil; China; Hong Kong SAR, China; Indonesia; Japan; the Republic of Korea; Malaysia; Malta; Oman; Singapore; Taiwan, China; and Thailand.

6. Pre-2000 data were not available for Libya. Some comparisons of Partnership countries in this report do not include Libya because of the absence of comparative data on that country.

References

Abulafia, David. 2011. *The Great Sea: A Human History of the Mediterranean.* New York: Oxford University Press.

Balassa, Bela. 1961. *The Theory of Economic Integration.* Homewood, IL: Richard D. Irwin.

Baldwin, Richard. 2011. "21st Century Regionalism: Filling the Gap between 21st Century Trade and 20th Century Trade Rules." CEPR Policy Insight 56, Centre for Economic Policy Research, London.

Braudel, Fernand. 1949. *La Méditerranée et le Monde Méditerranéen à l'époque de Philippe II.* 3 vols. Paris: Colin.

Chauffour, Jean-Pierre. 2011. "Trade Integration as a Way Forward for the Arab World: A Regional Agenda." Policy Research Working Paper 5581, World Bank, Washington, DC.

Commission on Growth and Development. 2008. *The Growth Report: Strategies for Sustained Growth and Inclusive Development.* Washington, DC: World Bank.

Dewatripont, Mathias, André Sapir, and Khalid Sekkat, eds. 1999. *Trade and Jobs in Europe: Much Ado about Nothing?* New York: Oxford University Press.

Dollar, David. 1992. "Outward-Oriented Developing Economies Really Do Grow More Rapidly: Evidence from 95 LDCs, 1976–1985." *Economic Development and Cultural Change* 40 (3): 523–44.

Dollar, David, and Aart Kraay. 2002. "Growth Is Good for the Poor." *Journal of Economic Growth* 7 (3): 195–225.

Dutt, Pushan, and Daniel A. Traca. 2005. "Trade and the Skill-Bias: It's Not How Much, but with Whom You Trade." CEPR Discussion Paper 5263, Centre for Economic Policy Research, London.

Edwards, Sebastian. 1992. "Trade Orientation, Distortions and Growth in Developing Countries." *Journal of Development Economics* 39: 31–57.

Fawzy, Samiha. 2003. "The Economics and Politics of Arab Economic Integration." In *Arab Economic Integration: Between Hope and Reality*, ed. Ahmed Galal and Bernard Hoekman, 13–37. Washington, DC: Brookings Institution Press.

Frankel, Jeffrey A., and David Romer. 1999. "Does Trade Cause Growth?" *American Economic Review* 89 (3): 379–99.

Hoekman, Bernard, and Patrick Messerlin. 2002. "Initial Conditions and Incentives for Arab Economic Integration: Can the European Community's Success Be Emulated?" Policy Research Working Paper 2921, World Bank, Washington, DC.

Hoekman, Bernard, and Khalid Sekkat. 2010. "Arab Economic Integration: Missing Links." CEPR Discussion Paper 7807, Centre for Economic Policy Research, London.

Kuran, Timur. 2004. "Why the Middle East Is Economically Underdeveloped: Historical Mechanisms of Institutional Stagnation." *Journal of Economic Perspectives* 18 (3): 71–90.

Lee, Eddy, and Marco Vivarelli. 2006. "The Social Impact of Globalisation in the Developing Countries." CSGR Working Paper 199/06, Centre for the Study of Globalisation and Regionalisation, University of Warwick, Coventry, U.K.

Levine, Ross, and David Renelt. 1992. "A Sensitivity Analysis of Cross-Country Growth Regressions." *American Economic Review* 82 (4): 942–63.

Lopez, Humberto J. 2004. "Pro-Poor Growth: A Review of What We Know (and of What We Don't)." World Bank, Washington, DC.

Luciani, Giacomo, and Steffen Hertog. 2010. "Has Arab Business Ever Been, or Will It Be, a Player for Reform?" Policy Paper 1, Arab Reform Initiative.

Malik, Adeel, and Bassem Awadallah. 2011. "The Economics of the Arab Spring." OxCarre Research Paper 79, Oxford Centre for the Analysis of Resource Rich Economies, University of Oxford, Oxford, U.K.

Niblett, Robin, and Claire Spencer. 2012. "Time to Build Bridges over the Mediterranean." *World Today* 67 (12): 12–13.

OECD (Organisation for Economic Co-operation and Development). 2011. *OECD Regional Outlook 2011: Building Resilient Regions for Stronger Economies.* Paris: OECD.

Pigato, Miria. 2009. *Strengthening China's and India's Trade and Investment Ties to the Middle East and North Africa.* Orientation in Development Series. Washington, DC: World Bank.

Rodriguez, Francisco, and Dani Rodrik. 1999. "Trade Policy and Economic Growth: A Skeptic's Guide to Cross-National Evidence." NBER Working Paper 7081, National Bureau of Economic Research, Cambridge, MA.

Togan, Sübidey. 2012. *The EU-Turkey Customs Union: A Model for Future Euro-Med Integration.* MEDPRO Technical Report 9, Mediterranean Prospects, Centre for European Policy Studies, Brussels.

World Bank. 2003. *Trade, Investment and Development in the Middle East and North Africa.* Washington, DC: World Bank.

World Bank. 2011. World Development Indicators (for figures) UNCTAD statistics 2011.

CHAPTER 2

Adapting to a Changing Trade and FDI Landscape

Trade and foreign direct investment (FDI) have experienced a global boom in recent decades, driven by large reductions in border barriers and technological changes that have lowered the costs of communications and transport. The resulting globalization of production, with its associated fragmentation of the supply or value chain, has lowered prices and increased the variety of imported goods and services for firms and consumers. It has also led to unprecedented interlinkages and interdependency among countries. As a group, developing countries are now a major driver of global trade. Many countries have benefited greatly from global integration, but the benefits are not necessarily distributed equally, either across countries or within them. The most dynamic countries have attracted large FDI inflows and are integrated into global value chains (GVCs).

Regional integration is another reality that is fast reshaping the world. Transoceanic integration in the post–World War II period was followed by North–South integration beginning in the 1970s. Today, there is a very swift trans-Eurasian integration under way in the supracontinental space anchored by the European Union (EU), Russia, China, Japan, and India, as well as an emerging trans-Pacific partnership. Sixty years after the founding of the General Agreement on Tariffs and Trade, the global trading landscape has changed beyond recognition.

Countries in the Middle East and North Africa (MENA) region have so far been less successful than countries in other regions in using trade as a means to create jobs, increase per capita incomes, and diversify their economies. Excluding petroleum exports, the MENA region, with over 400 million people, exports roughly the same amount as Switzerland. Similarly, FDI inflows in the MENA region are concentrated in the real estate and mining sectors. FDI in manufacturing—the type of investment richest in employment—has remained marginal, accounting for just a fifth of all FDI inflows in the region. The MENA region's trade and investment underperformance is particularly striking for intra-industry and intra-regional trade, the fastest-growing segment of global trade. Poor households and communities in lagging areas continue to confront major challenges in dealing with external shocks and rising food costs and in harnessing the opportunities offered by a more open world trading system. An Arab Factory of integrated supply chains and production networks akin to Factory Asia has yet to emerge in the MENA region. While all Partnership countries emphasize trade and investment in their competitiveness and development strategies, all are facing—and will need to adapt to—a fast-changing trade and investment landscape.

A New International Context

Trade is a key driver of growth and development. No country in the last 50 years has sustained high levels of growth and significantly increased per capita incomes without greatly expanding trade. Trade allows countries to exploit their comparative advantages. It permits firms to sell to customers in any country and to source goods, services, and technologies from the most efficient suppliers, in the process generating better jobs and raising household incomes, thus helping to reduce poverty. While trade has only temporary direct effects on a country's growth rate, the indirect productivity effects associated with opening markets to new imported varieties of goods typically account for 10–25 percent of a country's per capita income growth (Broda, Greenfield, and Weinstein 2006).

Developing countries are new drivers of global trade. Trade grew rapidly in the 1990s and 2000s (figure 2.1), driven by a mix of technological change and policy reforms (Hummels 2007; WTO 2008). Global merchandise trade in 2009 was approximately $13 trillion, up from $3.5 trillion in 1990 (in constant dollars). Developing countries account for a steadily increasing share of the global total: their volume of exports rose more than fourfold between 1990 and 2009. Between 2000 and 2009 their exports rose by 80 percent, compared to only 40 percent for the world as a whole.[1] The rapid rise of South–South trade in the past decade is a reflection of the new market opportunities that have been created.[2] China has become the world's largest exporter and will be the world's largest economy in terms of gross domestic product (GDP) purchasing power parity by a significant margin in 2020; India is projected to be the third largest, after the United States. The growth of China significantly changes the trade landscape for other developing countries. China, together with the large and rapidly growing nations of Brazil and India as well as other middle-income countries, creates major opportunities for diversification and likely prospects for sustained higher prices for natural resource-based

FIGURE 2.1

Increase in Trade Integration, 1985–2010, and South–South Trade, 1990–2009

a. Total trade as share of GDP, low- and middle-income countries compared to global average, 1985–2010

b. Imports from global South as share of total world imports and of total South imports, 1990–2009

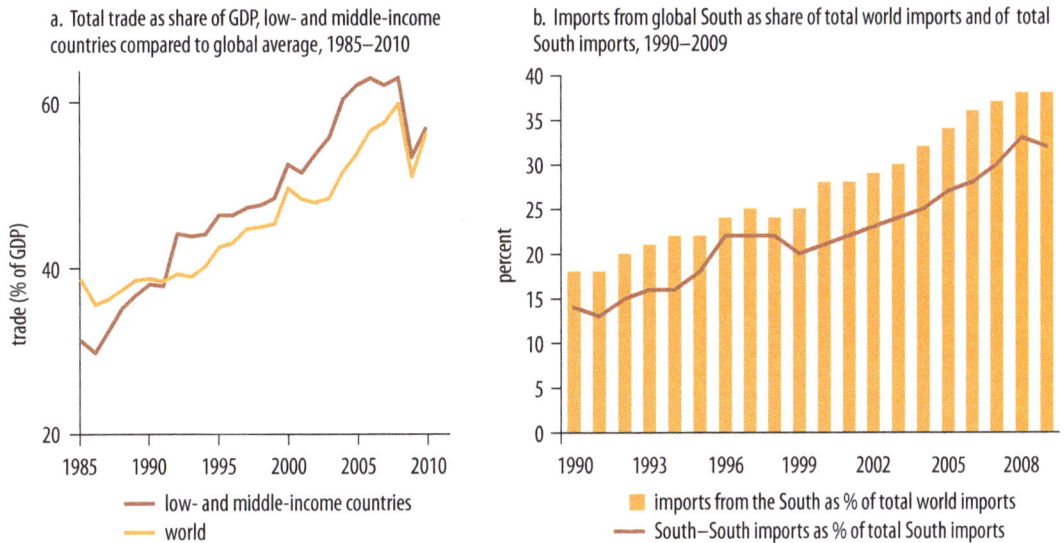

- low- and middle-income countries
- world

■ imports from the South as % of total world imports
— South–South imports as % of total South imports

Source: World Bank, World Development Indicators 2011.

exports (Canuto and Giugale 2010). But these nations are also a potent source of competition, putting greater pressure on firms in other developing economies to improve productivity and reduce their costs, as well as making it more difficult to attract FDI.

The structure of global production has been transformed. While many firms have had international operations and trading relationships for decades, GVCs have become much more prevalent and elaborate in the past 10–15 years.[3] Their expansion has created both new opportunities and challenges. Characterized by ever more refined degrees of specialization, GVCs have allowed developing and developed countries alike to better exploit their respective comparative advantages.

Entering into GVCs requires considerable competence on the part of suppliers and a capacity to move goods cost-effectively to where they are needed, according to tight manufacturing schedules. GVCs contain tightly integrated activities, often managed on a day-to-day basis. Just-in-time manufacturing practices mean that firms and workers in widely separated locations affect one another more than they have in the past. Moreover, this form of production is more sensitive to disruptions in trade credit. If component exporters cannot get credit, then assemblers cannot get parts, and the production cycle is interrupted. Even a limited financial disruption can affect the entire chain. Evidence points to GVCs being geographically consolidated after the global economic crisis (Milberg and

Winkler 2010), contributing to fiercer competition for developing countries seeking to enter or upgrade within a value chain. Developing countries new need strategies to benefit from the growing importance of these production networks (Cattaneo, Gereffi, and Staritz 2010).

Many MENA countries continue to depend on a small number of exports. Many countries in the world have benefited greatly from global integration, using trade and FDI as elements of a successful growth strategy. Many of the most dynamic developing countries have integrated into GVCs—often associated with inward FDI—and have become exporters of parts and components as locations for the assembly of finished goods. Others, including many countries in the MENA region, have benefited less, with only limited shifts away from traditional exports of primary commodities. Most MENA countries continue to rely on a highly concentrated export bundle, comprising mainly natural resources and low-transformation products, exported to just a handful of markets. Much of the trade dynamism of developing countries as a group is driven by Asian economies, which have collectively more than doubled their share of global exports since 1990. Other regions have seen much smaller increases in market share. Most of the recent Arab trade growth is due to increases in natural resource exports, both in volume and value (better terms of trade).

In many developing countries, export structures have remained highly concentrated, not only in terms of products and markets but also in terms of the number of exporters (Freund and Pierola 2010). Export diversification[4] remains a key means for developing countries to leverage trade for growth. In the past decade, a much better understanding of the links between diversification and economic growth has developed (see, e.g., Broda, Greenfield, and Weinstein 2006; Broda and Weinstein 2006; Felbermayr and Kohler 2006; Newfarmer, Shaw, and Walkenhorst 2009). Diversification is also a way to help manage the risks that can come with openness. Countries with more diversified export bundles exhibit a weaker link between openness and increased volatility of output growth (Haddad, Harrison, and Hausman 2010). To some extent, the process of market diversification is already well under way with the rise of South–South trade. There is still great scope to intensify the process, however, and in particular to further diversify at the product level.

Trade in services, particularly business services, has become a dynamic component of trade as well as a source of export diversification for many developing countries. During 2000–07, trade in services grew as fast as trade in goods, at an average rate of 12 percent per year. India's success is well known: exports of software and business process services account for approximately 33 percent of India's total exports. Many other countries have also increased services exports, but there remains significant scope for further growth (Cattaneo et al. 2010).

Openness brings opportunities, but it also brings vulnerability to global shocks. Globalization creates immense opportunities for countries to leverage global demand for goods and services. It allows countries to benefit from the knowledge and technologies that have been developed anywhere in the world, whether embodied in machinery, intermediate goods, FDI, or people. At the same time it greatly increases the need for governments to ensure that citizens are able to benefit from these opportunities: workers must be able to acquire the needed skills, firms need to access credit to finance profitable investment opportunities, and farmers need to be connected to markets (Porto and Hoekman 2010). Greater openness also increases the vulnerability of countries to global shocks. This has potentially major adverse consequences for the poorest households that do not have the savings needed to survive a period of unemployment or sharp falls in the prices of their outputs (and thus their incomes) resulting from global competition. The recent financial crisis demonstrated the importance of complementing greater openness with domestic policies and mechanisms to help poor households (Haddad and Shepherd 2011). Commodity markets are experiencing strong and sustained demand from developing countries, especially China. Price prospects looking forward are strong in energy and agricultural markets alike. Although this is good news for commodity exporters, for agricultural commodity importers food insecurity could have severe implications for their populations, particularly among the poor.

Tariffs are no longer the centerpiece of the policy debate. The policy responses to the recent crisis suggest that the incentives to use traditional trade policies have changed. In contrast to the last global recession, in the early 1980s, this time there was no widespread resort to import tariffs and quotas to support domestic production (Evenett, Hoekman, and Cattaneo 2009; Kee, Neagu, and Nicita, forthcoming). Instead, the focus of policy was on supporting domestic demand and providing specific industries with financial assistance. Insofar as trade policies are being used extensively in a manner that distorts global markets, this is largely limited to agriculture, where both import protection and export restrictions are used by net exporting countries.

This does not mean that import tariffs and other border barriers have become irrelevant. For example, barriers frequently arise in those MENA countries where tariff peaks persist and in those sectors where ad hoc import bans and quotas are sometimes used to ensure that domestic production is consumed first. Concluding the long-running Doha Round of trade negotiations would provide a boost to the world economy. It would create greater security of market access through the negotiation of policy disciplines, such as placing tighter limits on the level of permitted tariffs and outlawing agricultural export subsidies. The primary deliverable would be policy bindings—enforceable commitments by governments that they will not raise production of or support for domestic industries above a given level and will not use certain policies at all. Maintaining an open trade regime is, therefore, an important foundation for the global recovery and for the necessary reorientation of global supply and demand. This is especially true for developing countries, as so many depend on export markets to finance growth-stimulating imports of goods, services, and technologies.

One reflection of this is the engagement of governments in reciprocal preferential trade agreements (PTAs), which have come to be the major focal point for international cooperation on trade and investment policies. In contrast to the PTAs negotiated in the 1990s, the recent agreements seek to integrate markets for services and investment as well as for goods. Much of the policy focus of PTAs—including those between low-income countries—centers on regulatory cooperation and convergence and on actions to reduce trade costs.

More generally, reducing the costs that limit the "connectivity" of firms, farmers, and households to markets and supply chains is critical for trade opportunities to generate the investments and economic activities that can help reduce poverty. Disciplines to reduce such costs are on the agenda of the World Trade Organization (e.g., disciplines on trade and investment in services, nontariff barriers, and trade facilitation), but they are also increasingly taking center stage in regional trade agreements. "Connectivity" is often also a critical domestic constraint, especially in large countries and island economies.

Longer-term challenges loom on the horizon. Climate change poses major challenges of mitigation and adaptation for developing countries. There are likely to be important consequences for patterns of production and trade in agricultural products and for food security. Climate-related policies may have implications for trade, especially if they involve direct restrictions in the flow of goods and services at the border. Trade also offers opportunities to adapt to a changing climate, including through the acquisition and use of technology.

In short, policy makers in developing countries now confront a more complex trade agenda. International trade negotiations increasingly revolve around behind-the-border regulatory policies, not just import tariffs. Research findings also show that trade success is determined by behind-the-border factors such as low internal transaction and transport costs and efficient access to quality services inputs (Djankov, Freund, and Pham 2010). One implication is that traditional trade policies (tariffs and nontariff barriers) are instruments of diminishing utility for industrial or economic development policy (Harrison and Rodríguez-Clare 2010; Pack and Saggi 2006). Another implication is that the international trade and investment policy agenda increasingly lies outside the traditional domain of trade ministries. Instead it spans a plethora of policy areas that are the responsibility of other parts of government, including a variety of regulatory agencies. These bodies do not always consider the trade repercussions of their actions. The challenges of assessing and understanding this impact, identifying possible modalities for international cooperation to reduce trade costs without undermining regulatory objectives, and obtaining a national consensus on policy reforms that will support larger, more integrated markets can be daunting for any country, but especially for poor developing countries with limited administrative capacity.

The Trade and FDI Landscape in Partnership Countries

Trade

The Deauville Partnership has been launched against the backdrop of a changing Arab world that is not reaping the benefits of a globalized world economy. Although countries in the MENA region have made progress in recent years in exploiting their comparative advantages, the region's share in total world exports of non-oil goods has remained flat at around 2–3 percent for more than 20 years (figure 2.2). Despite doubling its ser-

FIGURE 2.2

Evolution of Regional Shares of Global Exports, 1988–2008

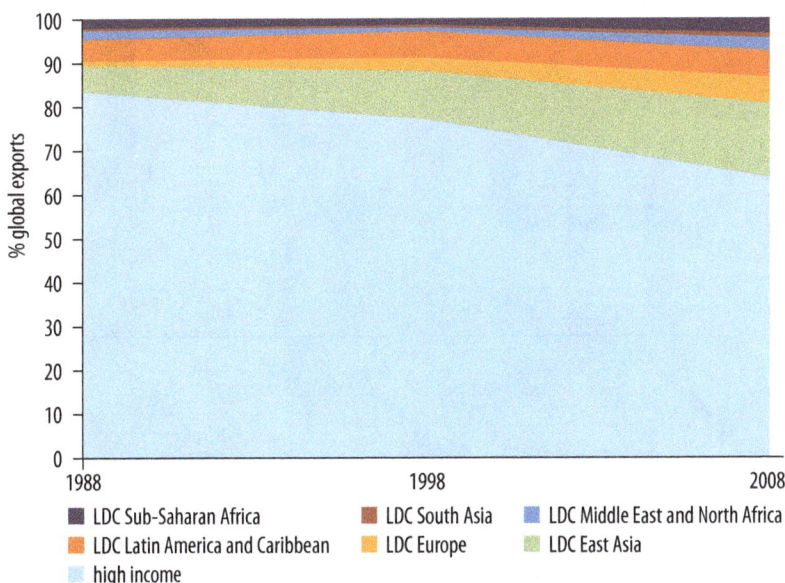

Legend:
- LDC Sub-Saharan Africa
- LDC South Asia
- LDC Middle East and North Africa
- LDC Latin America and Caribbean
- LDC Europe
- LDC East Asia
- high income

Note: LCD = less developed countries.

vices exports, the region has seen its share in total services trade also stagnate at around 2.8 percent during the period from 1990 through 2006.[5] These outcomes reveal serious competitiveness issues and suggest that the region has missed opportunities to integrate into the world economy, increase growth, and create new productive jobs. This general assessment also applies to individual Partnership countries, notwithstanding their heterogeneities in trade policy and trade outcomes.

A more detailed analysis of the MENA region's trade performance suggests that exporters in the region find it particularly difficult to expand their intensive margin, that is, to export more of their existing products to existing markets. In comparison to other regions, the MENA region is no less capable of exploiting the extensive margin, that is, exporting to new markets or exporting new products. It is in exploitation of the intensive margin, by growing their exports of existing products to existing markets, that the region underperforms in comparison to other regions, except Sub-Saharan Africa (figure 2.3). In contrast, the Asian miracle has relied on full exploitation of the intensive margin, including within Asia as part of global supply chains.

In part for this reason, intra-regional trade in MENA has not taken off. For many Arab countries, regional trade accounts for less than 10 percent

FIGURE 2.3

Growth of Non-Oil Merchandise Exports in Value Terms by Types of Margin, Selected World Regions, 1998–2008

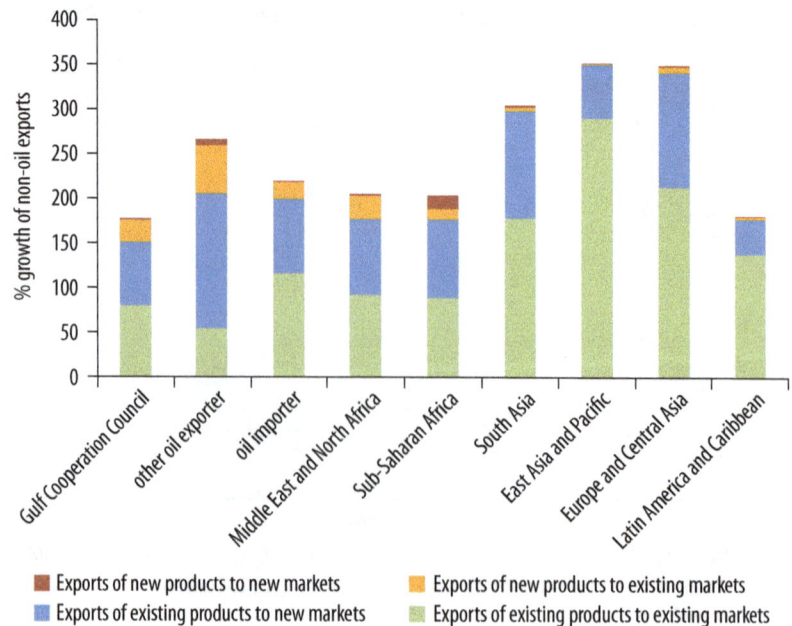

Exports of new products to new markets
Exports of existing products to new markets
Exports of new products to existing markets
Exports of existing products to existing markets

Sources: Ianchovichina, Gourdon, and Kee 2011; World Bank 2011b.

of total trade. At less than 5 percent, the Maghreb countries had the lowest share of intra-regional non-oil merchandise trade (figure 2.4), and this share has increased only marginally since 2000. Intra-regional trade in the Mashreq and Gulf Cooperation Council (GCC) countries represents a somewhat larger share of trade. In the case of the Syrian Arab Republic and the Republic of Yemen, regional markets account for more than half of all non-oil exports; for Bahrain, Lebanon, Oman, and the United Arab Emirates, it is in the 35–40 percent range; while it is more than 25 percent for the Arab Republic of Egypt, Jordan, Kuwait, and Saudi Arabia.

Despite a "spaghetti bowl" of overlapping PTAs (box 2.1), the Arab world is less integrated than many other regions. Overall, the share of

FIGURE 2.4

Export Share by Destination (Excluding Oil) for Maghreb and Mashreq Countrties, 2000 and 2007

a. Maghreb countries

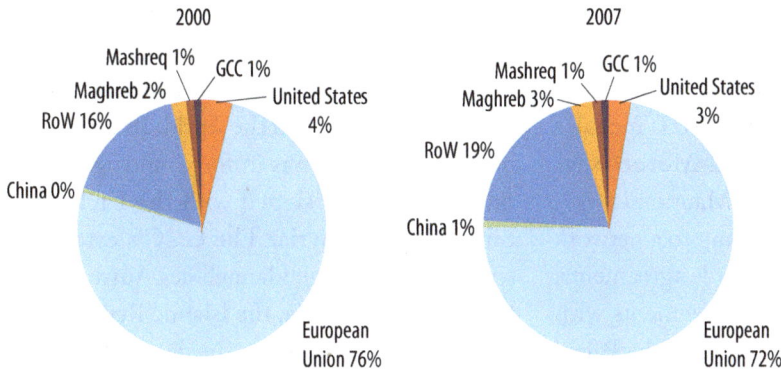

b. Mashreq countries

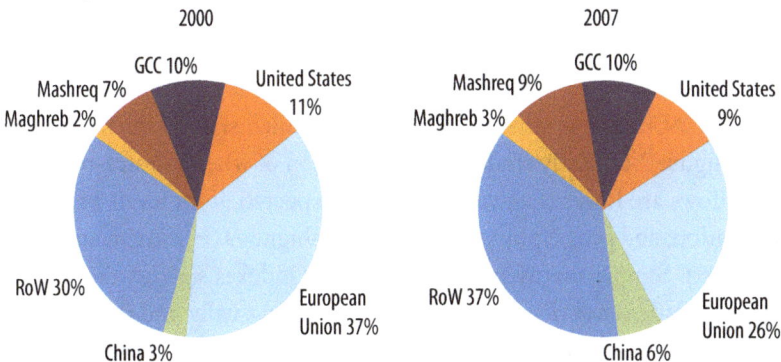

Source: World Bank calculations from UN Comtrade.

Note: RoW = rest of world.

BOX 2.1

PTAs Involving the Arab World

The idea of regional integration among Arab countries has been pursued for decades. Efforts to integrate the Arab world regionally date back to the 1950s, earlier than in any other developing region. Examples are the 1957 Arab Economic Unity agreement and the 1964 initiative by Egypt, Iraq, Jordan, and Syria to form an Arab Common Market. Today, the key multilateral trade agreements are the Agadir Agreement between Egypt, Jordan, Morocco, and Tunisia, which has been in force since 2007; the Gulf Cooperation Council Customs Union, in force since 2003; and the Pan-Arab Free Trade Area (PAFTA), in force since 1998, which includes members of the GCC and Agadir as well as other members of the Arab League. In addition, the Arab Maghreb Union (AMU) includes Agadir parties Tunisia and Morocco, as well as Algeria, Libya, and Mauritania.

Arab countries also belong to a network of intra-regional bilateral trade agreements. For instance, Jordan has agreements with Bahrain, Egypt, Israel, Morocco, the Palestinian Authority, Sudan, Syria, Tunisia, and the United Arab Emirates, and is negotiat-

ing with the GCC. Tunisia has agreements with Egypt, Iraq, Jordan, Libya, and Morocco. Egypt has agreements with Iraq, Jordan, Lebanon, Libya, Morocco, the Palestinian Authority, Syria, and Tunisia.

Links with countries outside the region are also expanding. Several countries are part of the Euro-Med process of agreements with the EU and the European Free Trade Association (EFTA). In addition, the United States has negotiated agreements with Bahrain, Jordan, Lebanon, Morocco, and Oman, and is currently negotiating with the United Arab Emirates. While individual members of the GCC have signed agreements with or are negotiating with the United States, the GCC as a group is also negotiating with a large number of partners around the world. Its agreement with Lebanon is in force, and agreements have been signed with the EFTA, Singapore, and Syria. The GCC's extensive negotiating agenda includes Australia, China, the EU, India, the Islamic Republic of Iran, Japan, Jordan, the Republic of Korea, MERCOSUR, New Zealand, Pakistan, and Turkey.

intra-MENA trade is small and has even declined slightly during 1998–2008 (figure 2.5). Early studies on the question of whether intra-regional trade flows are lower than what would be expected given levels of GDP, population, and geography are somewhat ambiguous (Hoekman and Sekkat 2009). Simple shares and trade intensity indexes suggest that intra-regional trade is not that low, yet gravity models usually find that trade is less than what would be expected. A more recent update of the gravity model suggests that there has been a noticeable change in the last few years, with trade now larger than what the standard gravity model would

BOX 2.1 (continued)

BOX FIGURE B2.1.1

The Network of MENA Regional Agreements

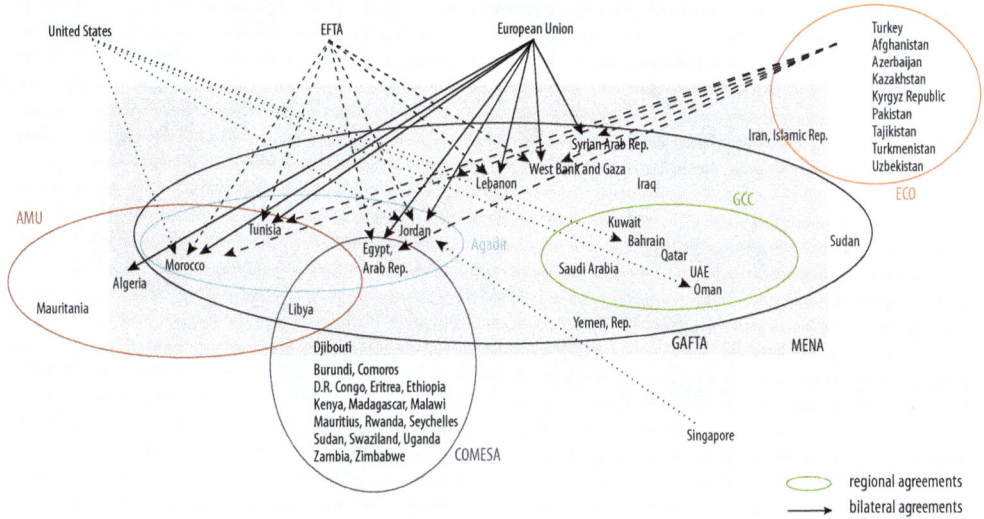

Source: World Bank 2008.

Note:

AMU: Arab Maghreb Union (5)

GCC: Gulf Corporation Council (6)

GAFTA: Great Arab Free Trade Agreement (18)

ECO: Economic Cooperation Organization (10)

COMESA: Common Market for Eastern and Southern Africa (19)

EFTA: European Free Trade Association (4), includes Iceland, Switzerland, Norway, and Liechtenstein

Agadir: Agadir Agreement for the Establishment of a free trade zone between Arabic Mediterranean Nations (4)

predict (Abedini and Péridy 2008). Yet in a world where trade is growing fast, one would expect more intra-regional trade regardless of regional agreements. In the case of the GCC, the increased integration seems to reflect the progress made in converging on common norms and policies in some regulatory areas and in integrating both factor and product markets.

The lack of intra-regional trade integration is as much a cause as a consequence of the region's economic difficulties. Low trade integration could be the result of poor production complementarities and other ex-

FIGURE 2.5

Distribution of MENA Trade by Region, 1998 and 2008

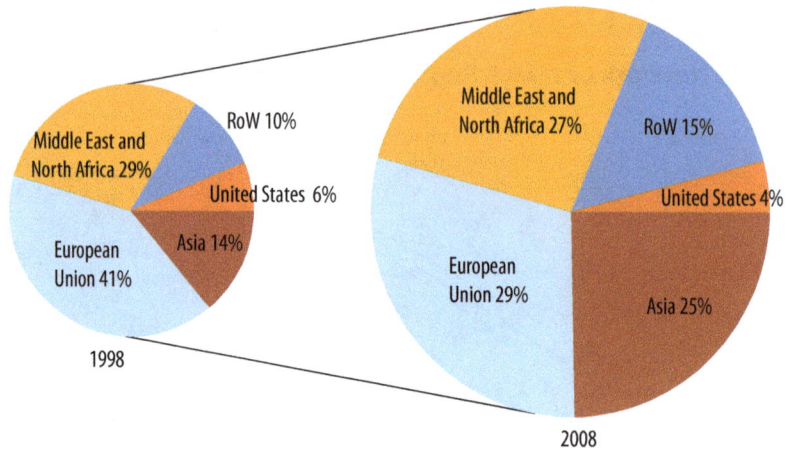

Sources: Ianchovichina, Gourdon, and Kee 2011; World Bank 2011b.
Note: RoW = rest of the world.

ogenous factors. Indeed, a number of Arab countries have similar resource endowments, production capabilities, and export structure. They may find it difficult to use regional integration as a means to establish patterns of specialization and diversification, but the lack of intra-regional trade is also to some degree policy-driven. As recently analyzed, public sector governance and participation, accountability and transparency, and rents and privileges remain key impediments to private sector development in the region (World Bank 2009). The very same causes also impede the region's capacity to export. Without improved rule of law, participation, and governance, trading across borders is difficult and trade cannot flourish on a sustainable basis. In turn, the lack of integration and exposure to new technologies, innovation, and ideas hampers more rapid progress in the region and helps explain many economic and social shortcomings: poor resource utilization, insufficient human capital, gender inequality, high unemployment, oversize governments, unfavorable investment climate, limited foreign investment, and, eventually, lackluster private sector performance.

In their destination of trade, Morocco, Tunisia, and to a lesser extent Egypt are mainly oriented toward the EU, while Jordan trades more with other Arab countries, including the GCC. Morocco and Tunisia trade predominantly with the EU, though the EU share has declined markedly in recent years (table 2.1). This has also been the trend in Egypt. Jordan trades less with the EU than the other three countries do. The EU represents less than 5 percent of Jordan's exports, but more than 20 percent

TABLE 2.1

Direction of Trade: Deauville Partnership Countries' Exports to and Imports from Selected Countries, 2000 and 2008

Partnership country	Canada		China		EU27		GCC		Japan		Turkey		United States		MENA excluding GCC	
	2000	2008	2000	2008	2000	2008	2000	2008	2000	2008	2000	2008	2000	2008	2000	2008
Direction of exports (% of total merchandise exports)																
Egypt, Arab Rep.	0.2	0.2	0.8	1.3	40.9	35.5	4.9	8.6	2.0	3.4	1.8	3.0	8.5	4.8	7.2	14.4
Jordan	0.1	0.2	0.0	1.8	5.8	4.2	19.3	15.0	1.4	2.6	1.5	0.5	6.6	16.8	17.9	24.3
Morocco	0.4	0.2	0.5	0.8	75.7	59.3	1.0	1.1	3.8	1.1	0.7	1.5	3.4	3.9	2.8	2.6
Tunisia	0.1	0.1	0.0	0.3	80.3	72.1	0.8	0.7	0.3	0.4	0.9	1.6	0.7	1.7	7.5	10.0
Direction of imports (% of total merchandise imports)																
Egypt, Arab Rep.	0.6	1.0	4.6	8.4	37.5	27.1	8.4	11.0	3.1	3.5	1.4	2.2	15.0	10.8	1.8	3.0
Jordan	0.8	0.5	4.2	10.4	36.4	20.9	6.0	25.1	4.5	2.9	2.2	2.6	11.3	4.6	7.5	8.0
Morocco	2.0	0.8	2.3	5.7	59.1	51.8	5.3	7.7	1.7	1.8	0.9	2.5	5.6	5.1	10.2	7.8
Tunisia	0.2	0.4	1.2	3.7	71.7	57.3	1.2	2.0	2.0	1.3	1.8	3.0	4.6	3.0	6.6	9.0

Source: World Bank calculations from UN Comtrade data.
Note: Data for Libya were not available. EU27 refers to the 27 EU member states.

of its imports. Jordan trades more with the MENA region than any other Deauville Partnership country. Exports to MENA, including the GCC, averaged about 40 percent of Jordan's total exports in 2008. Jordanian exports to the United States rose to 17 percent of total exports in 2008, from 7 percent in 2000. Exports from the Deauville Partnership countries to China have on average doubled between 2000 and 2008 but remain very low as a share of total exports.

Notwithstanding the relatively weak trade performance of the MENA region, and despite disruptions from regional conflicts, overall trade flows of Deauville Partnership countries have grown steadily since the early 2000s. The value of total exports and imports of goods and services has expanded over the past decade, and most of the growth has occurred since 2003. The global economic crisis had a significant impact on trade in 2009–10 (table 2.2). However, the net contribution of exports to economic growth has remained weak or even negative. The export-import coverage ratio of goods and services has been hovering around 100 percent for Egypt and Tunisia in recent years (figure 2.6, panel a). Morocco saw a significant drop in its import coverage during 2007–09 but has recovered since then. Jordan has been experiencing a steady decline since 2003, with an average export to import ratio of 65 percent between 2007 and 2010. Except for Morocco, most of the trade expansion has been driven by the primary and secondary sectors. For instance, Jordan and Tunisia have significantly expanded exports of textiles and pharmaceuti-

TABLE 2.2

Growth of Goods and Services Trade in Deauville Partnership Countries, 1996–2010

Partnership country	Export growth (%)			Import growth (%)			Trade (% of GDP)		
	1996–2003	2004–08	2009–10	1996–2003	2004–08	2009–10	1996	2005	2010
Egypt, Arab Rep.	4.1	23.8	−8.7	2.1	23.6	−10.5	46.9	63.0	47.5
Jordan	3.9	4.0	2.5	2.2	10.1	−0.4	131.0	146.9	110.4
Libya	NA	NA	NA	NA	NA	NA	52.5	94.7	NA
Morocco	6.6	8.7	0.7	4.7	11.0	−1.4	56.5	70.2	75.9
Tunisia	4.3	5.8	−1.4	4.0	5.1	−1.7	85.7	90.3	102.7

Source: World Bank, World Development Indicators 2011.

Note: NA = Not available.

FIGURE 2.6

Export Coverage of Imports and Share of Exports in Total Trade of Deauville Partnership Countries, 1996–2010

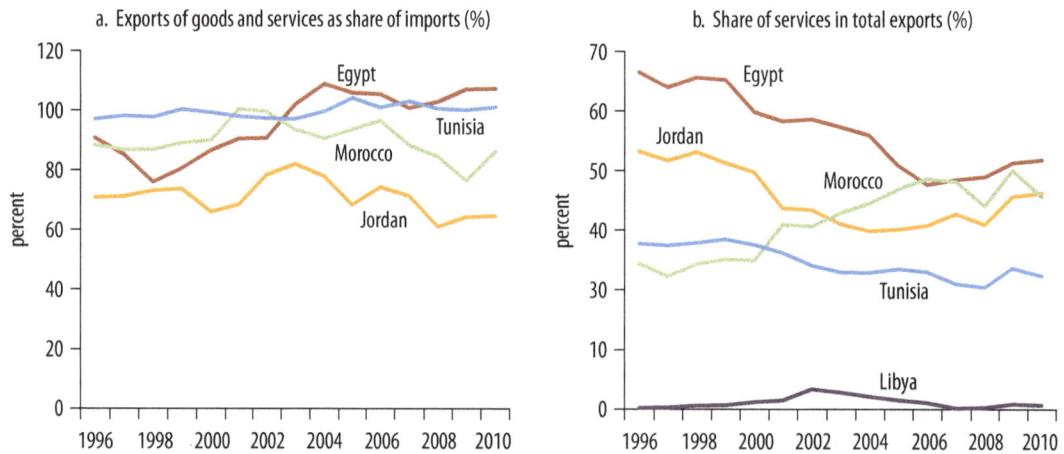

a. Exports of goods and services as share of imports (%)

b. Share of services in total exports (%)

Source: World Bank, World Development Indicators 2011.

cals. In contrast, Morocco witnessed a significant increase in its services trade (figure 2.6, panel b).

Relative to their potential, Jordan, Morocco, and Tunisia have been among the top achievers in the MENA region. These three Partnership countries (together with Bahrain and the United Arab Emirates) have been quite successful in maximizing their trade potential, on a par with the performance of successful emerging economies in Asia (Malaysia), Africa (Mauritius), and Latin America (Chile), although from a much lower potential basis (figure 2.7). In contrast, Egypt has been seriously underperforming in recent years, despite some opening up and liberaliza-

FIGURE 2.7

Non-Oil Export Performance Relative to Potential, MENA Countries and Selected Comparators, 1998–2007

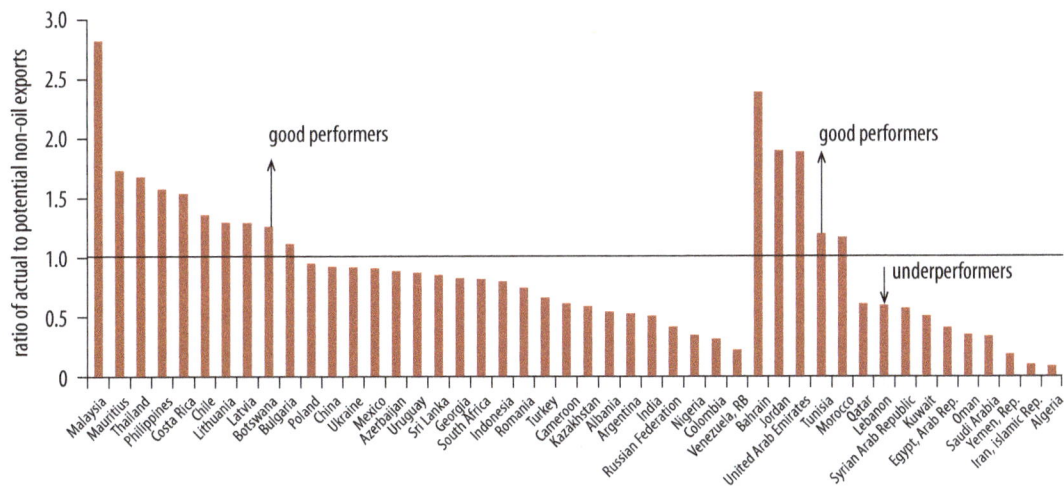

Sources: Ianchovichina, Gourdon, and Kee 2011; World Bank 2011b.

tion of the economy and the implementation of market-oriented reforms. Jordan, Morocco, and Tunisia have managed to expand both their intensive and extensive margins: they were able to export more of the same products to the same destinations and also to expand to new markets, though not so much to export new and more sophisticated products (i.e., the quality margin). The productivity content of Partnership countries' exports is estimated to have increased only moderately since 1990 (box 2.2) and their exports concentrated in peripheral clusters such as petroleum, garment, textile, and agricultural products (Appendix A).

Notwithstanding their relatively good export performance, both Morocco and Tunisia have been able to penetrate only a fraction of their potential markets. To be sure, no country would ever be able to supply all the world's imports of the products it exports. This would mean an export market penetration (IEMP) of 100 percent. The Federal Republic of Germany, one of the world's most successful exporting nations, exploits around 60 percent of its potential, and this can serve as a best-case benchmark. China and to a lesser degree India have been able to increase their IEMPs substantially between 1999 and 2008 (figure 2.8). In comparison, the IEMPs of Tunisia and Morocco have remained extremely low and flat at around 2–3 percent since 1999. Such low IEMPs point to serious competitiveness issues regarding product quality and the trade infrastructure and logistics needed to bring products to their potential buyers.

BOX 2.2

Have the Export Baskets of the Partnership Countries Diversified Toward Higher-Value-Added Goods?

Partnership countries have gradually become more sophisticated in terms of the knowledge and technology content of their exports, but they have lagged behind the fast-growing emerging economies of Asia. Several recent studies provide empirical evidence that countries which export higher-productivity goods will grow faster (Hausmann, Hwang, and Rodrik 2007; Krishna and Maloney 2011). The figure below illustrates the evolution over time of the productivity content of Partnership country exports relative to those of selected East Asian countries, using the methodology from Hausmann, Hwang, and Rodrik to derive an indicator ranking traded goods in terms of their implied productivity content (EXPY).

The productivity content of Partnership country exports has increased only moderately since 1990. Egypt's jump in 2005 was due to its diversification into petroleum gases and other gaseous hydrocarbons (mostly exported by rich countries) following the 2003 opening of the Arab gas pipeline that exports Egyptian natural gas to Jordan, Syria, Lebanon, and Israel. The sophistication of Libyan exports over the last decade reflects the productivity content of oil exports, although data are limited. The relative stagnation of export sophistication since 2004 in all Partnership countries except Egypt is particularly striking compared to the evolution of the index in China, Thailand, and Vietnam. For instance, Thailand had the same level as Morocco in the early 1980s, but by 2004 Thailand's export sophistication index exceeded those of Egypt, Jordan, Morocco, and Tunisia by almost 50 percent. Vietnam's export sophistication index started well below the indexes of Jordan and Morocco but exceeded both in 2005.

FIGURE B2.2.1

Productivity Content of Exports (EXPY) from Deauville Partnership Countries and East Asian Comparators, 1980–2008

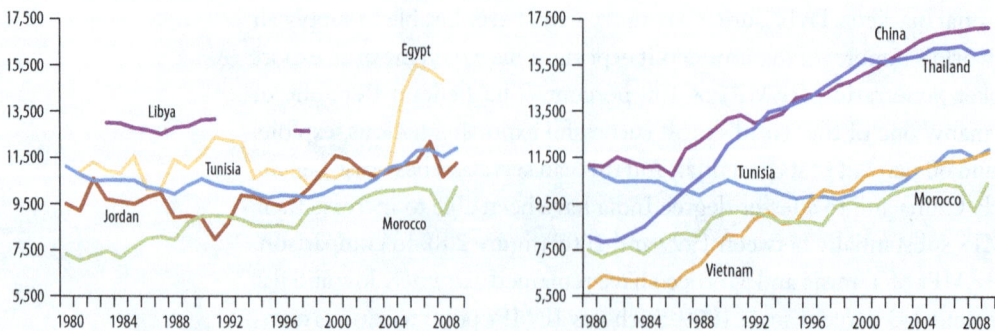

Source: World Bank calculations based on Comtrade data.

FIGURE 2.8

Index of Export Market Penetration in Tunisia, Morocco, and Selected Comparators, 1999 and 2008

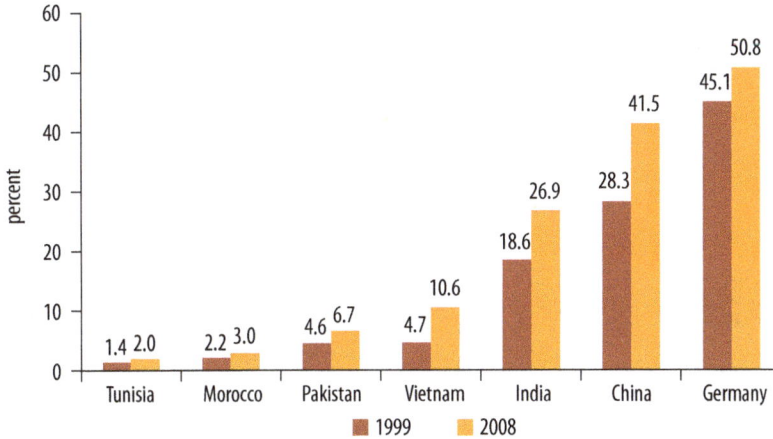

Source: World Bank calculations based on Comtrade data.

Foreign Direct Investment

As a share of GDP, FDI increased markedly in Partnership countries between the 1990s and the 2000s, although from a relatively low base. The FDI takeoff in the MENA region was apparent after 2002 (figure 2.9). In the oil importers with strong GCC links—Djibouti, Jordan, and Lebanon—FDI has increased so much that it now represents a major share of private investment. Among Partnership countries, Tunisia and Jordan were more successful than the average MENA economy in attracting FDI flows (measured as a share of GDP), while Egypt, Libya, and Morocco lagged behind the average. Inflows reached a peak in the two years preceding the global financial crisis and declined rapidly with the onset of the crisis.

In terms of nominal inflows, most of the FDI received by MENA has gone to the GCC countries. FDI flows have been concentrated in three countries: Saudi Arabia and the United Arab Emirates, which received 23 and 22 percent respectively of all MENA FDI inflows, and Egypt, which attracted 12.3 percent during this period. The other Partnership countries, being smaller economies, received considerably lower FDI inflows for this period. Jordan and Morocco each received 4 percent of total MENA FDI inflows, while Libya and Tunisia each received 3 percent of the total. There has been a shift in the destination of FDI from MENA's oil importers, which received over half of all MENA FDI during 1993–97, to MENA's oil exporters, which received 70 percent of all MENA

FIGURE 2.9

FDI in MENA Countries, 1990–2010

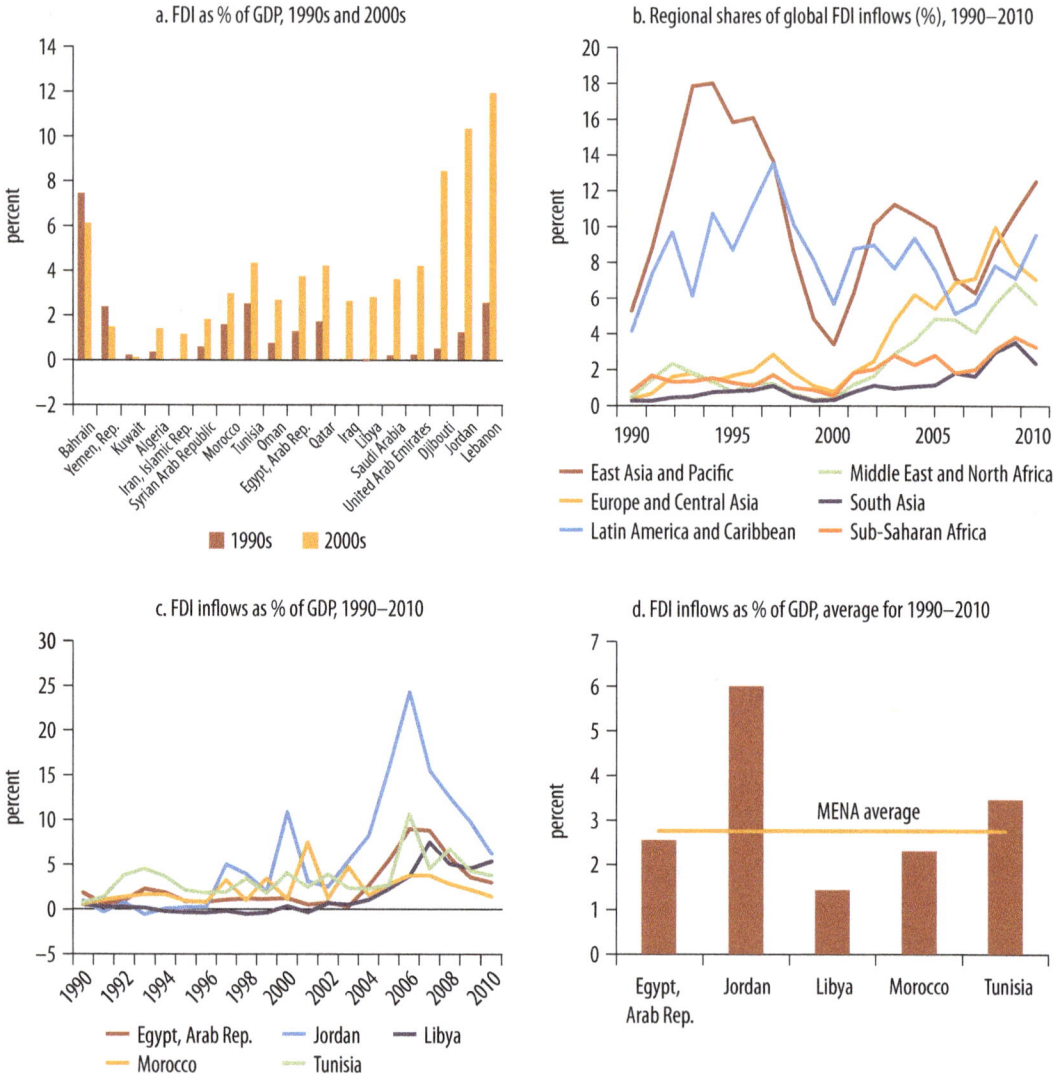

a. FDI as % of GDP, 1990s and 2000s

b. Regional shares of global FDI inflows (%), 1990–2010

c. FDI inflows as % of GDP, 1990–2010

d. FDI inflows as % of GDP, average for 1990–2010

Sources: World Bank 2011a; UNCTAD data; World Bank estimates.

Note: MENA = Middle East and North Africa.

FDI during 2003–07. The shift toward oil exporters is not surprising given rising oil prices during most of the 2000s. There is a strong positive relationship between the growth in oil prices and growth of MENA FDI (figure 2.10). High oil prices make oil exploration more attractive and thus draw FDI into the oil and gas sector. Other factors that stimulated

FIGURE 2.10

Growth in Oil Prices and FDI Inflows to MENA, 1992–2010

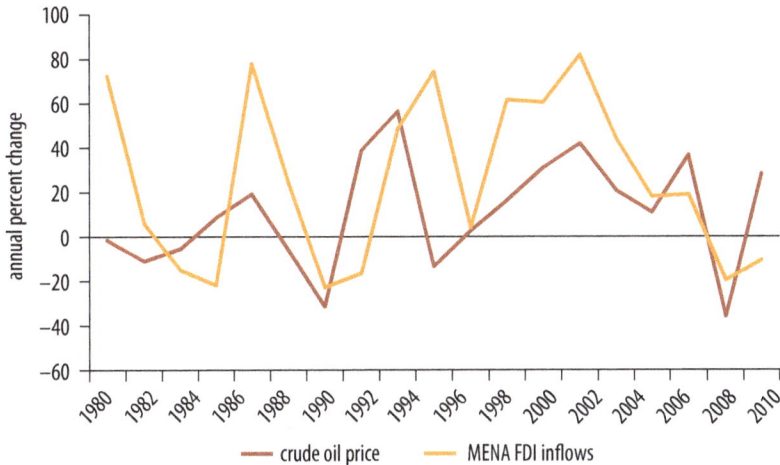

Sources: World Bank 2011a, using UNCTAD data.

Note: Crude oil price is the simple average of prices of Bent, Dubai, and West Texas Intermediate.

the rise of foreign investment in the MENA region were excess liquidity in global financial markets, reforms in business environments, and the launch of privatization initiatives.

FDI inflows to MENA economies are concentrated in two sectors: real estate and mining. According to the online database fDi Markets, which covers data on greenfield FDI values by country and sector, real estate activities and mining activities, including coal, oil, natural gas, and minerals, each received close to one third of all MENA FDI inflows in the period 2003–11 (figure 2.11). Manufacturing and tourism (the latter includes transportation services) also attracted FDI flows, but to a much lesser extent than real estate and mining. In the GCC economies, real estate, mining, and manufacturing each attracted approximately one fourth of all FDI inflows during the 2000s, while tourism attracted close to one fifth. Over the same period, among developing oil exporters, the mining sector attracted close to half of all FDI inflows, while the real estate sector received one third. Among oil importing countries the real estate sector was the top FDI recipient, accounting for half of all inflows, while the FDI shares of mining, manufacturing, and tourism were between 10 and 15 percent.

In Egypt, Jordan, and Libya, in 2003–11, most of the greenfield FDI was directed to the real estate and construction sector, while in Morocco the majority went to the mining sector. Only in Tunisia was the distribu-

FIGURE 2.11

FDI Inflows and FDI-Related Jobs in MENA, by Sector, 2003–11

a. Distribution of FDI flows and FDI-created jobs, by sector (% of total)

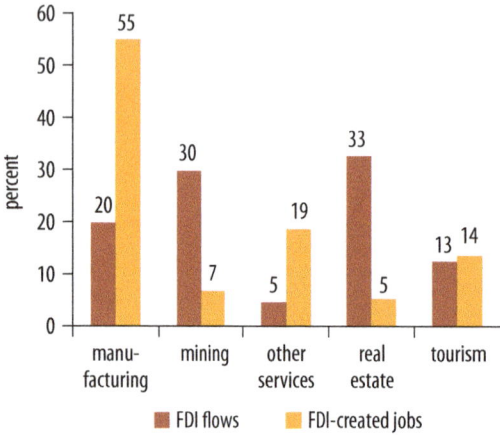

b. Distribution of FDI inflows, by country group and sector (%)

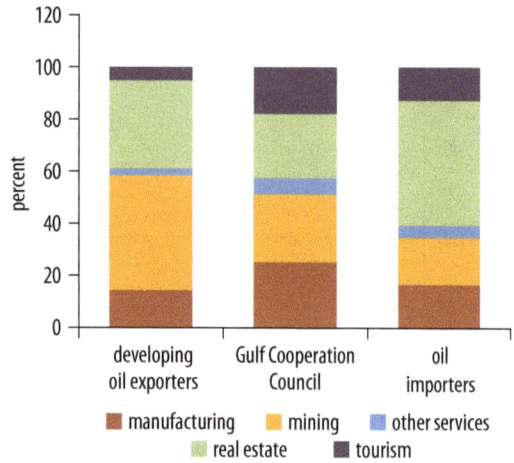

c. Distribution of FDI flows and FDI-created jobs, by country group (% of total)

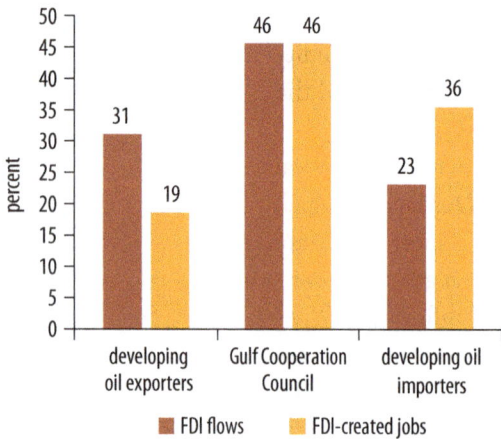

d. Number of FDI-created jobs, by sector and country group

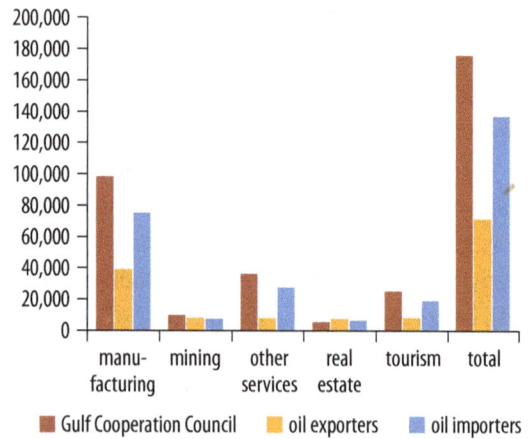

Source: World Bank 2011a.

Note: The mining sector includes the coal, oil, and gas industries, including petroleum refining, as well as mining of other products.

tion of greenfield FDI inflows fairly evenly distributed among sectors (figure 2.12, panel a). The GCC group of economies was the main source of greenfield FDI in Egypt, Jordan, Tunisia, and Libya (figure 2.12, panel b). The share of FDI supplied by the GCC averaged nearly 60 percent in Egypt, 70 percent in Jordan and Tunisia, and 50 percent in Libya. In Morocco the GCC accounts for only a quarter of FDI, while the EU plays a dominant role, with a share exceeding 40 percent. The United

FIGURE 2.12

Greenfield FDI Inflows to Deauville Partnership Countries as Shares of Total, 2003–11

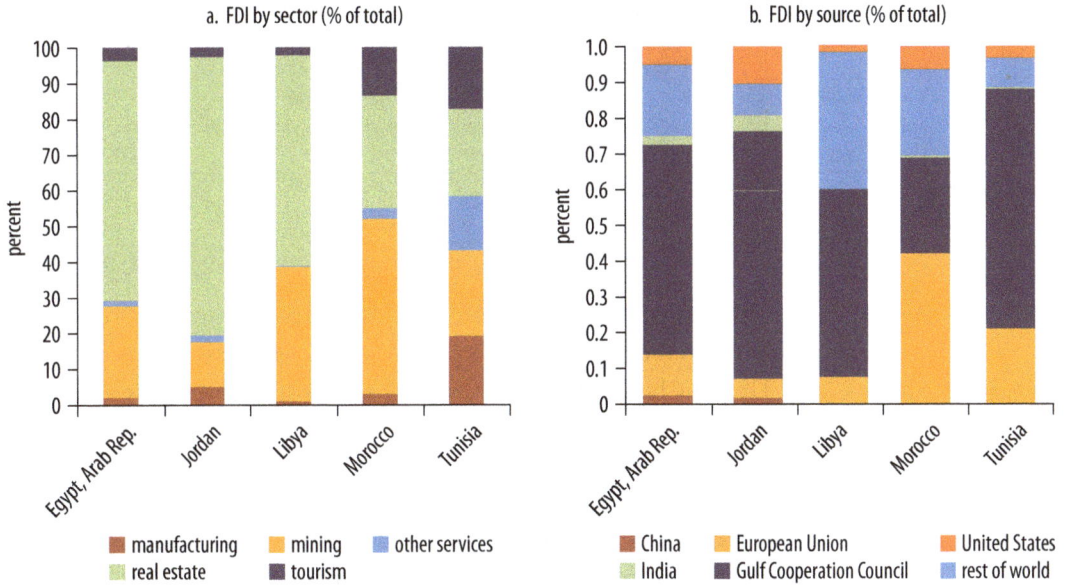

a. FDI by sector (% of total)

b. FDI by source (% of total)

Legend (panel a):
- manufacturing
- mining
- other services
- real estate
- tourism

Legend (panel b):
- China
- European Union
- United States
- India
- Gulf Cooperation Council
- rest of world

Source: World Bank estimates based on fDi Markets data.

Arab Emirates and Bahrain are the top investors in the Partnership countries. Among European countries, the United Kingdom is among the top five investors in Egypt, Libya, Morocco, and Tunisia, while Italy and France are among the top five investors in Tunisia (table 2.3).

Because of their concentration in mining and real estate, FDI inflows have not generated much employment in Partnership countries or in the MENA region more broadly. The comparatively large FDI in mining and real estate activities accounted for only 7 and 5 percent of all FDI-related jobs, respectively (figure 2.11, panel a). By contrast, the smaller FDI in manufacturing created most of the FDI-related jobs in the region in the period 2003–11. In particular, the labor-intensive food processing, consumer products, and textile industries accounted for the largest shares of FDI-related jobs created in the MENA region's manufacturing sector in this period. This outcome is consistent with the existing literature on the relationship between FDI, growth, and employment (Harrison and Rodríguez-Clare 2010). The FDI implications of productivity growth and employment depend on the particular sector and industry receiving FDI, the impact on employment in competing domestic firms, the nature of FDI, and the scope for spillovers.

TABLE 2.3

Top Investors in Deauville Partnership Countries

Investor rank	Egypt, Arab Rep.	Jordan	Libya	Morocco	Tunisia
1	United Arab Emirates	United Arab Emirates	Bahrain	Bahrain	United Arab Emirates
2	Qatar	United States	United Kingdom	United Kingdom	Bahrain
3	United Kingdom	Bahrain	Indonesia	Indonesia	Italy
4	Kuwait	India	United Arab Emirates	United Arab Emirates	France
5	United States	Saudi Arabia	Qatar	Qatar	United Kingdom

Source: fDi Markets.

Given that the manufacturing sector accounts for just a fifth of all FDI inflows to the region, there is potential to expand manufacturing-related FDI in the future and thus boost job creation in the region. Besides being a source of direct capital finance, FDI inflows can potentially lead to transfers of new technology and management know-how that can spur productivity and allow a country to catch up technologically. Foreign manufacturing firms tend to be larger and more productive and to have better access to markets than domestic firms. Thus, they may also be more successful in creating jobs. By fostering linkages with domestic

FIGURE 2.13

FDI-Related Jobs in MENA Countries, 2003–11

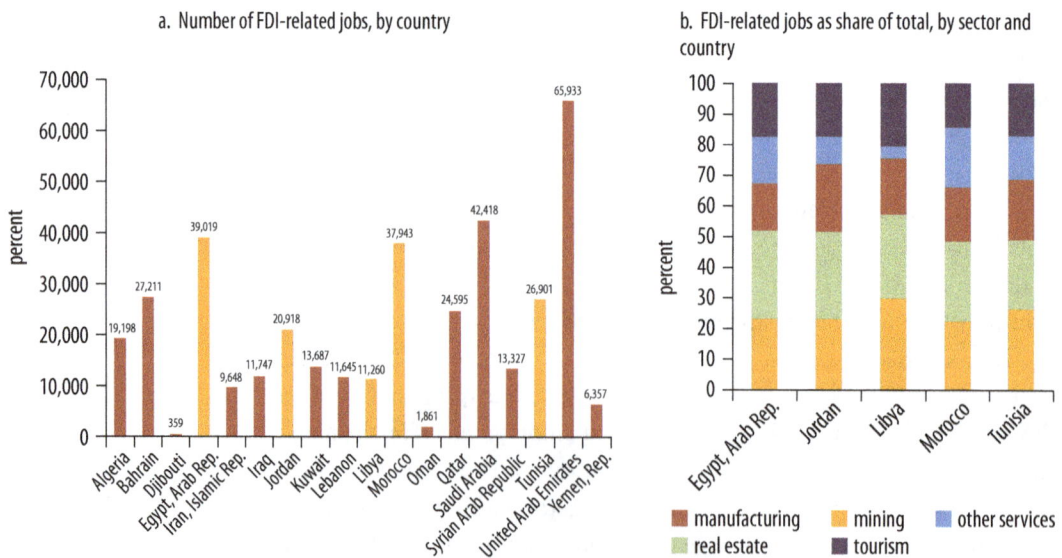

Source: World Bank estimates based on fDi Markets data.

firms, FDI can potentially create spillover benefits for other firms within and outside the sector that receives foreign investment.

Notwithstanding the composition of their FDI inflows, the Partnership countries have begun to reap some benefits from their FDI in terms of employment. To be sure, the GCC economies have been more successful than other MENA countries in attracting FDI and reaping the benefits in terms of job creation. The countries that gained the largest number of FDI-related jobs in 2003–11 were the United Arab Emirates and Saudi Arabia (figure 2.13, panel a). This reflects the magnitude of the FDI flows involved. Yet the Partnership countries (with the exception of Libya) were more effective at creating jobs through FDI. With less than a quarter of regional FDI, they generated nearly 40 percent of all MENA FDI-related jobs. They achieved this outcome largely because of FDI-linked jobs in manufacturing. In Partnership countries, around half of the FDI-related jobs were created in the mining and real estate/construction sectors. However, manufacturing jobs accounted for 20 percent in Jordan and slightly lower percentages in the other Partnership countries. In Libya, jobs in tourism accounted for 20 percent of all FDI-related jobs (figure 2.13, panel b).

Overall, the trade and investment performance of Partnership countries in this fast-changing landscape points to serious competitiveness challenges. The mixed economic performance of the past is due in large part to half-hearted domestic reforms and the capture of benefits by a few. When an economic opening is not accompanied by domestic reforms to promote competition and transparency in the domestic market, by the reallocation of factors through market flexibility, and by the adjustment of relative prices, the effect is often to displace rents rather than reduce them. Under such circumstances, the gains from economic liberalization can be captured by a well-connected few. In the same vein, the benefits of economic opening cannot be fully reaped if the design and governance of public policies, including sectoral policies, distort economic decisions and stifle competition.

A new integration strategy through trade and FDI should therefore show a clear break from the past (box 2.3). Such a strategy will need to confront political and political economy challenges, both from vested interests that benefit from markets not open to greater competition and from groups that have an instinctive resistance to inward FDI and greater imports. It should only support public policies that are designed and governed to foster growth and welfare (Aghion et al. 2011). The road ahead is promising—provided that the mistakes of the past are not repeated. Special attention should be given in the new strategy to promoting equity of opportunities so that the reform process benefits, and receives support from, the overwhelming majority of citizens.

Trade and Investment Promotion, a Cornerstone of Partnership Countries' Action Plans

Egypt, Jordan, Morocco, and Tunisia each submitted an action plan at the G8 Finance Ministers' Meeting in Marseille in September 2011. While the plans will no doubt be refined by the governments that subsequently took office in all Partnership countries, their broad focus on inclusive growth and employment is likely to remain unchanged.

Egypt, the Way Ahead: Facing Current Challenges and Building for the Future

Egypt's medium-term program under the Deauville Partnership focuses on sustainable growth, job creation, trade facilitation, and investment promotion, all to be pursued through regional and global integration. The program focuses on fostering investment through business-friendly policies and public investments. Public investments will be accelerated under public-private partnerships and build-operate-transfer arrangements, particularly in projects with the highest developmental and social returns.

Egypt is seeking opportunities to increase its exports in G8 markets and extend the Qualifying Industrial Zones umbrella to new areas. Egypt considers it crucial to associate trade facilitation with investment promotion, improved market institutions, and trade infrastructure to avoid supply bottlenecks and inflationary pressure.

Jordan: The Way Forward: Country Action Plan

Jordan's economic development program identifies improving the investment environ-ment as one of its seven priority pillars. Jordan is seeking the application of revised and simplified rules of origin with partner countries, including the regional convention on Pan-Euro-Mediterranean rules of origin with the EU. While the majority of Jordan's free trade agreements (FTAs) contain services liberalization rendezvous clauses, only the Jordan-U.S. and Jordan-Singapore FTAs contain a services chapter. In this respect, Jordan is seeking to advance services liberalization, including through signature of the Protocol on Trade in Services with the EU.

The program emphasizes that trade partners are to assist Jordan in addressing the barriers that impede entry of its products into international markets, including through twinning projects and capacity building for conformity with relevant standards. It also stresses the importance of facilitating movement of business people. Jordan seeks support from the Deauville Partnership through (a) loan guarantees; (b) partnership and investment in venture capital funds; and (c) partnerships and investment facilitation in key development projects.

Moroccan Plan for the Deauville Partnership

Morocco aims to achieve growth of 6 percent per year to reduce unemployment, eradicate poverty, and improve economic and social welfare. Morocco's expectations from the Deauville Partnership are (a) short-term support to consolidate the macroeconomic framework, including direct budgetary support, in particular to mitigate the impact of higher subsidization costs and de-

BOX 2.3 *Continued*

terioration of external balances by establishing compensatory facilities and a stabilization fund; (b) medium- and long-term support to bolster growth and job creation through financing and technical assistance; and (c) implementation of support through an approach that ensures donor harmonization and alignment with country systems.

At the trade level, the Deauville Partnership should help remove obstacles to increased trade, promote trade facilitation, and participate in the restoration and consolidation of external balances and development in general. Morocco seeks the removal of tariff and nontariff barriers to take full advantage of existing FTAs. These include rules of origin and restrictive standards affecting industrial goods; quotas, pricing regimes, and sanitary and phytosanitary standards affecting agricultural goods; and inadequate recognition of skills and qualifications affecting services trade.

Tunisia: Economic and Social Program: The Jasmine Plan

Tunisia's top priority in its economic and social program is to tackle unemployment, particularly among graduates in the less-developed regions, through investment programs. At the trade level, Tunisia aims to advance its integration into the world economy. This is identified as one of the 10 strategic targets in the medium-term economic and social program. Specifically, Tunisia is seeking to obtain advanced status with the EU and to expand FTAs with its main trading partners. Tunisia is also seeking to become an investment hub for Europe, Africa, the Middle East, and Asia.

In the Ennahda party's economic and social program, key trade and investment priorities are to increase the share and contribution of exports in the economy; upgrade the legal and administrative framework for international trade; diversify the economy by strengthening trade policy and representations abroad; promote trade in services, especially toward the African, Arab, Asian, and American markets; extend FTAs to countries in Asia and in the Americas; and consolidate trade among Maghreb countries through FTAs.

Notes

1. World Trade Organization, "Millennium Development Goals: Trade and Development," http://www.wto.org/english/thewto_e/coher_e/mdg_e/development_e.htm
2. The share of low- and middle-income countries in total world imports has nearly tripled, from 12 percent in 1996 to 31 percent in 2008. The global import share of the BRICs (Brazil, Russia, India, and China) more than tripled, from 4 to 12 percent. Consequently, high-income countries now account for less than 70 percent of world imports, compared with nearly 90 percent a little over a decade ago (Hanson 2011). From 2000 to 2008, Africa's exports grew

by 18 percent per year, mainly driven by exports to low- and middle-income countries, with exports to the BRICs increasing by over 30 percent per year during this period.

3. The term "value chain" describes the full range of activities that firms and workers do to bring a product from conception to end use and further disposal. This includes activities such as design, production, marketing, distribution, and support to the final consumer. The activities that constitute a GVC can be contained within a single firm or divided among different firms, may involve goods or services, and are often spread over a large number of countries.

4. "Export diversification" refers to producing and exporting existing products to new markets and new products to new markets (the so-called extensive margin of trade).

5. For a recent discussion of economic developments in the MENA region, see World Bank (2012).

References

Abedini, Javad, and Nicolas Péridy. 2008. "The Greater Arab Free Trade Area (GAFTA): An Estimation of Trade Effects." *Journal of Economic Integration* 23: 848–72.

Aghion, Philippe, Mathias Dewatripont, Luosha Du, Ann Harrison, and Patrick Legros. 2011. "Industrial Policy and Competition." GRASP Working Paper 17, Growth and Sustainability Policies for Europe. Previously published as CEPR Discussion Paper 8619, Center for Economic Policy Research, London.

Broda, Christian, Joshua Greenfield, and David E. Weinstein. 2006. "From Groundnuts to Globalization: A Structural Estimate of Trade and Growth." NBER Working Paper 12512, National Bureau of Economic Research, Cambridge, MA.

Broda, Christian, and David E. Weinstein. 2006. "Globalization and the Gains from Variety." *Quarterly Journal of Economics* 121 (2): 541–85.

Canuto, Otaviano, and Marcelo Giugale. 2010. *The Day after Tomorrow: A Handbook on the Future of Economic Policy in the Developing World.* Washington, DC: World Bank.

Cattaneo, Olivier, Michael Engman, Sebastián Sáez, and Robert M. Stern. 2010. "Assessing the Potential of Services Trade in Developing Countries: An Overview." In *International Trade in Services: New Trends and Opportunities for Developing Countries,* ed. Olivier Cattaneo, Michael Engman, Sebastián Saez, and Robert M. Stern, 1–28. Washington, DC: World Bank.

Cattaneo, Olivier, Gary Gereffi, and Cornelia Staritz, eds. 2010. *Global Value Chains in a Postcrisis World: A Development Perspective.* Washington, DC: World Bank.

Djankov, Simeon, Caroline Freund and Cong S. Pham, 2010. "Trading on Time," The Review of Economics and Statistics, MIT Press, vol. 92(1), pages 166–173, February.

Evenett, Simon J., Bernard M. Hoekman, and Olivier Cattaneo. 2009. *Effective Crisis Response and Openness: Implications for the Trading System.* Washington, DC: World Bank.

Felbermayr, Gabriel J., and Wilhelm Kohler. 2006. "Exploring the Intensive and Extensive Margins of World Trade." *Review of World Economics (Weltwirtschaftliches Archiv)* 142 (4): 642–74.

Freund, Caroline, and Martha Denisse Pierola. 2010. "Export Entrepreneurs: Evidence from Peru." Policy Research Working Paper 5407, World Bank, Washington, DC.

Haddad, Mona, Ann Harrison, and Catherine Hausman. 2010. "Prices vs. Quantities in the Great Trade Collapse." VoxEU.org.

Haddad, Mona, and Ben Shepherd, eds. 2011. *Managing Openness: Trade and Outward-Oriented Growth after the Crisis.* Washington, DC: World Bank.

Hanson, G. 2011. "Changing Dynamics in Global Trade." In *Managing Openness: Trade and Outward-Oriented Growth after the Crisis*, ed. Mona Haddad and Ben Shepherd. Washington, DC: World Bank.

Harrison, Ann, and Andrés Rodríguez-Clare. 2010. "Trade, Foreign Investment, and Industrial Policy for Developing Countries." In *Handbook of Development Economics*, vol. 5, ed. Dani Rodrik and Mark Rosenzweig, 4039–214. Amsterdam: Elsevier.

Hausmann, Ricardo, Jason Hwang, and Dani Rodrik. 2007. "What You Export Matters." *Journal of Economic Growth* 12 (1): 1–25.

Hoekman, Bernard, and Khalid Sekkat. 2009. "Deeper Integration of Goods, Services, Capital, and Labor Markets: A Policy Research Agenda for the MENA Region." Policy Research Report 32, Economic Research Forum, Cairo.

Hummels, David. 2007. "Transportation Costs and International Trade in the Second Era of Globalization." *Journal of Economic Perspectives* 21 (3): 131–54.

Ianchovichina, Elena, Julien Gourdon, and Hiau Looi Kee. 2011. "Anatomy of Nonoil Export Growth in the Middle East and North Africa Region." Paper presented at the 14th Annual Conference, "Global Trade Analysis," Venice, Italy, June 16–18.

Kee, Hiau Looi, Cristina Neagu, and Alessandro Nicita. Forthcoming. "Is Protectionism on the Rise? Assessing National Trade Policies during the Crisis of 2008." *Review of Economics and Statistics.*

Krishna, Pravin, and William F. Maloney. 2011. "Export Quality Dynamics." Policy Research Working Paper 5701, World Bank, Washington, DC.

Milberg, William, and Deborah Winkler. 2010. "Trade Crisis and Recovery: Restructuring Global Value Chains." Policy Research Working Paper 5294, World Bank, Washington, DC.

Newfarmer, Richard, William Shaw, and Peter Walkenhorst, eds. 2009. *Breaking into New Markets: Emerging Lessons for Export Diversification.* Washington, DC: World Bank.

Pack, Howard, and Kamal Saggi. 2006. "The Case for Industrial Policy: A Critical Survey." Policy Research Working Paper 3839, World Bank, Washington, DC.

Porto, Guido, and Bernard M. Hoekman, eds. 2010. *Trade Adjustment Costs in Developing Countries: Impacts, Determinants and Policy Responses.* Washington, DC: Center for Economic and Policy Research and World Bank.

World Bank. 2008. *MENA Economic Developments and Prospects: Regional Integration for Global Competitiveness.* Washington, DC: World Bank.

———. 2009. *From Privilege to Competition: Unlocking Private-Led Growth in the Middle East and North Africa.* MENA Development Report. Washington, DC: World Bank.

————. 2011a. *Middle East and North Africa: Investing for Growth and Jobs: A Regional Development and Prospects Report*. Washington, DC: World Bank.

————. 2011b. *Middle East and North Africa: Sustaining the Recovery and Looking Beyond: A Regional Economic Developments and Prospects Report*. Washington, DC: World Bank.

————. 2012. *Middle East and North Africa: Enabling Employment Miracles: A Regional Economic Developments and Prospects Report*. Washington, DC: World Bank.

WTO (World Trade Organization). 2008. *World Trade Report 2008: Trade in a Globalizing World*. Geneva: WTO.

CHAPTER 3

Improving Market Access and Regulations

The ability of the Partnership countries to use trade and foreign direct investment (FDI) to advance their development objectives and increase employment depends in part on the market access conditions that confront their exports and on the policies affecting their imports of goods and services. On both fronts, the Deauville Partnership could help lower trade and investment costs, spur economic growth and employment, and promote the economic integration of Partnership countries at both the regional and global levels. Rules and discipline are key to market access opportunities that are predictable, transparent, and nondiscriminatory. There are six priorities for the Deauville Partnership in this area:

- Improve market access for *agricultural products* and encourage investment to upgrade sanitary and phytosanitary (SPS) standards, promote agricultural research and extension, and deliver efficient irrigation services.

- Reduce tariffs on *manufactured goods;* streamline unnecessary nontariff measures (NTMs) to reduce trade compliance costs, red tape, and discretion; adopt simpler and more liberal rules of origin in preferential trade agreements (PTAs); and upgrade industrial norms and standards, testing, and certification procedures.

- Enable *services trade* to move up the value chain by fostering services liberalization and regulatory reforms, improving regional connectivity and cooperation, and supporting the presence of global services providers.

- Promote *solar energy* exports, including through a multilateral agreement on concentrated solar power (CSP); upgrade and expand infrastructure to increase electricity capacity and synchronize power grids; and open up and encourage nondiscriminatory, transparent, and predictable access to national transmission systems.

- Formulate comprehensive *labor mobility* strategies and open a sensible dialogue on ways to achieve a mutually beneficial increase in labor mobility through new mobility schemes, especially for less-skilled workers, based on incentive-compatible design under the principle of shared responsibility.

- Promote the process of institutional change through *regulatory convergence* of norms and standards and other behind-the-border regulations related to competition policy, government procurement, and other trade- and FDI-enhancing aspects of the regulatory environment.

Agriculture

Key issues

The share of agriculture in gross domestic product (GDP) is relatively modest for many Partnership countries, ranging from 3 percent in Jordan to 16 percent in Morocco, but its significance for job creation and social inclusion is much greater. Some 30 percent of employment across the Middle East and North Africa (MENA) region is in the farm sector, while agricultural growth is around 2.5 times more efficient at reducing poverty than growth in other sectors. Partnership countries compete successfully in international markets for fruits, vegetables, olive oil, cotton, and other produce. However, despite a comparative advantage founded on climate, seasonality, and labor costs, export growth has been impeded. Global agricultural trade is highly protected, and European Union (EU) tariffs average more than 15 percent on agricultural goods compared with 4 percent on nonagricultural goods. The Deauville Partnership has a potential role to play in opening or relaunching negotiations to liberalize agricultural, processed agricultural, and fisheries trade. This would involve progressive abolition of tariff-rate quotas, reference prices, seasonal import restrictions, and other nontariff barriers. For Partnership countries, the greatest benefits would arise through domestic reform. The Arab Republic of Egypt, Morocco, and Tunisia are among the 15 most protected economies in the world for agricultural goods. Reducing import protection unilaterally, as well as on a reciprocal basis, would improve consumer welfare and produce net welfare gains.

Complementary policies can enhance these benefits. Gains from trade liberalization increase when producers can reallocate land, labor, and capital from formerly protected sectors to newly profitable sectors. This calls for measures to streamline issuance of land and construction permits, modernize land titling, improve credit access, and build capacity to implement EU standards. Price supports and input subsidies that are used extensively have a large fiscal cost and fail to reach intended beneficiaries, as well as reward overuse of water. Partnership countries can more effectively use targeted programs such as cash transfers and public works in the context of a shift to greater openness.

Agriculture in Middle East and North Africa (MENA) countries has the potential to become competitive in both export and domestic markets, helping diversify the sources of employment and reducing poverty. With the possible exception of Libya, all Partnership countries have a comparative advantage in producing fruits and vegetables—provided that market access, domestic institutions, and regulation, including in the area of water management and SPS standards, allow for efficient marketing chains. Across the region, the modern horticulture sector is becoming a key force for market-oriented reforms. In Morocco's El Guerdane project, for example, export farmers are driving private participation in development and management of an irrigation scheme, following a public-private partnership investment in a new desalination and irrigation plant to improve water supply to a vital agricultural region. Farming efficiency needs to improve beyond these market niches, and rural populations need to move toward higher productivity and higher-wage activities. This could be achieved by creating the conditions for competitive agriculture and the emergence of nonfarm income activities to diversify the rural economy, and by providing rural people with critical supports, such as education, health, and information, that can help them take advantage of the economic opportunities available.

The recent rise in food prices has brought the issue of food security and the possibility of "Arab" self-sufficiency to the forefront of the policy debate. Agricultural production, especially of cereals, faces significant water constraints in the MENA region. This is particularly so in Partnership countries. With the exception of Morocco, they are net food importers and import a large share of their most important food staples, such as soft wheat. Nonetheless, many countries continue to encourage farmers to produce basic staples through a combination of tariffs and price supports. Over time, agricultural trade liberalization will lead to higher prices for some commodities, and through substitution effects will likely lead to an increase in prices for most other agricultural commodities. Allowing farmers to respond to such price increases may be the best way to address food staple scarcity over the long term. For short-term concerns, governments need to optimize their food security strategies by removing policy and infrastructure bottlenecks, improving the management of inventories, and using financial instruments to reduce exposure to price volatility.

An Untapped Agricultural Potential

The agricultural sector in the MENA region is more significant than its share in gross domestic product (GDP) would suggest. The production of crops and livestock in MENA is relatively small, ranging from 3 percent of GDP in Jordan to 15 percent in Morocco (table 3.1). To this, one should add the agricultural processing sector, which is closely linked to and dependent on agricultural production. Although statistics on the value of agricultural processing are scarce, the value added in the manufacture of food, beverages, and tobacco (a narrower concept that excludes the processing of nonfood crops such as cotton) ranges from 2.8 percent of GDP in Egypt to 4.6 percent in Jordan. Nonetheless, all these figures understate the importance of the agricultural sector in MENA. There are four main reasons.

First, the proportion of national employment in agriculture is larger than the sector's share of GDP. For example, 41 percent of the labor force in Morocco works in the agricultural sector. For the MENA region as a whole, about 30 percent of employment is in the agricultural sector. The rural population, much of which depends directly or indirectly on agriculture, varies from 22 percent of total population in Jordan and Libya to 57 percent in Egypt.

Second, poverty rates are generally higher in rural areas. For example, in Egypt and Morocco, rural poverty rates are approximately three times higher than urban poverty rates. As a result, more than 70 percent of the poverty in these two countries is found in rural areas (table 3.2). Chronic rural poverty is concentrated in certain social groups, such as female-headed households and landless households, and in defined regions, such as Upper Egypt, the mountains and steppes of Morocco, and northwest Tunisia. This gives MENA governments the opportunity to adopt clearly

TABLE 3.1

Role of the Agricultural Sector in Selected MENA Countries, 2010

Indicator	Egypt, Arab Rep.	Jordan	Libya	Morocco	Syrian Arab Republic	Tunisia	MENA developing	Global middle-income	World
Agriculture, value added as % of GDP	14.0	2.9	—	15.4	—	8.0	—	9.8	3.2
Manufacturing, value added as % of GDP	15.8	19.3	—	15.3	—	18.0	—	20.4	16.4
Food, beverages, and tobacco									
% of value added in manufacturing	17.8	23.7	—	19.7	—	17.3	—	—	—
% of GDP	2.8	4.6	—	3.0	—	3.1	—	—	—
Rural population as % of total population	57.2	21.5	22.1	43.3	45.1	32.7	42.0	51.5	49.1
Employment in agriculture as % of total employment	31.6	3.0	—	40.9	19.1	—	29.7	35.2	—

Source: World Bank, World Development Indicators 2011.

Note: Data refer to 2010 except for food, beverages, and tobacco, which refer to 2006. — = not available.

TABLE 3.2

Urban and Rural Poverty Rates in Egypt, Jordan, and Morocco, 2005–08

Country	Year	Poverty rate (%)			Rural population (%)	Share of poor (%)	
		Rural	Urban	Total		**Rural**	**Urban**
Egypt, Arab. Rep.	2005	27	10	20	57	78	22
Egypt, Arab. Rep.	2008	30	11	22	57	78	22
Jordan	2006	19	12	14	22	31	69
Morocco	2007	15	5	9	44	70	30

Source: World Bank, World Development Indicators 2011.

targeted rural and social development programs as instruments for the elimination of poverty. Above all, there is a strong link between the performance of the agricultural sector and progress in reducing poverty in Partnership and other MENA countries.

Third, international cross-country studies suggest that agricultural growth is 2.5 times as effective in reducing poverty as growth in other economic sectors (Ligon and Sadoulet 2007). This is because the benefits of agricultural growth accrue disproportionately to lower-income groups in society. China and Vietnam are examples of countries where agricultural policy reforms have led to high rates of agricultural growth and substantial progress in poverty reduction. On a smaller scale, the export of horticultural crops and other high-value exports have contributed to poverty reduction in countries as diverse as Kenya, Ghana, and Thailand (World Bank 2007).

Fourth, the gains from trade liberalization are generally greater in the agricultural sector than in other sectors. Although trade liberalization has reduced barriers to trade in numerous sectors, the agricultural sector remains highly protected in many countries, including those in the Deauville Partnership. Most countries use a variety of measures, including tariffs, tariff-rate quotas, and nontechnical barriers, to protect their farmers from import competition. As a result, agriculture is one of the most distorted sectors in the world economy. This is also true for Deauville Partnership countries. Economic theory and most empirical studies suggest that the benefits of trade liberalization exceed the costs, at least on aggregate. However, policy makers are reluctant to reduce trade protection for their own industries and farmers unless they are sure that other countries will reciprocate.

Given the high level of protection in agricultural markets around the world, market access barriers for agricultural exporters, and especially for poor agricultural exporters, are much higher than in other sectors. Even taking into account preferences, developing country exporters face an average tariff of 15.6 percent for agriculture and food as compared to 9.3 percent for textiles and clothing and just 2.5 percent for other manufactures (Anderson and Martin 2006). Given their trade orientation, Partnership countries have been particularly affected by the EU tariff protection for agricultural and fishery products. A recent review of EU trade policy by the World Trade Organization (WTO) found that the EU had 1,998 tariff lines for agricultural products. The average tariff for agricultural products is 15.2 percent, compared to just 4.1 percent for nonagricultural products. In addition, the EU uses non–ad valorem tariffs, tariff-rate quotas (in which the tariff varies depending on the level of imports), reference prices, seasonal restrictions, domestic and export subsidies, and other nontariff barriers to agricultural trade. Seasonal tariffs are applied to fresh fruits and vegetables to protect EU growers during the European growing season. Partnership countries therefore have a strong interest in promoting greater market access for the agricultural commodities that they export, especially fruits and vegetables. Tunisia would also benefit from a reduction in EU tariffs on olive and olive oil imports, while Egypt would gain from reduced domestic support by the United States and (to a lesser extent) the EU for their cotton growers.

Partnership countries would benefit greatly from further liberalization of agricultural markets in the EU and other Deauville partners. Although the EU is the largest trading partner of all Partnership countries, Partnership countries often feel that the bilateral Association Agreements have not fully delivered the expected welfare gains. One important reason is that until now the agricultural sector has largely been excluded from these agreements (a comprehensive Morocco-EU agreement was just approved in early 2012). Simulation studies confirm the economic intuition that the gains from the agreements would be much larger if the agreements included liberalization of the agricultural sector (Minot 2012). Easing of EU tariff and nontariff barriers to imports of fruits, vegetables, olive oil, and sugar would be particularly beneficial to the Partnership countries. In particular, they would benefit from liberalization of the complex EU regulations regarding horticultural imports and from increased technical assistance to help them comply with the complex and extensive SPS regulations regarding meat, fruits and vegetables, and other food imports.

Partnership countries would gain even more from the liberalization of their domestic agricultural markets. Partnership countries have relatively high levels of protection for farmers: Egypt, Morocco, and Tunisia are among the 15 most protected economies in the world (Bouët 2006). The commodities that are the most protected are wheat, sugar, dairy, and livestock products. While recognizing the political sensitivity of agricultural prices, leaders in Partnership countries should also keep in mind that most of the benefits of an expanded Association Agreement or Deep and

Comprehensive Free Trade Area (DCFTA) with the EU will be related to the degree of domestic liberalization within their own countries. To be sure, the benefits will be larger if domestic liberalization is combined with a reduction in the trade barriers to agricultural imports in the EU (which is the rationale for insisting on reciprocity), but unilaterally reducing import protection for agriculture will increase overall welfare, aggregate output, and employment. Under fairly plausible assumptions, it is easy to demonstrate that the static benefits of lower domestic prices to consumers are greater than the static losses to producers (Minot 2012).

There is scope for trade reform outside the context of reciprocal trade agreements. This is illustrated by Egypt's trade reforms of 2004. In addition, a number of MENA countries unilaterally reduced import tariffs on wheat products and other staples during the 2007/08 food crisis. While a legitimate concern is that poor farmers in Partnership countries cannot compete with large-scale, technologically advanced farmers in developed countries, particularly if the latter are protected by tariff and nontariff barriers and receive production subsidies, evidence suggests that Partnership countries can indeed compete in markets—even distorted markets—where they have comparative advantages. Egypt is a competitive exporter of fresh vegetables and rice; Morocco exports fresh fruit to Europe; and Tunisia is a major exporter of olive oil. Small farmers in Partnership countries can compete in the market for many fresh fruits and vegetables because their costs for labor and land are lower and because they enjoy a climate that is more suitable for the production of some crops, particularly during the European winter. Furthermore, as described below, studies suggest that agricultural protection is a costly and imprecise tool with which to address the problem of rural poverty.

There is also scope for further liberalization of South–South agricultural trade. The benefits of regional integration within the MENA region have been limited to date. Regional agreements such as the Pan Arab Free Trade Area (PAFTA) and South–South bilateral agreements either exclude trade in agricultural products or tend to be fairly flexible, allowing numerous exceptions for sensitive goods, permitting protection to vary by season, and granting countries the right to suspend tariff reductions under certain circumstances. Since the costs of protection rise more than proportionately with the level of protection, allowing a relatively small number of exceptions can largely negate the gains from trade liberalization. To generate significant gains for member countries, PAFTA and other regional bilateral agreements will have to insist on a greater level of discipline on tariffs and nontariff barriers. One approach might be to reduce the maximum level of tariff protection gradually, thus constraining the highest tariffs first. For instance, in Morocco tariff rates on agricultural imports peak at more than 300 percent for a number of livestock products.

Agricultural trade protection is an ineffective instrument for poverty reduction. However, the effect of global agricultural trade liberalization on poverty is ambiguous and varies widely across countries. First, the effect of trade liberalization on agricultural prices is uncertain. Global agricultural trade reform is likely to increase world agricultural prices, but domestic trade liberalization will reduce domestic agricultural prices relative to world prices. The net effect of liberalization on domestic agricultural prices depends largely on the initial level of protection. If the level of domestic protection is high (as in Morocco and Tunisia), then full trade liberalization is likely to reduce domestic agricultural prices. If, on the other hand, domestic protection is modest (as in Egypt and Jordan), then full trade liberalization may have no effect on or may slightly increase domestic agricultural prices. Second, the impact of changes in agricultural prices on poverty is also uncertain. The impact of trade liberalization on certain agricultural producers may be substantial, and vulnerable households should be supported through targeted safety programs.

One option for reducing the distorting effects of agricultural support policies while maintaining support to farmers is decoupled payments. Currently, Partnership countries offer their farmers guaranteed prices for staple and industrial crops, as well as a large gamut of input subsidies. The political aims are to improve food security and reduce rural to urban migration. Price supports for key staples and energy subsidies (for pumps) are also common across the region. However, price supports and untargeted subsidies are not focused on the poor, have a large fiscal cost, reward low-value cropping, and encourage the overuse of water.

One way to implement a socially acceptable and politically feasible reform is to replace payments to farmers linked to current production, as well as price supports, with payments decoupled from these measures. Such decoupling policies have been implemented in a number of developed countries and in some emerging countries such as Mexico and Turkey (Baffes and de Gorter 2004). For instance, Turkey was providing $6.4 billion in support for agriculture in 2000, of which $1.4 billion was price support and input subsidies and $5 billion was in the form of import protection. In 2001 Turkey launched the Agricultural Reform Implementation Program and introduced direct income support payments to farmers, decoupled from production decisions, while phasing out agricultural price supports and input subsidies. Between 2001 and 2004, the payments increased, while price supports and input subsidies were phased out (Cakmak 2004; Olhan 2006). However, decoupled payments are not necessarily pro-poor: they exclude poor nonfarmers, such as agricultural wage laborers, owners of microenterprises, and the urban poor. Furthermore, among farmers, benefits are generally proportional to farm size and thus are likely to be greater for richer farmers than for poor farmers. Finally, the fiscal burden of decoupled payments can be quite high, particularly when a large proportion of the population is involved in agricultural production. If the objective is to assist poor and vulnerable households regardless of their occupation, different types of program should be considered.

Existing universal food subsidy programs in Partnership countries impose high fiscal costs with little return in terms of poverty reduction and food security. The cost of such programs ranges from 0.7 percent of GDP in Morocco to 2 percent of GDP in Egypt (World Bank 2011a). Making certain basic staples such as bread, wheat flour, cooking oil, and sugar available at below-market prices to all consumers, sometimes using separate government-managed supply channels, is a highly regressive and inefficient policy that generally benefits the nonpoor more than the poor (Coady, Grosh, and Hodinott 2002). In addition to leakage, these programs suffer from undercoverage, as they often exclude rural households. Targeted food subsidy programs that make subsidized food available to selected households through low-price shops located in poor neighborhoods or through ration cards have had mixed results. Egypt, Jordan, Tunisia, and more recently the Islamic Republic of Iran have attempted to introduce targeting into their food subsidy programs (Coady 2004). In the Egyptian experience, though, corruption and political pressure led to a situation in which large numbers of nonpoor households held ration cards, and efforts to narrow eligibility faced strong political opposition (Kherallah et al. 2000). As in the case of assistance to poor farmers, other more effective programs should be considered, such as well-targeted school food programs, food-for-work programs, and targeted cash transfer programs (see chapter 6).

To increase its benefits, the liberalization of agricultural trade requires the implementation of complementary measures to facilitate this trade. It is by now well established that the gains from trade liberalization increase when consumers and producers have the capacity to respond to new opportunities and new prices. Studies of trade liberalization in Morocco and Tunisia show that when factor markets are flexible, the benefits of trade liberalization are three to five times greater than when factor markets are rigid (Dennis 2006b). Flexible factor markets allow factors of production (such as land, labor, and capital) to be reallocated from formerly protected sectors to newly profitable sectors. The agricultural sector in Partnership countries would therefore benefit from countrywide reforms to facilitate the use of temporary workers and expatriates, streamline the application for and issuance of land and construction permits, lower capital requirements for starting a new business, modernize land titling systems, and facilitate access to credit. Complementary policies more specific to the agricultural sector involve measures to reduce the transaction costs related to domestic and international trade, including excessive documentation requirements, authorizations from multiple agencies, unclear or subjective criteria for the application of duties, and delays and uncertainties related to customs clearance. Trade facilitation measures also include the provision of effective agricultural services such as well-functioning input and output markets, extension services, and market information systems that provide farmers with useful information about the agronomic and economic aspects of shifting into new commodities. Indeed, even under agro-climatic constraints, farmers are usually able to respond to incentives to shift into new crops when input and output prices or technologies change.

Improving Food Security

Despite the scope for progress in facilitating trade, food security concerns in Partnership countries are likely to continue to dominate all considerations. Agricultural policy in the MENA region and in the Partnership countries in particular is not only about market access, tariff liberalization, and adoption of international SPS standards. The MENA region is highly dependent on food imports and is perhaps the region most threatened by high and volatile grain prices. Net food imports, expressed in caloric terms, as a percentage of consumption are over 50 percent in Libya, Morocco, and Tunisia and over 25 percent in Egypt and Jordan, among the highest in the world (Breisinger et al. 2010). Since the global food crises of 2007/08 and 2010/11, international prices of wheat, rice, maize, and other commodities have been higher and more volatile than in the first part of the decade. It has been estimated that the import price increases of 2010 imposed a cost equivalent to 0.6 percent of total GDP on the region (World Bank 2011a). The range of policy responses in the MENA region includes programs to stimulate agricultural production, decisions to release public food reserves in the short run (and build them up in the long run), restrictions on food exports, reduced taxes and import tariffs on food and fuel, expanded cash transfer programs, and other safety net programs (World Bank, FAO, and IFAD 2009). In spite of the debate on the merits of each policy measure, there is agreement that greater attention must be paid to the agricultural sector to reduce vulnerability to global food commodity price shocks.

Some policymakers within the MENA region (and elsewhere) consider food self-sufficiency an important strategy for achieving national food security. The argument is that if a country can meet its own consumption requirements for food, particularly staple grains, then it will be less vulnerable to fluctuating international prices and possible disruptions of supplies. Indeed, food imports represent between 9 and 19 percent of the value of total merchandise imports in Partnership countries. This is higher than the global average of 7 percent (table 3.3). Morocco is the only net food exporter. Egypt imported 45 percent of its domestic wheat requirements, while Tunisia and Morocco imported more than 60 percent of theirs, and Libya and Jordan imported virtually all of their wheat requirements. Furthermore, trends in population, income growth, and urbanization, combined with limited land and water resources, suggest that the level of cereal and food import dependence will likely rise in the coming decade (Magnan et al. 2011).

Policies that promote food self-sufficiency and maintain public food reserves may be considered a form of insurance. However, it is important to evaluate the cost of these policies relative to the amount of risk reduction achieved. This requires country-specific analysis of policy options, but several general observations can be made. First, partial self-sufficiency does not break the link between domestic food prices and world markets. Many MENA countries adopt an intermediate goal of increasing grain self-sufficiency to a certain level. However, increasing grain self-sufficiency from, say, 40 to 65 percent cannot be expected to protect the domestic market from fluctuations in world markets. Second, even full self-sufficiency will not eliminate price volatility; instead, it changes the source of volatility. For a closed economy that is fully self-sufficient in wheat, changes in world prices will not have a direct effect on domestic prices, but changes in domestic supply will. The volatility associated with weather-related changes in the size of the harvest can be as large as or larger than volatility associated with international markets (Minot 2012).

TABLE 3.3

Measures of Food Import Dependence in Selected MENA Countries, 2010

Indicator	Egypt, Arab Rep.	Jordan	Morocco	Syrian Arab Republic	Tunisia	Global middle-income	World
Imports (constant 2000 US$, billions)	55.0	9.6	23.3	10.7	12.5	3,568	12,742
Food imports (constant 2000 US$, billions)	10.5	1.6	2.7	—	1.2	271	944
Exports (constant 2000 US$, billions)	48.4	5.8	18.7	8.0	11.8	3,795	13,203
Food exports (constant 2000 US$, billions)	8.3	1.0	3.6	—	0.9	395	1,079
Food imports as % of total imports	19	16	11	—	9	8	7
Food exports as % of total exports	17	17	19	—	8	10	8
Ratio of food imports to food exports	1.27	1.64	0.75	—	1.29	0.68	0.87
Net food imports as % of total exports	22	27	14	—	10	7	7

Source: World Bank, World Development Indicators 2011.

Note: Data for Libya were not available. — = not available.

Third, the opportunity cost of grain self-sufficiency can be quite high. Currently, MENA countries export a variety of high-value agricultural commodities, which generate foreign currency and help "pay for" the importation of wheat and wheat flour. For example, Morocco exports fresh fruits and vegetables, Tunisia olive oil, and Egypt cotton, vegetables, and rice. Given the constraints on arable land, expanding domestic production of wheat and other grains would require displacement of these high-value crops.

Policy makers in Partnership countries are understandably concerned about the high and volatile prices of wheat and other staple foods in world markets. Policy responses to these price trends include temporary reduction of import tariffs on imported staple foods, increased consumption subsidies, and rapid buildup of public grain stocks. While understandable from the point of view of an individual country, temporary changes in trade restrictions tend in aggregate to be pro-cyclical in that they exacerbate the volatility in world prices of wheat and other commodities. They also create uncertainty and unpredictability in domestic grain markets, discouraging private sector storage and trading activity.

A more cost-effective approach to reducing the volatility of domestic prices of wheat and other staple foods would be to improve import supply chains and explore modern risk management tools such as forward delivery contracts, futures markets, and call options. Such an approach would serve the dual objectives of improved food security and modernization of the agricultural sector. Recent studies suggest that average transit time of a ton of wheat in MENA countries is 78 days, and transit costs are approximately $40 per metric ton. For comparison, in the Netherlands average transit time is 18 days and costs are $11 per metric ton, while in Korea average transit time is 47 days and costs are $17 per metric ton. While there are differences in performance of the import supply chains in different countries, significant efficiency improvements can potentially be gained by reducing the time it takes to import wheat, the base cost of importing wheat, and product loss, which can be as high as 5 percent. Jordan and Morocco have started to explore the use of these modern risk management tools. Risk management also requires accurate, timely, and spatially disaggregated information on rainfall, local harvests, market prices, and internal commodity flows. Partnership countries would benefit from strengthening market information systems to include weather and crop production data and from investing in supply chain infrastructure, which can bring down the cost of moving and storing the grain and reduce the time to restock. In all these areas, the Group of Eight (G8) and other Deauville partners could usefully provide the necessary technical assistance and capacity-building support needed for the development of effective modern risk management tools such as forward delivery contracts, futures markets, and call options.

One of the most constraining factors for agricultural production in Partnership countries is low and variable rainfall (table 3.4). Less than 10 percent of the agricultural land in most MENA countries is irrigated, although Egypt is an exception in that virtually all crops grow under irrigation. In spite of the small percentage of arable land that is irrigated, it is estimated that 60 percent of the food grown is produced under irrigation. In spite of the importance of irrigation, water use systems suffer a number of problems, including low surface delivery due to leakage and evaporation, inequity in distribution, insufficient maintenance, and inadequate drainage leading to salinization and waterlogging (World Bank 2011a). The absence of market-based water fees or adequate quantitative controls encourages wasteful use of water by those who have access, as well as overextraction of groundwater. It also reduces the incentives to invest in water-saving technology and develop drought-resistant crop varieties. As a result, water withdrawals in the MENA region represent 67 percent of renewable water resources, compared with 8 percent for the developing world overall. A related problem is that the agricultural sector is likely to be adversely affected by climate change in the coming decades. Most climate models predict that rainfall in the MENA region will decline by up to 20 percent, resulting in lower yields for rainfed agriculture and increasing scarcity of water for irrigation systems (Breisinger et al. 2010).

Public investment in the agricultural sector is both a necessity and a smart choice given the expected long-term return. While policy makers may be tempted to provide additional assistance to farmers in the interest of alleviating poverty and as compensation to ensure political support for trade reform, these are often shortsighted policies that do not serve the long-term interest of farmers. In the long run, there is no substitute for improvements to public infrastructure—both hard and soft—as a means of modernizing agriculture in the region. Partnership countries with the

TABLE 3.4

Agricultural Land Resources in Selected MENA Countries, 2009

Indicator	Egypt, Arab Rep.	Jordan	Libya	Morocco	Syrian Arab Republic	Tunisia	MENA developing	Global middle-income	World
Agricultural land as % of land area	4	12	9	67	76	63	23	38	38
Agricultural irrigated land as % of total agricultural land	—	9	—	5	9	4	—	—	—
Arable land as % of land area	3	2	1	18	25	17	6	11	11
Arable land (hectares per person)	0.04	0.03	0.28	0.25	0.23	0.26	0.16	0.18	0.21
Average precipitation in depth (mm per year)	51	111	56	346	252	207	—	—	—

Source: World Bank, World Development Indicators 2011.

Note: — = not available.

support of the G8 and other Deauville partners should explore options for increasing public and private investment in irrigation and other water management infrastructure. In particular, public investments need to put a higher priority on establishing institutions to ensure maintenance of the irrigation network and incentives to reduce water wastage. Promoting private investment in irrigation entails creating a more favorable investment climate, establishing clearer property rights to agricultural land and water, and facilitating water cost recovery. In parallel, there is a need to develop soft infrastructure in support of agricultural research and extension, pest and disease control, marketing and promotion services, marketing infrastructure, public stockholding for food security, disaster relief, income insurance and safety net programs, environmental protection, and regional assistance programs. In particular, investing in agricultural research and extension can yield very high returns.[1] Yet countries in the region tend to invest a smaller share of agricultural GDP in agricultural research and extension than the rest of the world. This is probably one reason why cereal yield growth in the region lags behind global averages. Clearly, investment in agricultural research and extension would have a higher rate of return over the long run than can be expected from most alternative uses of public funds.

Agriculture: Key selected recommendations

Short-term:

- Improve Partnership countries' access to the agricultural, processed agricultural, and fisheries markets of Deauville partners, particularly for fruits, vegetables, and olive oil. Steps should include progressive abolition of quotas, reference prices, seasonal restrictions, and other nontariff barriers to agricultural trade.

- Scale up technical assistance and other capacity-building efforts to support Partnership countries in the adoption of principles contained in the WTO's SPS Agreement and corresponding procedures applied domestically by Deauville partners, focusing on mutually agreed priorities.

- Analyze the trade-offs in investing in cereals production and consider improved use of modern risk management tools and financial instruments (hedging, futures and others) to reduce vulnerability to fluctuations in world prices of wheat and other staple foods.

Medium-term:

- Expand Partnership countries' public investment in agricultural research and extension, irrigation, plant protection services, and market information systems.

- Open up the agriculture and fisheries sector in Partnership countries by phasing out tariffs on a most favored nation (MFN) basis and limiting nontariff barriers to those necessary for food and plant safety, consistent with WTO rules.

- Reform Partnership countries' water regulations to clarify water rights, improve cost recovery and maintenance, expand private investment in irrigation and drainage, and create incentives for efficient use of agricultural water.

- Facilitate the development of marketing partnerships to strengthen quality, predictability, and speed of supply for all actors in the value chain, especially for dairy products, fruits, and vegetables. Regular surveys of agricultural enterprises carried out in collaboration with farmer and private sector organizations could help identify constraints and possible solutions.

Long-term:

- Phase out agricultural price supports. If politically necessary, this could be implemented in conjunction with the introduction of decoupled payments to farmers. Scale back universal food subsidies in conjunction with the expansion of safety net programs targeted to low-income households.

Manufacturing

Key issues

Unlike agricultural goods, manufactured goods generally face tariffs of less than 5 percent on entry to G8 markets, while barriers to Gulf Cooperation Council (GCC) markets are also low due to PAFTA. Nonetheless, survey data from Partnership countries show that firms encounter significant difficulties owing to rules of origin and NTMs intended to protect health, safety, and the environment. An estimated 15 percent of Jordan's manufactured exports during 2000–07 did not use advantageous trade preference rates owing to the difficulty of proving adherence to rules of origin. Addressing these issues and building capacity for stronger technical standards application can boost export volumes and help develop regional production networks within the MENA region.

Partnership countries have made great progress in reducing domestic tariffs for manufactures through both preferential liberalization and lower MFN rates. Nonetheless, the agenda remains unfinished, with the region ranking second only to South Asia for levels of tariff restrictiveness. By reducing tariffs to the level of competing economies in Asia, Eastern Europe, and Latin America, Partnership countries would foster productivity growth, lower costs of intermediate and capital goods, and promote inward technology transfer. A

(continued on next page)

Key issues *(continued)*

reasonable goal in the medium term would be to gradually adopt MFN rates not exceeding 5 percent.

A major factor affecting manufacturing trade is the prevalence of NTMs that aim to protect health, safety, or the environment but can restrict market access and protect rents. Key reforms designed to streamline NTMs have been adopted but remain incomplete. These range from making technical improvements in border management without a change in enforcement culture to the creation of dialogue structures that remain largely empty shells for lack of political drive. Building on past initiatives, Deauville partners can support the development of a competitiveness-focused regulatory reform agenda based on public-private dialogue. In the long run, mutual recognition agreements and Agreements on Conformity Assessment and Acceptance are key ways to harmonize industrial standards across countries and upgrade quality, labeling, packaging, and traceability standards. Deep integration trade agreements with key trading partners offer significant opportunities in this area.

Regarding trade in manufactured goods, G8 markets are quite open as far as tariffs are concerned. The main issues faced by Partnership countries relate to the rules of origin applicable under different PTAs and compliance with technical norms and standards that protect human health, safety, and the environment. In general, G8 country tariffs on manufacturing goods are low, averaging less than 5 percent, with little dispersion in terms of tariff peaks or tariff escalation. Tariffs in advanced economies therefore pose no obstacles to the penetration of those markets—a situation of which China has taken full advantage. But Partnership countries find it difficult to use the preferences provided by their trade agreements with the EU and other preferential trading partners and to develop intra-regional production networks and value chains because of overly complex and restrictive rules of origin (Ilahi and Mati 2011). MENA exporters to the EU face lengthy procedures for obtaining the certificate of origin and difficulty in calculating the raw material value. As a result, it is estimated that over the 1996–2006 period, as much as 18 percent of Jordan's exports to the EU that should have been duty-free in fact were subject to duties, possibly because of the high costs associated with obtaining certificates of origin (Ayadi et al. 2009). Existing rules of origin are often excessively restrictive with respect to (a) raw materials that can be used; (b) countries where products can originate (there are problems, for instance, in determining the origin of vessels that catch fish to be processed and exported from Morocco, or the origin, usually in Asia, of textile inputs used in Tunisia); and (c) difficulties in complying with the required double transformation rule in textile (spinning/weaving or weaving/assembly). In addition, imports from the new EU member states are not accepted as a proof of a product's European origin (that is, the EUR1 certification cannot be used, particularly for temporarily admitted products).

The EU and to a lesser degree the United States could facilitate the use of preferences and the emergence of intra-regional production networks by relaxing the stringent rules of origin regarding country of origin, transformation, or value addition. Partnership countries would benefit from adopting the regional convention on preferential Pan-Euro-Mediterranean rules of origin, which replaces the network of about 60 bilateral protocols on rules of origin in the Pan-Euro-Med zone and bases the diagonal cumulation of origin on a single legal instrument. Yet the proposed regional convention on preferential Pan-Euro-Mediterranean rules of origin that allows for cumulation and single transformation to qualify for preferential treatment could be further improved and made consistent with the rules implied by the EU agreements with accession countries (box 3.1). An improved regional convention would enable the contracting parties (current participants in the cumulation zone) to enter into production networks, thus promoting regional integration. Also, partner countries and international institutions could scale up their technical assistance and capacity-building programs to help Partnership countries adopt the necessary regulations, standards, and testing and certification procedures to ensure the protection of human health and safety and the environment according to international norms and standards.

In contrast to the advanced economies and other regions, the Arab region tends to be further insulated by restricted access to its markets for world exporters. The level of trade policy restrictions confronting exporters from a country in other markets can be measured by the Market Access Overall Trade Restrictiveness Index (MA-OTRI).[2] This index measures the uniform tariff faced by exporters in all external markets in a manner that is consistent with the current aggregate export of a country. Given trade preferences and the composition of goods exported, most countries have good market access to the markets of high-income countries (figure 3.1). By contrast, market access in the MENA region is quite restrictive, particularly for exporters from Latin American and Sub-Saharan African countries.

An Unfinished Tariff Agenda

Significant progress has been made in reducing tariffs on goods in the MENA countries. Over the last decade, preferential liberalization under PAFTA and other PTAs has been complemented by reductions in MFN tariffs. As a result, the average uniform tariff equivalent of all tariffs (ad valorem and specific) for the region fell from 14.7 to 6.7 percent between 2002 and 2007. Despite mounting protectionist pressures during the

BOX 3.1

Improving the New Regional Convention on Pan-Euro-Mediterranean Rules of Origin

The June 2011 convention on Pan-Euro-Mediterranean rules of origin proposes to replace the current network of about 60 bilateral protocols on rules of origin in the Pan-Euro-Mediterranean zone with a single legal instrument in the form of a regional convention on preferential rules of origin.[a] It is hoped that the new regional convention will allow for a simpler, more liberal, and more consistent system.

The Pan-Euro-Med preferential rules of origin allow for cumulation of origin for countries that have an Association Agreement with the EU. Inputs that have originating status in one of the countries in the Pan-Euro-Med cumulation zone may be used in products originating in any other country for the purpose of certifying origin within the free trade area. This will make it easier to integrate production structures among MENA countries and will facilitate trade among the Partnership countries and with the EU. However, the provision comes with certain conditions that suggest scope for improvement:

- A "variable geometry" stipulation states that Pan-Euro-Med cumulation can only be applied if the countries of final manufacture and final destination have concluded free trade agreements (FTAs) with all the countries in the zone that have participated in the production process. For example, if Egypt originates a product using components that have EU origin and exports it to Jordan, where it is incorpo-

rated into a machine that also contains components with Turkish origin (Turkey has an FTA with Jordan), the machine produced in Jordan obtains Jordanian origin, since the components used to produce it all originated in the zone. However, if there were no FTA between Turkey and Jordan, Turkish materials could only be incorporated into originating products if a sufficient "working and processing" rule were satisfied.

- Under the "no full cumulation" rule, a product's country of origin will be the place where the "last working or processing" was carried out, so long as the operations concerned were more than minimal. If, on the other hand, inputs imported from one or more other countries in the Pan-Euro-Med zone are not subject to more than minimal working or processing in the country of final manufacture, then the origin of the final product will be the country contributing the highest value. This is also a feature of EU arrangements with Morocco and Tunisia.

- The certification process is not fully simplified, as a new EUR-MED certificate is now needed as proof of origin under the Pan-Euro-Med agreement to indicate whether the preferential origin is based on cumulation of goods from one or several participating countries. Administrative costs of proving compliance remain high for certain companies.

Source: Ilahi and Mati 2011.

a. Council of the European Union, "Proposal for council decision on the signature of the regional Convention on Pan-Euro-Mediterranean preferential rules of origin," Brussels, 25 March 2011.

FIGURE 3.1

Market Access Overall Trade Restrictiveness Index, by Exporters and Markets, 2008–09

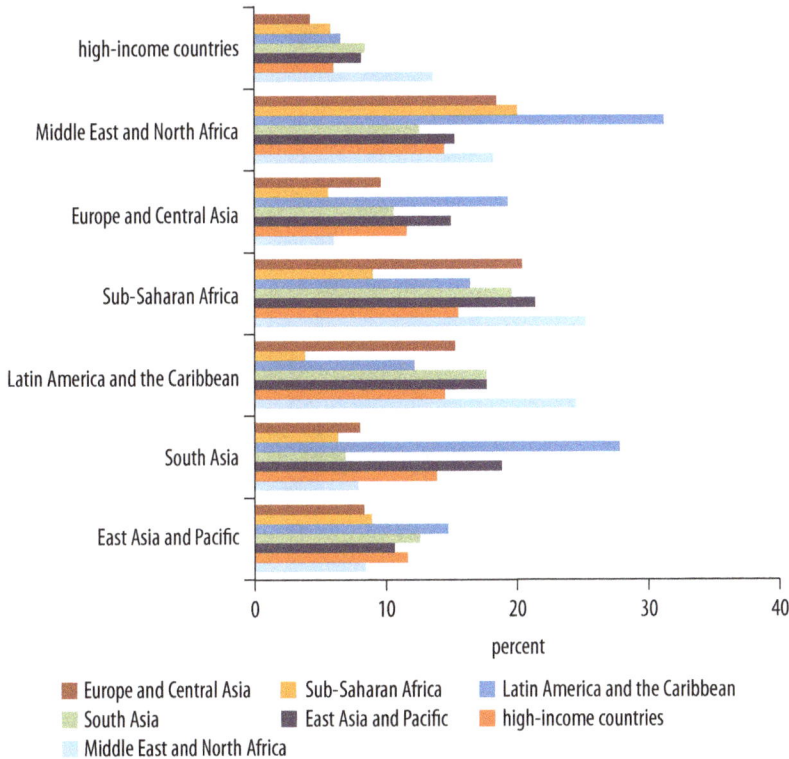

Source: Kee, Neagu, and Nicita, forthcoming.

Note: The percentage value signifies the tariff and ad valorem equivalent of nontariff measures. The higher the percentage, the higher the restriction.

global economic crisis, tariffs in the MENA region decreased by another 0.8 percentage point in 2008/09. The MENA region was actually the region where tariffs decreased the most during the financial crisis, especially on manufactured goods (figure 3.2). This improvement has been confirmed by private sector operators. In a survey conducted in 2001, tariffs were ranked as one of the most important barriers to intra-regional trade by firms in the region (Zarrouk 2002). In a follow-up survey conducted in 2009, they were ranked last (Hoekman and Zarrouk 2009). A majority of respondent companies reported that tariffs on intra-regional trade have largely been removed and that there has been a marked improvement in procedures related to customs clearance.

Notwithstanding the progress made in the last decade, the level of tariff protection in the MENA region remains relatively high by international standards. According to the Tariff-only Trade Restrictiveness Index (TTRI),[3] only the South Asia region had a level of tariff restrictiveness

FIGURE 3.2

Changes in Tariffs by Region on Total Trade, Agriculture, and Manufacturing, 2008–09

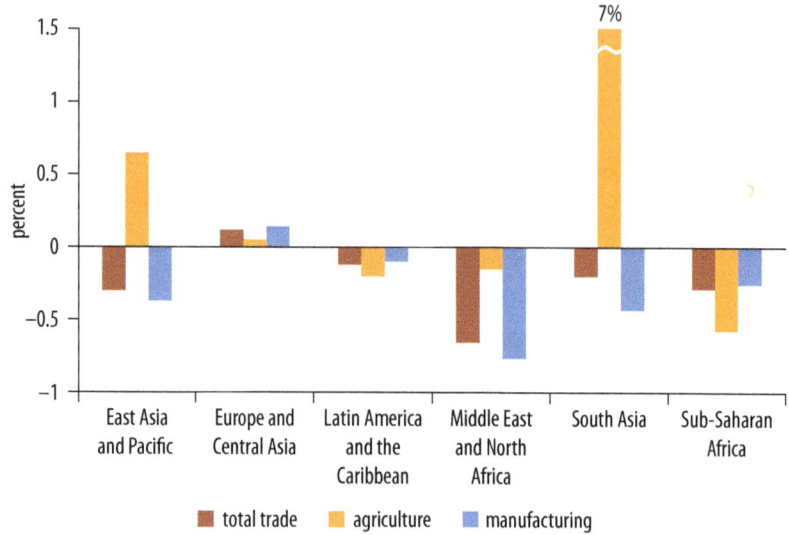

Source: Kee, Neagu, and Nicita, forthcoming.

Note: South Asia agriculture is 7 percent.

FIGURE 3.3

Tariff-Only Trade Restrictiveness Index, by Region, 2008

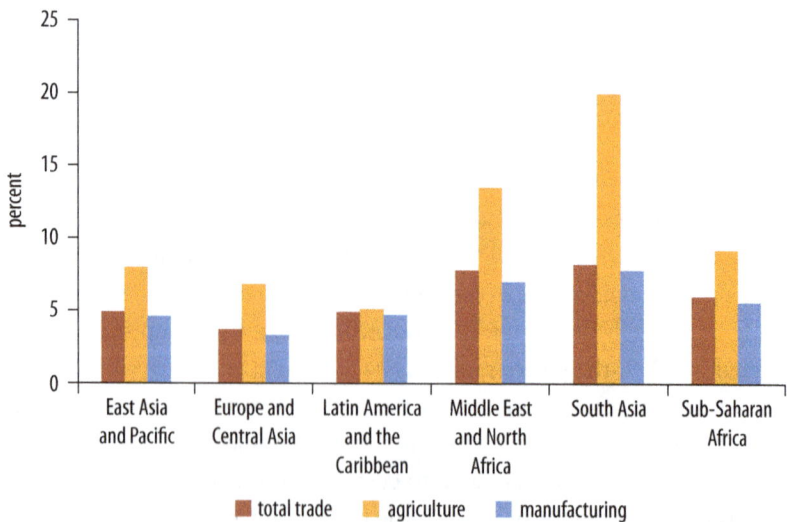

Source: Kee, Neagu, and Nicita, forthcoming.

Note: The percentage value signifies the tariff. The higher the percentage, the higher the restriction.

higher than that of the MENA region in 2008 (figure 3.3). The MENA region compares unfavorably with its main competitors in Eastern Europe and Central Asia, Latin America and the Caribbean, and East Asia and the Pacific—the new dynamic poles of the world economy. In particular, as noted in the preceding section, agriculture in the Arab world is still heavily protected by high tariffs. Further external liberalization is all the more important as some countries may be adversely affected by trade diversion, and the economic size of the Arab world is limited. The combined GDP of the Arab countries that are members of PAFTA is a little less than the GDP of Spain. Given these relatively small domestic markets, trade and investment liberalization is key to help integrate the region into production sharing or processing-type trade, where each country specializes in its areas of comparative advantage and factor endowment to serve bigger markets. A precondition for this, however, is a substantial increase in the efficiency of logistics and other trade services, as discussed below.

Partnership countries would gain by lowering their tariff protection to the level of their main competitors in Asia and other emerging markets. Based on past empirical evidence, a number of sectors rich in potential employment, such as textiles, chemicals, and food, would benefit from a lower effective protection. Bhattacharya and Wolde (2010) incorporated the Trade Restrictiveness Index (TRI) of the International Monetary Fund (IMF) into a gravity model applied to the region and found that the coefficient of the TRI is negative and significant not only for imports but also for exports; this means that restrictive policy reduces export opportunities in the region. Sekkat and Varoudakis (2002) also investigated the impact of trade policy but at the sector level for Egypt, Morocco, and Tunisia. They considered the three most important sectors in these countries (textiles, chemicals, and food) and an extension of the IMF's TRI. The regression results show that the coefficients of the trade liberalization indicator are always significant and positive, implying that trade liberalization improves export performance. The level of the coefficient is highest for textiles and chemicals and lowest for food. Further calculations show that the adoption of the trade liberalization strategy has increased the ratio of sector exports to GDP by around 70 percent for textiles, 64 percent for chemicals, and 36 percent for food.

For such opportunities to materialize, however, the regulatory environment for business should also be improved (see chapter 4). Freund and Bolaky (2008) confirmed that increased trade is associated with higher income but showed that this relationship is magnified in well-regulated countries and breaks down in the most heavily regulated economies. In order for trade to improve living standards, the regulatory environment, especially for business entry, must be improved in heavily regulated countries. Interestingly, these authors found that relaxing re-strictions to business entry as a complementary policy to trade is a more important means to improve living standards than relaxing labor restrictions. In Partnership countries, Sekkat (2008) found that manufacturing exports are highly and increasingly specialized in food products, wearing apparel, and textiles and that these industries typically exhibit high mark-ups and low productivity growth. These two variables are highly related: productivity growth is significantly and negatively affected by the lack of competition. Such lack of competition is due in part to the near absence of effective competition policy and in part to a very slow process of firms' entry and exit in the market concerned. The latter is affected in turn by high barriers to entry—both natural (capital intensity and wage level) and strategic (concentration of incumbents); by limited access to funds and to adequate human resources; and by government interventions (Sekkat 2010).

As in the rest of the world, NTMs have become more significant barriers to trade in the MENA region. NTMs are difficult to measure, as they affect trade in many different ways. Examples range from excessive delays resulting from lengthy clearance and inspection processes—even straightforward border closures—to multiple documents and signatures needed to process a trade transaction, to frequent problems with customs and other government authorities (box 3.2). Compared to the average of 30 countries for which data are available, the MENA region does not stand out as an outlier user of NTMs in terms of either frequency ratio or coverage ratio (figure 3.4). Data available for five MENA countries (Egypt, Lebanon, Morocco, Syria, and Tunisia) show that NTMs cover on average about 40 percent of the products imported by the region and 50 percent of the value of its imports. These frequency ratios are quite similar to what is observed in other regions of the world, and significantly lower than the ratios for the EU. NTM frequency ratios vary substantially across countries in the region, however, with the lowest rates for Lebanon (15 percent), Tunisia (22 percent), and Morocco (25 percent), and the highest for Egypt, at more than 90 percent. In terms of coverage ratio, Morocco is the least affected (21 percent), implying that, compared to other MENA countries, Morocco tends to impose NTMs on relatively low-value items.

In many MENA countries, the existence of NTMs has had the perverse effect of complicating the reform of subsidy systems. For instance, the Moroccan government maintains price-raising measures simultaneously with other distortionary measures aimed at containing the cost of living. Prominent among those is an array of price measures that amount to import subsidies, in particular for fuels. Figure 3.5 shows that these measures are extremely costly, peaking at 4.5 percent of GDP in 2008 (or

BOX 3.2

Measuring Nontariff Barriers

The impact of NTMs on market access and competitiveness is typically assessed along two dimensions: incidence and severity. Their incidence is measured by either the frequency ratio (the proportion of product categories covered by one or more NTMs) or the coverage ratio (the proportion of imports covered). Severity is measured by ad valorem equivalents. Product categories are customarily defined at the harmonized system's 6-digit level, which comprises a nominal total of over 5,000 goods. Most countries trade fewer than that. An ad valorem equivalent is the rate of an ad valorem tariff that would have the same effect on imports.

Estimation of either incidence or severity requires prior measurement, which has historically proved difficult because NTMs are, unlike tariffs, complex legal instruments with multiple objectives. Several sources of information are available, none of them perfect. Private sector surveys should be interpreted carefully, as respondents sometimes are imperfectly informed and sometimes manipulate answers strategically. Moreover, surveys rarely have rigorous sampling frames and are therefore informative rather than representative.

Objective measurement is provided by official sources. The first and foremost is notifications of measures by member states to the WTO secretariat. These notifications, which are mandatory but subject only to weak disciplines, are meant to provide other members with time and information to react to measures with the potential to restrict market access. However, the process suffers from various weaknesses, including a basic incentive problem: by notifying, countries expose themselves to criticism. Thus, coverage is haphazard; for instance, since the 1994 Marrakesh agreement, Morocco has given notice of only 26 measures. Moreover, most notifications are too vague in their wording to be exploited for statistical purposes.

Promoted by the United Nations Conference on Trade and Development (UNCTAD), a formal database of NTMs is progressively taking shape. A first wave of data collection led to the TRAINS database, with one year of data (2001) for about 100 countries. A new wave of data collection was initiated in 2009 by the Multi-Agency Support Team (MAST), based on a new classification of measures. After a pilot phase, data collection is now progressing rapidly. In particular, for the MENA region, 2010 data are available for Morocco, Tunisia, Egypt, and Lebanon. Partial data are also available for Syria. The data include measures coded according to the MAST classification with the HS-6 codes of all products affected, in addition to legal references.

18.3 percent of current expenditures). These subsidies also tend to be regressive, disproportionately benefitting the well-off, and they reward negative externalities such as urban traffic jams and pollution. Worse, because they are contingent on dollar oil prices, they have both a high

FIGURE 3.4

NTM Frequency and Coverage Ratios in Tunisia, Morocco, and Selected Comparators

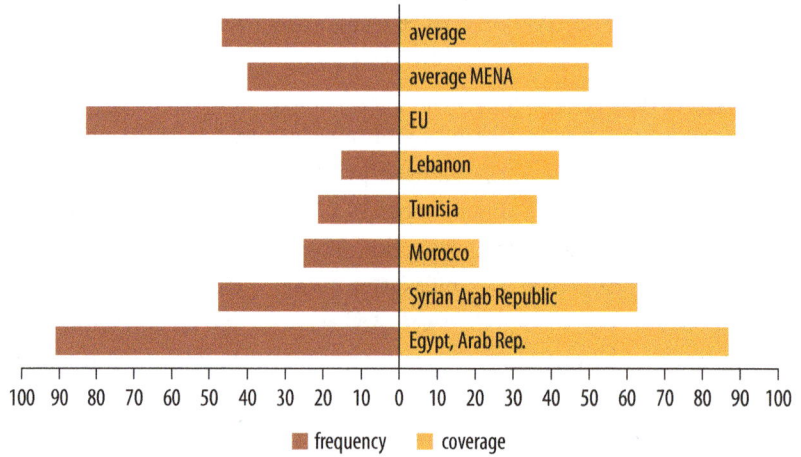

Source: World Bank/UNCTAD NTM data.

Note: Covers measures coded A to E in the MAST classification. The frequency ratio measures the proportion of products covered. The coverage ratio measures the proportion of import value covered.

FIGURE 3.5

Cost of Morocco's Import Subsidies as Share of GDP and Current Expenditure

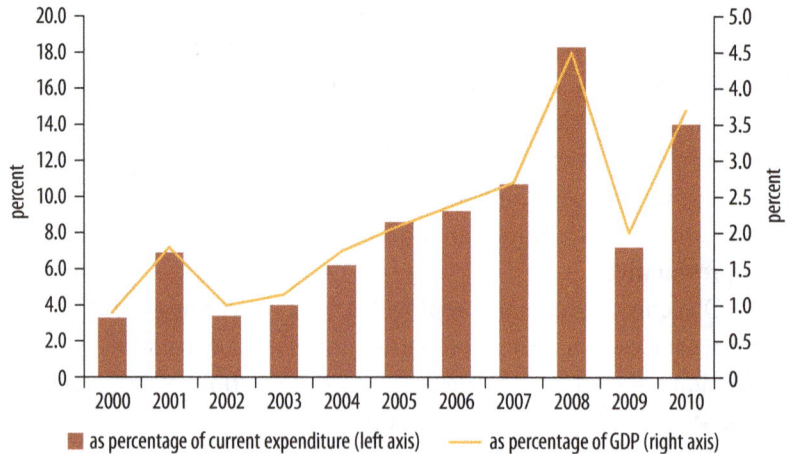

Source: Morocco Central Bank.

built-in volatility, which affects fiscal management, and high elasticity to the exchange rate. For this and other reasons, they loom in the background of any discussion of competitiveness and contribute to policy deadlock.

The composition of NTMs has changed in recent decades, with a reduced use of command-and-control instruments (such as quantitative
restrictions, prohibitions, and anticompetitive measures) and the emergence of technical regulations (SPS and technical barriers to trade) as the
main source of NTMs. As a matter of fact, technical regulations have
replaced all other measures in the majority of cases. On the one hand, this
development can be taken as a modernization of the NTM apparatus in
Partnership countries, marking a shift from protectionist measures to
regulatory ones. On the other hand, it could also hide the increasing use
of technical regulations as barriers to trade through complex design that
ends up being discriminatory de facto although not de jure. Frequency
and coverage ratios bunch together products covered by one measure and
products covered by many (figure 3.6). Figure 3.7 attempts to break this
down by type of measure, the assumption being that several measures of
different types imposed on the same product may generate a particularly
heavy compliance burden. Tunisia stands out as a user of multiple measures, suggesting that a possible lack of internal coordination between
government administrations compounds the problem.

Most of the Partnership countries' NTMs are applied on a nondiscriminatory basis, and there is no evidence that they affect regional trade
by design. They might still affect it de facto if their incidence was borne
disproportionately by products accounting for a large part of intra-re-

FIGURE 3.6

Frequency Ratios for Core NTMs in Selected MENA Countries, 2001 and 2010

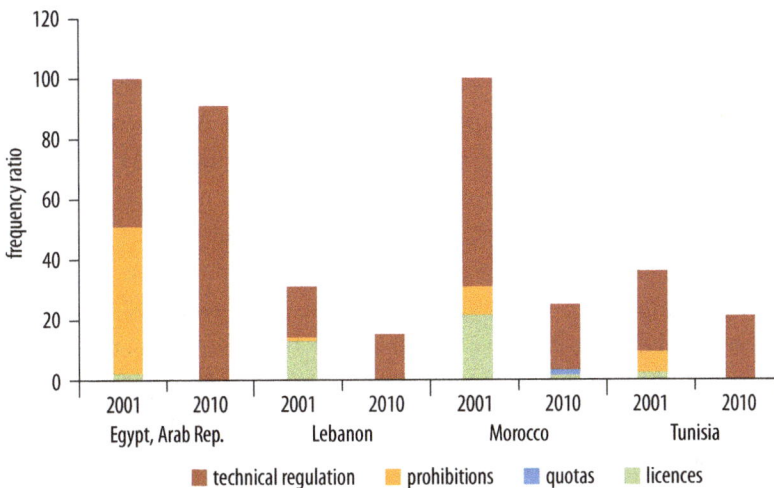

Source: World Bank/UNCTAD NTM data.

FIGURE 3.7

Average Number of NTMs Imposed per Product in Selected MENA Countries and the European Union

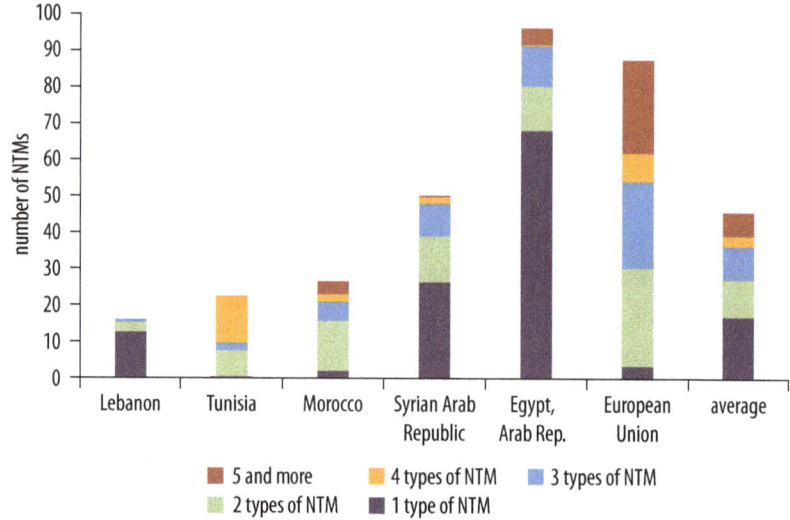

Source: World Bank/UNCTAD NTM data.

Note: Types of measures are defined by the MAST nomenclature at the one-letter, one-digit level (e.g., A100).

gional trade. Figure 3.8 verifies this conjecture by plotting NTM coverage ratios in terms of total imports (horizontal axis) versus intra-regional imports (vertical axis) for all countries with data worldwide, regions being defined by the World Bank's categories. Points above the 45-degree line mark NTM structures falling disproportionately on intra-regional imports; those below the line show disproportionate impact on extra-regional imports. It can be seen that Egypt and Syria—whose data must be interpreted very cautiously—are the only two countries within MENA with NTM structures that penalize regional trade. Morocco, Tunisia, and Lebanon are outliers in the other direction, with NTM structures penalizing out-of-region imports.

Conceptually, NTMs could have two main adverse direct effects on the home economy, contributing to an increase in poverty and a reduction in productivity. When imposed on consumer goods, NTMs affect poverty and the distribution of income. These effects are sometimes nontrivial, in particular when domestic producers of substitute products have market power—which is likely to be the case in Partnership countries, given their small market sizes. When imposed on intermediate products, NTMs affect the competitiveness of domestic firms. By making foreign sourcing costlier, NTMs tend to reduce productivity, growth, and em-

FIGURE 3.8

NTM Incidence by Type of Trade (Intra-Regional vs. Total Trade)

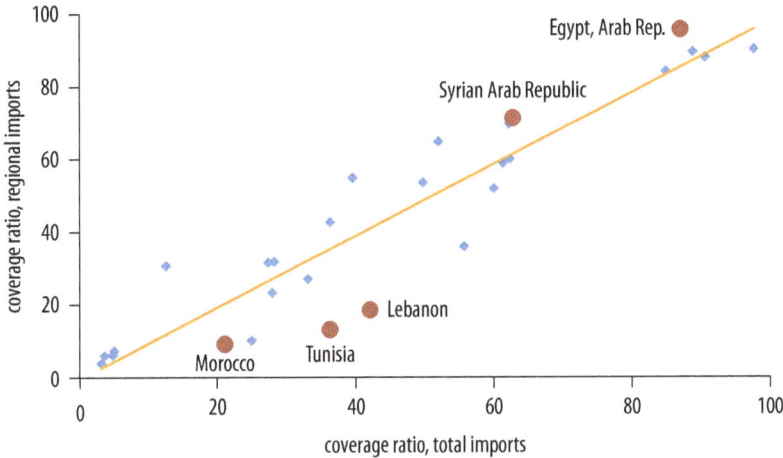

Source: World Bank/UNCTAD NTM data.

ployment. NTMs are a particular instance of a wider syndrome of heavy and ill-targeted intervention in the economy, resulting in inefficiency and sometimes even paralysis. By segmenting markets and raising the domestic prices of affected products, NTMs also may indirectly generate countervailing demands for other distortionary policies to contain the cost of living. The combination of these distortionary measures generates inefficiency and policy deadlock. In that sense, they open the door to a broader agenda of regulatory reform, with a double aim of reducing trade costs directly and creating a culture of competitiveness-oriented dialogue between public administrations and the private sector.

Whatever their form and intent, like all trade instruments, NTMs create wedges between domestic and world prices. In the case of quantitative restrictions, these wedges generate rents for distributors or holders of licenses. In the case of technical regulations, the wedges will typically (though not always) reflect compliance costs, making NTMs "dissipative barriers," although differences in compliance costs may generate rents for some firms.

Available econometric studies suggest that the wedge introduced by NTMs between domestic and world prices is typically large in Morocco and fairly large, albeit somewhat lower, in Tunisia (Augier, Cadot, and Dovis 2011). SPS measures are responsible for a good proportion of the wedge in Morocco, whereas other technical regulations are more important in Tunisia.[4] In Tunisia, the wedge ranges from zero to 105.2 percent (lamb meat), mainly due to technical regulations and price control measures. Simple averages across products are 62.6 percent for Morocco and 13.4 percent for Tunisia. Once zero-wedge products are taken out, simple averages rise to 87.6 and 37.4 percent respectively. That is, in Tunisia relatively few products are affected by NTMs, but for those products the implied price wedge is substantial, although much less so than in Morocco.

When NTMs are included in the calculation of the Overall Trade Restrictiveness Index (OTRI), the MENA region comes across as quite restrictive, with Partnership countries such Egypt, Jordan, and Tunisia more restrictive than Sub-Saharan Africa.[5] This overall result is driven by high NTMs on agricultural goods (figure 3.9), but also on manufactures. According to the surveys of firms mentioned above, transport-related infrastructure and real trade costs (i.e., trade facilitation) have become the most important constraints to trade in the region. This confirms recent analytical studies that conclude that the magnitude of Arab trade flows is

FIGURE 3.9

Overall Trade Restrictiveness Index for Deauville Partnership Countries and Selected Regions, 2008

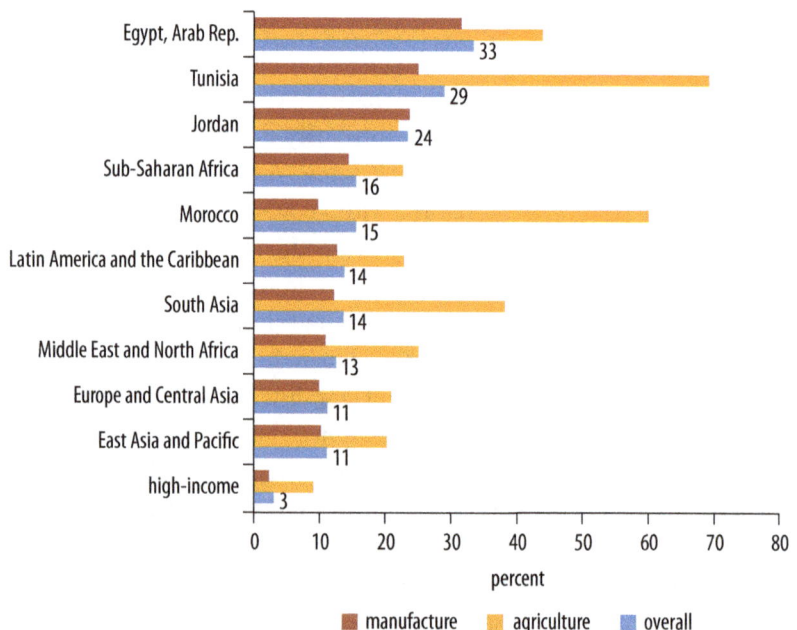

Source: Kee, Neagu, and Nicita, forthcoming.

Note: The OTRI captures the trade policy distortions that each country imposes on its import bundle. It measures the uniform tariff equivalent of the country tariff and nontariff barriers that would generate the same level of import value for the country in a given year, taking into account the composition of import volume and import demand elasticities of each imported product.

significantly lower than it would otherwise be as a result of high real trade costs (Dennis 2006a; Harb 2007; Péridy 2007).

Around the world, the prevalence of NTMs, unlike tariffs, tends to rise with income levels, reflecting stiff agricultural NTMs in developed countries. The pattern emerging from studies estimating the wedge or ad valorem equivalent of NTMs is one with substantial peaks—larger than for tariffs—and overall averages between 5 and 10 percent. While cross-country evidence suggests that NTMs represent, on average, substantial barriers to market access, they are not necessarily illegitimate. They often have nontrade objectives, such as to protect public health and safety or the environment. Yet in some cases, NTMs are just protectionist instruments in disguise. Given these varied possibilities, a balanced assessment of the need for reform must be made. Because of their complexity, NTMs have a strong obfuscation potential and are therefore easily captured. This suggests that the search for transparent governance processes and checks on their illegitimate use can have strong returns in terms of trade openness.

In particular, Partnership countries are facing important NTMs on their exports to the EU. The EU imposes NTMs on 83 percent of its products and 89 percent of its imports, making it the champion NTM user in the sample of 30 economies for which data are available. The vast majority of these measures are SPS and technical regulations. Indeed, a recent survey of Tunisian private sector operators (E-Marsoum 2008) shows that technical regulations, conformity assessment, and SPS measures are perceived as the biggest hurdles by exporters, irrespective of destination, with about half of the exporters (to the EU or other Arab countries) pointing to "inefficiency or even obstruction" in the border administration of technical regulations. One-third of the problem cases had to do with conformity assessment procedures and about another quarter with testing and certification. Among SPS measures, hygienic requirements, testing, and traceability requirements appear as the most frequent sources of problems. This is to be expected given the rising demands of consumers and retailers (in the EU and elsewhere) for more assurances in all three areas.

These NTMs are substantial sources of complications and costs for Partnership countries' exports to the EU (Aloui and Kenny 2004; Ghoneim 2009; Mandour 2006). The cost of EU SPS certification is over $1,000 per farm, and to that must be added the cost of investments in equipment and infrastructure needed to comply with requirements on traceability, record-keeping, waste and pollution management, worker health, and environmental protection. This makes EU SPS certification unaffordable for farmers with less than 100 hectares in vegetables and tomatoes or even several hundred hectares in citrus production (Aloui and Kenny 2004). Traceability adds to production and exporting costs and also has the side effect of shifting the burden of quality risk management upstream to the farmer, with potentially adverse consequences for income security (Frohberg, Grote, and Winter 2006). In addition, some MENA-based exporters face particular difficulties due to "homegrown" problems such as brown-rot disease in fresh potatoes and high aflatoxin levels in nuts from Egypt, and it is sometimes difficult to ascertain whether highly restrictive EU regimes at the product level reflect extreme risk aversion, demands for protection from EU domestic interests, or a mixture of both.

Given the sensitivity of SPS issues in the EU and other advanced economies, it is unrealistic to expect any relaxation of current rules in the name of market access for Partnership countries. However, the EU can provide financial and technical assistance to help MENA producers, in particular small-scale ones, adapt their products to both private and official standards. In agriculture, packing houses are one of the key points in the value chain that should be targeted for quality training. The EU has indeed put in place technical assistance programs, including the Pesticides Initiative Program and a number of Mise à Niveau (upgrading) programs. However, the efficacy of these programs in MENA remain to be evaluated.[6]

Different regions of the world have taken different approaches to the streamlining of NTMs. Because countries typically have large numbers of regulations on the books, many with potential trade effects, streamlining NTMs is a long and difficult undertaking. Regional trade agreements and regional institutions can help in several respects, as suggested by the experiences of other regions. First, as in the EU, supranational institutions like the European Commission and the European Court of Justice can play a leading role in fostering the elimination of NTMs, at least on intra-bloc trade, and promoting a general streamlining and harmonization of regulations. Second, as in the North American Free Trade Agreement (NAFTA), the agreement itself can serve as a political anchor to the reformists. That is, if the PTA enjoys strong multipartisan backing, it can be used as a justification for domestic reforms even when they hurt particular interests (e.g., the elimination of NTMs benefits domestic producers). Third, as in the Association of Southeast Asian Nations (ASEAN), regional institutions can provide a useful forum in which to exchange experiences, suggest directions for further moves, and motivate reformers by overcoming their isolation at home. Finally, a guillotine approach to reviewing, streamlining, eliminating, and updating regulations without the need for lengthy and costly legal action on each regulation could be adopted, as in Eastern European countries during their transition.[7]

In Partnership countries, progress has been made in streamlining NTMs, but reforms remain incomplete. They range from the adoption

of technical improvements in border management without a change in enforcement culture to the creation of dialogue structures that remain largely empty shells for lack of political drive. Several reforms have been introduced since the mid-2000s, including the reengineering of border management procedures, computerization of most paperwork, and reform of the administration in charge of standards and intellectual property. However, according to private sector operators, enforcement on the ground has remained haphazard, discretionary, and nontransparent. In Morocco, although some progress has been achieved in reducing regulatory interference in international trade, neither of the structures established to promote dialogue between national authorities and the private sector (the Commission consultative des importations and the Conseil national du commerce extérieur) has emerged as a powerful driver of reform or even a credible counter-power. In Egypt, progress is even slower, and the Competitiveness Council has not come up with a credible action plan, in spite of funding for NTM transparency and streamlining from the United States Agency for International Development (USAID).

Agreements on Conformity Assessment and Acceptance of Industrial Products (ACAAs) and mutual recognition agreements are key ways of harmonizing industrial standards across countries and reducing the market fragmentation effect of NTMs, especially technical regulations. These agreements would ensure that Partnership countries have state-of-the-art product quality, labeling, packaging, and traceability standards. However, because such agreements require a high degree of cooperation and confidence between national regulatory systems, they typically involve countries with similar income levels or those engaged in deep integration, such as through common markets. The prospect of a greater integration of Partnership countries with the EU and the United States—i.e., through DCFTAs and the Middle East/North Africa Trade and Investment Partnership (MENA TIP)—and with other developed countries and Turkey offers significant opportunities in this area. For instance, Article 51 of the FTA between the European Community (EC) and Morocco states that "the Parties shall cooperate in developing: (a) the use of Community rules in standardization, metrology, quality control and conformity assessment; (b) the updating of Moroccan laboratories, leading eventually to the conclusion of mutual recognition agreements for conformity assessment; (c) the bodies responsible for intellectual, industrial and commercial property and for standardization and quality in Morocco." The EC-Tunisia FTA contains identical language. Likewise, the EC-Jordan agreement states that "cooperation in this field will be aimed in particular at: (a) increasing the application of Community rules in the field of standardization, metrology, quality standards, and recognition of conformity." The EC-Egypt agreement contains no suggestion of that type. Instead, harmonization is expected to take place on the basis of international standards. Nonetheless, the Egyptian Organization for Standardization and Quality claimed in 2008 that it had completed the harmonization of over 80 percent of its technical regulations with those of the EU, and in January 2008 it became an affiliate member of CEN, the European standards body.

Still, harmonization with developed country standards is a double-edged sword. Harmonization can be a way for Partnership countries to reduce quality uncertainty and hence improve market access. Yet the adoption of stringent standards as part of a PTA with a developed country risks raising the costs of domestic production and pricing producers out of other Southern markets where such stringent standards confer no competitive advantage (Cadot, Disdier, and Fontagné 2012). This could even reinforce the so-called "hub-and-spoke" structure of international trade flows, with the Partnership countries becoming spokes less able to trade with other spokes, that is, neighboring Southern countries. This may be a particular adverse effect of the existing EU Association Agreements with Partnership countries, which encourage the adoption of EU regulations even for products aimed at the domestic market or at non-EU export markets. Although it is probably unwise to question alignment with the EU Community acquis, at least in the medium run, Partnership countries may want to adapt the speed of convergence to the needs of particular industries, depending on the existing and predictable evolution of sales patterns.[8] In sectors where EU markets constitute the primary destination of expansion, harmonization should be prioritized. In sectors where Southern markets offer a larger potential for expansion, harmonization might implemented a bit more slowly, or adapted with escape clauses for exports when needed.[9]

The Deauville Partnership could build and support a reform agenda around the notion of trade governance. There is an urgent need to deal with NTMs, which can constitute latent protectionist weapons. In good times, they are mostly set through technical processes meant to protect consumers from hazards and market failures. In bad times, however, with other instruments constrained (e.g., tariff hikes) or perceived to be politically visible (e.g., contingent protection), the high obfuscation and nuisance power of NTMs makes them tempting instruments that can be used to protect nonperforming producers on demand or even to make up for uncompetitive exchange rates and other macroeconomic distortions. In the current climate of macroeconomic and political uncertainty, it is thus crucial to frame the NTM-setting process in a way that ensures good governance and limits the scope for hijacking.

Streamlining NTMs in Partnership countries should not be thought of as a search for quick wins to reduce trade costs by a few percentage points. The factual analysis suggests that, with some exceptions, the stakes on that front alone may not be decisive. Instead, streamlining NTMs should be viewed in a more holistic and ambitious way, as an entry to a wide-ranging regulatory improvement agenda whose real aim is to put in place good governance and dialogue practices. In a context of newly established democracy, such an agenda—in the area of regulatory governance, as in others—is key to ensuring that the democratic process does not remain confined to shallow electioneering but instead goes deep into the heart of government action.

Manufacturing: Key selected recommendations

Short-term:

- Strengthen private-public partnership structures in Partnership countries to review, monitor, and streamline regulatory impediments to the business environment (e.g., NTMs) and conduct market surveillance. Examples include Morocco's National Committee on Investment Climate (CNEA) and the Egyptian Regulatory Reform and Development Activity (ERRADA). Use NTM monitoring structures as forums for permanent dialogue with the private sector on a broad set of competitiveness-related issues, and consolidate existing parallel initiatives in this area.

- Negotiate mutual recognition agreements, such as Agreements on Conformity Assessment and Acceptance of Industrial Products (ACAAs), between Partnership countries and Deauville Partners to reduce the market fragmentation effect of technical barriers to trade, especially in priority sectors such as mechanical and electric industries and construction materials.

- Scale up the EU's and other Deauville partners' technical assistance and capacity-building programs to upgrade infrastructure and procedures for technical regulations, standards, testing, and certification in line with best international practices.

- Adopt and implement flexible rules of origin in PTAs between Partnership countries and Deauville partners, including the EU regional convention on preferential Pan-Euro-Mediterranean rules of origin.

Medium-term:

- Open up the manufacturing sector in Partnership countries by gradually reducing MFN tariff rate levels and dispersion on manufacturing goods to the level of key competitors in emerging markets.

- Put in place arbitration structures to make binding decisions on regulatory changes in conformity with the results of analytical assessments.

Services

Key issues

Services are major inputs in any kind of economic activity. Access to high-quality and moderately priced services is a key condition for becoming more competitive in domestic and foreign markets and participating more actively in global production networks. However, the MENA region is one of the least open in the world to services trade. Levels of commitment in the WTO's General Agreement on Trade in Services remain low on average. Regulatory restrictions are extensive on all four modes of supply: cross-border trade, consumption abroad, commercial presence, and presence of natural persons. The integration of services markets lags far behind the progress achieved for goods within PAFTA, where most tariffs and duties have been removed.

Greater integration can affect the economy through two channels: direct export of services and the indirect role of "backbone services" in expanding the export base for manufactures. Partnership countries have a strategic trade interest in information technology–enabled services, business services, professional services, and tourism. While the share of services in GDP doubled on average for Partnership countries during the 2000s, and tripled in the case of Egypt, this increase was disproportionately driven by tourism, suggesting a need for diversification. However, the growing prevalence of intra-firm and intermediate services trade means export growth will be inhibited unless Partnership countries further open their own services markets.

Both for direct exports and for backbone sectors such as transport, telecommunications, and energy, foreign establishment and movement of service providers are key factors of technology and knowledge transfer. Deep integration with selected G8 partners could help Partnership countries offer a bundle of tasks with high-value-added content at key points in global value chains. The Deauville Partnership can foster trade liberalization and regulatory reform, including in the context of high-quality trade agreements with Deauville partners and in the context of the Agadir Agreement.

Ease of access to high-quality, efficient, and moderately priced services has become essential to global trade integration and competitiveness and, in turn, to sustainable economic growth and job creation. Services are inputs into any kind of economic activity and production: accessible, affordable financial services, for example, are essential to economic activity and growth (see chapter 5). It has been estimated that services could represent up to 20 percent of industrial production costs (Hodge 2002). A recent study by Arnold et al. (2012) found that banking, telecommunications, insurance, and transport reforms in India all had significant, positive effects on the productivity of manufacturing firms: a one-standard-deviation increase in the aggregate index of services liberalization resulted in a productivity increase of 11.7 percent for domestic firms and 13.2 percent for foreign enterprises. Gains expected from increased services trade also include knowledge spillovers and FDI inflows. Benefactors are the local consumers of services, including firms that use services in their production.

A country cannot become a major services exporter unless it is open to services imports. Opening up trade in services, if implemented in a proper regulatory and competition environment, could remedy supply-side constraints and increase competition in the domestic market, resulting in a more diversified and competitive local supply of services. First, services exports include about 15 percent of imported services inputs (Miroudot and Ragoussis 2009); second, about a quarter of cross-border services trade is intra-firm (Lanz and Miroudot 2010). Thus, a country that is not open to trade in services automatically excludes itself from a significant part of world services trade, significantly increasing its trade costs to the detriment of its competitiveness and remaining outside of major global value chains and intra-firm trade.

With the fragmentation of production in different stages and the development of trade in tasks, services efficiency all along the production chain has become a key determinant of integration. Improving the efficiency of services is important to any strategy of trade integration (or export-led growth) and is necessary to compete with cost-efficient emerging countries. About 75 percent of services trade is in intermediate services, suggesting that services trade primarily takes place in global value chains (Miroudot, Lanz, and Ragoussis 2009). A recent study by the Swedish National Board of Trade (2010) revealed that 40 different services tasks are involved when a manufacturing firm internationalizes its production. Participation in global production networks will depend on the country's ability to efficiently supply those services, either onshore or offshore: in relation to the EU, Partnership countries' geographic proximity and just-in-time production are a major comparative advantage that relies on sophisticated supply chain management.

In a globalized economy, the quality and efficiency of services "links" (e.g., transportation and logistics, telecommunications) have a strong influence on production location and trade routes. This is particularly the case in global value chains, where final and intermediate goods cross borders a number of times before reaching the final consumer. Recent analysis suggests that progress on trade facilitation could generate more gains for developing countries than anything else emerging from the Doha negotiations (Hoekman and Nicita 2010). The relatively weak logistics performance of most Partnership countries, as discussed in chapter 5, suggests that a further liberalization of transport and logistics services could generate significant gains for the region: it would not only help reduce the costs of trade, but would also make the region more attractive to global buyers and retailers and increase participation in global value chains.

Services themselves have become increasingly complex, and trends toward consolidation of global value chains suggest that countries able to supply a bundle of services tasks are more attractive to FDI. Trade in intermediate services and tasks has created new prospects for international division of labor and productivity growth. A country can specialize in different tasks and progressively move up the value chain, for instance from business process outsourcing (BPO) to knowledge process outsourcing (KPO) (Gereffi and Fernandez-Stark 2010). Starting with call centers, Partnership countries could move to exporting knowledge if market access were granted by key trading partners. Recent studies suggest, however, that not all tasks can be performed independently and/or offshore (Lanz, Miroudot, and Nordås 2011) and that countries able to offer a bundle of tasks to multinational firms increase their prospects of integrating global value chains (Staritz, Gereffi, and Cattaneo 2011). Thus, it is not enough to liberalize the performance of one specific task when it is bundled with other tasks: services reform strategies should be holistic, or countries may miss opportunities to enter global production networks and move up the value chain. In the MENA region, the objective could be to create a production platform with intermediate goods and services traded within the region, providing the basis for a competitive offer to the rest of the world. The goal is not to compete with China and other emerging countries, but to offer a bundle of tasks with high-value-added content at key points in global value chains. This will require more freedom of trade in services and an increased efficiency of services links to allow a new division of labor, as well as important technology and knowledge transfers that enable the Partnership countries to move up the value chain.

Beyond the economics, the development of services trade has important social dimensions that should be taken into consideration when designing domestic regulatory services reforms and regional trade integration strategies. While the social issues related to increased economic integration are discussed in chapter 6, it is worth noting here the particular role of services trade in promoting gender, employment, and regional opportunities.

The development of services trade could contribute to expanding the female labor force. As noted in *World Development Report 2012*, two service sectors alone, communication services and retail/hotels/restaurants, represent more than half of all jobs held by women worldwide—52 percent, compared to 33 percent of jobs held by men. The report suggests that increases in female employment between 1995 and 2005 were correlated with increases in international trade and new opportunities in the services sector (male employment did not correlate with increases in trade). In particular, new services jobs enabled by information and communication technologies (ICTs), such as information processing in banking, insurance, printing and publishing, and call centers, were mainly taken up by women. Moreover, telework offered new opportunities for men and women to better balance their family and professional lives (World Bank 2011b).

Increased services trade could also help ease the unemployment problem. New jobs created by trade are prominently in the services sector and benefit both women and youth, the latter being the group most severely affected by unemployment in the MENA region. Greater economic integration increases the demand for skilled workers and could benefit young graduates. Upgrading within global services value chains—e.g., from BPO to KPO—could also serve the same objective, justifying an emphasis in services trade negotiations not only on low-skilled but also on high-skilled labor movements and a further liberalization of trade in professional services. A better regulation of services sectors could also help address the issue of informality that affects these sectors (and women workers in particular) more than manufacturing.

Services trade integration strategies could also include regional planning as a legitimate domestic policy objective. Important wealth and development disparities between subnational regions in Partnership countries are a source of economic distress and social unrest, as illustrated by the eruption of the Tunisian revolution in the central part of the country (Gafsa, Sidi Bouzid). In Morocco, for instance, the Atlantic coast, site of the economic and administrative capitals, has traditionally been the economic driver of the country. This area is the objective of an ambitious spatial planning policy, backed by services trade integration projects, to develop new growth poles: Tanger-Tétouan and Fès-Meknès as trade platforms oriented to Europe and the Maghreb, respectively; Marrakesh and Agadir for tourism; Ouarzazate for solar power. Larger projects such as cross-border transport, energy, and telecommunications networks could allow the construction of adequate infrastructure and the development of efficient and competitive services available to a larger share of the population. Services trade, under all four modes of services supply (i.e., cross-border trade, consumption abroad, commercial presence, and presence of natural persons), could be used to serve spatial planning objectives.

Despite recent progress, services trade in the MENA region remains insufficiently open, and its potential is largely unexploited. Restrictive regulations on all four modes of services supply constitute a major obstacle to regional integration and to the region's participation in the new division of labor. Moreover, governments in the region have retained a considerable degree of regulatory discretion in the implementation of their policies. As discussed in chapter 4 in the context of the overall business environment, de jure openness has not always translated into de facto openness. Thus a key reform issue will be to reconcile regulatory discretion—to the extent that it serves legitimate domestic policy objectives—with the need to establish clear and predictable rules for foreign and domestic service providers (Borchert, DeMartino, and Mattoo 2010). The lack of openness has been evidenced by services trade restrictiveness indexes recently developed by the Organisation for Economic Co-operation and Development (OECD) and the World Bank. In 2009, a first assessment of the barriers to trade in services in the MENA region (Marouani and Munro 2009) found that significant regulatory reforms had taken place, but a broad range of restrictions remained. At the same time, the World Bank developed a Services Trade Restrictiveness Index that contained detailed and comparable information on policy and regulatory measures affecting international trade in services in 103 countries. This index confirms the scope for further opening of services in the MENA region, especially in the GCC countries (figure 3.10). All the Partnership countries, with the exception of Morocco, appear more restrictive than the world average, with Egypt and Tunisia being the most restrictive of the sample countries.[10]

The relative lack of openness in services trade contributes to the region's difficulty in developing trade in intermediate goods. The integration of services markets in the region lags behind the progress that has been achieved for goods, for instance within PAFTA, where most tariffs and duties on intra-regional trade have been removed. In contrast, the prevailing services protection in MENA countries is spread across major services sectors, notably in those key to integration in global value chains, such as financial, transportation, telecommunications, professional, and retail services (figure 3.11). For example, barriers to establishment (such as strict nationality requirements) and movement of persons in professional services could constrain production relocation decisions (FDI) in some industries; barriers to trade in retailing and distribution (such as interdiction of foreign franchises and pervasive zoning laws) could be an impediment to backward linkages in the industry and agriculture sectors (when the lead firm is a global retailer); absence of adequate protection of data could be an obstacle to services offshoring. Specifically, in telecommunications, governments continue to limit the number of providers and the extent of foreign ownership. In both banking and insurance, the allocation of new licenses is often opaque and highly discretionary. Transport and professional services remain a bastion of protectionism. In mari-

FIGURE 3.10

Services Trade Restrictiveness Index, by Region, 2008–11

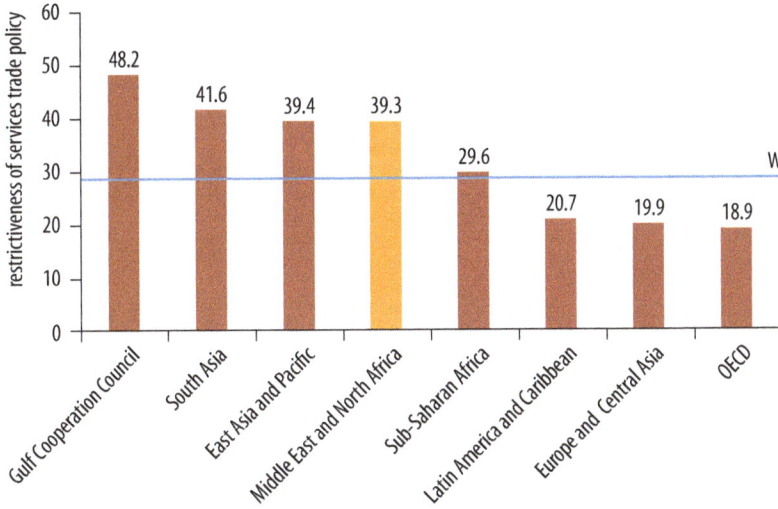

Source: Borchert, Gootiiz, and Mattoo 2012.

Note: W = world average (across 103 countries). The index is 0–100, with higher numbers signifying higher restrictions.

FIGURE 3.11

Services Trade Restrictiveness Index, by Region and Sector, 2008–11

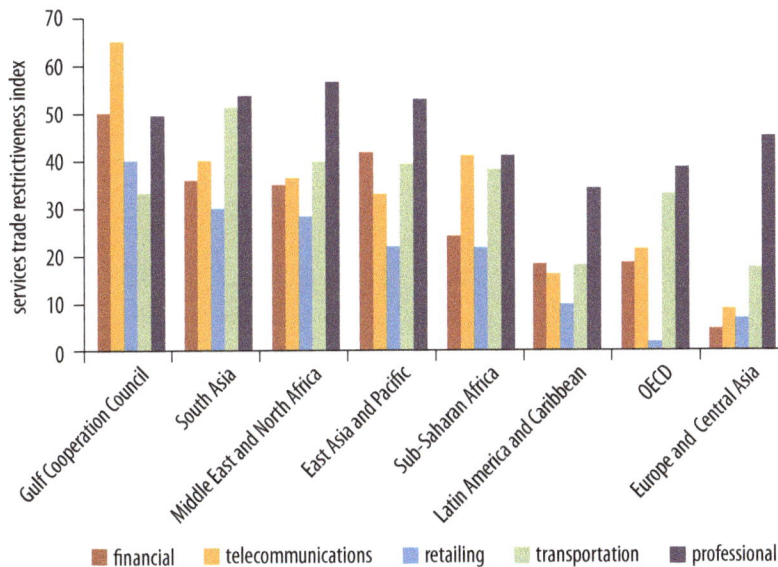

Source: Borchert, Gootiiz, and Mattoo 2012.

time transport, even though international shipping is quite open today, entry into cabotage and auxiliary services such as cargo handling is restricted in many countries. In air transport, investment in the supply of international and domestic air passenger services is restricted.

This relative lack of openness of the MENA region in services trade is also reflected, but to a lesser extent, in the countries' commitments made in the General Agreement on Trade in Services (GATS). While the MENA countries' GATS commitments are lower than those of the OECD and Europe and Central Asia countries, they are higher than those of the rest of the world (figure 3.12). However, MENA countries' offers on the table in the Doha negotiations are among the least ambitious, and it appears that they are reluctant to narrow the gap between their Uruguay round commitments and their actual policies. By contrast, OECD countries would reduce this gap by three quarters, and countries in the Europe and Central Asia region by more than half. Thus, MENA countries still have significant margin to improve their GATS offers without going further than consolidating the status quo. Among the Part-

FIGURE 3.12

Existing Commitments, Doha Offers, and Actual Policy, by Region

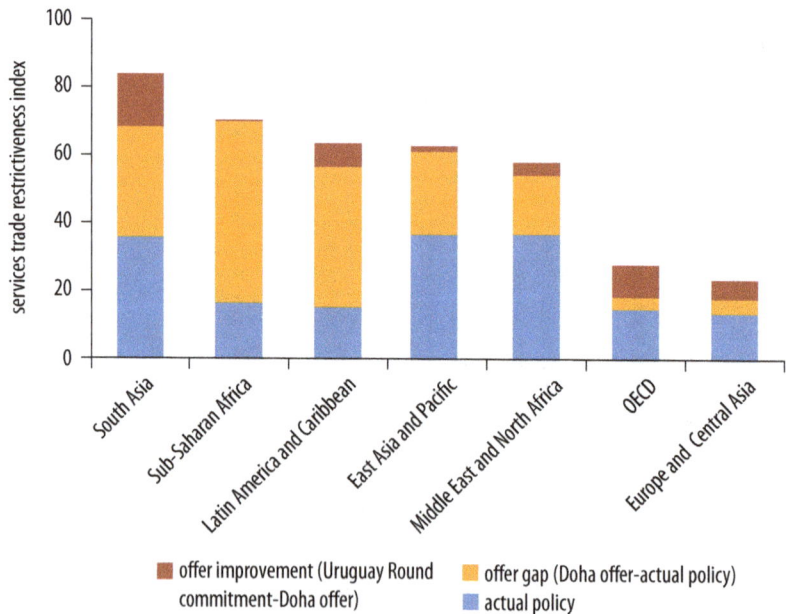

Source: Gootiiz and Mattoo 2009.

Note: If countries have not made a Doha offer, existing commitments are used.

nership countries, Libya still has to complete its accession to the WTO and make initial commitments in this context.

Turning to Partnership countries, services trade, whether embedded in goods or stand-alone, represents an important source of diversification and growth potential. Partnership countries have long been dependent on the export of raw materials and low-value-added industrial goods, confined to the bottom of the productivity chain as emerging countries moved up the value chain (Müller-Jentsch 2005). Yet during the 2000s, Morocco, Tunisia, and (in the early part of the decade) Egypt made a modest leap forward. In Morocco, for instance, the share of services trade in GDP increased by almost 30 percent during 2002–10 (figure 3.13). Services trade also appears to have been more resilient than merchandise trade during the 2008 global economic crisis, suggesting that this specialization could be more sustainable than a too-heavy reliance on agriculture and manufacturing (Borchert and Mattoo 2009). As a result, Egypt, Morocco, and Tunisia rank among the world's 30 largest net exporters of services (in value). With the exception of Libya, all the Partnership countries run a services trade surplus, which helps to partially offset their current account deficit in merchandise trade (figure 3.14).

Still, Partnership countries' services exports have been mainly concentrated in transport and travel, that is, tourism. Travel alone represents 50

FIGURE 3.13

Trade in Services as a Share of GDP, Deauville Partnership Countries, 2002–10

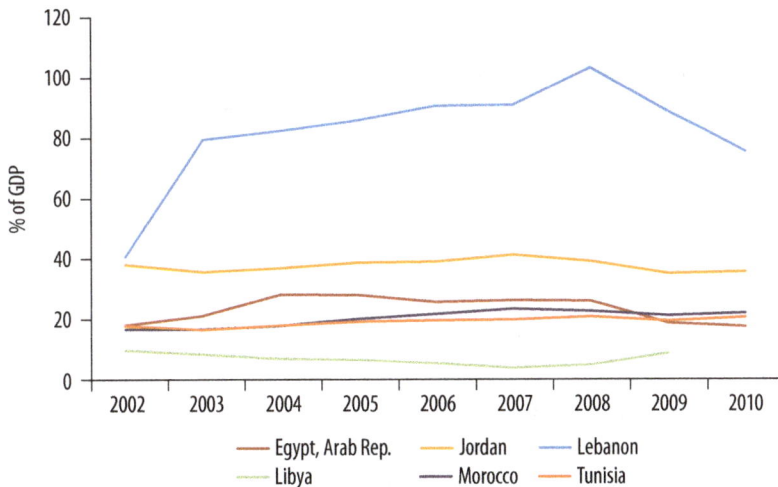

Source: World Bank, World Development Indicators 2011.
Note: 2010 data for Libya are not available.

FIGURE 3.14

Trade in Services Net Surplus, Deauville Partnership Countries and Lebanon, 2010

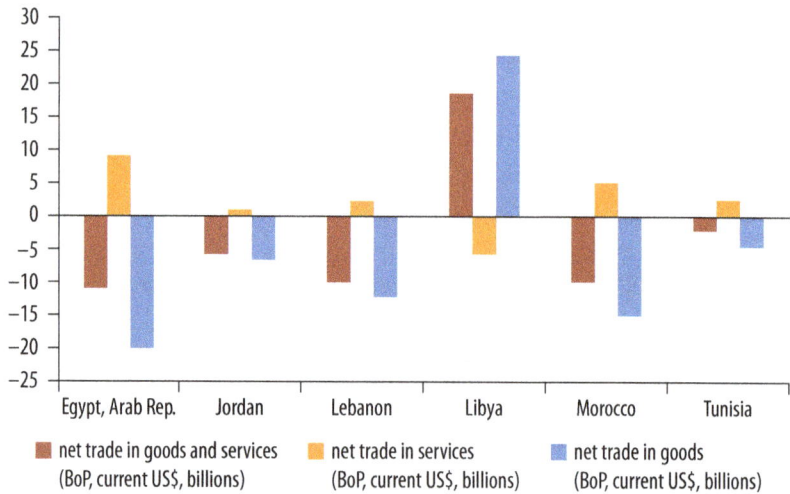

net trade in goods and services
(BoP, current US$, billions)

net trade in services
(BoP, current US$, billions)

net trade in goods
(BoP, current US$, billions)

Source: World Bank, World Development Indicators 2011.
Note: BoP = balance of payments.

percent or more of the services exports in Egypt, Jordan, and Morocco and close to 50 percent in Tunisia, compared to 25 percent or less, on average, for the rest of the world and the OECD (figure 3.15). In Libya, transport services account for more than 60 percent of total services exports. The share of Partnership countries' exports in other types of services, such as financial and communications services, remains well below the world average, suggesting a need for further diversification (figure 3.16).

Despite the number of trade agreements that involve the Partnership countries, progress in the liberalization of services trade has been limited (box 3.3). The main advancements on a GATS basis have been achieved through the U.S. free trade agreements concluded with Morocco and Jordan (table 3.5). Negotiations among Arab states and with the EU, the Common Market for Eastern and Southern Africa (COMESA), and other trading partners are still under way. Nonetheless, additional agreements outside the scope of free trade agreements per se, such as bilateral investment treaties or open skies agreements, have also helped liberalize some aspects of services trade.

The Deauville Partnership could help promote services trade and investment among Partnership countries and with Deauville partners by fostering liberalization and regulatory reforms, including through deep and high-quality trade agreements; improving regional connectivity and

FIGURE 3.15

Travel and Transport Services as Shares of Total Services Exports, Deauville Partnership Countries and Selected Comparators, 2010

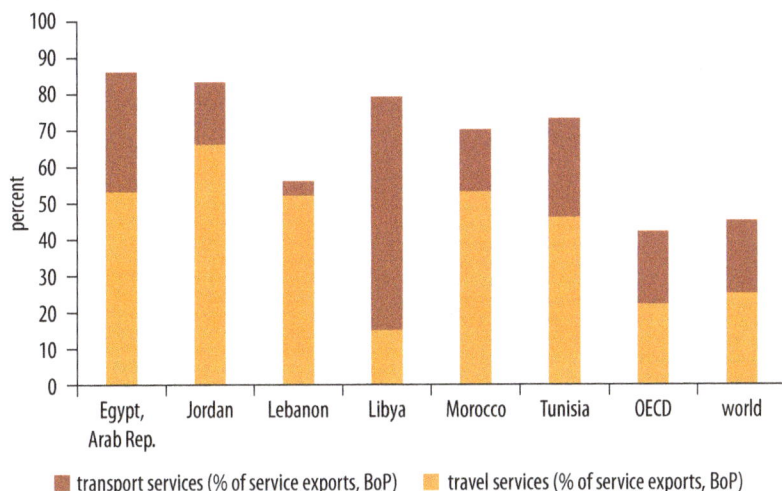

■ transport services (% of service exports, BoP)   ■ travel services (% of service exports, BoP)

Source: World Bank, World Development Indicators 2011.
Note: BoP = balance of payments.

FIGURE 3.16

Insurance/Financial and Communications Services as Shares of Total Services Exports, Deauville Partnership Countries and Selected Comparators, 2010

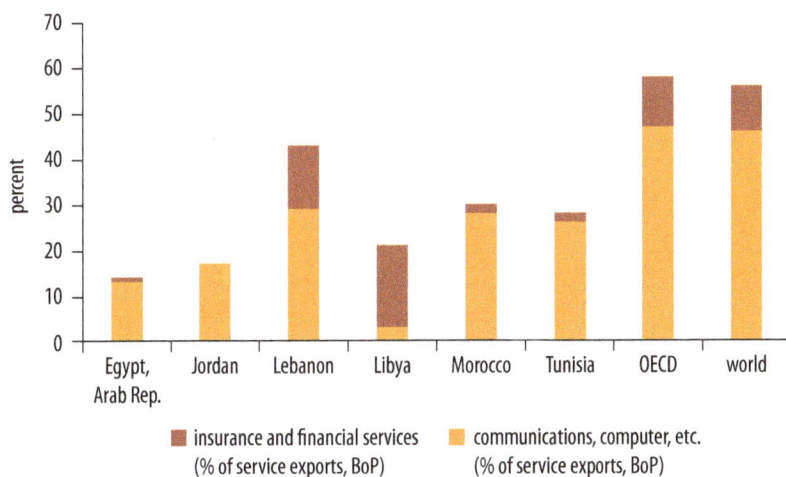

■ insurance and financial services   ■ communications, computer, etc.
   (% of service exports, BoP)   (% of service exports, BoP)

Source: World Bank, World Development Indicators 2011.
Note: BoP = balance of payments.

BOX 3.3

Services Trade Provisions in Partnership Country Trade Agreements

With the exception of the U.S.-Morocco FTA, only limited liberalization or integration has been achieved in Partnership countries through plurilateral or bilateral agreements. The best progress has been achieved at the sectoral level, for instance in air transport.

Selected plurilateral agreements

The 2004 Agadir Agreement (Egypt, Jordan, Tunisia, Morocco): Article 5 pertaining to trade in services does not require further liberalization of services trade. Instead, it states that members will respect WTO commitments and "seek to expand the scale of trade in services between them," with the Ministers' Committee playing a monitoring role.

The 1989 Arab Maghreb Union (Tunisia, Morocco, Libya, Algeria, Mauritania): Article 2 of the Treaty of Marrakesh provides for progressive liberalization of services trade, but without stating details of implementation mechanisms. The group has nonetheless undertaken a number of infrastructure projects and coordination efforts that pertain to services (e.g., telecommunications).

The 1997 Pan-Arab Free Trade Agreement (Agadir members plus Libya, Lebanon, GCC countries, West Bank and Gaza, the Republic of Yemen, Iraq, Sudan, Syria): PAFTA does not cover trade in services, but a separate framework agreement based on a GATS approach was concluded in 2003 (Regional Agreement on Liberalizing Trade in Services). Between 2004 and 2011, four rounds of negotiations were completed but no agreement was reached. Egypt and Jordan suggested a new approach aimed at fully liberalizing selected sectors (e.g., education, computer services, and telecommunications), but nothing concrete has yet materialized (Ghoneim 2012).

The 1993 COMESA agreement (Egypt, Libya, and 16 other African countries): COMESA initially focused on trade in goods, but the objective is to create by 2014 a common market that includes free movement of services, capital, and persons. A COMESA services framework was adopted in 2009. Following certain guidelines and a GATS approach (positive list and requests/offers), negotiations are underway on seven priority sectors (finance, business, communications, transport, energy, tourism, and construction and related engineering).

Selected bilateral trade agreements

The 2004 U.S.-Morocco FTA: This is the most ambitious agreement signed by a Partnership country with respect to services. It is based on a negative list approach (i.e., top-down, list it or lose it). Morocco made significant additional opening efforts compared to its GATS position, as demonstrated in its decisions not to maintain any restrictions on telecommunications and open sectors such as ICT-enabled services, BPO, insurance, and postal/courier services. The agreement includes chapters on services trade liberalization, financial services, telecommunications, procurement, investment, and e-commerce.

BOX 3.3 *Continued*

The 2000 U.S.-Jordan FTA: This is the only U.S. FTA that adopted a positive list approach (GATS-like, bottom-up). Unlike Morocco, Jordan did not make significant additional commitments in the FTA. However, this could be explained by Jordan's significantly higher level of GATS commitments that automatically reduce the marginal trade liberalization allowed by the FTA.

The Euro-Med process: The Euro-Mediterranean trade partnership was launched with the 1995 Barcelona Declaration and boosted in 2004 with the European Neighbourhood Policy. Its objective is to create a free trade area through substantial liberalization of trade both between the EU and Southern Mediterranean countries (North–South) and between the Southern Mediterranean countries themselves (South–South). All the Partnership countries have concluded Association Agreements with the EU. While these agreements essentially cover trade in goods, services negotiations have also been opened. In 2012, the European Commission will start negotiations with Egypt, Jordan, Morocco, and Tunisia to establish Deep and Comprehensive Free Trade Areas that should supplement a GATS Article V–compatible agreement on services with key disciplines on competition, government procurement, and investment.

Partnership countries have concluded other bilateral agreements among themselves and with other countries. For example, Tunisia has concluded bilateral agreements with Algeria, Egypt, Jordan, Libya, Mauritania, Morocco, Senegal, and Turkey. However, these include no services commitment other than to pursue further cooperation on services trade.

Bilateral investment treaties

Bilateral investment treaties could also have an impact on services trade and could overlap with some commitments made in the GATS or PTAs (Mode 3). According to the International Centre for Settlement of Investment Disputes database on bilateral investment treaties, as of January 2012 Egypt had concluded 91 such treaties, Jordan 42, Libya 14, Morocco 40, and Tunisia 54.

Selected sector agreements

A number of sector agreements affect the regulation and openness of services. For instance, it was recognized early that the implementation of the Yamoussoukro Decision on air transport liberalization would mainly depend on regional initiatives to be carried out by the Regional Economic Communities. In North Africa, both the Arab Maghreb Union and the League of Arab States have played a role in the regulation and liberalization of air transport: 17 open skies agreements have been concluded among Arab League members, and a plurilateral Arab League Open Skies Agreement was concluded in 2004. A number of agreements were also reached with the rest of the world: for instance, Morocco first signed an open skies agreement with the EU in 2005, and Tunisia is finalizing its own agreement (Schlumberger 2010).

TABLE 3.5

Comparison of Selected WTO and PTA Liberalization Commitments

	Bahrain (U.S.-Bahrain PTA)	Oman (U.S.-Oman PTA)	Morocco (U.S.-Morocco PTA)	Jordan (U.S.-Jordan PTA)	Jordan (Singapore-Jordan PTA)
GATS commitments	27.97	48.46	17.85	50.25	50.25
PTA commitments	83.84	80.69	75.25	55.61	51.19

Source: Ghoneim 2012.

Note: The index score is on a scale of 1–100 for each sector, with 100 representing full commitments (no limitations) across all relevant subsectors. "GATS" reflects the index value for both GATS commitments and services offers in the ongoing Doha Development Agenda. "PTA" reflects the index value for a member's highest PTA commitments across all PTAs concluded, for each subsector. The index value is for both Mode 1 and Mode 3 (WTO Dataset of services commitments in regional trade agreements, 2010).

cooperation through the creation of hard (infrastructure) and soft (institutional) networks; and enhancing the competitiveness and export performance of Partnership countries.

First, foster liberalization and regulatory reforms, including through deeper services integration in the context of high-quality trade agreements with Deauville partners. This would involve a number of phases, starting with the preparation of a diagnostic study of competition, regulation, and market access conditions prevailing in Partnership countries. Deauville partners could provide technical assistance support, including for efforts to build public platforms for dialogue and coordination and to improve services trade statistics and capacity within relevant ministries and institutions, including negotiation skills. Part of the services strategy would be to identify the sequence and optimal level of reforms: this would involve a mix of unilateral, regional, and multilateral reforms (box 3.4). Partnership countries should assess the contestability of their markets and improve the competition framework before opening. They could also consider a parallel exercise to liberalize services trade among themselves in the context of the Agadir Agreement. Partnership countries would also benefit from adopting a pragmatic approach to the sensitive matter of the temporary movement of service providers in the region. The Deauville Partnership could facilitate the dialogue with a view to developing mutually acceptable standards and criteria for licensing and certification of professional services suppliers on the basis of factors such as educational background, qualifying examinations, and experience.

Second, improve regional connectivity and cooperation through the creation of hard (infrastructure) and soft (institutional) networks. With the coordinated assistance of the Deauville partners, Partnership countries could develop regional infrastructure for telecommunications, energy, transport, and other backbone services, as well as strengthen cooperation among services regulatory agencies and/or create joint agencies where appropriate. The case for such cooperation is twofold. First, the

BOX 3.4

The Right Mix of Unilateral, Regional, and Multilateral Reforms to Further Integrate Partnership Countries into Regional and Global Services Markets

Partnership countries should only adopt EU rules when they are in line with best practices, help remove significant nontariff barriers, can be implemented at reasonable cost, and help overcome the resistance of vested interests to domestic reforms. This will have to be assessed on a case-by-case basis. As Partnership countries need to simultaneously tackle domestic adjustment, regional integration, and multilateral liberalization, integrated reform strategies need to be developed and priorities set. Generally speaking, economic adjustment and multilateral liberalization should be at the top of the agenda. While harmonization with EU rules for its own sake should be avoided, gradual participation in the EU Single Market through a well-defined program of regulatory convergence seems desirable. The right mix of national, regional, and multilateral reforms will vary considerably across sectors and policy areas.

Transport and logistics. The role of multilateral liberalization in creating a regional transport space seems limited, given the limited coverage under GATS. In maritime and land-based transport services, domestic sector reforms will suffice, and there is little need for regulatory harmonization. The main exception is cross-border transport corridors, along which infrastructure investments and facilitation measures should be coordinated (see chapter 5). In air transport, cross-border liberalization will require a modification of bilateral air services agreements, while

national-level reforms—such as the restructuring of airlines, the privatization of airports, and the liberalization of ground handling—could be anchored through bilateral or regional agreements. The removal of transport frictions at national borders is largely a question of domestic reforms, including streamlining of customs procedures, but it should be complemented by administrative cooperation with neighboring countries, including information exchange between customs authorities.

Financial services. At the multilateral level, financial services are the second most frequently committed sector under the GATS. Nonetheless, the small size of most MENA domestic markets highlights the need for greater regional integration. However, the EU Community acquis might not be an adequate template for financial reforms in Partnership countries: many EU rules are complex pieces of legislation for modern securities markets, while simpler banking and insurance reforms are the priority of most Partnership countries. These countries could nonetheless encourage linkages between banks, stock markets, and insurance companies across the Mediterranean, as well as encourage South–South integration.

Telecommunications. As far as multilateral liberalization is concerned, telecommunications is one of the service sectors where negotiations have progressed farthest. Required domestic reforms should therefore be

(continued on next page)

BOX 3.4 *Continued*

anchored by extended GATS commitments. In telecommunications, there seems to be relatively little value added in regional integration measures at the policy level, except for the exchange of best practices between policy makers and regulators. The general principles and many regulatory instruments developed in the EU context could well be replicated in Partnership countries, but full regulatory harmonization seems less of a short-term priority.

Electricity. Electricity is one sector where deeper forms of integration can only be achieved at the regional level. Such integration could have substantial benefits. First, cross-border power transfer for emergency support and peak demand allows countries to lower expensive reserve margins. Second, economies of scale, different load profiles, and complementary energy endowments can give rise to further gains from trade. And third, private investors tend to be more willing to invest in large markets. Much progress has already been made on the interconnection of national grids, but deepening of regional trade is a priority (see chapter 3).

ICT-enabled and business services. EU firms are among the world leaders in many business services; as such, they could help Partnership countries upgrade their business environment and benefit from knowledge spillovers and transfers. However, much of the liberalization that would be required in this sector has to take place at the national level (unilat-

erally) or through the GATS (multilaterally). Only on issues such as mutual recognition do additional integration measures at the regional level seem merited.

Distribution/retail services. Reforms in the distribution sector have broad economic and social implications and should be gradual. There is a strong case for comprehensive liberalization in wholesale distribution, where economies of scale are large and repercussions on small shopkeepers are minor. Where retailing is concerned, stores serving the urban middle class would be an obvious place to start. The gap between developed and developing countries' GATS commitments is wide, allowing for more multilateral liberalization. An opening of the distribution sector in Partnership countries would most likely lead to an extension of European retail networks to the South: this would enhance competition and would be associated with significant infrastructure investments, knowledge spillovers, and human capital formation. The agriculture and industry sectors could benefit from backward linkages.

Tourism services. Most of the required reforms of the tourism sector have already been undertaken unilaterally due to the importance of the sector for the Partnership countries' economies. Regional commitments remain important in the field of transport and South–South integration of tourism infrastructure.

scale of operation of service providers is often regional or global; the market of reference is therefore broader than the domestic market, and it would make sense to issue regional licenses or reach conclusions on competition litigations with a larger market of reference. Second, beyond the economies of scale allowed by regional networks, cooperation allows information sharing and promotes liberalization through approximation of rules and practices. Cooperation should extend beyond the public sphere to include professional bodies and other entities that contribute to the regulation of services. For instance, business associations have a key role to play in the development of mutual recognition agreements.

Third, enhance the services competitiveness and export performance of Partnership countries. Partnership countries, with support from the Deauville partners, would benefit from the adoption of accompanying measures aimed at improving the competitiveness and global presence of their service providers. This involves efforts to adapt education and training to the needs of export-oriented services sectors, for example by developing new fields of study in technologies or promoting the teaching of foreign languages. Enhancing competitiveness in services also involves improving the overall ease of doing business, as well as taking specific steps to promote high-value and quality services exports, including through knowledge transfers and innovation. For instance, the protection of intellectual property and data is essential to promote BPO and KPO.

Services: Key selected recommendations

Short-term:

- Modernize the regulatory regimes of key services sectors in Partnership countries (e.g., trade facilitation and transport, including air services, energy, tourism, banking and finance, and information and communication) consistent with best international practices.

- Negotiate between Partnership countries and Deauville partners specific sector commitments on labor mobility, especially for skilled workers, as part of Mode 4 on the movement of natural persons in future deep and high-quality trade agreements with Deauville partners.

- Define reform priorities for the most important service sectors in Partnership countries based on a diagnostic of competition, regulation, and market access conditions. This can be assisted by Deauville partners and could be reinforced by creating a pilot multi-stakeholder services knowledge platform to share experience and analysis on a regional basis.

(continued on next page)

Services: Key selected recommendations *(continued)*

Medium-term:

- Open up the services sector in (and between) Partnership countries in all four modes of services supply beyond the GATS commitments, including in the context of deep and high-quality trade agreements with Deauville partners.

- Negotiate acceptable standards and criteria for licensing and certification of professional service suppliers, with a view to agreeing on mutual recognition of qualifications and skills and portability of benefits.

- Develop regional (soft and hard) infrastructure for telecommunications, energy, transport, and other backbone services in Partnership countries to improve regional connectivity and cooperation, including cooperation among services regulatory agencies and/or the creation of joint agencies where appropriate.

- Adopt accompanying measures aimed at improving the competitiveness and global presence of Partnership countries' service exports, including through education, training, business climate reforms, and improved backbone and intermediate services.

Energy

Key issues

Regional integration and trade in the energy sector can help MENA countries meet growth in energy demand, which is projected to exceed 6 percent per year and result in the need for 150,000 megawatts of additional capacity by 2020. In addition to a strong endowment of hydrocarbon resources, with around 57 percent of proven oil and 41 percent of proven natural gas reserves, the region has vast exploitable solar energy potential, which is more evenly distributed across countries. The division between energy surplus and deficit countries implies the potential for mutually beneficial trade at levels greater than currently prevail.

Electricity trade between Partnership countries and their neighbors can be increased. The Maghreb regional interconnection scheme, linking Morocco, Algeria, and Tunisia, and the Eight-Country Interconnection between Egypt, Iraq, Jordan, Libya, Lebanon, West Bank and Gaza, Syria, and Turkey, can both be reinforced. Efforts to synchronize electricity networks and improve cross-border interconnections can reinforce energy security and lower costs to consumers and industry. Cross-border trade can be facilitated by a sector reform agenda, including making transmission grids accessible to independent firms and reforming electricity tariffs that are set below cost recovery level.

The Arab world is making a major contribution to scaling up solar energy technologies that can ease supply constraints domestically and contribute to global environmental goals. The deployment of CSP in Morocco, Algeria, Tunisia, Egypt, and Jordan could create 80,000 jobs in those countries alone. For oil and gas importers, solar power offers energy security, while for exporters it offers the chance to free up fossil fuels for higher-value-added usage and export. The growth of CSP is necessarily a regional issue, requiring commitment from partners including European industry and government. Deauville partners can offer crucial support by sending long-term, critical signals about market access and demand, including through government-backed commitments to import CSP.

Reliable access to efficient energy services is a key precondition for sustaining economic growth. Energy is a critical factor of production in the agriculture, mining, and manufacturing sectors. It is a source of investment and therefore a direct contributor to economic growth and growth potential. The efficiency with which energy is used in the economy also has indirect effects on total factor productivity. From the perspective of trade and FDI, improved access to reliable and efficient regional energy markets is another powerful mechanism of economic integration that can help accelerate economic growth and employment. Regional integration and trade in the power sector can both help MENA countries meet energy demand and improve the security of supply.

The MENA region has a strong comparative advantage in energy resources—both traditional and renewable. The region is endowed with about 57 percent of the world's proven oil reserves and 41 percent of proven natural gas resources. It also has unique solar potential. The distribution of the oil and gas endowment is highly unequal within the region, however, with some countries rich in natural resources while other countries depend on imports of such resources. With the exception of Libya, Partnership countries are mainly in the second category. Solar potential is naturally more evenly spread and offers great prospects for Partnership countries. Overall, in these countries, there is much scope for improving the efficiency of energy supply and energy conservation, as well as for developing renewable energy resources. The rest of this section focuses on electricity and gas.

Electricity

Several bilateral and subregional initiatives are under way to interconnect the electricity networks of the Partnership countries. The primary regional interconnection schemes specific to Egypt, Jordan, Libya, Morocco, and Tunisia are the Maghreb regional interconnection between

Morocco, Algeria, and Tunisia, and the Eight-Country Interconnection (ECI) between Egypt, Iraq, Jordan, Lebanon, Libya, Syria, Turkey, and West Bank and Gaza.

The *Maghreb* regional interconnection was initiated in the 1950s and has evolved into multiple high-voltage transmission interconnections between the three countries. Morocco was connected to Spain in the late 1990s, and Morocco, Algeria, and Tunisia are now all synchronized with the pan-European high-voltage transmission network.

The *ECI* was initiated in 1988 by Egypt, Iraq, Jordan, Syria, and Turkey as part of an effort to upgrade their electricity systems to a regional standard. Lebanon, Libya, and the Palestinian National Authority later joined the interconnection, extending the agreement to eight economies. Turkey is expected to fully synchronize with the European grid in early 2012, furthering the efforts to synchronize the ECI network with the grids in Europe.

Although the Maghreb and Eight-Country interconnections have existed for some time, electricity trade between partner countries has remained modest. Electricity trade cannot currently take place between the ECI and the Maghreb via the interconnection between Tunisia and Libya because the Maghreb and ECI systems are not synchronized. Currently, the GCC countries are unable to trade with other MENA countries because they are not physically interconnected. Although the Maghreb countries (except Libya) are fully interconnected and synchronized, transfers of large amounts of power across Northern Africa are not currently possible; for example, Algeria-Tunisia transfers are limited to 150 megawatts. The Mediterranean Ring project is attempting to synchronize the electricity networks of all European and MENA countries bordering the Mediterranean Sea. The project envisions linking the power systems from Spain to Morocco and the remaining Maghreb countries, on to Egypt and the Mashreq countries, and from there to Turkey. From Turkey the network would loop back into the European grid via Greece or through newly interconnected Eastern European country grids. This project would increase energy security in the region and enable more efficient and lower-cost power production. Over the long term, this would pave the way for the ECI to synchronize and join the EU market.

One of the most significant bottlenecks in developing new power generating capacity in Partnership countries is the supply of fuel. In the MENA region, electricity demand is forecast to grow sharply in the coming years. The demand for electricity is projected to increase by an average annual rate of more than 6 percent, resulting in a need for over 150,000 megawatts of new generating capacity by 2020, excluding the capacity that would be needed to replace retired plants. The investment cost for such new generating capacity could approach $225 billion. When one factors in the transmission and distribution facilities needed to meet the increased demand, the total investment cost for new infrastructure in the MENA power sector could top $450 billion by 2020. While the share of gas in power generation doubled to about 50 percent during the last decade, it will be difficult to continue to significantly increase this share in the coming years, given the increased constraint on the amount of natural gas available for power generation (discussed further below).

The solar energy potential of the MENA region offers a unique opportunity to diversify sources of energy and at the same time limit the carbon footprint of the region. Unlike oil and gas, solar energy is evenly spread across MENA countries—including all the Partnership countries. For oil and gas importers, renewable energy would provide energy security, whereas for oil and gas exporters it could free up fossil fuels for higher-value-added usage and exports. The prospect for exporting green energy to Europe at high prices reinforces the vision that renewable energy could become an important and reliable source of revenue for the Partnership countries. Concentrated solar power could create tens of thousands of jobs in Partnership countries over the medium term, as well as FDI opportunities (box 3.5).

Notwithstanding the existing interconnections and potential for developing solar energy, electricity trade in Partnership countries and in the region more generally is still impeded by a number of physical and institutional challenges. In addition to the lack of interconnection and synchronization of existing transmission lines, the electricity systems of some MENA countries have not been designed to meet minimum standards, meaning there may be reliability and security risks associated with expanding interconnection capacity in the region. Only three countries—Algeria, Morocco, and Tunisia—are currently synchronized with the EU grid. There is a limited amount of surplus power available to support long-term trade. At the institutional level, there is no coordination of the generation and transmission operation for the subregions, making it difficult to determine the potential for further trade. The electricity markets in Partnership countries remain mostly vertically integrated in the framework of state-owned utilities. There are no "eligible customers" with the opportunity to choose their supplier. As a result, international transactions take a long time to negotiate and are unable to respond to short-term opportunities, such as sudden changes in generation availability. Private sector participation in electricity markets is generally limited to independent power producers. By providing third-party access to the transmission grid and regional trade, the private sector would, however, be in a position to contribute to financing the new generation projects.

To promote electricity integration, a key priority is to improve and expand capacity and synchronize the power grids. The necessary infrastructure improvements include reinforcement of existing cross-border interconnections and upgrading of national transmission networks. An-

BOX 3.5

Comparative Advantage, Integration, and Technology: Solar Power from the Deserts of the MENA Region

There have long been dreams of harnessing the incredible solar energy potential of the deserts of MENA, but now those dreams are becoming a reality. A "commodity" in which MENA countries have clear global comparative advantage is beginning to be exploited, to regional and global benefit. That development is motivated by objectives of employment creation, climate change mitigation, regional integration in the Mediterranean and GCC space, and energy security. These objectives are reflected in the Union for the Mediterranean's "Mediterranean Solar Plan" and in the DESERTEC and MEDGRID initiatives.

MENA countries from Saudi Arabia to Morocco are taking steps to scale up solar power. Strong emphasis is being placed on CSP, a highly transferable technology that could create tens of thousands of jobs in the MENA region over the medium term, as well as FDI opportunities. CSP has the advantage of being fully available during daylight hours without significant interruption, and increasingly at night also, as heat storage technology develops. The Arab world is making a major contribution to the development of a technology that can be deployed globally once economies of scale have brought the costs down—helping the world reduce its long-term dependence on fossil fuels.

This scale-up of CSP is being supported in five MENA countries—Morocco, Algeria, Tunisia, Egypt, and Jordan—by a multidonor group consisting of the African Development Bank, World Bank Group, Islamic Development Bank, EU Neighbourhood Investment Facility, and European Investment Bank, as well as Japanese and other European donors, including the governments of the Federal Republic of Germany and France. Catalytic funding is being provided by the highly concessional Clean Technology Fund, and private investment is being mobilized in partnership with the public sector. The package includes about 1,200 megawatts of CSP generation and also cross-border interconnections for export, with a total estimated cost of $5.6 billion. With replication based on the strong initial signal to markets that CSP is taking off in the region, it is estimated that more than 80,000 jobs could eventually be created in CSP equipment manufacturing and construction in those five countries alone.

A crucial question still being resolved is whether green energy markets in Europe will allow access to imports of CSP energy from MENA countries on terms equivalent to those provided to EU producers. Opening these profitable markets will be essential to the takeoff of CSP in Mediterranean MENA. It will require adoption of some implementing regulations, and ultimately some transmission investments once a high level of imports is foreseen. But the first step is for European offtakers—with government financial and political support—to commit to importing CSP. That action would have a powerful and immediate demonstration effect throughout the region, signaling that Europe is willing to open important markets to create much-needed employment and revenue in the MENA region.

other component involves construction of new international interconnections and expansion of generation capacity for export to other market destinations, particularly renewable energy. A number of new international interconnection projects that would contribute to regional power market integration are under consideration. A key transmission project for the MENA region and Partnership countries would be construction of the proposed Egypt–Saudi Arabia interconnection. This would open the door to trade between the GCC countries and the ECI, and ultimately beyond, to the Maghreb and Europe. A number of grid-strengthening projects are under study in the region, including 400-kilovolt interconnections between Morocco and Algeria, Algeria and Tunisia, and Tunisia and Libya. Consideration has also been given to establishing new interconnections between the Maghreb region and Europe, with the interconnection between Tunisia and Sicily being the most promising. The project will contribute to an increase in electricity trade between Tunisia and Europe, including support for sustainable development of renewable energy in the region. Finally, reinforcement of the transmission networks of the ECI, and in particular the Egypt-Jordan-Syria transmission corridor, will be necessary to increase the level of electricity trade and renewable energy development in the Mashreq region and the region's future interconnection with Turkey and Europe.

A barrier to increased regional trade and cooperation as well as private sector participation in power generation has been the significant subsidization of pricing in the power sector. As in other MENA countries, electricity price distortions are large in Partnership countries, and tariffs are set below their cost recovery level. This has led to inefficient use of supply, high energy intensity in energy use, increasing environmental problems, and a rapidly increasing burden on government finances. In particular, most Partnership countries have had difficulty coping with high oil prices. This situation makes it difficult to find a creditworthy offtaker, since many power companies have poor financial performance. It also makes it difficult to find a buyer, since potential customers are paying prices for power that are below cost. A potential customer is unlikely to buy power at international prices when it can purchase power at subsidized prices domestically.

Gas

Natural gas has emerged as an important source of energy in Egypt, Jordan, and Tunisia over the last three decades, but it has not increased significantly in Libya and Morocco. The growth in gas demand can be attributed to three factors: a rapid increase in electricity demand, as noted above; the diversion of gas into energy-intensive industries, mainly petrochemicals; and the policy of maintaining low gas prices (Fattouh and

Stern 2011). Table 3.6 outlines the growth of natural gas as a percentage of total primary energy supply in the five countries.

In particular, Jordan, Tunisia, and Morocco have realized that their domestic gas production together with their current gas imports are not sufficient to meet the needs of their power sectors. This has triggered a search for alternative energy, particularly renewable energy, as well as for sources of imported gas and/or electricity. Gas trade in the Arab world has been dominated by the objective of exporting gas in the form of lique-fied natural gas (LNG) to buyers outside the region, especially to Asia, Europe, and North America. Algeria and Qatar have been the largest gas exporters, exporting significant amounts of gas in the form of both LNG and piped gas. Egypt also successfully completed construction of two LNG plants. Gas trade within the region is limited, however, to rather small-volume gas movements from Algeria to Tunisia and Morocco; from Egypt to Jordan, Syria, and Lebanon; and from Qatar to the United Arab Emirates—all through pipelines. Against these small volumes of gas trade, there are significant needs for imported gas, and therefore the po-tential for gas trade within the Arab world is large.

As for electricity, the low price of gas regionally has been a key factor in limiting gas trade. Gas prices in most MENA countries are on the order of $1 per million metric British thermal units (MMBtu), though certain con-sumer categories in a few countries pay $3–4 per MMBtu. Such pricing schemes were adopted when most countries were considered gas-surplus countries. However, there is now a new reality—gas shortages—and gas prices therefore need to be adjusted to reflect the cost of supply. The most immediate effects of an adjustment would be more efficient use of gas, more domestic supply, and less dependence on oil. This will also facilitate gas imports, which seem to be necessary for Jordan, Tunisia, and Morocco.

There is some potential to expand existing gas pipelines in the region, but the prospects for LNG facilities for gas export are rising. Potential gas pipe-

TABLE 3.6

Share of Natural Gas in Total Primary Energy Supply of Deauville Partnership Countries, 1980–2008
(% of total primary energy supply)

Country	1980	1990	2000	2008
Egypt, Arab Rep.	10.45	21.15	39.38	49.10
Jordan	—	3.13	4.32	38.58
Libya	35.98	35.75	25.03	24.65
Morocco	1.13	0.62	0.37	3.16
Tunisia	10.74	24.95	37.39	43.94

Source: IEA Energy Balances.

Note: Share of natural gas in Jordan in 1980 was negligible; precise data not available. — = not available.

line projects could include the expansion of the existing pipelines between Algeria and Tunisia and between Algeria and Morocco. There is some scope as well for expansion of the Egypt–Jordan pipelines, but this would be limited, at least in the short term, by constraints on gas export from Egypt. New pipeline projects could also include a gas pipeline from Libya to Tunisia, and in the long term, from Iraq to Jordan. However, given the complexity and long lead time for developing cross-border gas pipelines, the delays associated with cross-border pipeline delivery, and the limitation of gas supply through existing pipelines, countries in the region such as Jordan, Lebanon, Morocco, Saudi Arabia, and Bahrain are now considering developing LNG gas export facilities. The LNG option may appear more costly than gas pipelines but the option would offer a number of benefits, including increased supply diversification, flexibility, and reliability.

Energy: Key selected recommendations

Short-term:

- Launch negotiations on a multilateral agreement on solar energy imports from MENA countries that will govern how parties share the burden of paying for the incremental cost of solar imports. (European subsidies for renewable energy could be made available for imports, with appropriate adjustments.) The agreement could be concluded initially between Morocco and interested EU member states, such as Germany, Spain, France, Italy, and potentially others. Other Partnership countries could be invited to join the agreement, depending how fast they move with CSP projects.

- Start harmonizing (a) technical codes and standards for the national energy systems; (b) regulation in the national energy sectors; (c) goals and milestones for energy sector reform relating to, in particular, open access and consistent and fair pricing of transport; and (d) energy pricing and taxation.

- Identify an independent process and procedure for resolving disputes related to regional energy transactions.

Medium-term:

- Open up and encourage nondiscriminatory, transparent, and predictable access to national transmission systems by implementing reforms to ensure reciprocity and a level playing field. These should be backed by technical and financial documentation and governed by high-level institutions with the expertise and authority to guide and enforce consistency and fairness across the region.

- Upgrade and expand infrastructure to increase electricity capacity and synchronize power grids, including by reinforcing existing cross-border interconnections, upgrading national transmission networks, and constructing new international interconnections.

Labor Mobility

Key issues

In the Mediterranean basin, labor mobility is restricted (especially for less-skilled workers) and politically sensitive to the extent that large opportunities for mutually beneficial exchanges are missed. At the global level, there is evidence that labor market restrictions impose a greater burden on economies than trade or FDI restrictions. In the region, the declining labor forces of migrant-receiving EU countries and the excess supply of young workers from Partnership countries suggest strong conditions for mutually beneficial exchanges. The Deauville Partnership is an opportunity for dialogue on the ways and means of achieving a beneficial increase in labor mobility between the two rims of the Mediterranean and beyond.

At the regional level, the Deauville Partnership could usefully strengthen the migration framework for increased intra-Arab mobility, especially to the GCC and Libya. However, it is in relation to the EU that a regional avenue for increased labor mobility is most promising. New Mobility Partnership discussions have been launched with the EU, and the EU could take on commitments for liberalizing labor-intensive services in future DCFTAs. Partnership countries have an interest in obtaining provisions similar to the most generous that exist in EU trade agreements—notably those with Chile and CARIFORUM—covering movement of personnel.

At the bilateral level, the G8 and other Deauville partners could develop new migration schemes by drawing on best practices in program design, implementation, and organizational capacity as exhibited by circular migration schemes in Canada, Australia, and New Zealand. As with the concept of "aid for trade," G8 countries could provide the financial and technical assistance to strengthen behind-the-border systems to manage labor outflows. Indeed, this would seem essential for any sustainable implementation of bilateral labor mobility agreements from the receiving country perspective. On their side, Partnership countries need to strengthen public agencies for job prospecting and placement and align training priorities with the skills that are demanded in the private marketplace.

Migration, which until recently was the exclusive domain of domestic immigration policy, has become central to the policy debate on economic integration and development. Indeed, some have argued that nothing separates an individual from the benefits of development so much as lack of a work visa (Clemens, Montenegro, and Pritchett 2008). Yet economic theory predicts that under certain conditions the free movement of goods is a substitute for the free movement of the factors embodied in the production of those goods—hence trade in goods that are highly labor-intensive should do the same for wages as a physical movement of people, accomplishing a result close to factor price equalization in the end. This is not borne out by reality, in part because the conditions listed in textbooks are not present in the real world. Evidence shows that differences in productivity do not explain away the differences in wages across locations; rather, wages are highly location-specific, which means that where you are often matters more than who you are (Clemens 2011). This leads to a ready stock of migrants willing to raise their incomes by moving to, or working in, high-wage locations.

There is strong evidence that labor market restrictions are imposing a much greater burden on the global economy than trade or investment restrictions. The gains from economic integration are based on harnessing economic advantage from differences in endowments. Today, goods, capital, and to a growing extent services are able to cross international borders and thus deliver substantial economic gains worldwide. It has been estimated that the gains from eliminating barriers to labor mobility would dwarf the gains from eliminating other types of barriers. While the full liberalization of trade and capital flows could increase world GDP by up to 4 percentage points, it is estimated that removing labor mobility barriers could increase world GDP in the range of 50–150 percent.[11] Migration helps industrialized countries address specific sectoral shortages and the economic and social challenges presented by their ageing populations. Simultaneously, it can yield enormous benefits for the residents of developing countries—the migrants themselves, most obviously, but also those left behind, who benefit from remittances, diaspora investment, and the transfer of knowledge.

There is a potentially strong, mutually beneficial complementarity in the demographics of the Northern and Southern Mediterranean. Given the geographic proximity and history of migration between Europe and its North African neighbors (box 3.6), there is potential for a North–South demographic arbitrage in the Mediterranean. Most migrant-receiving countries in the EU face stagnating populations and expect their labor force to decline as a consequence of sustained below-replacement fertility rates. In the absence of immigration flows, three main trends will transform Europe's demographic profile over the next two decades: a sharp decline in the share of the population below age 40, a stagnant share of the population aged 40–60, and a strong growth in the population aged 60 and over (Fargues 2005). Meanwhile, MENA countries as a group will continue to experience significant labor force increases. Moving further down the road, the World Bank's (2009) projections indicate that such opposite trends in the evolution of the labor force in the two regions are likely to persist over the long term (figure 3.17).

The projected decline in the EU labor force is likely to generate persistent labor market shortages at all skill levels, providing opportunities

The Migration Landscape around the Mediterranean Basin

With about 8 million migrants living abroad out of a combined population of 135 million, North Africa (Morocco, Algeria, Tunisia, and Egypt) has an emigration rate of about 5.5 percent, almost double the world emigration rate (World Bank 2010). Morocco's migration rate is the highest, at more than 9 percent of the population, but all four countries have higher than average rates of emigration. Maghreb migrants are concentrated in EU countries. In 2000, more than half of North Africa's migrants and about 75 percent of Maghreb migrants were in EU countries, with France as the main destination: more than 60 percent of Algerian and Tunisian migrants were located in France. Although Egypt has a low migration rate to the EU compared to its Maghreb neighbors (around 9 percent of Egyptian migrants are in EU countries), it is high in absolute terms, with about 200,000 migrants in the EU in 2000. Maghreb migrants are predominantly low-skilled workers, with more than 70 percent having primary education or less. The majority of Egyptian migrants are also low-skilled, but almost 30 percent have higher education.

Skilled emigration from MENA to OECD countries grew significantly in absolute numbers between 1990 and 2000: from 674,000 in 1990 to 1,135,000 in 2000. At the same time, skilled emigration rates (the percentage of the domestic stock of high-skilled workers who emigrate) of MENA countries as a whole have actually fallen, from 11.3 percent in 1990 to 9.2 percent in 2000, reflecting an overall increase in educational attainment in the individual countries. Skilled emigration rates to the EU counties in 2000 were 7.1 percent for Algeria, 0.9 percent for Egypt, 13.3 percent for Morocco, and 9.6 percent for Tunisia. In comparison, the skilled emigration rate to OECD countries in 2000 was 7.3 percent for developing countries worldwide.

for both skilled and less-skilled migrants. Migration from MENA countries could only partially offset the labor force decline in the EU, depending on the evolution of the MENA labor force by education level (figure 3.18). Between 2005 and 2016, more than 61 million jobs are expected to become available in the EU25, with the greatest number of job openings arising in the major European economies: the United Kingdom, Germany, Italy, and France (Özden, Sewadeh, and Wahba 2009). Figure 3.19 shows the number of projected job openings in the EU generated by replacement demand (due to exit of workers for retirement and other reasons) and expansion demand (due to economic and technological changes). The growth will be particularly significant in the business and other ser-

FIGURE 3.17

Projected Change in Labor Force, 2005–50, by Country and Age Group, EU and MENA

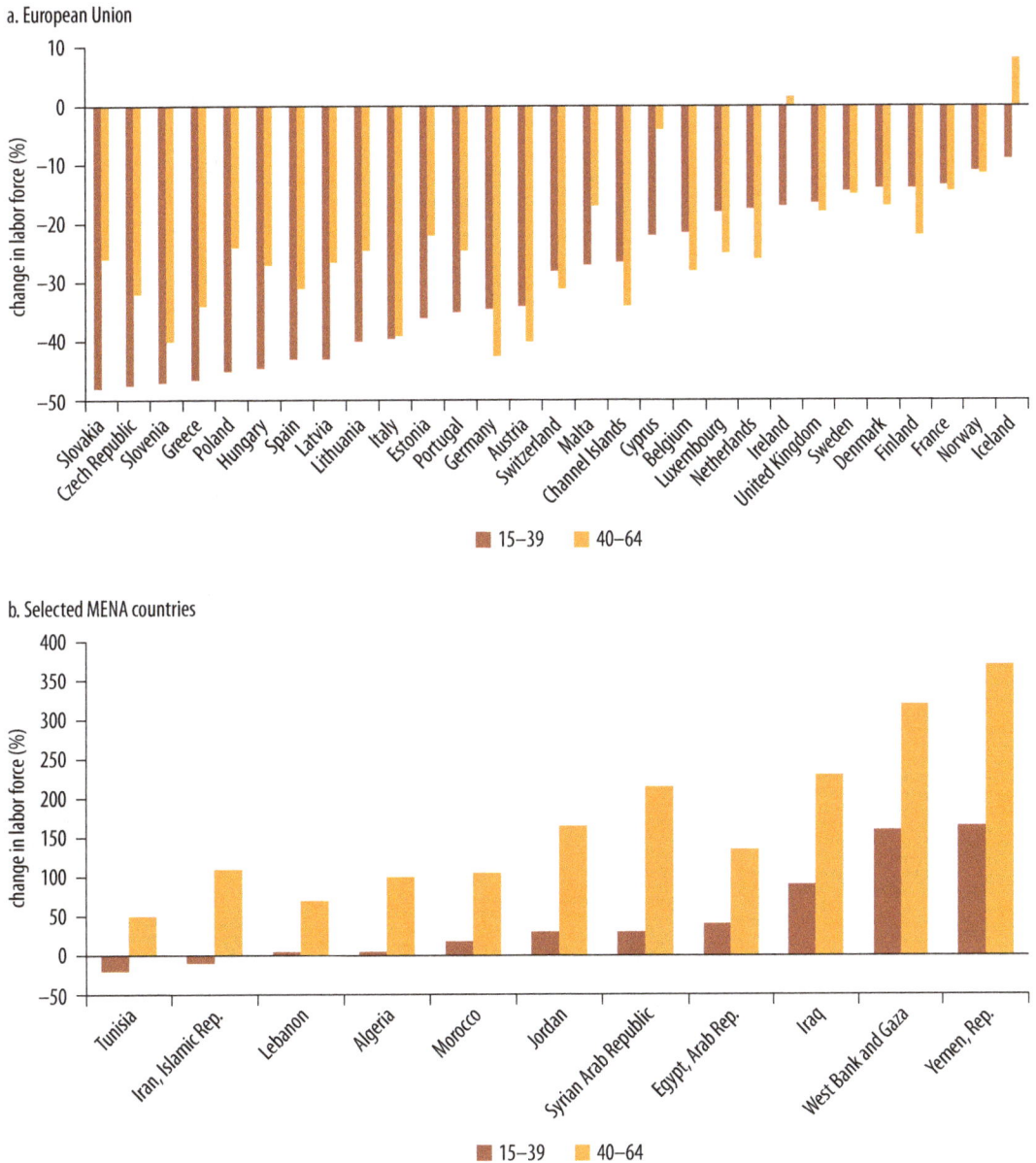

a. European Union

b. Selected MENA countries

Source: World Bank 2009.

vices sector. The number of employees in that sector will grow significantly from a little under 5 million in 2006 to over 54 million in 2015
(Özden, Sewadeh, and Wahba 2009). Figure 3.20 also shows that job
creation will mainly happen in business services, though some growth is
also expected in distribution and transport. In contrast, job losses are ex-

FIGURE 3.18

Projected Change in Labor Force, 2005–50, by Age Group and Education Level, EU and MENA

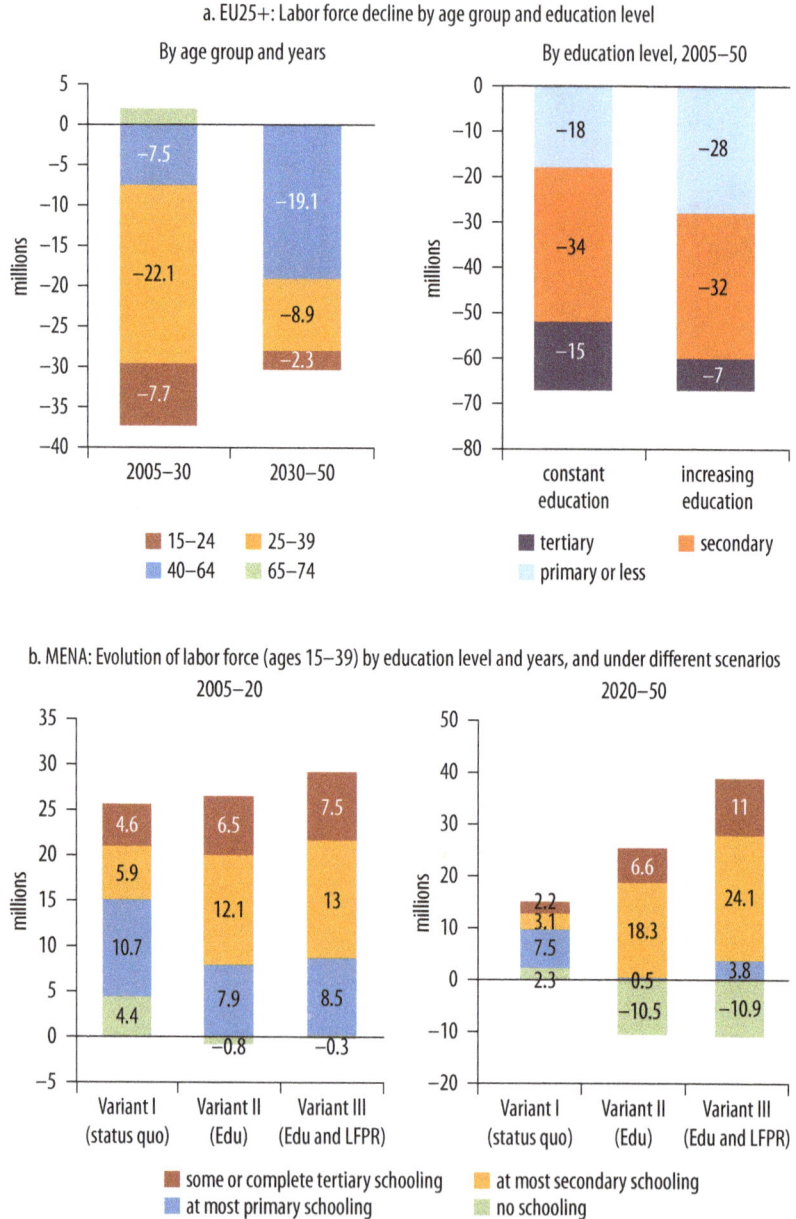

a. EU25+: Labor force decline by age group and education level

b. MENA: Evolution of labor force (ages 15–39) by education level and years, and under different scenarios

Source: World Bank 2009.

Note: Variant I: Unchanged education rates (Edu) and labor force participation rates (LFPR). Variant II: Unchanged LFPRs, education rates converging to France, Greece, Italy, Portugal, and Spain. Variant III: Both education rates and LFPRs converging to EU-Mediterranean peers.

FIGURE 3.19

Total Job Openings in the EU Due to Replacement and Expansion Demand, 2006–15

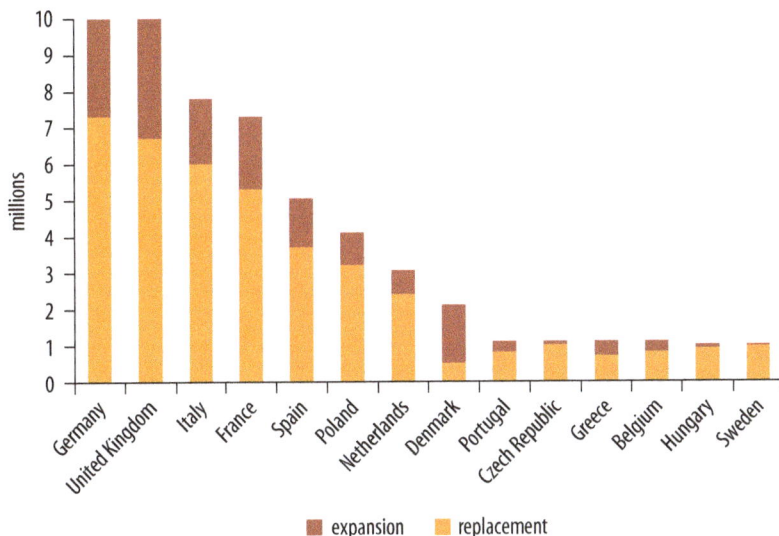

Source: Özden, Sewadeh, and Wahba 2009.

pected in the primary sector and in manufacturing and production industries. Industrial restructuring and technological developments are expected to increase demand in knowledge-intensive industries. Demand for routine workers in agriculture and manufacturing is expected to fall, while demand for technicians, skilled professionals, services workers, and unskilled workers in elementary occupations will see a sharp increase (figure 3.21). Managers, technicians, and professionals are expected to account for 42 percent of total EU employment in 2020.

North African and other MENA countries have an excess supply of young workers with medium and high qualifications who could potentially meet Europe's future labor needs. As a result of the persistent incapacity of their economies to absorb labor force increases, migrant-sending countries in MENA are characterized by high unemployment rates among young labor market entrants (21 percent in MENA and 25 percent in North Africa). This is especially the case at medium and high qualification levels, where labor needs are highest in Europe. The share of unemployed adults who are tertiary-educated is particularly high in North African countries and has increased significantly over the last decade in Tunisia (figure 3.22). Given existing wage differentials between MENA and Europe, historical migration patterns between the two re-

FIGURE 3.20

Employment Trends by Industry in the EU25, 2006 and 2015

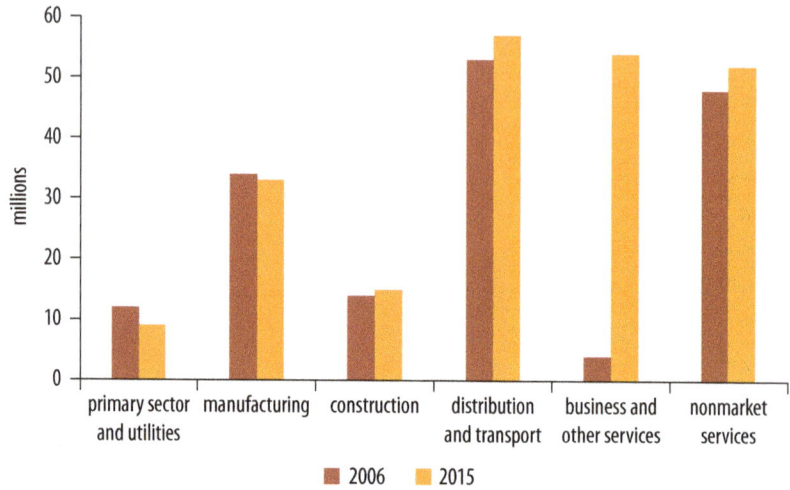

Source: Özden, Sewadeh, and Wahba 2009.

FIGURE 3.21

Levels and Growth of Employment by Occupation in the EU, 2006–15

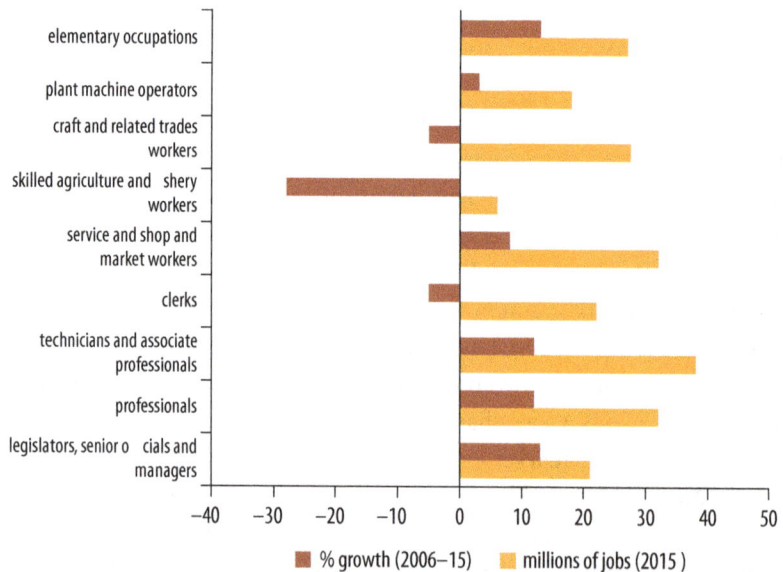

Source: Özden, Sewadeh, and Wahba 2009.

gions, and the broad desire to emigrate among young and educated job seekers from North Africa, EU countries could potentially use this excess supply of labor in their Southern neighborhood to meet their labor shortages in the short and medium term through a combination of temporary and permanent labor migration.

But young Arab workers may find it difficult to match the skills needed to compete for jobs in advanced, largely knowledge-based economies. Despite impressive advances in access to education at all levels of instruction over the last 40 years, MENA countries' educational attainment remains low compared to that of East Asian and Latin American countries at similar levels of economic development (World Bank 2009). Illiteracy rates in MENA remain twice as high as in East Asia and Latin America. The Trends in International Mathematics and Science Study confirms that MENA students score much lower on standardized mathematics tests at the end of secondary education than students in countries like Malaysia, Thailand, or Korea, for example. A few MENA countries (Jor-

FIGURE 3.22

Share of Unemployed Adults Who Hold a Tertiary Degree, Selected MENA and European Countries, 2000 and 2010

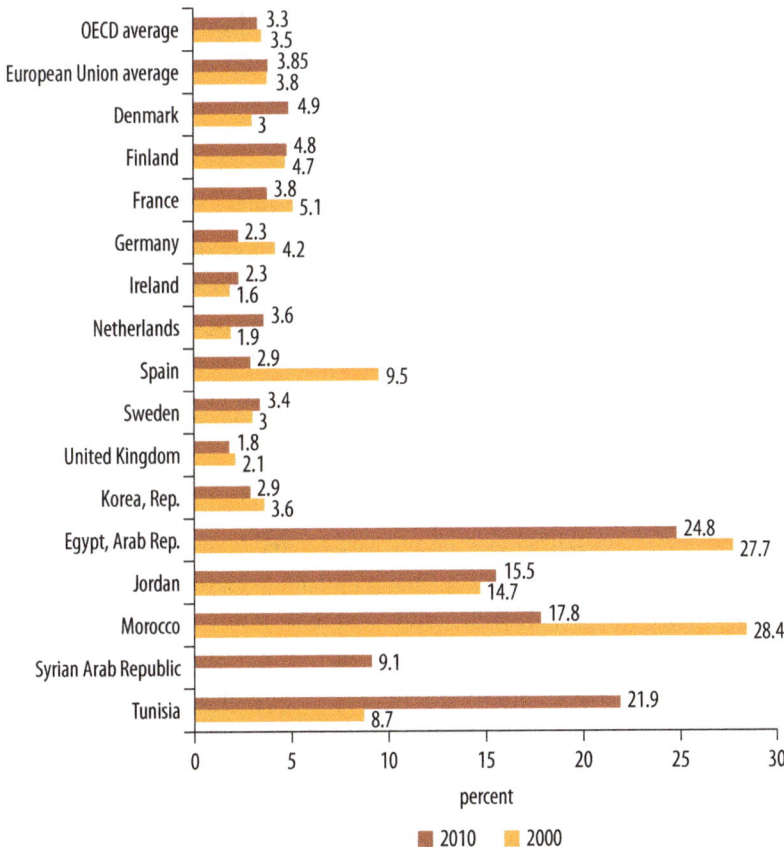

Source: Kosarajo and Zaafrane 2011.

dan, Qatar, and Tunisia) have participated in the OECD's Programme for International Student Assessment. The program found that in these countries, cognitive skills acquired at the secondary level in reading, mathematics, and science are quite low compared to the OECD average (OECD 2010). On the demand side, results from enterprise surveys show that firms identify worker skills and education as among the top five constraints to business climate in the region, especially in Arab Mediterranean countries. Employers express dissatisfaction about lack of technical skills and relevant professional experience, but also point to deficiencies in soft skills such as language, interpersonal skills, personal habits, workplace attitudes, and so forth.

The mismatch between MENA workers' skills and private sector demand calls for an urgent adjustment of education and training programs. Education systems in MENA countries are skewed toward the humanities and social sciences at the expense of technical, scientific, and business training, which is what matters most for innovation and knowledge creation in Europe. Beyond the choice of curricula, there is also evidence that higher education systems in MENA do not develop the critical skills needed for innovation in the knowledge economy (World Bank 2009). Whereas pedagogical methods are evolving worldwide toward inquiry-based learning, problem solving, student-centered learning, and critical thinking, MENA countries continue to use traditional, passive models of pedagogy based on unilinear transmission from teacher to student. Moreover, secondary and higher education curricula do not provide enough flexibility and diversity to allow for multiple learning paths along the life cycle, as is increasingly possible in more innovative economies (World Bank 2009). Part of the explanation for high unemployment rates among university graduates in MENA countries could lie in the inadequacy of skills acquired at university for jobs in the private sector. If observed at home, such a lack of employability can be expected in EU labor markets as well.

Last but not least, labor migration faces huge obstacles in many advanced countries due to high unemployment rates and fierce political opposition to low-skilled immigration. Squeezed by a tight job market, young Americans have suffered bigger income losses than other age groups and are less likely to be employed than at any time since World War II. Similarly, in the context of the eurozone crisis, European countries are experiencing persistently high unemployment rates, especially among the most vulnerable groups; youth unemployment was above 20 percent in the EU and 40 percent in Spain in the first quarter of 2011. As a consequence, domestic options focusing on the unemployed are likely to be favored over increased labor immigration among European voters and their governments. Current governments in major EU economies such as France and the United Kingdom have already set restrictive targets on labor migration at all skill levels, and especially at lower skill levels, where political opposition to immigration is fierce. Unlike their tertiary-educated peers, low-skilled workers in MENA countries could easily become employable in Europe for low- to mid-skilled jobs in agriculture, tourism, construction, and routine service occupations, as long as they receive sufficient language training and predeparture orientation. But in a context of high unemployment rates, unsatisfactory labor market and social integration of immigrants and their children, and strained welfare systems in European economies, low-skilled immigration will continue to face steep political obstacles. Data from the European Social Survey indicate that European citizens express increasingly negative perceptions of immigrants over the last decade, driven primarily by concerns that immigrants are a fiscal burden and abuse the generosity of welfare states. Low-skilled and low-income groups in the EU are the most concerned about the fiscal implications of migration (Boeri 2010).

The Deauville Partnership is therefore an opportunity to open a sensible dialogue on the prospects for increased labor mobility between the two rims of the Mediterranean. Gradually liberalizing the movement of persons will complete the long-term vision of a common Mediterranean economic area with the free movement of goods, services, capital, and labor. It entails large opportunities for mutually beneficial exchanges, especially for less-skilled workers. There are two levels at which the liberalization of labor markets in the Mediterranean is already being pursued and could be further enhanced: regional and bilateral. A third alternative, the multilateral level, is not practical in the context of the Deauville Partnership. Indeed, WTO members have made only a few commitments to liberalize the movement of natural persons (Mode 4 in the WTO agreement on services), and 70 percent of those commitments are in high-skilled service occupations; within these, one fourth target executives and managers in high-ranking and high-income positions. Therefore, Mode 4 in the context of the WTO framework is not seen as a vehicle that can deliver development dividends for countries with surplus low-skilled labor in the foreseeable future. The reason lies mainly in the fundamental principle of "most favored nation" in the WTO, which implies that once access is negotiated, it must be granted on an unconditional basis to all nations. Granting all WTO members unconditional access to their labor markets does not sit well with most countries, which feel compelled to balance the liberalization of labor markets with domestic economic and social concerns.

At the regional level, the Deauville Partnership could usefully strengthen the migration framework for increased intra-Arab labor movements, especially to the GCC and Libya. Historically, one important route for MENA labor migration has been toward the GCC countries. This reached a peak in the 1970s, when Arab workers made up 72 percent of all migrant workers in the GCC. However, this proportion has fallen steadily to around 20 percent in 2010, according to the International Organization for Migration, mainly on account of competition from other labor-sending countries in Asia. More recently, GCC countries such as Saudi Arabia and Qatar have been solidifying ties with post-revolution North African economies, and discussions on investment and labor are ongoing. Another important destination for North African Arab workers has been Libya, which until 2007 allowed visa-free circulation of people as part of the Union of the Arab Maghreb. The Libyan workforce has historically included a sizeable foreign contingent, comprising approximately 1 million formal and informal workers as of 2009. Since the conflict, however, a substantial proportion of the South Asian and Sub-Saharan African labor force has left Libya, and job opportunities for migrants from neighboring countries, including Tunisians and Egyptians, would need to be assessed. Given the geographic and cultural proximity of Tunisia and Libya, the support provided by Tunisia to the Libyan people during the armed conflict, and the availability of a large pool of Tunisian unemployed workers at all skill levels, significant employment channels could be opened under a visa-free regime for Tunisian workers within the framework of bilateral cooperation with Libya.

However, it is in relation to the EU that a regional avenue for increased labor mobility is the most promising and attractive for Partnership countries. With respect to labor mobility, the current Euro-Med Association Agreements with the EU only go as far as reaffirming each party's (limited) obligations under the GATS. The agreements with Morocco and Tunisia also include commitments on nondiscrimination with respect to working conditions, remuneration for dismissal, and social security payments for nationals of these countries who are legally employed in the EU. Both agreements also call for regular dialogue on legal and illegal migration. The agreements with Algeria and Jordan provide for limited movement of key personnel (such as certain employees of Jordanian companies established in the EU). There is therefore scope for improvement, and a first step could be to extend to Partnership countries what the EU has already granted to other countries. For instance, the CARIFORUM-EU Economic Partnership Agreement signed with a number of Caribbean countries includes firm commitments on the movement of contractual service suppliers and independent professionals—something that the Euro-Med Agreements do not provide. The 2002 EU-Chile agreement contains provisions on the temporary movement of business service sellers in about 30 sectors, though it remains skewed toward highly skilled workers. Partnership countries have an offensive interest in obtaining similar provisions and extending them to include the mutual recognition of academic and professional qualifications in as many sectors as possible.

An effort to push the EU-wide policies into further liberalization of labor mobility from the South would require some inclusion of specific commitments to liberalize labor-intensive services under Mode 4 on the temporary movement of natural persons in future DCFTAs and MENA TIP, as well as the expansion of Mobility Partnerships. It will also require extending the period of stay beyond six months to allow costs of movement to be recouped. This would require garnering some support inside the EU from certain sectors that need such labor and are important to EU constituencies. In this endeavor, the Global Approach to Migration (GAM) could be used to promote an EU-wide approach to migration. The GAM was proposed in 2005 to minimize tensions in EU migration policy by promoting cooperation with countries on legal migration, combating illegal migration, and addressing the development dimension of migration. Mobility Partnerships are one of the operational instruments of the GAM that could be further developed in the context of Deauville. These are nonbinding multilateral declarations signed by the EU, a willing member state, and a partner country that aim to find innovative ways to improve the management of legal movement of people. As such, they can advance the political and technical dialogue on migration matters. In early 2012, discussions on potential Mobility Partnerships were launched with Tunisia and Morocco.

G8 countries and other Deauville partners could offer Partnership countries more generous bilateral migration agreements, especially for less-skilled workers, under the principle of shared responsibility. The key idea behind current bilateral agreements is that responsibility for migration management is shared by the sending and receiving countries. When sending countries are involved in preventing irregular migration and enforcing return, it becomes more politically acceptable for receiving countries to open access to their labor markets, especially for low-skilled temporary migration, where the risk of overstay is important. The principle of shared responsibility can be seen as a risk prevention and mitigation mechanism that is absent from multilateral or regional trade agreements, which are biased toward labor market access for skilled workers. Such bilateral agreements offer a mechanism for the negotiating parties to spell out, articulate, and balance their key interests and policy objectives with respect to migration (Holzmann and Pouget 2010). They are also effective instruments for organizing recruitment in a safe and orderly manner. Such a comprehensive migration strategy is currently being formulated in Tunisia.

The main downside of bilateral agreements is that the border management approach takes precedence over a more strategic and demand-driven labor market approach. Second-generation bilateral agreements in Europe do not really increase the liberalization of cross-border labor mobility because their first and foremost objective is to control immigration, notably through quotas and readmission agreements (box 3.7). Some agreements only ease labor market access within already existing national admission schemes in receiving countries, for example in France and Italy. Most of the migration flows still happen outside of those bilateral schemes under unilateral admission schemes or irregular migration.

BOX 3.7

The Resurgence of Old Migration Tools in the Euro-Med Context

The first generation of guest worker programs in the 1950s through the 1980s in France and Germany generally failed to manage the risk of overstay in low-skilled temporary migration, turning it into permanent migration then followed by family reunification (Castles 2006). In a context of rising irregular migration flows since the 1980s and increasingly restrictive admission policies among EU countries, a new generation of bilateral agreements has emerged to manage temporary migration between Europe and North Africa. Over the past decade, such agreements have become more comprehensive in addressing the different dimensions of migration management: irregular migration, labor market access, and development impacts. It is not surprising that such agreements are mainly used by the European countries most exposed to irregular migration flows, namely Spain, France, and Italy. They all embody a partnership approach in which migration management responsibilities are shared between receiving and sending countries.

France has signed 14 such agreements with countries in Sub-Saharan Africa and Eastern Europe, and most recently with Tunisia (2008). Spain has concluded bilateral labor agreements with countries in West Africa and Latin America, as well as with Morocco. Italy currently uses a system of quotas to regulate legal immigration from Tunisia and Egypt. There is no agreement with Tunisia, and the annual quota is used to regularize the situation of Tunisians already working in Italy irregularly and to ensure the cooperation of Tunisian authorities on border control. The situation is different with Egypt: Italy has cooperated since 2005, in the framework of the EU-Egypt Association Agreement, in an online system to match up Egyptian workers with Italian employers.

Quid pro quo. Such regulatory agreements typically allow controlled labor market access for temporary migrant workers conditional

(continued on next page)

BOX 3.7   *Continued*

---

on commitments by the sending countries to prevent and control irregular migration while enforcing return and readmissions.

Legal arrangements. Bilateral agreements can take the form of either formal treaties or nonbinding memoranda of understanding. But what ultimately determines the effectiveness of a bilateral agreement is not its legal nature but how it is implemented and enforced in practice.

Scope. The new generation of bilateral agreements provide for shared responsibility between source and destination countries in a single framework embracing readmissions, visa policy, border management and security, technical assistance, diaspora policy, return provisions, and development aid. A key innovation of the second-generation agree-

ments as compared to the old guest worker programs is to bring together different quotas for different categories of workers across sectors, skill levels, and qualifications into a single framework to better control labor migration as a whole (Panizzon 2010).

Size. The bilateral agreements signed by European countries remain quite limited in terms of admission quotas. For instance, among the bilateral agreements signed by France, the one with Tunisia provides the largest quota, amounting to 9,000 entries annually in different categories: 2,500 for seasonal workers, 1,500 for young professionals, 3,500 for skilled workers in shortage occupations, and 1,500 for talented workers. In comparison, Italy's annual quotas in 2009 were 4,000 for Tunisian workers and 8,000 for Egyptian workers.

EU member states could further improve their migration programs for Partnership countries by drawing on best international practices in program design, implementation, and institutional capacity. The circular migration schemes in Canada and New Zealand, for example, present elements of best practice in program design (box 3.8). These include the buy-in of sending-country governments and employers in implementation of the scheme, from recruitment to return, in an "incentive-compatible manner." Elements include training, information, screening, and skills matching; adequate salary conditions and social protection provisions for migrants; high rates of return and repeat employment (i.e., circularity); and commercial viability for farmers in Canada and migrant workers in terms of saving opportunities. The importance of incentives to ensure return upon completion of the job contract is best exemplified by the EU-sponsored circular migration program between Spain and Morocco for strawberry picking in the province of Huelva. The initial rate of return was less than 50 percent, which spurred a change in the

BOX 3.8

Elements of Best Practice in Circular Migration Schemes in Canada and New Zealand

Canada's Seasonal Agricultural Workers Program (SAWP) builds on bilateral agreements to bring about 20,000 workers from Mexico, Central America, and the Caribbean annually to do seasonal work on Canadian farms for up to eight months, with compulsory return at the end of the work period. The program offers repeat employment opportunities over the years if both migrant and employer comply with the program's rules. Employers provide free housing and cover part of the travel costs. Seasonal workers are offered the same wage and work conditions as Canadian workers doing the same job and enjoy similar social benefits, including health insurance. Sending-country governments are in charge of screening and recruiting the workers and monitor their living and working conditions in Canada through consular services. On the receiving side, farm employers apply to local centers run by Human Resources and Skills Development Canada (HRSDC) for certification to employ foreign workers, subject to a labor market test. The grower association, Foreign Agricultural Resource Management Services (FARMS), is in charge of arranging recruitment with sending countries once approval from HRSDC has been received. The rates of return and repeat employment are very high, signaling that both employers and workers are complying with the scheme's rules. Canadian employers benefit from a secure labor supply, allowing them to expand

their activities, and the return of experienced workers reduces screening and training costs. Evidence shows that Mexican migrants are able to accumulate significant savings and then invest in agricultural land and small businesses in Mexico.

In addition to the SAWP, the Province of Québec's association of agricultural seasonal labor recruiters, the Foundation of Enterprises for the Recruitment of Foreign Labor (FERME), has signed an agreement with the government of Guatemala to recruit seasonal workers. The International Organization for Migration in Guatemala has supported the implementation of this project. The Guatemalan Ministry of Labor is in charge of screening and recruiting workers, and the Guatemalan consulate in Montreal provides support and supervision to the seasonal migrants during their stay in Québec. This ensures low intermediation costs for the migrants (about $270 for a medical exam, passport, and visa, plus an exit tax). On the receiving side, HRSDC delivers certifications to farm employers willing to hire seasonal migrants. Most of the migrants are married men with families left behind, and the return rate is close to 100 percent. Even though the numbers remain small, admissions have grown steadily from 215 in 2003 (the first season) to about 2,000 per season currently.

New Zealand's Recognised Seasonal Employer Work Policy was introduced in 2006

(continued on next page)

BOX 3.8   *Continued*

by the Department of Labour, the Ministry of Social Development, and New Zealand Agency for International Development (NZAID) in collaboration with ministries of labor and community leaders in five Pacific Island countries: Kiribati, Samoa, Tonga, Tuvalu, and Vanuatu. It aims to create a mutually beneficial circular migration scheme where employers in the New Zealand horticulture and viticulture industries can access a secure labor supply in order to circumvent local labor shortages and remain competitive in world markets, while selected Pacific Island workers can secure access to the New Zealand labor market and contribute to economic development in their home countries through remittances and employment experience abroad. The government of New Zealand has collaborated with the World Bank to monitor and evaluate the outcomes of this policy scheme from its inception. This monitoring and evaluation (M&E) component has made it possible to revise and

significantly improve the design and implementation of certain aspects of the scheme, including enhanced pre-departure training sessions and new pooled savings and remittance transfer mechanisms. Evaluation findings indicate positive development impacts, with significant improvements in per capita income and economic welfare, increased remittance flows, access to financial services, house improvements, and an increase in children's school attendance. The scheme already involves one third as many workers as the Canadian SAWP, and the M&E component has provided legitimacy, leading to plans to scale up the scheme and replicate it in Australia. Other elements of best practice in this scheme include incentive-compatible design, multi-stakeholder consultations and involvement in pilot phases, shared responsibility of sending and receiving countries in implementation, development of trust-building mechanisms, and institutional capacity building in sending countries.

rules: only mothers with children in Morocco became eligible, and those departing at the end of the season were guaranteed the right to return to Spain for the next harvest season. Of the 5,000 women selected for the 2007 season, 85 percent returned voluntarily to Morocco at the end of the season. However, such a mechanism to enforce return raises strong concerns about the protection of migrants' rights. In the current functioning of the French-Tunisian agreement, the costs of hiring Tunisians for seasonal work seem too high for French employers, who need to go through a lengthy labor market test that slows the recruitment process to the extent that they cannot use foreign workers to fill their labor needs in time (box 3.9). As a result of such burdensome procedures, only 1,000 seasonal migrants out of a quota of 2,500 were hired in 2010. In the Egyptian-Italian agreement, the major impediments to effective labor matching seem to be the low level of soft skills and qualifications available in Egypt

BOX 3.9

Bottlenecks and Areas of Progress in Implementation of the French-Tunisian Agreement

The French-Tunisian agreement is considered the main model for labor migration management with EU countries, even though its implementation needs to be improved in several areas to fully exploit its potential. This agreement offers the possibility for 9,000 Tunisian workers to enter the French labor market every year. There are subquotas in different categories under existing French admission schemes: (a) a scheme for young professionals with postsecondary education offers a 3- to 12-month contract, extendable to 24 months, with compulsory return at the end of the contract; (b) a talented workers scheme ("Carte Compétences & Talents") offers a three-year renewable contract with family reunification and streamlined procedures; (c) a shortage list scheme offers employment-based admission without a labor market test for 77 occupations experiencing labor shortages; and (d) a seasonal employment scheme offers a three-year permit with the possibility of working for three to six months per year in seasonal activities, subject to a labor market test. The French Office for Immigration and Integration (OFII) in Tunis is in charge of the administrative and medical procedures for admission and integration.

Actual flows of workers remain far below the levels offered by the agreement. In 2010 only 2,500 Tunisian workers signed a job contract in France. They included 350 entries in the young professionals scheme (subquota 1,500); 70 entries in the talented work-

ers scheme (subquota 1,500); 1,000 entries in the shortage list scheme (subquota 3,500); and 1,000 entries in the seasonal workers scheme (subquota 2,500). The core difficulty for Tunisians is that emigration candidates need to secure a job offer before applying for a work permit in France. Tunisian authorities have not been able to ensure matches between their job seekers at home and job openings abroad. The international division of the Tunisian public jobs agency, Agence Nationale pour l'Emploi et le Travail Indépendant (ANETI), has no representation in France and therefore has limited capacity to reach out to French employers. Coordination on skills matching between technical partners on both sides is lacking. The regular transmission of job offers by the French public employment agency (Pôle Emploi) to ANETI seldom leads to the emigration of Tunisian workers, as few Tunisians are able to meet specific skill profiles, which may include prior professional experience in France. As a result of limited public intermediation capacities, most of the selected emigrants mobilize Tunisian social networks in France to secure a job offer.

Beyond job-matching difficulties, the Tunisian Bureau of Emigration reports significant administrative delays; it can take up to six months for the French authorities to process an application. The OFII in Tunis collects the applications of Tunisian candidates from ANETI or the Bureau of Emigration (in charge of young professionals) and sends

(continued on next page)

BOX 3.9 *Continued*

them to France for verification and approval. Of 1,000 applications of young professionals sent to OFII in 2010, only 350 were accepted. The main reasons for rejection were the inability of the employer to host a foreign worker, often because the firm was too small, had not settled its fiscal situation, or was unable to provide adequate supervision. Some cases of fake certifications were reported. A specific constraint for seasonal workers is the labor market test, a cumbersome administrative procedure that slows the recruitment process to the extent that employers are not able to use foreign workers to fill their labor needs in time. Hence, despite latent demand among French farmers for seasonal workers, the subquota remains unfilled.

In view of the bottlenecks described above, improvements are needed in several key areas: (a) building capacities on the Tunisian side for better job prospection and placement services, especially in partnership with the private sector; (b) improving the cooperation between ANETI and Pôle Emploi at the technical level for better skill-matching mechanisms; (c) improving the screening of applicants on the Tunisian side; and (d) lowering transaction costs linked to complex recruitment procedures and high recruitment costs, especially for seasonal workers and skilled workers in shortage in France.

and insufficient screening of emigration candidates by the validation unit of the Ministry of Manpower and Emigration.

As in "aid for trade," financial and technical assistance to establish or strengthen behind-the-border systems to manage labor outflows is essential to improve the implementation of bilateral agreements by sending countries. This includes adequate legal frameworks for international recruitment, funding to support migrants throughout the migration cycle, relevant training programs, remittance transfer infrastructure, interagency or interministerial coordination mechanisms and oversight, marketing strategy and communication tools to promote domestic workers abroad, data management, and M&E. Such capacities are clearly insufficient in Partnership countries and deserve to be reinforced, as already initiated through EU-sponsored programs with public intermediation agencies in Egypt, Tunisia, and Morocco. On their side, receiving countries should be able to identify the domestic labor market needs that can be addressed effectively through temporary migration schemes, and they should strive for transparent and reliable admission procedures to avoid undermining the functioning of bilateral schemes. Finally, technical coordination mechanisms between the public agencies of sending and receiving countries are essential to ensure a smooth implementation of bilateral agreements.

Labor mobility: Key selected recommendations

Short-term:

- Improve the design and implementation of existing bilateral labor mobility agreements between Partnership countries and Deauville partners by (a) strengthening the capacities of public agencies for job prospecting and placement abroad; (b) by upgrading training and screening of emigration candidates; (c) by improving technical coordination between sending and receiving countries on skill-matching procedures and information sharing; and (d) by lowering the transaction costs on firms and workers related to slow and complex administrative procedures.

- Partnership countries, if they have not yet done so, should formulate a comprehensive labor emigration strategy with clear policy objectives that go beyond diaspora engagement and remittances.

Medium-term:

- Launch labor Mobility Partnerships or similar mobility schemes between Partnership countries and Deauville partners, including visa facilitation for some categories of workers, readmission, concerted border management, and easier access to the job market of the Deauville partners, especially for less-skilled workers. The EU should include specific sectoral commitments on labor mobility, especially for less-skilled workers, as part of the Mode 4 liberalization of services in the future DCFTAs and MENA TIP.

- Partnership countries should consider using embassies and consulates in G8 countries to support labor emigration strategies and improved job prospecting.

Long-term:

- Align educational priorities in source countries to better meet the requirements of employers in destination countries and upgrade soft skills and qualifications of emigration candidates in critical sectors.

- Include mutual recognition of skills qualifications and portability of benefits in future agreements. This may also require streamlining the mandates of the European Commission on migration and establishing a monitoring mechanism for cooperation between the EU, its agencies, member states, and third countries.

Regulatory Convergence

Key issues

Competition policy and effective public procurement systems are key areas of regulation that can maximize the gains from trade and FDI. Until now, the MENA region has suffered from discretionary implementation of policies and unequal treatment of traders and investors, often biased toward the politically connected. This weak competitive environment is reflected in high markups for core industries such as processed food, textiles, and clothing. Where competition is weak, incumbent firms capture large rents to the detriment of consumers. In addition, evidence from Partnership countries shows that the process of firm entry and exit, in which new competitors drive up productivity, takes place with less intensity than in competing economies.

Effective use of competition policy can address such issues to the benefit of consumers and aggregate productivity growth. While Partnership countries have enacted or strengthened their competition laws, enforcement has remained weak. This reflects institutional structures such as ministerial discretion to pursue or drop cases. Inclusion of competition issues in trade negotiations with the EU, the United States, and other partners could strengthen implementation. Competition provisions could also be negotiated in the context of the Agadir Agreement and, in the long run, extended to other members of PAFTA.

In Morocco, public procurement was equivalent to around 16 percent of GDP in 2006, representing more than 12,000 contracts awarded. As with competition policy, Partnership countries would benefit from pursuing efficient, transparent, and nondiscriminatory government procurement in the context of their regulatory convergence with the EU and other advanced economies. Successful reform experiences have reduced costs by more than 40 percent for categories of goods in other countries. In addition, Partnership countries can examine the experience of Central and Eastern European countries and Turkey in establishing coordination mechanisms for economic integration. Upgraded mechanisms of interministerial coordination, together with support from specialized civil service units, can overcome administrative bottlenecks and foster effective action across departmental boundaries.

In order to reap the full benefits of their greater trade and FDI integration, Partnership countries should consider accelerating the convergence of their regulatory frameworks with best international practices. Beyond the free movement of goods, services, capital, and persons discussed in previous sections, this would involve the gradual alignment of a number of behind-the-border regulatory issues dealing with competition, government procurement, and other aspects of the EU Community acquis. The acquis, which is at the center of the enlargement of the EU to include countries in Central and Eastern Europe, comprises the accumulated legislation and case law that new member states are required to transpose into national law.[12] The remainder of this section discusses three topics of particular relevance to a trade and FDI agenda: competition policy, government procurement, and institutional mechanisms for integration.

Competition Policy

Competition policy needs to become an essential complement to the trade agenda. It goes hand in hand with consumer protection policy. Competition or interfirm rivalry is essential to ensure that consumers enjoy freedom of choice, low prices, and good value for money; it also promotes innovation and higher standards. Competition policy improves the allocation of resources toward their most efficient uses through many different channels. Increased competition is expected to provide managers with incentives to improve their enterprise's performance (Djankov and Murrell 2002), to reap the most benefits from trade reforms, to enhance the attractiveness of an economy in terms of FDI (Maskus and Lahouel 2000), and to prepare and enable domestic firms to compete successfully in international markets (Porter 1990). Empirical evidence from several studies tends to confirm that higher competition has a positive impact on welfare. Using panel data on manufacturing firms in Indonesia from 1982 to 1995, Bartel and Harrison (2005) found that public sector firms that have been protected from import competition do not have a high level of productivity. Kim (2000) examines the impact of trade liberalization on productivity, market competition, and scale efficiency using panel data for 36 Korean manufacturing industries. Trade liberalization is found to improve productivity, increase competition, and promote scale efficiency. Pavcnik (2002) conducted a study on the relationship between competition, plant exit, and productivity in Chile and found that trade liberalization increases within-plant productivity in the manufacturing industries by 3–10 percent. Kahyarara (2004) showed that various aspects of competition policy played an important role in improving Tanzania's economic performance. Kahyarara found a robust positive impact of government measures, aiming to stimulate competition and protect consumers against anticompetitive practices, on investment, productivity, and export performance.

Partnership economies have been suffering from a relatively weak competitive environment. Focusing on Morocco, Haddad, de Melo, and Horton (1996) found that concentration rates in manufacturing are relatively high and that concentration has a strong positive effect on profit margins, while import penetration is negatively correlated with the margins. They also identified a positive correlation between the productivity level and export orientation of a firm. Sekkat (2008), examining the state of competition and efficiency in Egypt, Jordan, Morocco, and Tunisia, found that these economies face important competition and policy issues. First, their manufacturing sectors are highly and increasingly specialized in food products, wearing apparel, and textiles (though less so for Jordan). Second, in Egypt and Tunisia, state-owned enterprises represent an important share of manufacturing output. This share has decreased over time but remains sizeable in Egypt and in some Tunisian industries. Third, the three industries (except for the apparel industry in Jordan) exhibit much higher markups than the rest of the manufacturing sector, suggesting weak intensity of competition in the respective markets, as well as low productivity growth—even negative in some cases. Considering the importance of markup and of the state-owned enterprises in an industry as indicative of weak competition and labor productivity, and total factor productivity growth as indicative of economic performance, Sekkat (2009) found that productivity growth is significantly and negatively affected by lack of competition.

Finally, Sekkat (2010) showed that the process of firms' entry and exit has helped improve industrial productivity in recent years in Jordan, Morocco, and Tunisia. This improvement took place through either the exit of less-productive firms or the entry of more-productive firms or both, but not through the productivity of survivors. Exit seems to cleanse industries of their less-productive plants, while entry allows replacement of these plants with more productive ones. Although the process of entry and exit has improved productivity in a similar way as in other emerging economies, inefficiency persists. The reason is in the intensity of the process (table 3.7). Comparing the intensity of entry and exit across the three countries and with other emerging economies shows that the intensity is much lower than in the latter. Hence, it seems that while the process has played a similar role as in other emerging economies, its limited impact on industries' productivity is due to its weak intensity. Further investigations show that entry is higher in those industries offering some opportunities (sales or productivity improvement) and lower in industries with high barriers to entry, both natural (capital intensity and wage level) and strategic (concentration of incumbents). Moreover, an analysis of the business environment and practices identified technological knowledge and economies of scale as the most important obstacles to doing business in the four countries. Access to funds and to adequate human resources poses a problem mainly in Jordan and Tunisia, while government intervention is seen as an important issue in Egypt and Morocco.

This weak competitive environment in Partnership countries has survived the enactment of competition and consumer protection laws because of lax implementation and enforcement practices. In 1991 Tunisia enacted a law on competition and prices to ensure free price setting and free competition and to control concentration and mergers. Morocco ad-

TABLE 3.7

Competition and Efficiency in the Food and Textile Industries in Deauville Partnership Countries, 2007 or Latest Available Data

Country	Industry		
	Food	Textiles	Wearing apparel
	Shares in manufacturing employment (%)		
Egypt, Arab Rep.	18	23	6
Jordan	15	3	8
Morocco	18	8	35
Tunisia[a]	18	35	
	Four firms concentration ratio (%)		
Egypt, Arab Rep.[a]	54	76	
Jordan	50	78	27
Morocco	20	13	10
Tunisia[a]	31	30	
	Markup (%)		
Egypt, Arab Rep.	173	120	113
Jordan	176	128	100
Morocco	112	105	109
Tunisia[a]	119	117	
	Total factor productivity growth (%)		
Egypt, Arab Rep.	−0.05	0.01	0.03
Jordan	−0.62	0.64	0
Morocco	−2.45	2.11	−1.25
Tunisia[a]	0.2	0.5	

Source: Sekkat 2008.

a. Textiles and apparel aggregated.

opted a competition law in 2001 to promote freedom of prices and free competition, economic efficiency and consumers' welfare, and transparency and loyalty of commercial relationships. In 2002 the Jordanian competition law entered into force with the aim of establishing and securing the principle of market forces and economic freedoms, especially freedom of prices. Egypt enacted its own competition law in 2003 to protect competition and prevent anticompetitive practices. Across these four countries, the provisions of the laws are fairly similar: they establish freedom of prices as a general rule, prohibit arrangements and acts that disrupt competition, prohibit abuse of dominant positions, regulate concentration, and provide for exemptions in specific cases. However, the laws differ on the degree of independence of the national competition authority and on provisions for enforcement. The independence of the competition authority is stipulated in the Tunisian law but not in the Egyptian and Moroccan laws. In Jordan, although the competition law only recently entered into force, the Competition Directorate has already dealt with a number of cases brought to it by industry. In Egypt and Morocco, by contrast, very few cases of competition issues have been dealt with by the authority thus far.

A well-designed regional competition agreement could act as a policy tool to create the national institutional and behavioral environment necessary to benefit from regional competition provisions while taking account of local realities. International trade may also give rise to uncompetitive practices and arrangements in the form of import distribution monopolies and cartels, dominant firms from abroad, export cartels overseas, and regional market sharing. These market failures can be difficult to deal with on a unilateral basis, depending on where the unlawful conduct takes place and where the evidence is located. Where an abuse of dominant position extends beyond one national market, as in the case of the EU, there is a clear administrative case for regional cooperation. Negotiating competition provisions in a future DCFTA with the EU could therefore have great development benefits, especially for Southern partners. It would help strengthen implementation, especially if the more developed party offers appropriate technical and capacity-building assistance. Given that Partnership countries have difficulty implementing their own competition rules, a DCFTA or similar agreement with another advanced economy would help establish a culture that values competition at the national or subregional level in the region.

Partnership countries could consider negotiating regional competition provisions in the context of the Agadir Agreement and, in the long run, expand the agreement to the other members of PAFTA. This would create an incentive to implement national regimes with a view to creating policy lock-in, increasing FDI, gaining technical assistance, and learning by doing. These can potentially generate beneficial regional public goods. Partnership countries working together could induce beneficial cross-border spillover effects, such as in the provision of information or cooperation in enforcing competition law in the region. Moreover, scale economies can be realized by regional agencies. To be sure, the economic and human resources necessary to implement even a minimal decentralized competition regime would be significant. Deauville partners could usefully step in and assist this institutional improvement. In any case, the actual economic and welfare costs associated with cross-border anticompetitive practices are likely to be higher than any implementation costs. Short-term political costs should be weighed against the understanding that the long-term and sustainable benefits of a strongly enforced regional competition regime will almost always outweigh its costs.

Partnership countries could also opt for more decentralized agreements that only require the existence of a local competition law and authority, as in the case of NAFTA. This option would not be as economically demanding as a regime that establishes a fully centralized law with a supporting regional authority, as in the EU or COMESA. Competition provisions included in customs union agreements are, in general, more specific and demand higher commitments. The economic burdens of implementation can be offset if the parties are able to exchange information effectively and avoid duplications and conflicting decisions. If cooperation leads to a successful investigation, then the costs are justified by greater access to data and by avoidance of conflicting enforcement activities. For instance, the Caribbean competition regime indicates potential economies of scale provided by regional cooperation because its provisions allow for resource pooling among neighboring countries when national capacity is insufficient to implement and enforce the regional framework.

In the area of competition policy, given the large potential benefits and relatively low costs in terms of loss of sovereignty, Partnership countries may want to adopt the norms of their more advanced trading partners. In the "hegemonic" convergence model, a large economic partner is essentially able to impose its own model, not necessarily through coercion but through the force of its market size. This appears to be happening already with Morocco and Tunisia, which are achieving convergence with the EU in many areas through the deepening of existing FTAs, the European Neighbourhood Policy, the Mediterranean Union, and so on. An alternative solution would be "competition between rules," that is, acceptance by governments of differing policies as equivalent. In the United States, specific provisions of competition policy differ across states. The European provisions on competition apply only if a given practice affects the trade between member states. A careful analysis is therefore needed to highlight the costs and benefits of these alternative "models" and identify the types of institutions and mechanisms that could better help Partnership countries implement strong competition rules.

Setting up competition observatories could increase the public support for trade and FDI openness under strengthened competition rules. Regular monitoring of implementation enables policy makers to assess the effects of regulatory changes and take the necessary corrective actions in case of difficulties. Without information on the extent of implementation, it is difficult for governments either to respond to concerns on the part of consumers, workers, and businesses regarding the impacts of trade and FDI agreements or to make a compelling case that economic integration leads to superior growth and employment outcomes. As trade and FDI reforms are implemented and specific trade and FDI barriers are removed, other constraints to trade and investment become more important. Policy makers need up-to-date information on these constraints in order to decide whether and how they might best be removed. The Aga-

dir Agreement could be a natural venue for a coordination of this institutional strengthening.

Government Procurement

Government procurement is another determinant of a competitive economic environment where all economic actors—domestic and foreign—
compete on a level playing field. Public procurement policy in all countries responds to a mix of targets, including value for money (typically
taken to mean minimizing procurement costs) but also macroeconomic
management, national security, redistribution to the poor, industrial and
regional development, promotion of small and medium enterprises, and
support for state-owned enterprises and their employees. In practice,
pursuit of any except the first target means designing procurement systems that sacrifice the value-for-money goal, in whole or in part, for some
other objective. Despite, or perhaps because of, the variety of government
objectives for public procurement policy, most jurisdictions, international
accords, and pronouncements of international organizations on public
procurement tend to refer to a core set of four principles for the implementation of national policy in this area: efficiency (value for money);
equality of opportunity to compete for state contracts (nondiscrimination); transparency (control of corruption, accountability); and encour-
agement of investments and partnerships (public-private partnerships).

The principles of openness, transparency, and nondiscrimination in
government procurement may be pursued and codified in national constitutions but also in bilateral or plurilateral trade agreements and multilateral agreements. One such binding but voluntary agreement is the
WTO's Government Procurement Agreement (GPA). However, no
Arab country is a member of the GPA. Bahrain, Oman, and Saudi Arabia
are observers. However, Partnership countries and other Arab countries
have included government procurement provisions in their PTAs (table
3.8). For instance, the U.S.-Jordan PTA contains a single commitment
on government procurement to the effect that the parties support Jordan's accession to the WTO GPA. Yet surveys of government procurement provisions in PTAs worldwide indicate that the most comprehensive regimes—for example, the EU-Chile PTA, NAFTA, and the
Dominican Republic-Central America FTA—do contain detailed provisions on government procurement and related issues, such as dispute
settlement. So far, PTAs entered into by the EU have not included clauses
committing a party to accede to the GPA. Instead, their negotiated texts
tend to set reciprocal and gradual liberalization of procurement markets
as a goal without specifying the scope or coverage of the agreement. This
is the case with the EU-Morocco Association Agreement, which states

TABLE 3.8

PTAs with MENA Countries Containing Government Procurement Provisions

MENA country	Partner
Egypt, Arab Rep.	EFTA
Jordan	EFTA
Lebanon	EFTA
Morocco	EFTA
Tunisia	EFTA
Algeria	European Union
Egypt, Arab Rep.	European Union
Jordan	European Union
Morocco	European Union
Jordan	United States
Egypt, Arab Rep.	Turkey
Morocco	Turkey
Syrian Arab Republic	Turkey
Tunisia	Turkey
Bahrain	United States
Morocco	United States
Oman	United States

Source: Preferential Trade Agreements policies for development, WTO data.

Note: Includes PTAs notified to the WTO as of December 2009. EFTA = European Free Trade Association.

that the council set up by the agreement must implement the mutual opening of procurement markets.

For many developing countries, the inefficiency and opportunity cost of suboptimal levels of competition in national procurement regimes can be substantial. For an average developing country that spends about 15 percent of its national income on goods and services, a 10 percent saving on procurement contracts is equivalent to 1.5 percent of GDP—an amount that may exceed the total amount of aid received by many developing countries (Dawar and Evenett 2011). Available data in Partnership countries show that procurement contracts represent a similar share of GDP. In Morocco, for instance, public procurement was equivalent to about 16 percent of GDP in 2005 (Cherkaoui 2011). In terms of transactions, this represented more than 12,000 government contracts awarded, about 90 percent of them through open tendering. Both Moroccan and foreign firms can compete for public procurement contracts. As to the benefits from more transparent and competitive procurement processes, it has been estimated, for instance, that Colombia achieved a saving of 47 percent in the procurement of certain military goods by improving transparency and procurement procedures (Anderson and Kovacic 2009). The saving in the cost of purchasing medicines in Guatemala, due to similar improvement, was 43 percent. Chen and Whalley (2011) estimate that membership in the WTO GPA has a positive impact on trade in both goods and services between parties as well as on outward foreign affiliate service sales.

In recent years, Partnership countries have undertaken reforms of their national procurement systems to promote transparency. Such reforms emphasize integrity in related administrative processes, that is, preventing corruption on the part of public officials, as well as effective competition among alternative suppliers, including by preventing collusion among suppliers. For instance, Morocco launched a series of public procurement reforms in 2007. The reforms began with modification of the legislative framework and issuance of a new decree that set conditions and terms for the award of government contracts as well as rules on their management and control. The decree covers not only the tendering phase but also the prior needs assessment and postaward contract performance monitoring stages of the procurement cycle. It applies to local government as well as to central agencies. The decree has increased transparency in the procurement process by requiring officials to publish tender notices, inform firms of tender results, and maintain records of awarded contracts. This decree brought Morocco's procurement system up to the standard of the WTO GPA and the European Union Public Procurement Directives. The establishment of the Public Procurement Review Board in 2008 completed the country's strategy for safeguarding integrity in public procurement. The board is responsible for reviewing complaints and advising on actions to be taken. The government is also considering reinforcing the review mechanisms for procurement and pushing forward its e-procurement project by completing it with a database on suppliers.

Yet many governments still view public procurements as trade and industrial policy instruments to support domestic firms by creating demand that enables businesses to improve performance. It is sometimes argued that public procurement can support the cost of risky activities such as research and development (R&D). Government-supported R&D often leads to positive spillover effects on private R&D expenditures, thus improving the welfare of society as a whole (Becker and Pain 2003; Cozzi and Impullitti 2006). It is well documented, for instance, that the superiority of the U.S. information technology industry owes much to military procurements. Government procurement can also be used to affect the pattern and intensity of a country's specialization (Trionfetti 2000). In numerous cases where markets alone have failed to select an optimal standard, governments have fostered adoption of such standards through government procurement (Cabral et al. 2006). Government procurement can also be used as an instrument of trade policy in conditioning access to the domestic market (Evenett and Hoekman 2005).

Public procurement is also at the core of many political economy issues best resolved through high-quality institutions and governance. A procurement decision is not always based on rational arguments; rather, it often reflects a political preference or priority. The literature provides ample evidence that politicians and regulators, even when not involved in abuse of power or corruption, are subject to an incentive system that may not lead to socially desirable outcomes. From the perspective of political economy and governance, government procurement raises a number of issues. First, like other public spending, government procurement can be used for electoral purposes even at the expense of economic efficiency. The vast literature dealing with political cycles shows that governments may choose policy instruments, and thereby affect economic outcomes, based on political considerations, such as the desire to win elections or promote ideologies. Second, another branch of the political economy literature points to the role of lobbying and the risk of capture of public authorities by the private sector (Laffont 1997). Third, various researchers (e.g., Compte, Lambert-Mogiliansky, and Verdier 2005; Laffont and Tirole 1991) have shown that favoritism and corruption may emerge as an equilibrium outcome in procurement auctions: since many objects of bidding are very complex and have major quality differences, delegation is inevitable. That is why the concepts of transparency and accountability in public administration are important in the field of public procurement.

As in the case of competition policy, Partnership countries would benefit from pursuing efficient, transparent, and nondiscriminatory government procurement in the context of their regulatory convergence with the EU and other advanced economies. In the first instance, to promote and lock in the principles of openness, transparency, and nondiscrimination, Partnership countries could usefully join the WTO GPA. In parallel, Partnership countries could explore the benefits of negotiating government procurement provisions with their main advanced trading partners, starting with the EU and the United States in the context of the DCFTAs and MENA TIP, respectively. The motives for negotiating and agreeing on public procurement provisions with the EU would not be limited to market access. Partnership countries might strategically accept binding rules on their national procurement regime as the most effective way of reforming national practices. Partnership countries could also initiate a similar government-procurement best practice in the context of the Agadir Agreement and later on within PAFTA.

Deauville partners should step up and provide the necessary technical assistance and capacity to help Partnership countries set up effective government procurement regimes. This would require establishing specialized institutional frameworks and expertise. For example, transparency provisions that require signatories to publish all relevant procurement regulations in a foreign language will require translators with legal expertise, and retaining the specialized legal talent to adjudicate complaints on procurement matters and present appeals before tribunals is a distinct resource challenge. Technical assistance requirements related to government procurement in PTAs may be quite substantial. For example, NAFTA requires the parties to provide, on a cost-recovery basis, information concerning training and orientation programs relevant to their government procurement systems and to grant nondiscriminatory access to any programs they conduct. Such activities include training of government personnel directly involved in government procurement procedures; training of suppliers interested in pursuing government procurement opportunities; an explanation and description of specific elements of the party's government procurement system, such as its bid challenge mechanism; and information about government procurement market opportunities.

Institutional Mechanisms for Regulatory Convergence

Taking advantage of DCFTA negotiations with the EU and similar initiatives from other G8 and Deauville partners entails behind-the-border reforms that can be hard to implement. Yet the process is far from unprecedented. MENA countries could usefully examine the experience of Central and Eastern European (CEE) countries and Turkey in creating high-level administrative bodies, connected to upgraded systems of ministerial responsibility and coordination, to drive forward reforms. Poland, Slovenia, and Lithuania are among countries with successful historical experiences. In the contemporary period, Serbia presents a model that draws on the lessons of earlier reformers. Turkey's Secretariat General for EU Affairs (later Ministry for EU Affairs) has overseen technically demanding reforms necessary to achieve substantial reductions in trade costs by means of the EU-Turkey Customs Union. Deauville Partnership countries could establish similar mechanisms as a route to effective implementation of deep integration commitments.

The CEE countries adopted different responses to the challenge of domestic reform that came with EU accession, but all of them took two steps: (a) elevating EU coordination to a high position in the political hierarchy, and (b) establishing administrative units within the civil service to support this process. The location of EU coordination units varied: several countries established a Ministry of EU Integration, while others established civil service units in the Cabinet Office, Prime Minister's Office, or Foreign Ministry. These efforts relied on upgrading ministerial-level coordination and civil service capacity in parallel. Since many accession reforms required regulatory changes that cross departmental borders, the process involved considerable consultation at the cabinet level. Individual ministries can stall such processes, blocking progress elsewhere in the administration. Many CEE countries created new interministerial committees to monitor progress and agree on action plans. The Czech

Republic is one example: a deputy prime minister for legislation chaired the committee and led the process.

To support the role of ministerial "point person," many CEE countries set up dedicated units in the civil service. These carried out a range of functions, including monitoring progress on rule adoption, focusing attention and flagging problems, giving opinions on draft acts regarding their compliance with EU law, preparing accession negotiations, and enhancing communication between the government and the EU. The units often had high status within the administration. They had upgraded authority in a number of areas, allowing them to require information and status updates from line ministries and to propose implementation plans for EU directives requiring action by multiple line agencies. In a number of cases, these bodies were highly effective, ensuring levels of political attention and administrative coordination that were higher than in older member states. Following completion of the EU's enlargement from 15 to 25 members in 2005, the European Commission's Internal Market Scoreboard concluded that new member states "perform better in transposing Internal Market directives on time than the EU-15 Member States, despite having had to absorb the whole acquis in a short time frame" (European Commission 2005). Research finds that countries with more effective coordination mechanisms tend to be systematically better at applying EU rules (Dimitrova and Toshkov 2009).

Two examples illustrate the role such administrative units played in the CEE region. In the late 1990s Poland established the European Integration Committee (KIE), an interministerial committee chaired by the deputy prime minister. During the preaccession period it oversaw a large volume of administrative and legal reforms, and it retains an important role in supervising the implementation of EU rules and directives. Poland also created an Office of the European Integration Committee (UKIE), whose staffing peaked at above 200. It developed a rigorous approach to collecting information from line ministries and addressing bottlenecks to implementation.

In 2004, Serbia created an upgraded system for regulatory convergence, having reviewed best practices among other EU accession countries. The deputy prime minister was given coordination responsibility for EU integration and chaired an interministerial committee that included the ministers of finance, foreign affairs, agriculture, interior, justice and others. Working groups on each of the 35 chapters (negotiating areas covering the EU acquis) report to the committee, which is supported by a civil service unit, the Office for European Integration (SEIO). Functions of this office include monitoring progress on transposing EU rules, providing opinions on draft acts, providing technical assistance to line ministries, coordinating use of EU and other donor funds, and organizing "twinning" exchanges with EU agencies.

Turkey's regulatory convergence with the EU deepened to reflect the reform demands associated with the EU-Turkey Customs Union. Establishing a customs union entails lifting all customs duties, quantitative restrictions, and charges with equivalent effect between the relevant trading partners, and applying a common external tariff. Yet beyond these measures, the EU-Turkey Customs Union Decision (CUD) of 1995 (and its preceding negotiations) initiated or reinforced a wide range of behind-the-border reforms in areas that include customs reform, technical barriers to trade, competition policy, and intellectual property. The CUD included time-bound requirements to demonstrate the application of EU competition policy rules, including provisions on state aid, and EU rules on technical barriers to trade. Subsequent standards reform and the 1997 creation of the Competition Authority have been associated with reduced trade costs and a decrease in market concentration in key sectors (Togan 2012). Significant interdepartmental and interministerial coordination has been instrumental to achieving these wide-ranging reforms. Partnership countries can examine the experiences of both CEE countries and Turkey with a view to identifying institutional features that support their own integration goals. Where political leadership is sufficiently strong, Deauville partners can assist by supporting the capacity building necessary to establish strong integration mechanisms within the government and civil service.

Regulatory convergence: Key selected recommendations

Short-term:

- Adopt comprehensive competition legislation in Partnership countries with an effective competition agency in charge of implementation consistent with future deep and high-quality trade agreements.

- Adopt efficient, transparent, and nondiscriminatory government procurement legislation in Partnership countries, with effective implementation mechanisms consistent with future deep and high-quality trade agreements.

- Review mechanisms for interministerial coordination on trade and FDI integration with a view to creating upgraded committee structures, led at the cabinet level and supported by specialized civil service units.

Medium-term:

- Achieve a gradual regulatory convergence of the Partnership countries with the rules and regulations in place in their main Deauville partners, including through alignment with relevant WTO discipline and gradual approximation of the EU Community acquis, focusing on mutually agreed priority areas.

Notes

1. It has been estimated that the median rate of return worldwide is 48 percent per year for agricultural research and 63 percent for extension services (Alston et al. 2000). In studies of the returns for agricultural research in Arab countries, the average rate of return was 36 percent.

2. MA-OTRI = Market Access Overall Trade Restrictiveness Index (tariff only (MA-TTRI) and tariffs + AVEs of NTMs (MA-OTRI)). Tariff preferences are taken into account. MA-OTRI measures the restrictiveness faced by exports. It captures trade distortions that the rest-of-the-world trade policies impose on the export bundle of each country. These indexes and indicators are provided for OVERALL trade, AGRICULTURE, and MANUFACTURING.

3. The TTRI is calculated as a weighted sum of ad valorem tariffs and ad valorem equivalent of specific duties, where the weights are import volumes and import demand elasticities.

4. Results should be interpreted with caution, but in the case of Morocco, they suggest that the wedge ranges from zero to over 373 percent (rice), with the bulk of the effect generated by SPS measures.

5. The OTRI adds NTMs to the TTRI to calculate an overall trade restrictiveness index.

6. To our knowledge, Mise à Niveau programs have not been evaluated formally in MENA countries. Outside the MENA region, a formal impact evaluation of the pesticides program on Senegalese horticulture exporters found that, although Senegal's horticulture exports indeed grew vigorously after the program's implementation, a comparison of the performance of beneficiary firms with that of a control group showed a statistically significant effect only on horticulture exports to the EU, with no externality on other exports (Jaud and Cadot 2011).

7. The guillotine approach provides both a quick fix for the most critical problems of inefficient and antimarket regulations and a permanent system for quality control of new business regulations to avoid reoccurrence of the same problems. It can be used to improve future legal security by establishing a central electronic regulatory registry with positive security.

8. The Community acquis is the accumulated body of EU legislation and case law, including all regulations and directives passed by EU institutions, that is applied by the 27 member states. During successive EU enlargements, countries that joined were required to transpose the acquis into national law and demonstrate its effective enforcement. The European Neighbourhood Policy, introduced in 2005, promotes alignment with the acquis for relevant countries to the EU's east and south on the basis of "everything but institutions" (i.e., deep integration that does not end in membership).

9. In some sectors, switching production processes to accommodate different standards is costly. For instance, accommodating different maximum residual levels of toxic chemicals on different production runs in the same facility can be tricky. In such cases, relaxing technical regulations for exports to certain destinations may do no good. Only very close collaboration between competent, technically trained regulatory bodies and technical industry representatives may yield real benefits.

10. The Services Trade Restrictions Database is at http://iresearch.worldbank.org/servicestrade/.

11. See, for example, Hamilton and Whalley (1984), Moses and Letnes (2004), Iregui (2005), and Klein and Ventura (2007).

12. For countries negotiating EU membership since 2007, the acquis is divided into 35 chapters. These cover free movement of goods, workers, and capital; right of establishment and freedom to provide services; public procurement; company law; intellectual property law; competition policy; financial services; information society and media; agriculture and rural development; food safety, veterinary, and phytosanitary policy; fisheries; transport policy; energy; taxation; economic and monetary policy; statistics; social policy and employment; enterprise and industrial policy; trans-European networks; regional policy; judiciary and fundamental rights; justice, freedom, and security; science and research; education and culture; environment; consumer and health protection; customs union; external relations; foreign, security and defense policy; financial control; financial and budgetary provision; institutions; and other issues.

References

Aloui, Omar, and Lahcen Kenny. 2004. "The Costs of Compliance with SPS Standards for Moroccan Exports: A Case Study." Agricultural and Rural Development Discussion Paper, World Bank, Washington, DC.

Alston, Julian M., Connie Chan-Kang, Michele C. Marra, Philip G. Pardey, and Tim J. Wyatt. 2000. *A Meta-Analysis of Rates of Return to Agricultural R&D: Ex Pede Herculem?* Research Report 113, International Food Policy Research Institute, Washington, DC.

Anderson, Kym, and Will Martin. 2006. "Agriculture, Trade, and the Doha Agenda." In *Agricultural Trade Reform and the Doha Development Agenda*, ed. Kym Anderson and Will Martin. New York: Palgrave Macmillan; Washington, DC: World Bank.

Anderson, Robert, and William Kovacic. 2009. "Competition Policy and International Trade Liberalisation: Essential Complements to Ensure Good Performance in Public Procurement Markets." *Public Procurement Law Review* 18: 67–101.

Arnold, Jens Matthias, Beata Javorcik, Molly Lipscomb, and Aaditya Mattoo. 2012. "Services Reform and Manufacturing Performance: Evidence from India." Policy Research Working Paper 5948, World Bank, Washington, DC.

Augier, Patricia, Olivier Cadot, and Marion Dovis. 2011. "Imports and Productivity at the Firm Level: The Role of Absorptive Capacity." CEPR Discussion Paper 7218, Centre for Economic Policy and Research, London.

Ayadi et al. (2009). http://trade.ec.europa.eu/doclib/docs/2009/october/tradoc_145214.pdf.

Baffes, John, and Harry de Gorter. 2004. "Experience with Decoupling Agricultural Support." In *Global Agricultural Trade and Developing Countries*, ed. M. Ataman Aksoy and John C. Beghin. Washington, DC: World Bank.

Bartel, Ann, and Ann Harrison. 2005. "Ownership versus Environment: Disentangling the Sources of Public-Sector Inefficiency." *Review of Economics and Statistics* 87 (1): 135–47.

Becker, Bettina, and Nigel Pain. 2003. "What Determines Industrial R&D Expenditure in the UK?" NIESR Discussion Paper 211, National Institute of Economic and Social Research, London.

Bhattacharya, Rina, and Hirut Wolde. 2010. "Constraints on Trade in the MENA Region." IMF Working Paper 10/31, International Monetary Fund, Washington, DC.

Boeri, Tito. 2010. "Immigration to the Land of Redistribution." 'Europe in Question' Discussion Paper 05, London School of Economics, London.

Borchert, Ingo, Samantha DeMartino, and Aaditya Mattoo. 2010. "Services Trade Policies in the Pan-Arab Free Trade Area (PAFTA)." Unpublished paper, World Bank, Washington, DC.

Borchert, Ingo, Batshur Gootiiz, and Aaditya Mattoo. 2012. "Policy Barriers to International Trade in Services: New Empirical Evidence." World Bank Policy Research Working Paper WPS6109, World Bank, Washington, DC.

Borchert, Ingo, and Aaditya Mattoo. 2009. "The Crisis-Resilience of Services Trade." Policy Research Working Paper 4917, World Bank, Washington, DC.

Bouët, Antoine. 2006. *How Much Will Trade Liberalization Help the Poor? Comparing Global Trade Models.* Research Brief 5, International Food Policy Research Institute, Washington, DC.

Breisinger, Clemens, Teunis van Rheenen, Claudia Ringler, Alejandro Pratt Nin, Nicholas Minot, Catherine Aragon, Bingxin Yu, Olivier Ecker, and Tingju Zhu. 2010. "Food Security and Economic Development in the Middle East and North Africa." IFRI Discussion Paper 985, International Food Policy Research Institute, Washington, DC.

Cabral, Luis M. B., Guido Cozzi, Vincenzo Denicolò, Giancarlo Spagnolo, and Matteo Zanza. 2006. "Procuring Innovation." CEPR Discussion Paper 5774, Centre for Economic Policy Research, London.

Cadot, Olivier, Anne-Célia Disdier, and Lionel Fontagné. 2012. "North–South Standards Harmonisation and International Trade." CEPR Discussion Paper 8767, Centre for Economic Policy Research, London.

Cakmak, Erol. 2004. "Structural Change and Market Opening in Turkish Agriculture." EU-Turkey Working Paper 10, Centre for European Policy Studies, Brussels.

Castles, Stephen. 2006. "Guestworkers in Europe: A Resurrection?" *International Migration Review* 40 (4): 741–66.

Chen, Hejing, and John Whalley. 2011. "The WTO Government Procurement Agreement and Its Impacts on Trade." NBER Working Paper 17365, National Bureau of Economic Research, Cambridge, MA.

Cherkaoui, Mouna. 2011. "Implementing Preferential Trade Agreements for Development: The Case of Morocco." Unpublished paper, World Bank, Washington, DC.

Clemens, Michael. 2011. "Economics and Emigration: Trillion-Dollar Bills on the Sidewalk?" Working Paper 264, Center for Global Development, Washington, DC.

Clemens, Michael, Claudio E. Montenegro, and Lant Pritchett. 2008. "The Place Premium: Wage Differences for Identical Workers across the U.S. Border." Working Paper 148, Center for Global Development, Washington, DC.

Coady, David. 2004. "Designing and Evaluating Social Safety Nets: Theory, Evidence and Policy Conclusions." Discussion Paper 172, International Food Policy Research Institute, Washington, DC.

Coady, David, Margaret Grosh, and John Hodinott. 2002. "Targeting Outcomes Redux." Discussion Paper 144, International Food Policy Research Institute, Washington, DC.

Compte, Olivier, Ariane Lambert-Mogiliansky, and Thierry Verdier. 2005. "Corruption and Competition in Procurement Auctions." *RAND Journal of Economics* 36 (1): 1–15.

Cozzi, Guido, and Giammario Impullitti. 2006. "Technology Policy and Wage Inequality." Working Paper 2008-23, Business School–Economics, University of Glasgow, Scotland.

Dawar, Kamala, and Simon Evenett. 2011. "Government Procurement." In *Preferential Trade Agreement Policies for Development: A Handbook*, ed. Jean-Pierre Chauffour and Jean-Christophe Maur. Washington, DC: World Bank.

Dennis, Allen. 2006a. "The Impact of Regional Trade Agreements and Trade Facilitation in the Middle-East North Africa Region." Policy Research Working Paper 3837, World Bank, Washington, DC.

———. 2006b. "Trade Liberalization, Factor Market Flexibility, and Growth: The Case of Morocco and Tunisia." Policy Research Working Paper 3857, World Bank, Washington, DC.

Dimitrova, Antoaneta, and Dimiter Toshkov. 2009. "Post-Accession Compliance between Administrative Co-ordination and Political Bargaining." In *Post-Accession Compliance in the EU's New Member States*, ed. Frank Schimmelfennig and Florian Trauner. European Integration Online Papers, vol. 13, special issue 2. http://eiop.or.at/eiop/index.php/eiop/article/view/2009_019a.

Djankov, Simeon, and Peter Murrell. 2002. "Enterprise Restructuring in Transition: A Quantitative Survey." *Journal of Economic Literature* 40 (3): 739–92.

E-Marsoum. 2008. *Projet Pilote de l'ITC et de la CNUCED sur les Mesures Non Tarifaires.* Tunis: E-Marsoum.

European Commission. 2005. *Internal Market Scoreboard, No. 14: Second Best Transposition Result Ever.* Brussels: European Commission. http://ec.europa.eu/internal_market/score/docs/score14/scoreboard14printed_en.pdf.

Evenett, Simon, and Bernard Hoekman. 2005. "Government Procurement: Market Access, Transparency, and Multilateral Trade Rules." *European Journal of Political Economy* 21 (1): 163–83.

Fargues, Philippe. 2005. "Temporary Migration: Matching Demand in the EU with Supply from the MENA." Analytic and Synthetic Note 2005/11, Euro-Mediterranean Consortium for Applied Research in International Migration (CARIM), European University Institute, Florence, Italy.

Fattouh, Bassam, and Jonathan Stern, eds. 2011. *Natural Gas Markets in the Middle East and North Africa*. New York: Oxford University Press.

Freund, Caroline, and Bineswaree Bolaky. 2008. "Trade, Regulations and Income." *Journal of Development Economics* 87 (2): 309–21.

Frohberg, Klaus, Ulrike Grote, and Etti Maria Winter. 2006. "EU Food Safety Standards, Traceability and Other Regulations: A Growing Trade Barrier to Developing Countries' Exports?" Paper prepared for the International Association of Agricultural Economists (IAAE), Queensland, Australia.

Gereffi, Gary, and Karina Fernandez-Stark. 2010. "The Offshore Services Value Chain: Developing Countries and the Crisis." Policy Research Working Paper 5262, World Bank, Washington, DC.

Ghoneim, Ahmed F. 2009. *Report on NTBs Facing Intraregional Arab Trade in Agriculture*. Report submitted to World Bank Institute, Washington, DC.

———. 2012. "Challenges of Services Liberalization in the Multilateral and Regional Contexts: The Case of Arab Countries." In *The Service Sectors, Trade Policy, and the Challenges of Development in the Arab Region*, ed. Kinda Mohamedieh and Ahmed Ghoneim. Beirut: Arab NGO Network for Development.

Gootiiz, B., and A. Mattoo. 2009. "Services in Doha: What's on the Table?" Policy Research Working Paper 4903, World Bank, Washington, DC.

Haddad, Mona, Jaime de Melo, and Brendan Horton. 1996. "Morocco, 1984–89: Trade Liberalisation, Exports, and Industrial Performance." In *Industrial Evolution in Developing Countries*, ed. Mark Roberts and James Tybout. New York: Oxford University Press.

Hamilton, Bob, and John Whalley. 1984. "Efficiency and Distributional Implications of Global Restrictions on Labor Mobility." *Journal of Development Economics* 14: 61–75.

Harb, Georges. 2007. "Trade Facilitation and Intra-Arab Trade: An Empirical Assessment." *Journal of International Trade and Diplomacy* 2 (2): 135–70.

Hodge, James. 2002. "Liberalization of Trade in Services in Developing Countries." In *Development, Trade and the WTO: A Handbook*, ed. Bernard Hoekman, Aaditya Mattoo, and Peter English, 221–34. Washington, DC: World Bank.

Hoekman, Bernard, and Alessandro Nicita. 2010. "Assessing the Doha Round: Market Access, Transactions Costs and Aid for Trade Facilitation." *Journal of International Trade and Economic Development* 19 (1): 65–80.

Hoekman, Bernard, and Jamel Zarrouk. 2009. "Changes in Cross-Border Trade Costs in the Pan-Arab Free Trade Area, 2001–2008." Policy Research Working Paper 5031, World Bank, Washington, DC.

Holzmann, Robert, and Yann Pouget. 2010. "Toward an Objective-Driven System of Smart Labor Migration Management." Economic Premise 42, World Bank, Washington, DC.

Ilahi, Nadeem, and Amine Mati. 2011. "Enhancing EU Association Agreements in the Wake of the Arab Spring." Unpublished paper, International Monetary Fund, Washington, DC.

Iregui, Ana Maria. 2005. "Efficiency Gains from the Elimination of Global Restrictions on Labour Mobility." In *Poverty, International Migration and Asylum*, ed. George J. Borjas and Jeff Crisp, 211–38. New York: Palgrave Macmillan.

Jaud, Melise, and Olivier Cadot. 2011. "A Second Look at the Pesticides Initiative Program: Evidence from Senegal." Policy Research Working Paper 5635, World Bank, Washington, DC.

Kahyarara, G. 2004. "Competition Policy Manufacturing Exports, Investment and Productivity: Firm-Level Evidence from Tanzania Manufacturing Enterprises." In *Competition, Competitiveness and Development: Lessons from Developing Countries*, ed. Philippe Brusick and Ana Maria Alvarez, 264–301. New York: United Nations.

Kee, Hiau Looi, Cristina Neagu, and Alessandro Nicita. Forthcoming. "Is Protectionism on the Rise? Assessing National Trade Policies during the Crisis of 2008." *Review of Economics and Statistics*.

Kherallah, Myele, Hans Lofgren, Peter Gruhn, and Meyra Reeder. 2000. *Wheat Policy Reform in Egypt: Adjustment of Local Markets and Options for Future Reforms*. Research Report 115, International Food Policy Research Institute, Washington, DC.

Kim, Euysung. 2000. "Trade Liberalization and Productivity Growth in Korean Manufacturing Industries: Price Protection, Market Power, and Scale Efficiency." *Journal of Development Economics* 62 (1): 55–83.

Klein, Paul, and Gustavo J. Ventura. 2007. "TFP Differences and the Aggregate Effects of Labor Mobility in the Long Run." *B. E. Journal of Macroeconomics* 7 (1): Article 10.

Kosarajo, S., and H. Zaafrane. 2011. "Benchmarking Higher Education in MENA." Paper presented at the Marseille Center for Mediterranean Integration, "Higher Education in the Mediterranean and Beyond," Marseille, France, January 23–25.

Laffont, Jean-Jacques. 1997. "Inflexible Rules against Political Discretion." *Nordic Journal of Political Economy* 24: 79–87.

Laffont, Jean-Jacques, and Jean Tirole. 1991. "Privatization and Incentives." *Journal of Law, Economics and Organization* 7 (0): 84–105.

Lanz, Rainer, and Sebastian Miroudot. 2010. "Intra Firm Trade: A Work in Progress." OECD Trade Policy Working Paper 114, Organisation for Economic Co-operation and Development, Paris.

Lanz, Rainer, Sebastien Miroudot, and Hildegunn Kyvik Nordås. 2011. "Trade in Tasks." OECD Trade Policy Working Paper 117, Organisation for Economic Co-operation and Development, Paris.

Ligon, Ethan, and Elisabeth Sadoulet. 2007. "Estimating the Effects of Aggregate Agricultural Growth on the Distribution of Expenditures." Background paper prepared for World Development Report 2008, World Bank, Washington, DC.

Magnan, Nicholas, Travis Lybbert, Alex McCalla, and Julian Lampietti. 2011. "Modeling the Limitations and Implicit Costs of Cereal Self-Sufficiency with Limited Data: The Case of Morocco." *Food Security* 3 (S1): 49–60.

Mandour, Dina. 2006. "Impact of EU Health and Environmental Standards on Egyptian Agro-Food Exports." Ph.D. diss., Ruhr University, Bochum, Germany.

Marouani, M. A., and L. Munro. 2009. "Assessing Barriers to Trade in Services in the MENA Region." OECD Trade Policy Working Paper 84, Organisation for Economic Co-operation and Development, Paris.

Maskus, Keith, and Mohamed Lahouel. 2000. "Competition Policy and Intellectual Property Rights in Developing Countries." *World Economy* 23 (4): 595–611.

Minot, Nicholas. 2012. *Agricultural Trade and Investment in Selected MENA Countries.* Report prepared for the Middle East and North Africa Region of the World Bank, International Food Policy Research Institute, Washington, DC.

Miroudot, Sebastian, Rainer Lanz, and Alexandros Ragoussis. 2009. "Trade in Intermediate Goods and Services." OECD Trade Policy Working Paper 93, Organisation for Economic Development and Co-operation, Paris.

Miroudot, Sebastien, and Alexandros Ragoussis. 2009. "Vertical Trade, Trade Costs and FDI." OECD Trade Policy Working Paper 89, Organisation for Economic Development and Co-operation, Paris.

Moses, Jonathon W., and Bjorn Letnes. 2004. "The Economic Costs to International Labor Restrictions: Revisiting the Empirical Discussion." *World Development* 32 (10): 1609–26.

Müller-Jentsch, Daniel. 2005. *Deeper Integration and Trade in Services in the Euro-Mediterranean Region: Southern Dimensions of the European Neighborhood Policy.* Washington, DC: World Bank.

OECD (Organisation for Economic Co-operation and Development). 2010. *PISA 2009 Results: What Students Know and Can Do.* Paris: OECD.

Olhan, Emine. 2006. "The Impact of the Reforms: Impoverished Turkish Agriculture." *Agricultural Journal* 1 (2): 41–47.

Özden, Ça lar, Mirwat Sewadeh, and J. Wahba. 2009. "Temporary Labor Migration from Egypt to the EU: Economic and Legal Background." Unpublished paper, World Bank, Washington, DC.

Panizzon, Marion. 2010. "International Law of Economic Migration: A Ménage à Trois? GATS Mode 4, EPAs and Bilateral Migration Agreements." *Journal of World Trade* 44 (6): 1–40.

Pavcnik, Nina. 2002. "Trade Liberalization, Exit, and Productivity Improvement: Evidence from Chilean Plants." *Review of Economic Studies* 69 (1): 245–76.

Péridy, Nicolas. 2007. "Toward a Pan Arab Free Trade Agreement." *Developing Economies* 43 (3): 329–45.

Porter, Michael. 1990. *The Competitive Advantage of Nations.* New York: Free Press.

Schlumberger, Charles. 2010. *Open Skies for Africa: Implementing the Yamoussoukro Decision.* Washington, DC: World Bank.

Sekkat, Khalid, ed. 2008. *Competition and Efficiency in the Arab World.* New York: Palgrave Macmillan.

———. 2009. "Does Competition Improve Productivity in Developing Countries?" *Journal of Economic Policy Reform* 12 (2): 145–62.

———. 2010. "Economic Policies, Firms' Entry and Exit and Economic Performance: A Cross Country Analysis." In *Market Dynamics and Productivity in Developing Countries: Economic Reforms in the Middle East and North Africa*, ed. Khalid Sekkat, 145–66. New York: Springer.

Sekkat, Khalid, and Aristomène Varoudakis. 2002. "The Impact of Exchange and Trade Policy Reforms on Manufactured Exports in North Africa." *Development Policy Review* 20: 177–89.

Staritz, Cornelia, Gary Gereffi, and Olivier Cattaneo. 2011. "Shifting End Markets and Upgrading Prospects in Global Value Chains." *International Journal of Technological Learning, Innovation and Development* 4 (1-2-3): 1–12.

Swedish National Board of Trade. 2010. *Servicification of Swedish Manufacturing*. Kommerskollegium 2010:1. Stockholm: National Board of Trade. http://www.kommers.se/upload/Analysarkiv/In%20English/New%20reports/Report%20Servicification%20of%20Swedish%20manufacturing.pdf.

Togan, Sübidey. 2012. *The EU-Turkey Customs Union: A Model for Future Euro-Med Integration*. MEDPRO Technical Report 9, Mediterranean Prospects, Centre for European Policy Studies, Brussels.

Trionfetti, Federico. 2000. "Discriminatory Public Procurement and International Trade." *World Economy* 23 (1): 57–76.

World Bank. 2007. *World Development Report 2008: Agriculture for Development*. Washington, DC: World Bank.

———. 2009. *Shaping the Future: A Long-Term Perspective of People and Job Mobility for the Middle East and North Africa*. Washington, DC: World Bank.

———. 2010. *Migration and Remittances Factbook 2011*. Washington, DC: World Bank.

———. 2011a. *Framework Document for Loans, Credits, Grants, and Guarantees for the Arab World Initiative for Financing Food Security*. Washington, DC: World Bank.

———. 2011b. *World Development Report 2012: Gender Equality and Development*. Washington, DC: World Bank.

World Bank, FAO (Food and Agriculture Organization), and IFAD (International Fund for Agricultural Development). 2009. *Improving Food Security in Arab Countries*. Washington, DC: World Bank.

Zarrouk, Jamel. 2002. "A Survey of Barriers to Trade and Investment in Arab Countries." In *Harnessing Trade for Development and Growth in the Middle East*, ed. Bernard Hoekman and Patrick Messerlin, 51–68. New York: Council on Foreign Relations.

CHAPTER 4

Fostering Competitiveness and Diversification

Partnership countries have not been able to enter foreign markets and save and invest in the future as much as the more successful emerging economies because of an overall lack of competitiveness and diversification. Competitiveness is central to harnessing private sector growth for sustainable employment, poverty reduction, and, ultimately, wealth creation. To reap the benefits of market opportunities, and for such opportunities to induce job creation, the regulatory environment for business should be improved, technological upgrading and skill availability should be fostered, and countries should boost their ability to enter new and sophisticated export markets. Firms, especially small- and medium-size ones, serving export and domestic markets in all sectors cannot exploit opportunities if they are burdened by costs outside their control that make them uncompetitive. Increasing the number and value of products produced, the number of markets served, and the survival rate of firms is conditional on lowering such costs, and Partnership countries need investment now. This requires economy-wide policies and regulations aimed at creating the proper business environment and investment climate, including trade policy (restrictions on imports and foreign direct investment [FDI]); trade in services as a new means to access international best practices and expand exports; and the design and implementation of specific actions to address market and information failures. There are four priorities for the Deauville Partnership in this area, including absolute priority for the recommendations aimed at attracting FDI and fostering domestic investment:

- Strengthen the *FDI regime* by phasing out de jure and de facto restrictions on foreign equity participation in most economic sectors; by simplifying and rationalizing investment regimes; by easing access to production factors (industrial land, foreign exchange, and expatriate workers); by completing privatization programs; and by launching negotiations with Deauville partners on investment.

- Improve the *domestic business climate* by fostering competition and limiting opportunities for rent seeking; by building strong rule-bound market institutions to reduce discretion and opacity; and by promoting new institutional dialogue among stakeholders on the design, implementation, and evaluation of policies.

- Address structural *economic governance* issues by fighting corruption, discretion, and the uneven implementation of policies; by restoring voice, accountability, and checks and balances; by strengthening the rule of law and the level playing field; and by promoting transparency through freedom of information.

- Foster the four pillars of a *knowledge economy* (KE) by harnessing more technological spillovers from existing and future FDI; by launching a major overhaul of education systems; by developing comprehensive knowledge and innovation strategies; and by further diffusing information and communication technologies (ICTs).

The FDI Regime

Key issues

Partnership countries have achieved considerable reductions in time required for investors to obtain permits and licenses to operate their businesses, including through initiatives such as one-stop shops. The Arab Republic of Egypt, Jordan, Morocco, and Tunisia all carried out major programs to improve their FDI environment in the past decade. Nonetheless, investment inflows are below potential as modeled by the countries' economic characteristics, and the precrisis surge in FDI was concentrated in real estate and petroleum to a greater extent than in manufacturing and services, which create more jobs per dollar invested.

Attracting more FDI can promote positive spillovers to the economy. As demonstrated by Tunisia's automotive and aerospace sectors, small and medium suppliers to multinational companies have an opportunity to absorb technology, increase their productivity, and create high-value jobs. While future FDI inflows will depend to an extent on political and social stability, Partnership countries will also need to address remaining barriers and incentive issues affecting foreign investors. These include sectoral caps on foreign equity holdings, the limited issuance of licenses in key sectors, and administrative devices such as Egypt's "investment pauses." The process could be reinforced by negotiating investment provisions with key trade partners.

Partnership countries' FDI and investment promotion regimes should be simplified and rationalized. A first step would be to establish or strengthen one-stop shops for foreign investors, while another approach is to study the reforms piloted in special economic zones with a view to extending their best features across the economy. Incentive schemes should be reviewed and reformed where they are complex and overlapping. In terms of broader reforms that can promote FDI, Partnership countries should review the regulations and information gaps around access to key production factors, including industrial land, foreign exchange, and expatriate workers. Attractiveness will also depend on the exit options available to investors. These can be strengthened through bankruptcy law, expropriation law, and dispute settlement mechanisms.

As noted in chapter 2, all Partnership economies benefited from and rode the surge of FDI in the mid-2000s. These trends in FDI flows to the five Partnership countries tell a compelling story. They show how reforms, after a time lag of 2–3 years, can raise the profile of an economy and bring it to the attention of investors, leading to FDI projects, economic activities, and jobs. Yet FDI flows to the five economies also point to a set of political economy, policy, and regulatory issues that are holding them back from benefiting fully from globalization. Those issues are within the power of the authorities to address, individually and collectively, and doing so could position these economies to take advantage of FDI for the economic and social development of their respective countries and of the whole region. The manufacturing and services sectors, where most jobs are generated, have not been able to attract their shares of FDI, compared to the petroleum and real estate sectors. Even when they do attract investment, there is still ample scope to increase the local added value of FDI projects through linkages to the host economy and to benefit from spillovers. All five countries are performing well below world averages and below their potential in attracting FDI. This underperformance, which offers opportunities for improvements and growth, has its roots in incomplete and slow reform processes. It is also the result of economic policies rooted in an era predating the prominence of emergent markets and the rise of globalization. Political economic factors affecting the stability of policies and business environment have also played a role in this suboptimum performance.

In the early part of the 2000s, all Partnership countries launched comprehensive reforms of their FDI environment. When Libya renounced its pursuit of nuclear capabilities, this opened diplomatic and economic doors. Egypt, Jordan, Morocco, and Tunisia either continued their efforts to improve their investment climate, including their FDI environment, or embarked on major reform programs. A case in point is the aggressive and wide-ranging program of reforms initiated in Egypt, offering a higher level of access to FDI through greenfield investment, mergers and acquisitions, and privatization. In addition, the program made substantial improvements in the institutional realm. The establishment of the Ministry of Investment sent a loud and clear signal to the domestic and private sectors, and more importantly, to the entire Egyptian administration that the authorities were serious about encouraging investment. The new ministry led the process of reforming the investment climate and brought a better coordination of policies and procedures related to domestic and foreign investment among various government agencies at the national level. An important investor-friendly measure was the establishment of the one-stop shop. This reduced substantially the time that investors had to spend making trips to various agencies to obtain the necessary permits and licenses to establish and operate their businesses.

Such political and economic improvements in the FDI environment paid off handsomely, with FDI inflows picking up in the early 2000s; yet performance remains below potential. Foreign investors took note of these reforms and stepped up their commitments to invest in all five economies. While global flows of FDI tripled from 2004 to 2007, those going to the Partnership economies increased at an even higher rate in most cases, albeit from a low base. Egypt saw its FDI flows increase by a factor of 9, Jordan by a factor of 4, Morocco by a factor of 3.3, and Tunisia by a factor of 2.5; Libya, starting from a very low base, increased by a factor of 35 (table 4.1). This performance notwithstanding, the Partnership countries still were not able to attract their potential share of global FDI flows, taking into account their economic and structural characteristics including gross domestic product (GDP) per capita, GDP growth rate, telecom infrastructure, exports of natural resources, and country risk. According to the Inward FDI Potential Index of the United Nations Conference on Trade and Development (UNCTAD), all five economies performed significantly below their potential (table 4.2). Morocco comes closest to reaching its potential, with Egypt not far behind.

TABLE 4.1

Inward FDI Flows to Deauville Partnership Countries, 2004–10
US$, millions

Country	2004	2005	2006	2007	2008	2009	2010
Egypt, Arab Rep.	1,253	5,376	10,043	11,578	9,496	6,712	6,386
Jordan	620	1,984	3,544	2,622	2,829	2,430	1,704
Libya	131	1,038	2,013	4,689	4,111	2,674	3,833
Morocco	853	1,654	2,449	2,805	2,487	1,952	1,304
Tunisia	639	783	3,308	1,616	2,758	1,688	1,513
North Africa[a]	5,270	12,236	23,143	24,775	24,045	18,468	16,926

Source: UNCTAD 2011.

a. 2003–10 cumulative FDI flows to North Africa amount to $131 billion.

TABLE 4.2

Inward FDI Potential Index, Deauville Partnership Countries, 1990–2009

Country	1990	1995	2000	2005	2006	2007	2008	2009	Average 2005–09
Egypt, Arab Rep.	67	79	70	85	87	88	92	88	88
Jordan	53	59	67	63	62	66	72	71	67
Libya	52	47	44	40	36	34	34	63	41
Morocco	74	94	94	88	89	93	94	95	92
Tunisia	65	72	71	62	65	68	68	72	67

Source: UNCTAD 2011.

Note: The Inward FDI Potential Index indicates whether an economy is attracting FDI according to its potential. The index takes into consideration 12 economic and structural variables. A score of less than 100 means that the economy is performing below its potential in attracting FDI.

The Partnership economies are missing valuable opportunities to attract FDI in the manufacturing sector, which, per dollar of investment, generates far more steady employment than either oil and gas or real estate. In addition, FDI projects in manufacturing can produce various types of spillovers that benefit the domestic economy. They offer substantial opportunities for adding local value through local supplies, which in turn fosters entrepreneurship and creation of small and medium enterprises (SMEs), generating even more employment. They are also a potential source of technology transfers to the host economy through backward linkages, training, and business spinoffs. As has been documented around the world, particularly in Asia and in Central and Eastern Europe, suppliers to multinational corporations in host economies are often able to raise their competitiveness to the point where they start to export. Like their East Asian competitors, Partnership countries could use FDI in manufacturing as a catalyst for industrialization and economic development—provided they can improve their investment climate, offer a stable and business-friendly policy environment, and adopt appropriate industry strategies.

All five Partnership economies have yet to take full advantage of their various international investment agreements. Despite a host of such agreements, including bilateral investment treaties (BITs) and double taxation treaties (DTTs), among themselves and with third parties, the intra-regional flow of FDI has remained marginal.[1] During 2003–10, about $8 billion of FDI was intra-regional to North Africa—a mere 6 percent of total FDI flows to the region. This low level of intra-regional FDI points to a de facto low degree of economic integration among Maghreb economies. It also points to missed opportunities: the geographic proximity, linguistic and cultural affinities, and economic complementarities among the Partnership economies all should provide regional multinational corporations an edge compared to those from outside the region. In addition, regional multinational corporations may offer more to the host countries, as they are in a better position to understand and service their neighboring markets, using more appropriate technologies and possibly fostering beneficial spillovers to those markets. Those opportunities could lead to a higher level of integrated supply chains and to the emergence of a regional Arab Factory similar to the Factory Asia developed over the last three decades in East Asia. This would contribute to a major push for economic development and to an increase in the region's economic competitiveness and attractiveness.

All Partnership countries are characterized by complex and de jure restrictive investment regimes in critical economic sectors, such as banking and insurance, electricity, and transport. In each country, different laws govern the approval and establishment of businesses, creating over time a patchwork of legal investment frameworks. Various investment regimes are offered for different subnational regions, economic zones, or economic sectors, often with elaborate or confusing sets of incentives, the effectiveness of which is largely unknown. The authorities seem to be aware of these issues, as the government of Egypt has shown by removing all incentives and lowering the income tax rate. Still, Egypt has at least three laws governing investment. According to the World Bank's Investing Across Borders (IAB) index, which measures de jure ownership restrictions in 33 different sectors, the three Partnership countries rated (Egypt, Morocco, and Tunisia) scored worse than world averages in a number of critical sectors, including banking (Egypt), media (Egypt), electricity (Morocco and Tunisia), and transport (Morocco). It is generally considered—though poorly documented—that Libya has a more restrictive regime, including in mining, oil, and gas; electricity generation, transmission, and distribution; construction; banking and insurance; and telecommunications.

In addition to the de jure restrictions, Partnership economies have strong de facto restrictions in the form of limited licenses issued in various sectors. These de facto restrictions are highly effective in closing market access, stifling competition, and impeding economic progress. While government interventions in the marketplace may be needed to provide public goods or manage natural monopolies, including public utilities, they are often used to protect sectors that would benefit from more competition. State-owned and quasi-state-owned enterprises still dominate a number of sectors in each of the five Partnership countries. Some are state-owned, and others are owned by government-related interests, such as the military. All such enterprises have enjoyed preferential treatment, thereby introducing distortions in markets and crowding out domestic and foreign private enterprises. Each of the five Partnership countries has a privatization program, but these are at different stages or levels of effectiveness and need strengthening. Jordan's privatization has been assessed as fairly successful in terms of process and outcome years (box 4.1).

Looking forward, the political, social, and legal stability of Partnership countries will be a key prerequisite to attract foreign investors and persuade them to establish and operate their businesses there. The five Part-

---

BOX 4.1

Jordan's Record in Privatization and Public-Private Partnerships

Fourteen privatization transactions and two public-privatization partnerships undertaken by the government of Jordan during 2000–07 successfully raised $2.6 billion in sales proceeds and otherwise benefited Jordan's macroeconomic stability, competitiveness, consumers, and labor.

The privatizations include the Jordan Telecommunications Company (2000, 2002), Arab Potash Company (2003), Jordan Phosphate Mines Company (2005), seven aviation sector businesses, including Royal Jordanian Airlines (2000–07), and three power sector companies (2007). The two partnerships include a management contract for the Port of Aqaba container terminal and a build-operate-transfer transaction to develop a new passenger terminal at Queen Alia International Airport.

Using most of the $2.6 billion in privatization proceeds to buy back Paris Club debt at a discounted rate, Jordan succeeded in reducing its external debt-GDP ratio from 100 percent in 2000 to 89 percent in 2004 to 60 percent in 2008. Thus, privatization contributed to lower interest charges and overall macroeconomic stability. In addition, as of 2008, these privatized companies made annual contributions to the Treasury—in the form of taxes, royalties, and dividends—amounting to about $380 million.

Following some restructuring in most cases, the privatized firms have shown gains in financial performance and productivity. Growth in sales revenue per employee during 2000–08 ranged from 50 to 200 percent at the electricity companies, Jordan Telecommunications Company, and Royal Jordanian Airlines.

Consumers have benefited as well. In telecommunications, fixed-line connect times and fees have dropped dramatically, and except for local peak-time calls, fixed-line tariffs have been halved since 1998. Leaving aside a fuel cost surcharge, electricity tariffs have grown in line with inflation, while the "lifeline" electricity tariff has actually declined in real terms. In air transport, Royal Jordanian has increased its destinations, frequencies, and customer satisfaction.

On worker protections, the government sought as a matter of policy to avoid involuntary retrenchments in the course of privatization. The 14 privatized firms saw only a 2 percent net loss in employment. This has been more than offset by indirect job gains elsewhere. The government estimates, for example, that privatization and other reforms in the telecommunications sector generated 25,000 additional jobs.

In most cases, privatization involved a foreign strategic investor who could improve

(continued on next page)

BOX 4.1   *Continued*

management and integration into global markets. The privatized firms made over $1 billion in capital investment during 2000–07, equivalent to 11.4 percent of overall FDI. The airport project is generating an additional $750 million in FDI.

These transactions improved Jordan's competitiveness. For example, private operation at Aqaba nearly doubled container throughput between 2003 and 2008 and practically eliminated waiting times. Lloyds now rates Aqaba as among the three best container terminals in the Middle East and South Asia.

Lead investors in these transactions were selected through open tenders. Internation-

ally recognized financial advisors and law firms helped structure and negotiate these transactions. Privatization was supported by regulatory reform in several cases, including in the telecommunications and electricity sectors. As part of electricity sector restructuring and reform, two independent power producers now operate in Jordan, and two more are planned. Substantial financial support for transaction advisors came from the U.S. Agency for International Development, while the World Bank provided advice and other support to Jordan's Executive Privatization Commission.

nership economies have experienced different levels of policy stability at different points in time. Frequent changes of government in Jordan have affected not only the stability of policies but also the consistency in implementation of whatever policy is already in force. For example, over the course of the 2000s, the Ministry of Industry and Trade, which oversees the investment environment in Jordan, was headed by nine different ministers. Restoring political stability in the aftermath of the regional turmoil of 2011/12 will be critical to reverse the recent collapse of FDI to the region. According to UNCTAD, in the first few months of 2011, FDI flows to North Africa registered a 50 percent decrease compared to 2010. Egypt suffered an 80 percent decrease, and FDI flows to Libya basically stopped for that period.

Equally important, foreign investors need compelling business opportunities to invest, and those opportunities are realized in a conducive investment climate. Countries compete to attract FDI based on their economic characteristics. Investors typically are attracted by a large or growing domestic market, an advantageous cost structure, the presence of natural resources, and strategic opportunities to conduct research and development (R&D) or acquire trademarks or distribution channels. Yet even these business opportunities may not lead to investment if the investment climate in the host country is seen as unfriendly to business or too risky. Over the last four decades, the world has seen example after example in which emerging markets made use of FDI as part of their efforts at economic and social development. This trend started with the five Asian "tigers," led by Japan, and soon expanded to include other Asian countries, most notably China and lately India. This phenomenon was not limited to Asia. Chile, Costa Rica, the Czech Republic, Ireland, Kenya, Rwanda, and Slovakia gave or are currently giving FDI a prominent role in their economic development, with considerable success (table 4.3). All of these economies have one feature in common: each in its own way conducted a sustained program to reform its investment climate over many years. As we saw earlier, all five Partnership economies enjoyed the effects of their partial reforms in the mid-2000s in terms of FDI inflows, even for the short period of time that those reforms were in place.

To enjoy the benefits of FDI, Partnership countries should make clear that they embrace economic openness and welcome foreign investors. Successful FDI destination countries typically share two characteristics. The first is strategic: a conscious understanding and belief that FDI, if handled in the right way, can contribute to national development. It can speed up the transfer of technology and management know-how, foster competitiveness and exports, and provide financial resources. The second is an understanding that, to attract more FDI and derive more benefits from it, countries must improve their climate for private investment, both domestic and foreign, leading to a positive-sum game that improves the general economic welfare of their people and of the investors. Successful countries have translated that understanding into sustained efforts to reform their investment climate over a number of years. Partnership countries could similarly benefit from FDI and draw inspiration from the experience of successful emerging markets. While some

TABLE 4.3

Inward FDI Performance Index, Selected Countries, 1990–2010

Country	1990	1995	2000	2005	2006	2007	2008	2009	2010
Bangladesh	105	117	103	109	121	130	117	120	114
Indonesia	56	53	139	74	119	119	111	117	79
Kenya	71	116	113	133	133	99	131	130	129
Malaysia	2	11	55	73	69	71	82	123	46
Slovakia[a]	n.a.	2	13	41	26	69	58	138	124
Turkey	78	110	126	89	71	91	94	102	108

Source: UNCTAD 2011.

Note: The Inward FDI Performance Index measures the extent to which an economy receives its share of global inward FDI relative to the size of its economy. A score of below 100 means the economy is attracting less than the global average. n.a. = not applicable.

a. In 1990, Slovakia was part of Czechoslovakia and not an independent country.

have already begun reforming their investment climate (see below), all could engage in wider, deeper, and sustained reform efforts aimed at enhancing the FDI environment.

All five Partnership countries could further open up their markets and eliminate the remaining market access restrictions on foreign investors. As we saw earlier, Egypt, Morocco, and Tunisia, covered by the IAB indexes, exhibited a level of de jure restrictions slightly below world averages. Jordan and particularly Libya present more restrictions. In addition, all five economies have pervasive systems of licenses and other administrative mechanisms that impose even more invasive de facto restrictions, particularly in the services sector, including in banking and insurance, tourism, and infrastructure. For instance, Egypt regularly imposes "pauses" on the issuance of licenses and permits in various sectors of the economy, including pauses on licenses to tourist boat operators, pauses on licenses to establish new banks, and similar pauses in the agribusiness and metallurgy sectors. While the official rationale is that the pauses allow for legal reviews of a given sector, they often reflect lack of openness and full competition. Licenses and other administrative mechanisms are often used to regulate the market in sectors dominated by public enterprises. They have introduced serious distortions in the economy and end up favoring narrow segments of business at the expense of the average consumer. In most cases, such licensing systems should be phased out and the affected sectors should be opened to private investors.

If done transparently, further privatization would also help create a level playing field for FDI across more economic sectors, and the presence of FDI in turn may foster greater competition in those sectors. Public enterprises continue to play a dominant role in various sectors in all five economies, including banking, mining, oil and gas, utilities, transportation, and tourism. In addition, quasi-state enterprises, controlled by public entities including the military, play an active role in the economy across many sectors. State and parastatal enterprises are particularly prominent in many sectors in Egypt, creating well-established vested interests. With its preferential treatment and special access to authorities, the state sector creates economic distortions and crowds out the domestic and foreign private sector, with a negative impact on economic efficiency and welfare. In Libya, the public sector economy cuts across most sectors. Egypt, Jordan, Morocco, and Tunisia all have privatization programs in place, some of which have shown good success. In general, however, the progress of privatization has been spotty and slow. In some cases privatization has met with strong resistance, as when controversial transactions have created an impression (or the reality) of cronyism. Finding ways to resume progress on a transparent footing would help level the playing field and enhance competition, a development that is likely to be noticed by the private sector, lowering its perception of investment risks in the country.

Except for Libya, the Partnership countries have already established various export and investment promotion mechanisms aimed at entering global networks, but with mixed results. All four countries have a variety of proactive export policies, such as exemption of taxes on profits or incomes, suspension of the value-added tax on local purchases, exemption of reinvested profits, duty-free imports of necessary raw materials and equipment, flexible labor contracts, and a one-stop shop to facilitate administrative processes. Moreover, the governments have created several trade support institutions that organize trade missions, in-country fairs, and exhibitions, provide matching grants to emerging and promising exporters, co-financing to professional associations, and so forth. However, such efforts should be complemented by more aggressive networking activities. For instance, Alvarez (2004), drawing on a survey of 295 small and medium-size exporters in Chile, provided evidence on what type of program, institutional setup, and financing is most likely to succeed. While trade shows and trade missions did not affect the probability of being a successful exporter, the formation of exporter committees turned out to have positive and significant impacts. These committees were composed of groups of firms with common objectives in international business, which cooperated on research, marketing, and promotion.

Effective presence of dedicated export promotion agencies in the target market is crucial. Export promotion agencies (EPAs) can accomplish various tasks, ranging from advertising, advocacy, information, and technical assistance to follow-up services. The latter is very important for their success and requires, even more than the other activities, an effective presence in the target market. Lederman (2007) examined the role of EPAs to identify the impact on exports of different institutional structures, objectives, and activities. Their evidence suggests that, on average, EPAs have a positive and statistically significant impact on national exports, but the impact is uneven across levels of development and across regions, with the Middle East and North Africa (MENA) agencies lagging behind. The use of office representation abroad also has a higher positive impact on exports than "onshore" offices. Hayakawa, Lee, and Park (2011), focusing on export promotion agencies from Japan and Korea, confirmed their success in boosting exports. Their results even suggest that establishing an EPA office in a country is equivalent in its impact to signing a free trade agreement with that country. Using data on exports from 22 important countries to 200 destination countries over 2002/03, Rose (2007) found that countries could use their foreign services network to their export advantage. The presence of foreign missions is positively correlated with exports: holding other things constant, each additional consulate boosts exports by an estimated 6–10 percent.

However, the success of dedicated export promotion bodies depends on certain conditions. Lederman (2007), using a cross-country analysis, and Macario (2000), focusing on Brazil, Chile, Colombia, and Mexico, both say that EPAs should target firms with new products or those entering new markets. Furthermore, they should emphasize cost and management sharing to ensure that programs are used only by those truly dedicated to exports. The Lederman study adds that the proliferation of small agencies within a country leads to a program that is less effective overall. Macario further recommends that support be given for a maximum of two to three years, to avoid turning it into a subsidy; programs should be submitted to external evaluation, and agencies should be subject to a mix of public and private management. Finally, using the experience of Colombia over the period 2003–06, Volpe Martincus and Carballo (2010) find that bundled services providing new exporters with comprehensive assistance throughout the process and building up buyer–seller relationships are more effective than isolated actions such as trade missions or fairs.

Partnership countries should simplify and rationalize their investment policies and foreign investment regimes. Multiple investment regimes are offered to investors under different laws and regulations governing the approval, establishment, and operation of enterprises, with often complicated sets of fiscal incentives (as described in the next paragraph). At times, a new investment law is added to introduce a new policy direction or address new investment needs or developments, yet the old laws and the investment regime they govern remain in place. The government may attempt to justify this by saying that it provides policy flexibility and stability for existing investments. However, the multiplicity of investment regimes is too complicated and confusing and is likely to be open to abuse, if not corruption. For example, in Egypt investors can choose from three different investment laws under which to establish their businesses, each with its own conditions and modalities. Partnership countries should adopt one investment law covering all the sectors of the economy, with a few specified exceptions (e.g., the extractive, finance, and utilities sectors). This is the approach currently being pursued in Jordan. Such a law should provide one investment regime driving the necessary rules and regulations to be applied to all businesses. It should be written to offer flexibility and stability for existing investors (e.g., through a stability clause, such as grandfathering). A single investment regime would have the indirect side benefit of being simple and easy to administer. In the interim, the authorities may wish to provide interpretation and clarification of current laws, rules, and regulations to investors when necessary. This would increase transparency, lower the level of uncertainty, and help investors make their decisions.

Partnership countries should also take steps to attract FDI inflows with high potential for technological and employment spillover effects on the domestic economy. Facilitating access to finance, especially for new and potential entrepreneurs who lack working capital, is key for reaping the positive demonstration, competition, and linkage effects of FDI that can help domestic producers upgrade their technologies and practices. This requires far-reaching reforms to improve financial access and stability in Partnership countries (World Bank 2011b). Expanding workers' training by firms could help upgrade the composition of exports toward more technologically advanced products. Given the high share of graduates who are unemployed, such an effort by firms—perhaps supported by active government policies—could yield positive results, both increasing exporters' productivity and reducing employment among skilled people. Strengthening trade and FDI support institutions, such as export promotion and investment agencies, to help private sector firms discover and exploit international market opportunities is another way to enter more sophisticated export markets. This often requires the presence of dedicated public-private representations in the targeted markets. Finally, by offering foreign investors access to a broader regional market, enhanced intra-Arab integration could reinforce the bargaining power of the host location and thereby influence the type of activities being outsourced, as well as the relationships with upstream and downstream domestic producers.

Spillover effects achieve their highest yields when multinationals establish links with local suppliers. An important source of development and technology inflow in developing and emerging economies consists of externalities resulting from the linkages that small local suppliers forge with large multinational corporations. However, various factors affect the extent and quality of these linkages. Banga (2006), in a study of the export-diversifying impact of FDI in India, found that FDI from U.S. investors led to diversification of India's exports while Japanese FDI had no significant impact. The reason seems to be that the U.S. firms have lower intra-firm trade and higher integration with domestic (Indian) firms than do the Japanese firms. This study highlights the importance of taking into account the heterogeneity of FDI according to origin when upgrading is a target. In addition, establishing such linkages often requires complementary government policies aimed at, among other things, domestic financial development. Omran and Bolbol (2003) note that FDI exerts demonstration, competition, and linkage effects on domestic producers that push them to invest in upgrading their technologies and practices. This requires, especially for new and potential entrepreneurs who lack internal funds, the presence of financial institutions that can provide access to external finance and can better allocate and monitor these funds. The development of domestic financial institutions is also crucial in determining to what extent foreign firms can borrow so as to extend their innovative activities to the domestic economy (Hermes and Lensink 2003; Rajan and Zingales 1998). Omran and Bolbol (2003) attribute the disappointing outcome of FDI in Arab countries in part to insufficient reforms to promote domestic financial development.

The prospects of an enhanced intra-Arab integration could help orient FDI toward activities with high technological spillover. Foreign investors look to fundamental economic variables in making decisions about which countries and activities to invest in, and in forging relationships with local producers, but the bargaining power of the host country is also important. For instance, China is able to implement an active selection of FDI and orient these investments toward the needs of its economy. The size of its market undoubtedly helps it do so. Intra-Arab regional integration would offer foreign investors access to the whole regional market instead of just to a single country's market—a more attractive package for foreign investors negotiating conditions of entry. The ability of the host country to influence the choice of activities or, at least, the relationships with upstream and downstream domestic producers is higher under regional integration, as well. Moreover, there may be gains from reducing competition between Arab countries to attract foreign companies. While competition in this context is generally positive, because it goes hand in hand with liberalization of the economy, it can sometimes have perverse consequences. Some countries may be tempted to set up barriers to entry to keep foreign products off their markets in the hope of providing a better incentive (i.e., the prospect of greater profit) to companies to locate in their country. But such strategies never pay off. When all countries adopt the same tactic, the expected individual benefit turns into an inevitable collective loss. The erection of barriers to trade by all the countries in the region makes the region globally less attractive.

Partnership countries should reconsider and streamline the set of incentives currently embodied in various regimes. All Partnership countries, with the exception of Egypt, offer an elaborate set of fiscal incentives to foreign investors. Fiscal incentives may vary according to the legal regime under which a business is established and governed, as well as by sector and by location in the country. Here too, the system is complicated and frequently open to abuse. In addition, the overall majority of fiscal incentives take the form of tax holidays. Studies have shown that in most cases tax holidays are ineffective, meaning that they rarely attract additional investments; they are also redundant, meaning that the investment would have been made in any case, even without the tax break. Because of the way tax holidays are granted, they are more open to abuse than other fiscal incentives. In Egypt, the amount of FDI inflows doubled and corporate income tax revenues increased shortly after the government dropped the old fiscal policy for investment and adopted a new policy of lower corporate income tax, with no incentives (outside the zones). The Partnership countries could draw lessons from international experience with the effectiveness of different types of fiscal incentives over time, including the performance of special economic zones (Farole and Akinci 2011). Such a review would help the authorities decide whether to continue to offer fiscal incentives—and if so, what types—or to do away with fiscal incentives and use the freed-up revenues to improve the investment climate in a way that benefits all investors. For instance, drawing on experiences with special economic zones, particularly as they relate to investment policy or practice, the authorities should consider scaling up the zone experience and making it available to the rest of the economy as part of reforming the national investment climate. Many countries, notably China, essentially piloted their policy reforms in special zones and then rolled them out over time to the rest of the economy.

One simple and practical way to streamline procedures and ease the regulatory burden on foreign investors is to create a one-stop shop. Investors save time when they do not have to travel to multiple government agencies for procedures to establish and maintain a business. According to the IAB indexes, Egypt and Morocco perform better than the global averages in terms of the number of procedures and the time required to establish a business. This was achieved following an effort to clean up some of the procedures and set up a one-stop shop. Yet much remains to be done in all Partnership countries to enhance their attractiveness to investors. The establishment of one-stop shops in Egypt and Morocco was a useful step, yet the procedures themselves remain cumbersome, nontransparent, and time-consuming for investors and administrators alike. The next steps should aim to retain or merge only those procedures that are absolutely necessary and administer them in an efficient manner. This should also be done for many of the recurring operational procedures required for the continuing operation of a business. If further reforms achieve high efficiency, the one-stop shop could eventually become unnecessary.

Another critical consideration for foreign investors making investment destination decisions is ease of access to production factors: industrial land, foreign exchange, and expatriate workers. There is a clear need to make it less difficult to access industrial land or information on land. According to the IAB indexes on this topic, Egypt, Morocco, and Tunisia scored above global averages on the strength of leasing rights in their respective countries, but not on ownership rights. (Jordan and Libya are not currently covered by the IAB indexes.) Egypt and Tunisia are below global averages on access to land information, and Egypt is below average on availability of land information. It takes substantially longer than the global average to lease either private or public land in Morocco, and this has been an impediment to investment. One reason for the establishment of special zones is to bring a temporary solution to the problem of accessing industrial land. Access to foreign exchange and capital and current accounts transfers are also essential to investors, particularly foreign investors, as foreign exchange is needed for imports of production inputs, and foreign investors operate across borders. A key consideration in investment decisions is a foreign exchange policy that guarantees investors a certain level of comfort, ensuring that they will be able to obtain and transfer foreign currencies, including for profit repatriation. Finally, labor and immigration policies and laws need to allow entry of expatriates with special skills and know-how, in reasonable numbers and for a reasonable length of time, to help set up and operate businesses. Foreign investors should be able to select individuals of any nationality to fill these roles.

The Deauville Partnership could offer an opportunity for countries of origin and recipient countries to jointly strengthen institutions in support of FDI. Over the past decade, Egypt, Jordan, Morocco, and Tunisia have made great strides in building up their investment promotion agencies (IPAs) and other FDI-supporting institutions. Each of these four IPAs has gone through more than one transformation and has improved its performance over time, but there is room to strengthen them further. All have experienced tension between their regulatory and promotion missions and functions. As their name suggests, IPAs should put the emphasis on promotion. Unfortunately, as all Partnership countries have complicated investment regimes that require a government institution to monitor or intervene in the establishment of businesses and the granting of incentives, the regulatory function has tended to crowd out the promotion function in their IPAs. For instance, although Egypt's GAFI is a hybrid agency charged with both regulation and promotion, it leans heavily to the regulatory part. As a result, Egypt lacks a true investment promotion function. For all the Partnership countries, a simpler, streamlined investment regime would be more effective, as mentioned earlier, and would allow the IPAs to focus on promotion. In terms of information, each Partnership country has set up a website, typically under the IPA, to provide information to potential and existing investors. All except Libya's are accessible, but all four websites would benefit from improvements. They need to be more user-friendly—to anticipate the types of information investors need and how they wish to access it. They need to contain accurate, complete, up-to-date data, with links to other relevant websites.

Each Partnership country would benefit from a strategic review of its international investment agreements within the context of Agadir and other regional and multilateral agreements. That review should be driven by the strategic foreign economic relationships that the country would like

to engage in—for instance, developing regional value chains in light manufacturing industries—with the goal of making the international investment agreements serve that purpose. This would require effectively implementing any existing BITs and DTTs, particularly those that fit in with the chosen strategy. Support for such an exercise may be offered by multilateral organizations and other Deauville partners. Whether through trade or investment, Partnership countries have tended to look north to the EU, west to the United States, or east to the Gulf. With a few exceptions, international economic relationships among the five Partnership economies have not reached anything close to their potential. The weak intra-regional flow of FDI, as noted earlier, is a case in point. If the Agadir Agreement is to serve its purpose, there is a need to go beyond the set of incentives it offers and make a deliberate effort to explore intrinsic, sustainable economic opportunities of common interest among Partnership countries.

The FDI regime: Key selected recommendations

Short-term:

- Adopt a timetable in Partnership countries for phasing out restrictions on foreign equity participation in all sectors, except for a short list of sectors with high degree of monopoly power, respecting the principle of national treatment.

- Review the impact of the reforms piloted in the special economic or offshore zones in Partnership countries with a view to extending them to the rest of the economy. Consolidate the legal framework for investment under one transparent and predictable investment code.

- Develop a national program to open up to competition and potentially privatize remaining sectors exhibiting monopolistic or quasi-monopolistic behavior, such as telecommunications, insurance, electricity production, postal services, and air transport.

- Improve access to information on land and its availability for business purposes, and take steps to substantially reduce transaction times.

- To enhance the benefits of inward FDI and increase its attractiveness to investors, Egypt should consider strengthening its National Suppliers Development Program by conducting an in-depth review of the program with a view to overhauling it. Morocco should study the establishment of a national suppliers development program in two or three selected sectors, one being the auto industry.

- Develop and implement training programs for government staff at the national and local levels to improve the administration of laws and regulations relevant to FDI, including expatriate work permits, commercial license renewals, infrastructure services, and customs.

(continued on next page)

The FDI regime: Key selected recommendations (*continued*)

Medium-term:

- Negotiate investment provisions in future deep and high-quality trade agreements to increase legal protection and provide a level playing field for investors, including common standards of treatment and rules.

- Review and develop strategic approaches in Partnership countries to international investment agreements to promote insertion in global or regional value chains and implement existing BITs that are not yet in force.

- Support the establishment of effective investor-to-state dispute settlement mechanisms through the arbitration provided for in BITs, when relevant, or through the establishment of a stand-alone arbitration law.

- Strengthen the coverage of expropriation laws in the national legal framework, including the principles of nondiscrimination and compensation. Develop and implement a comprehensive and modern bankruptcy law in Egypt and Jordan.

The Business Climate

Key issues

The benefits from open trade and FDI policy are greater where barriers to business entry have been relaxed, allowing new firms to enter the market and respond to growing export opportunities. A good business climate means that workers, capital, and land can be reallocated to the uses in which their value is greatest. However, firms in Partnership countries still confront a variety of obstacles to contesting new markets, including licensing restrictions, high costs of administrative transactions, and limited access to finance. Survey data show that companies experience wide variation in times taken to gain construction permits, clear customs, or access other administrative services, pointing to favoritism that benefits well-connected firms. Discretionary decision making can reinforce perceptions of exclusion and dampen competition. Indeed, Partnership countries are marked by a low rate of entry and exit in the business sector. Jordan resembles Croatia in population size but recorded five times fewer registrations of new firms during 2004–09.

A number of successful pro-competitive measures, such as Jordan's privatization process, suggest directions for future reform. Recent political changes offer an opportunity to build transparency and freedom of information practices that were lacking before the Arab Spring. The business climate can be improved by delegation of decision making to rule-bound institutions, reducing discretion and opacity, and through stronger reform alliances between government and private stakeholders.

To encourage FDI, a sound domestic investment climate is an essential complement to the foreign investment regime. One of the central challenges in reaping greater benefits from globalization lies in improving the domestic business environment: providing sound regulation of industry that promotes competition, overcoming bureaucratic delay and inefficiency, fighting corruption, and improving the quality of infrastructure. Evidence shows that the impact of trade on living standards is much higher in well-regulated economies than in the most heavily regulated economies. Interestingly, relaxing barriers to business entry as a complementary policy to trade seems more important as a means to improve living standards than relaxing labor restrictions. While the investment climate is clearly important for large, formal sector firms, it is just as important—if not more so—for SMEs and the informal sector, as well as for agricultural productivity and the generation of off-farm employment. Productive private employment is the central pathway out of poverty for workers and their families, so a vibrant and inclusive investment climate is critical to achieving poverty alleviation and social justice. Investment climate refers to the policy and institutional underpinnings of markets, including a broad range of policies and agencies. It also may include services such as infrastructure, or the regulatory framework for its provision.

Trade and FDI reforms cannot yield their full benefit in terms of economic development without complementary investment climate reforms. In MENA, the past decade has demonstrated that trade liberalization without reforms to improve the functioning of domestic markets and services will not generate substantial employment. Companion policies are needed to strengthen the investment climate and relax behind-the-border constraints, especially in trade-related services. These constraints increase the cost of doing business and limit the attractiveness of MENA as a place to invest (Dasgupta et al. 2002). Trade liberalization through the lowering of tariffs changes price signals to entrepreneurs and thus, in theory, their behavior, but only if other factors do not impede either the signal or their ability to respond. If trade is liberalized but product markets are not flexible, workers, capital, and land cannot be reallocated to markets or sectors where they are valued most highly. According to a study of Morocco and Tunisia, welfare gains from trade reforms under conditions of flexible factor markets can be as much as six times the gains under a rigid factor market scenario (figure 4.1). This is because while trade reforms may improve the incentive structure for resource reallocation, the extent to which resources move from less efficient to more efficient sectors of an economy depends on the degree of flexibility of factor markets (Dennis 2006). The implication is that addressing rigidities in labor, capital, and land markets should be considered an integral part of

FIGURE 4.1

Estimated Welfare Benefits of Trade Reforms in Tunisia and Morocco under Restrictive and Flexible Labor Markets

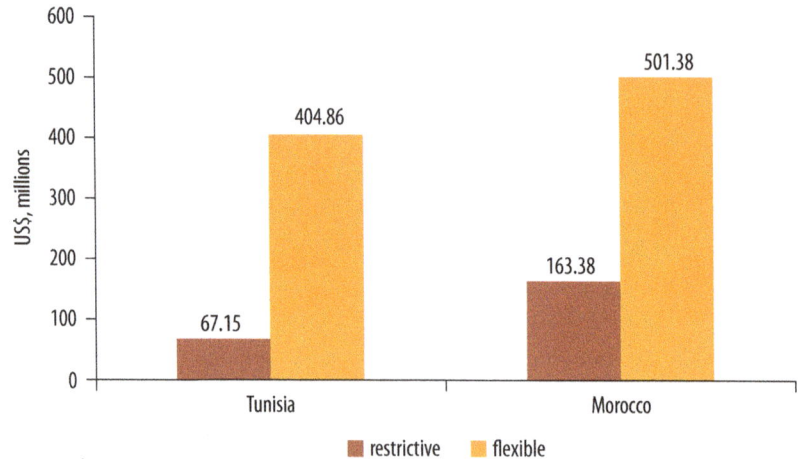

Source: Dennis 2006.

trade and structural reforms designed to promote growth and employment.

The benefits of trade liberalization risk being stifled in the absence of competitive product markets. As observed in Egypt and Tunisia, the co-alescence of political, economic, and military interests can lead to the accumulation of market power and its abuse. Abuses of power can include domestic and international cartels or price-fixing agreements; interfirm agreements that restrict pricing, market partner choice, or purchase choice; control of key inputs or distribution channels; or abuse of domi-nant position, for example through predatory pricing. Such exercises of market power deny consumers the benefits of international competition and insulate producers from having (or wanting) to respond to interna-tional price signals. Public policies too may restrain competition, includ-ing through various barriers to entry. These include the above-mentioned nontariff measures; antidumping laws; investment policies such as exclu-sionary lists, ownership restrictions, or licensing restrictions; and restric-tive sectoral regulations. Indeed, inappropriate regulation, whether de jure or de facto, can completely suppress the benefits of trade liberaliza-tion (Bolaky and Freund 2004).[2] Markets may also be segmented by transportation and transaction costs, by public policies, or by a number of anticompetitive business practices, each of which can protect incumbent firms from competition (and can inhibit new foreign investment) while limiting efficiency and consumer welfare gains from liberalization (Khemani 1997). Without an integrated approach to competition—one that embraces trade, regulation, and investment policies—the objectives of resource mobility, productivity gains, and improved consumer welfare may remain unrealized.

Similarly, in the absence of domestic competition and factor mobility, the benefits of FDI may be muted. To be sure, FDI in natural resource sectors (such as extractive industries) may be impervious to economic and political conditions and therefore somewhat insensitive to domestic investment climate conditions (Walsh and Yu 2010).[3] However, investment climate conditions matter a great deal in Partnership countries as they seek to develop their manufacturing and services sectors and diversify their economies. A recent analysis of FDI in the MENA region concludes that FDI is sensitive not only to market size, availability of natural resources, and level of foreign trade, but also to institutional and legal factors, including the levels of corruption, contract volatility, expropriation risk, ease of repatriation of profits, and payment delays (Mohamed and Sidiropoulos 2010).

Internationally, surveys show that certain investment climate variables matter most to foreign investors in choosing where to locate. For example, a 2002 international investor survey by the Multilateral Investment Guarantee Agency (MIGA) found that "market access" was the leading priority for foreign investors in their site selection, cited as critical by 77 percent of respondents. It was followed by "a stable political environment" (64 percent), "ease of doing business" (54 percent), and "reliability and quality of infrastructure and utilities" (50 percent). Other significant factors included availability of technical professionals and managers and the level of corruption (MIGA 2002). In addition, export orientation can be shaped by domestic conditions. For example, a recent Maghreb study revealed that a firm's export status depends in part on factors such as managers' education, the presence of quality certification, and the availability of export finance or overdraft facilities (Marchat 2011). In short, foreign investors are sensitive to multiple aspects of the domestic investment climate that go well beyond laws and policies directly governing trade and FDI.

Market Contestability

Barriers to firm entry and to sound competition—some due to government policies, and others to the discriminatory way in which rules are implemented and enforced—are key impediments to the emergence of a dynamic private sector in Partnership countries (World Bank 2009). At the policy level, while MENA governments have generally moved ahead on macroeconomic and tariff reform, regulatory reform came late, accelerating only after 2005. In spite of tariff reform, nontariff barriers and, especially, restrictions on trade in services persisted (Borchert, Gootiiz, and Mattoo 2012). States have been slow to withdraw from ownership in productive sectors. Elements of the legal system and commercial code have been overtaken by the evolution of corporations and transactions (De Meneval and Hanafy 2010). Governments have generally remained starkly opaque and, until the Arab Spring, have resisted freedom of information and other transparency measures. While progress in reforming the rules varies among countries, the region as a whole suffers from discretionary and arbitrary implementation of policies and from lack of political will to bring about real change in a deeply rooted status quo of privileges, including unequal treatment of investors.

In many countries, the problem is not insufficient or missing reforms, but rather their poor record of implementation. There is also a widespread belief that business regulations as they appear on the books do not apply equally to all. For instance, competition and commercial laws have been promulgated and competition agencies established in all the Partnership countries except Libya, but these have had little effect in terms of effective market contestability and competition on the ground (box 4.2). In multiple policy arenas, such as regulatory enforcement, markets for finance and land, and targeted programs of enterprise support or industrial policy, there is a substantial gap between stated policies and their implementation by institutions, which may engage in substantial discretion and favoritism. Thus, rules that are imperfect to begin with are subject to unequal and discretionary implementation and enforcement, hindering private sector development in the region.

Consequently, the region enjoys less competition than others, and the response of private investment to past reforms has been weaker than in other regions (figure 4.2). This is a sign that governments do not enjoy strong credibility with investors, who lack confidence that seemingly probusiness reforms will be applied to them fairly, predictably, and equitably. In terms of inclusiveness and coordination of policy making in the competitiveness area, Morocco and Egypt have already taken steps to address those issues: the Moroccan National Committee on Investment Climate (CNEA) and the Egyptian Regulatory Reform and Development Activity (ERRADA) provide a good model for the design and monitoring of investment climate reforms.

Favoritism and lack of competition are reflected in the characteristics of the region's firms. Figure 4.3 shows that Partnership countries have strikingly low firm entry densities when compared to other emerging economies with available data. Entry density is measured by the number of newly registered firms per 1,000 people ages 15–64. Data are available for 80 countries, and only 26 of these 80 countries, for example, had an entry density below that of Jordan. Croatia's working-age population is comparable in size to Jordan's, but the average number of newly regis-

BOX 4.2

Competition Laws and Competition Agencies in Partnership Countries

Competition policy is a natural complement to trade liberalization as a means to foster efficiency and resource mobility in domestic markets. With the exception of Libya, all Partnership countries have enacted a competition law and have a competition policy in place. Tunisia has had a competition law since 1991, Morocco since 2000, Jordan since 2004, and Egypt since 2005 (see table B4.2.1).

A recent review of competition policies in the region notes substantial progress by these authorities, but also some constraints to their efficacy (Sengupta and Mehta 2011). First, the competition agencies that have been established under the competition laws generally lack autonomy. They report to key political figures—the minister of trade or the prime minister—who retain final decision-making authority over prosecutions and, in some cases, budget and staffing. This invites political interference or simply constrains action in some areas, especially as regards the substantial role of state monopolies, state-owned industries, and policy-induced barriers to investment or entry. In addition, some competition agencies lack a mandate to carry out important roles. For example, in Egypt, the Competition Authority lacks a mandate to block mergers and acquisitions that would harm competition. Several of the authorities have not fully developed their role as policy advocates, and most have done relatively little to engage civil society stakeholders or effectively educate the public.

TABLE B4.2.1

Competition Laws and Agencies in Deauville Partnership Countries

Country	Competition law?	Legislation	Year of enactment	Competition agency	Since
Egypt, Arab Rep.	Yes	Law No. 3 of 2005, Law on the Protection of Competition and the Prohibition of Monopolistic Practices	2005	Egyptian Competition Authority	2005
Jordan	Yes	Competition Law No. 33 of 2004 (Provisional Law in 2002)	2004	Competition Directorate	2002
Libya	No	n.a.	n.a.	None	n.a.
Morocco	Yes	Competition (Antitrust), Law No. 06-99 of 2000	2000	Directorate of Competition and Prices & Competition Council	2001
Tunisia	Yes	Law No. 91-64 of 1991, on Competition and Prices	1991	Directorate General for Competition and Economic Surveys & Competition Council	1991

Sources: For Egypt, Jordan, Morocco, and Tunisia: Sengupta and Mehta 2011. For Libya: International Bar Association's Global Competition Forum.

Note: n.a. = not applicable.

(continued on next page)

BOX 4.2 *Continued*

In addition, most Arab countries have adopted commercial codes that include similar rules on key aspects of business law, including commercial contracts, registration of merchants, registration and governance of corporations (corporate law), means of payment, collateral, and insolvency and bankruptcy. These codes and laws, developed in the 1950s, are largely based on similar contract and commercial law principles of French origin, with adaptation to the local context and application of Shariah principles. A failure to keep up with evolving commercial practices means that most regional commercial codes suffer from structural flaws and numerous gaps: these include lack of adaptation to the latest banking and financing practices, cumbersome company registration procedures, ambiguous corporate governance rules, gaps in the collateral framework, and absence of implementing decrees. More generally, legal provisions relating to creditors, debtors, investors, and corporate managers often fail to clarify their respective rights and duties. Since the 1990s, most Arab countries have taken steps individually to reactivate and modernize their commercial codes and/or corporate laws, often with little success. Reformers across the regions tended to look separately for best international practices without acknowledging that common challenges could share common solutions. These efforts have rarely been successful due to weak local legal capacity and the complexity of the task. In fact, several reform initiatives implemented by Arab countries ended up lowering the quality and predictability of commercial rules in the region (De Meneval and Hanafy 2010).

FIGURE 4.2

Investment Response to Policy Reforms in Selected Regions

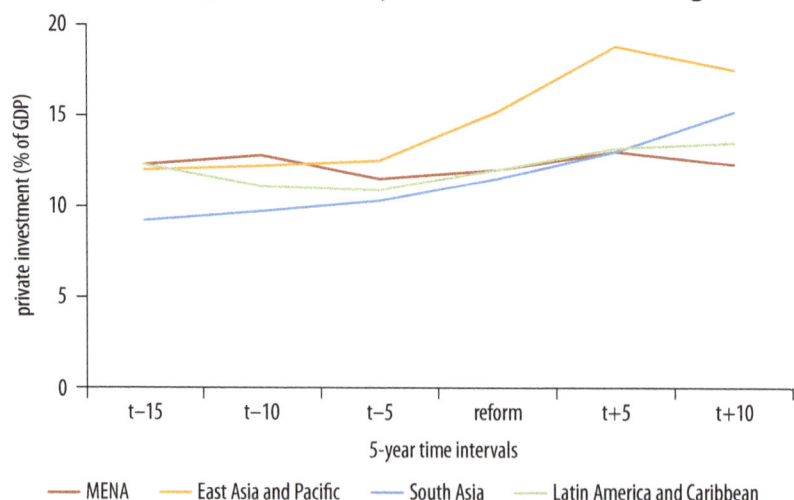

Source: World Bank 2009.

FIGURE 4.3

Average Entry Density for Selected Emerging Economies, 2004–09

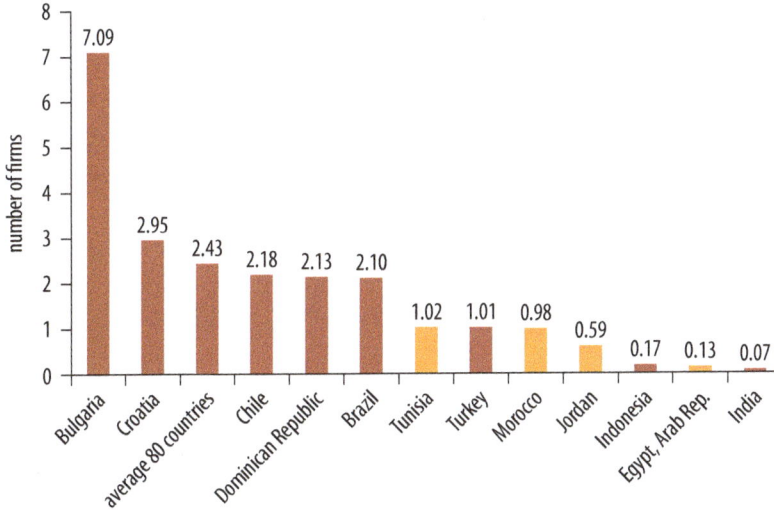

Source: Klapper and Love 2010.

Note: Entry density measures the number of newly registered limited liability firms per 1,000 population of working age (15–64).

tered firms in Croatia was almost five times higher in 2004–09. In our sample of emerging economies, only India and Indonesia had lower entry densities than MENA countries, and this was mainly due to India's and Indonesia's high shares of rural population and nonregistered (informal) firms. This situation is an unambiguous symptom of the MENA region's discriminatory business environment that favors established and connected firms and impedes firm entry or exit, thus distorting the process of "creative destruction" that could lead to job creation and technological upgrading. Enterprise surveys yield other indicators of lack of dynamism, including older than average firms and older than average senior managers of firms (World Bank 2009).

Doing Business

Partnership countries have mixed performance on a number of key indicators that measure the ease of doing business. According to the World Bank's 2012 Doing Business index, regulations typically impose significant barriers or burdens on firms, especially SMEs, which constitute the bulk of enterprises in every Partnership country. Egypt excels with respect to starting a business but lags in terms of getting construction permits, obtaining credit, enforcing contracts, and resolving insolvency. Jordan fares better than most countries with respect to getting electricity and paying taxes, but lags behind most in getting credit, enforcing contracts, and protecting investors. Morocco, which set a record for Doing Business reforms in 2011, has relatively efficient procedures for import and export (trading across borders), but lags in registering property, paying taxes, and getting electricity. Tunisia performs well across a variety of categories, led by trading across borders, resolving insolvency, getting electricity, and protecting investors. Libya is especially fast in granting construction permits and exceptionally weak in starting a business, registering property, and getting credit; in several other categories it cannot be rated.

The de jure business environment only partially explains the Partnership countries' lackluster performance in higher-value-added activities. When it comes to business regulations on the books, the Partnership countries are comparable to the more dynamic emerging economies of East Asia, Eastern Europe, and Latin America (table 4.4). The de jure regulations can at best only partly explain the Partnership countries' inferior performance relative to these countries. Discretion and favoritism in the implementation of rules and regulations in Partnership countries distorts the level playing field among nominal competitors and increases uncertainty for less-connected firms or potential new investors. Both the lack of competition and the higher uncertainty prevent firms from investing in new, riskier, higher-value-added products or technologies, resulting in a lack of economic dynamism. Thus, for many policy areas, the challenge is not necessarily to change legal regulations but to implement existing ones consistently and predictably for all firms.

Firm survey results for Morocco and Jordan reveal large variations in government officials' implementation of legal regulations across firms in

TABLE 4.4

Doing Business Rankings for Deauville Partnership Countries, 2011

Country	Overall	Starting a business	Dealing with construction permits	Registering property	Getting credit	Protecting investors	Paying taxes	Trading across borders	Enforcing contracts
Tunisia	46	56	86	65	98	46	64	32	76
Morocco	94	93	75	144	98	97	112	43	89
Jordan	96	95	93	101	150	122	21	58	130
Egypt, Arab Rep.	110	21	154	93	78	79	145	64	147
MENA	93	98	91	82	119	95	62	79	114

Source: World Bank Doing Business database, http://www.doingbusiness.org/rankings.
Note: The Doing Business index ranks economies from 1 to 183. For each economy, the rank is calculated as the simple average of the percentile rankings on each of 10 topics: starting a business, dealing with construction permits, registering property, getting credit, protecting investors, paying taxes, trading across borders, enforcing contracts, resolving insolvency, and, new in 2012, getting electricity. It does not account for an economy's proximity to large markets, the quality of its infrastructure services (other than services related to trading across borders and getting electricity), the strength of its financial system, the security of property from theft and looting, macroeconomic conditions, or the strength of underlying institutions (see World Bank 2011a).

both countries, relative to most other emerging economies. Table 4.5 summarizes the averages and dispersion of the number of days that firms had to wait for different regulatory services across countries. The average wait time to obtain a construction permit or import license or to clear customs for imports is among the lowest in Indonesia, Jordan, and Morocco. The firm survey results confirm that legal business regulations are, on average, relatively competitive in Jordan and Morocco.[4] However, there exist large variations across firms in both countries: the coefficient of variation in wait times for different regulatory services is higher than in most other emerging economies. In particular, the dispersion (uncertainty) of wait time for imports to clear customs, to obtain a construction permit, or to obtain an operating or import license across firms is among the highest in Jordan.[5]

Uncertainty about policy implementation discourages new entrants and imposes substantial costs on most incumbent firms, which have to undertake costly mitigating actions. The large variations in firms' access to regulatory services may stem in part from differences in the ways that public officials carry out their administrative duties. However, there is evidence that they also reflect the privileged access of a subset of firms, typically large, politically connected firms. To mitigate the higher uncertainty they face, less-connected firms pay bribes and spend more management time dealing with officials, showing that connections do indeed pay off.

In sum, the lack of market contestability and the difficulty of doing business help explain the poor yield of past reforms in Partnership coun-

TABLE 4.5

Averages and Dispersion (Coefficients of Variation) of Firms' Days Waiting for Regulatory Services in Jordan, Morocco, and Selected Comparators

Country	Average (days)				Country	Coefficient of variation			
	Construction permit	Operating license	Import license	Clear customs imports		Construction permit	Operating license	Import license	Clear customs imports
Indonesia	32	21	11	3	Bulgaria	1.04	1.59	1.17	1.10
Jordan	**43**	**6**	**5**	**9**	Brazil	1.31	1.14	1.25	1.10
Morocco	**61**	**4**	—	**4**	Indonesia	1.93	1.43	0.94	1.09
Croatia	182	26	12	2	India	1.33	1.40	1.82	1.02
India	28	29	15	14	Croatia	1.25	1.69	1.27	1.25
Bulgaria	94	62	21	3	Turkey	1.65	2.88	1.67	1.34
Turkey	42	37	21	10	**Morocco**	**1.72**	**1.87**	—	**1.46**
Brazil	139	83	43	15	**Jordan**	**1.75**	**2.33**	**2.14**	**1.50**

Source: World Bank Investment Climate Assessments in various years.

Note: Survey question: "What was the wait, in days, to obtain a construction permit, operating license, or import license, or to clear customs for imports?" The dispersions across firms are measured by the coefficient of variation (standard deviation divided by the mean). — = not available.

tries. Partnership countries have undertaken significant economic and trade liberalization reforms since the 1990s, with major privatization programs, important incentives for FDI and export-oriented firms, and the signing of free trade agreements. Despite these efforts, private investment in the region has remained stagnant and below the average of most other regions (figure 4.4). Although there are some differences between the countries in level and trend, the average level of domestic private investment has remained low in all five countries (between 7 percent of GDP in Jordan and 15 percent in Tunisia, on average). If one discounts investments in real estate and, in some countries, investments made by state-owned enterprises, the rates are even lower. This can be seen as reflecting a lack of confidence on the part of domestic investors in their governments and economic policies and a high level of risk aversion in the context of widespread corruption, arbitrariness, and even predation. The important share of domestic investments going to the less risky and exposed real estate sector in Tunisia, where the homeowner ratio is twice as high as in the Federal Republic of Germany, is another indicator of the negative impact of corruption and discretion on the business environment. In spite of an average record of policy reforms, the investment response in the MENA region has been weaker than in other regions. The

FIGURE 4.4

Trends and Composition of Private Investment

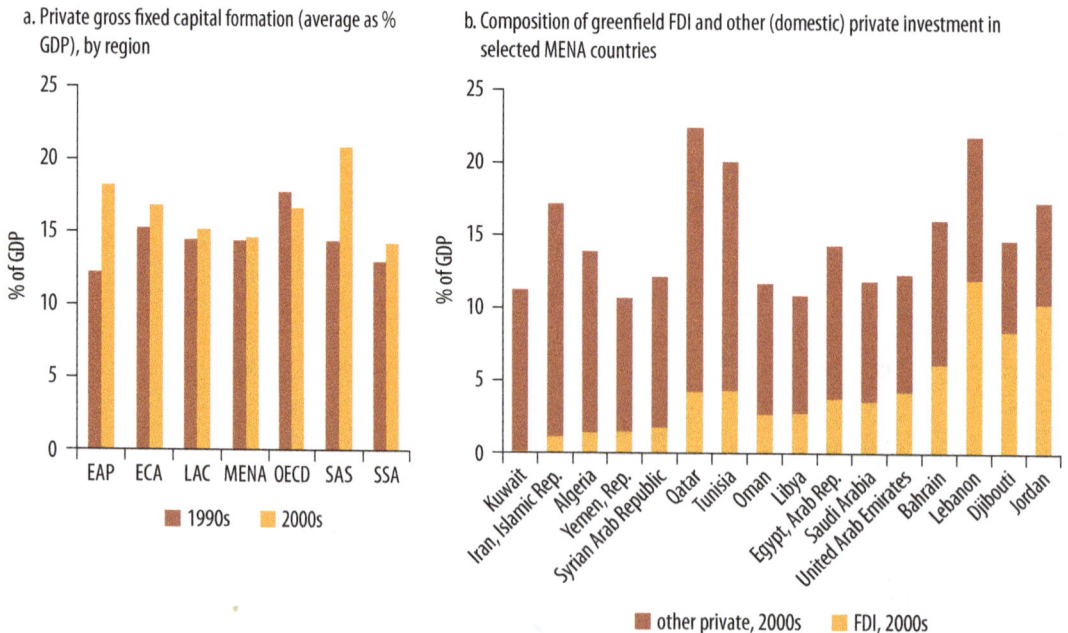

a. Private gross fixed capital formation (average as % GDP), by region

b. Composition of greenfield FDI and other (domestic) private investment in selected MENA countries

Source: World Bank, 2011c.

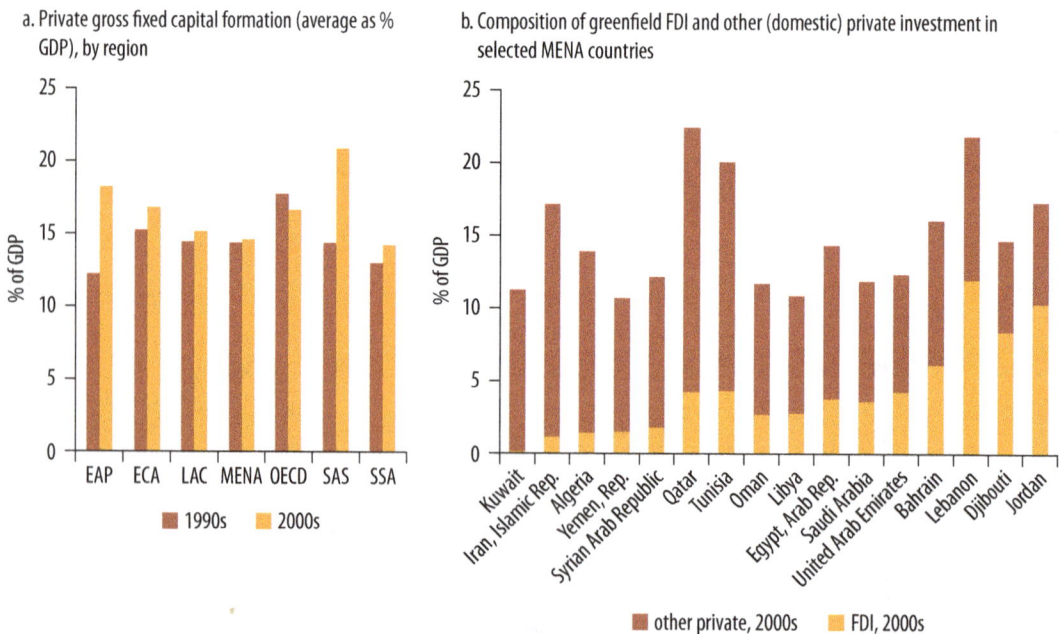

Legend (panel a): ■ 1990s ■ 2000s

Legend (panel b): ■ other private, 2000s ■ FDI, 2000s

region has lagged in terms of private investment rates, economic diversification, and technological sophistication of exports.

As a result, Partnership countries suffer from a lack of overall competitiveness in almost all dimensions rated by the World Economic Forum
(WEF) in its *Global Competitiveness Report*, perhaps with the exception of
health and primary education (figure 4.5). Where these countries lag
most is in the area of innovation—the single most important indicator of
vibrancy and creativity in societies. Tunisia, the top performer among the
four, ranked at 40, but it suffered an eight-place drop in ranking, reflecting "instability of the business environment," "heightened awareness of a
number of challenges," "a less favorable assessment of the quality of public and private institutions," institutions that are perceived as "more prone
to government corruption and favoritism," and a judiciary that is "less
independent." The biggest drop after its revolution was in security, but
its weakest general rating is in labor market efficiency. However, Tunisia
continued to perform well in a number of dimensions, including health,
education, and macroeconomic policy. Jordan declined slightly to rank at
71, lagging in labor market efficiency and macroeconomic management.
Morocco, ranked at 73, advanced slightly but lags in terms of the efficiency of its labor markets and education and training. The Arab awaken-

FIGURE 4.5

Global Competitiveness Report Ratings for Deauville Partnership Countries, 2011–12

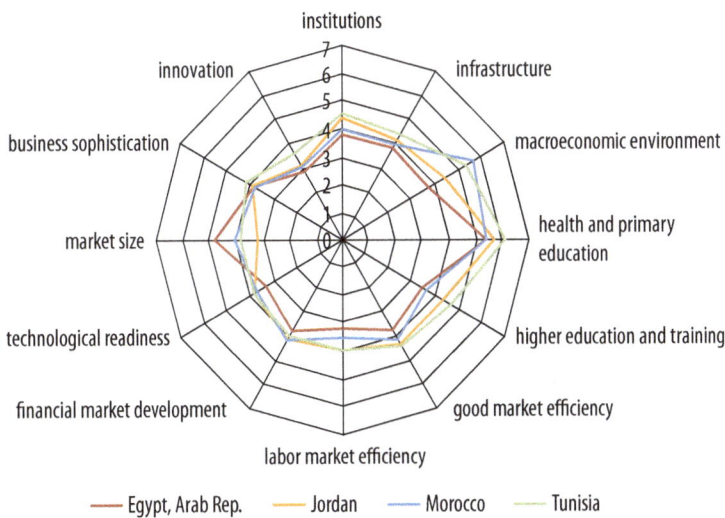

Source: WEF 2011.

Note: Higher numbers signify higher performance.

ing also brought a lower rating for Egypt, ranked at 94, which faces "several competitive challenges." These include its inefficient labor market and weak educational system, as well as its macroeconomic situation.

Labor markets in Partnership countries continue to face challenges in terms of supply and flexibility. As middle-income countries move up the value chain, the demand for skilled workers, technicians, and managers has grown ahead of the ability and responsiveness of the educational system to supply them (figure 4.6). With respect to education, while Jordan performed better than the average of middle-income countries, other Partnership countries lagged in terms of educational quality and efficiency, with Morocco and Libya facing particular challenges. Although labor markets are fairly flexible from an operational standpoint, Partnership countries have not generally introduced unemployment insurance, relying instead on severance restrictions and payments.

In spite of rapid recent progress, the financial sector in the MENA region is not yet fully equipped to serve the financial needs of firms, especially SMEs. The recent MENA financial sector flagship report from the World Bank observed the low share of total lending going to SMEs in this region (figure 4.7). Guarantee schemes designed to enhance SME access to finance (except in Jordan) are skewed toward larger average

FIGURE 4.6

Integrated Index for Educational Access, Equity, Efficiency, and Quality in Selected MENA Countries

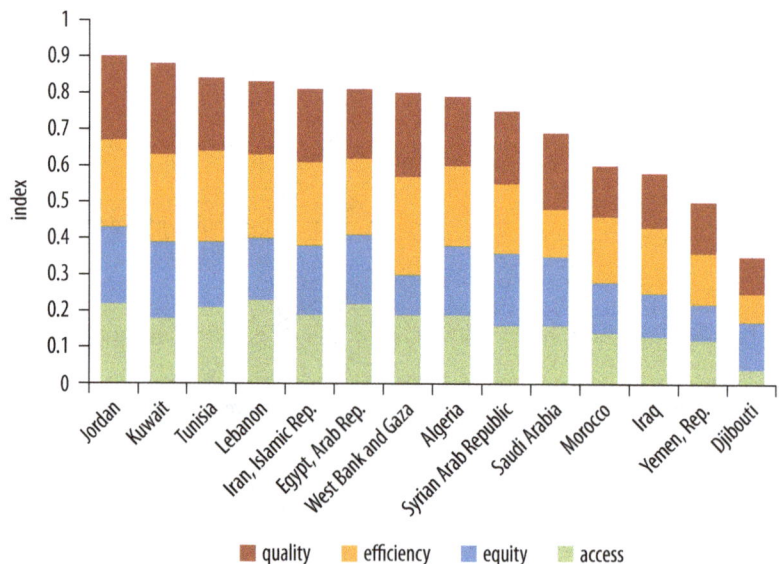

Source: World Bank 2008.

loans than in other regions (Hassani, Arvai, and Rocha 2010). The identified agenda for financial inclusion includes strengthening collateral systems and making them more efficient, extending credit information systems (including to cover microfinance institutions), improving banking techniques for risk assessment and risk management, removing regulations that deter bank lending to small business borrowers, establishing a clear legal and regulatory basis for commercial microfinance, and creating the legal basis for innovative finance with regulatory space for the use of agents and mobile phone technology and for a finance company model for microcredit and leasing (Pearce 2010). There remains substantial room to strengthen the legal and institutional underpinnings for nonbank finance, as well as to promote better corporate governance.

Looking forward, Partnership countries face a wide range of policy challenges for which there are no simple answers (table 4.6). Whatever their country-specific priorities, Partnership countries will need to develop a three-pronged strategy: they must effectively foster competition and limit opportunities for rent seeking, build strong market institutions, and mobilize key stakeholders and broad sectors of the public to support a long-term strategy. With the proper regulatory environment, governments can encourage entry of foreign and domestic investors alike in all

FIGURE 4.7

SME Loans as Share of Total Loans in Selected MENA Countries, 2009

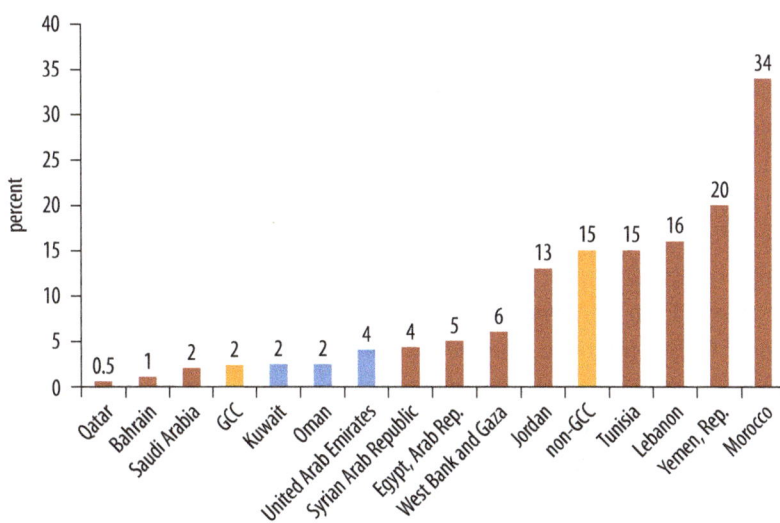

Source: Rocha et al. 2010.

Note: Reported numbers are weighted averages. Non-GCC average includes Iraqi banks that were not reported in the chart, as the coverage in Iraq is not more than 30 percent.

TABLE 4.6

Leading Constraints, by Country, from the World Bank's Investment Climate Survey (ICS) and the World Economic Forum's Global Competitiveness Report (GCR) Executive Opinion Survey

Egypt, Arab Rep. (ICS Update 2011)	Egypt, Arab Rep. (GCR 2011/12)	Jordan (ICS 2007)	Jordan (GCR 2011/12)	Morocco (2009)	Morocco (GCR 2011/12)	Tunisia (GCR 2011/12)	Libya (ICS 2010)
Macroeconomic uncertainty	Policy instability	Macro-economic uncertainty	Inefficient government bureaucracy	Tax rates	Access to financing	Inefficient government bureaucracy	Access to land
Political instability	Inadequately educated workforce	Tax rates	Access to financing	Access to land	Corruption	Access to financing	Regulatory policy uncertainty
Regulatory policy uncertainty	Access to financing	Political instability	Tax rates	Electricity	Inadequate supply of infrastructure	Government instability/ coups	Access to financing (e.g., collateral)
Corruption	Inefficient government bureaucracy	Business licensing and permits	Corruption	Practices of competitors in the informal sector	Inefficient government bureaucracy	Policy instability	Macroeconomic uncertainty (e.g., inflation, exchange rate)
Practices of competitors in the informal sector	Restrictive labor regulations	Corruption	Tax regulations	Access to finance	Tax rates	Restrictive labor regulations	Tax rates

Sources: World Bank, Investment Climate Surveys, and World Economic Forum, Global Competitiveness Report Executive Opinion Surveys, various years.

sectors of the economy by removing formal and informal barriers to competition. In conjunction with the governance agenda discussed above, substantial decision-making power over economic outcomes could be delegated to strong, rule-bound market institutions to reduce discretion and opacity, improve the quality of services provided to firms—hence reducing transaction costs—and increase transparency and accountability of all public bodies that interact with the private sector and regulate markets. Strong market institutions would also ensure equity in market governance, thereby reducing de jure and de facto barriers to competition.

A new form of partnership is also needed in each country between the government and the main stakeholders to underpin stronger reform alliances and broader participation in designing, implementing, and evaluating policies. Capable and inclusive business associations and an institutionalized, transparent, and inclusive process for private sector consultation should be engaged in the identification of policy issues, the design of reforms, and the monitoring and evaluation of their implementation.

The business climate: Key selected recommendations

Short-term:

- Modernize commercial codes in Partnership countries, adapt them to the latest banking and finance practices, and simplify company registration.

- Establish and/or strengthen public-private consultation mechanisms in Partnership countries to design, implement, evaluate, and monitor public policies and reforms.

Medium-term:

- Invest in capable, rule-bound market institutions to underpin the proper functioning of markets in Partnership countries, including regulatory authorities and public service providers. Such institutions should operate under the principles of transparency and accountability for results.

- Address existing policy gaps with respect to ease of doing business in Partnership countries and improve market access and contestability by removing barriers to entry, exit, and competition.

Economic Governance

Key issues

Partnership countries are engaged in ambitious and far-reaching efforts to improve the voice and participation of citizens and to create effective mechanisms for them to hold decision makers to account. Indeed, the governance challenges that prevailed before the Arab Spring, centered around exclusionary and opaque decision making that fostered corruption, was a key factor in the failure of past reform efforts to yield the growth and job creation expected of them. Empirical studies show that improved voice and accountability mechanisms can be strongly associated with higher long-term growth rates. As with successful transitions in Eastern Europe and East Asia, improved democratic and administrative safeguards can foster private sector confidence in a predictable business environment, promoting investment.

In general, Partnership countries have sufficient legal and administrative provisions for greatly improved economic governance, but they lack effective and credible enforcement of these rules. Competition authorities, tax and customs authorities, and anticorruption

(continued on next page)

Key issues *(continued)*

agencies have in the past been undermined by regulatory capture. Delegating power to key economic bodies, while ensuring a transparent and merit-based appointment of senior officials, can increase trust in impartial decision making. Practices concerning conflicts of interest, income and asset disclosure, and complaints mechanisms can reinforce accountability, while public performance contracts can be used to bind agencies based on objective and verifiable performance indicators.

Governance reforms are often difficult because beneficiaries of the status quo are better organized and more vocal than constituencies that lose out. To strengthen administrative integrity, experience suggests that one must address the chain of anticorruption actors, from investigation and prosecution to protection of whistleblowers. Moreover, transparency and access to information can be a powerful lever for reform, aligning leaders' incentives more closely with the interests of citizens through monitoring and scrutiny of official decisions. Partnership countries could benefit from the experience of countries that have adopted action plans documenting steps toward open government information and decision making, and from joining relevant international initiatives.

Modern governance principles of transparency, accountability, and participation in the decision-making process, along with solid anticorruption frameworks, are determinants of more productive economies that are capable of sustainable and long-term development. The interconnections between well-functioning markets, a healthy business environment, and democratic governance are a key consideration in addressing the structural weaknesses of past governance and development models in Partnership countries. Previous reform efforts aimed at liberalizing trade and investment and improving the business environment have failed to take this more holistic approach. Their outcomes were undermined by broad and unaddressed governance deficiencies, institutional weaknesses, and political economy issues. Most Partnership countries now acknowledge this fact, as evidenced by the focus on governance and private sector–led growth and investment in their Deauville action plans and by the overhaul of governance structures, initiated notably in Tunisia and Morocco.

The literature provides ample evidence of the detrimental impact of bad economic governance on growth and investment and the gains to be realized from good governance. Douglas North's historical analysis of the transition from natural states to open societies, which use economic competition rather than political institutions and rents to regulate social relations, is highly relevant here (North, Wallis, and Weingast 2009). It offers an illuminating framework in which to analyze the political economy issues of state capture, cronyism, and violence experienced in many MENA countries. Tunisia is a case in point. As a first step toward a more open society, the Tunisian people have reclaimed their citizenship rights and demanded equal access to economic and social opportunities. The next step toward more sustainable economic development outcomes consists of creating accountable and transparent political and economical institutions. Examples abound in which countries have achieved higher growth and improved welfare after modernizing their institutions, as was the case in the United Kingdom, Botswana, Chile, and Korea (Acemoglu and Robinson 2010). Some of these transformations took place in democracies, others in more autocratic regimes, and still others in both, as in Spain. The relationship between good governance and growth seems to transcend any particular political system as long as political parties are institutionalized, allowing for the contestability and smooth transition of leadership (Gehlbach and Keefer 2011). Such political institutionalization reduces the risk of corruption and discretion, enhances accountability and transparency, and fosters greater voice and accountability—three key governance challenges that are paramount in many MENA countries.

Discretion and Corruption

One revelation from the revolutions in Egypt and Tunisia was the degree and extent of discretionary decision making and corruption in the former regimes. The Tunisian and Egyptian development models favored an elite composed of closely linked politicians and business figures (Galal 2011). This collusion affected every sphere of society, influencing, for example, the selection of firms to win public tenders, regions to receive development projects, SMEs to receive loans, or individuals to be employed by the civil service or granted permits for street vending. Many governments in MENA countries were personalized and authoritarian and owed their longevity to a skewed social contract—the "authoritarian bargain"—in which citizens relinquished political freedom in exchange for public goods. Many regimes in the MENA region used welfare spending to circumvent pressures to liberalize politically.

Putting aside the more normative and deontological aspects of corruption, high levels of discretion and corruption can only have strong deterrent effects on trade, investment, and economic growth. Cross-country studies suggest that countries with lower discretion and corruption, as measured by the quality of institutions, achieved on average (and controlling for other factors) higher economic growth (figure 4.8). The growth premium of moving from the low- to the high-quality institution group

FIGURE 4.8

Control of Corruption and per Capita Income, Selected Countries, 2009

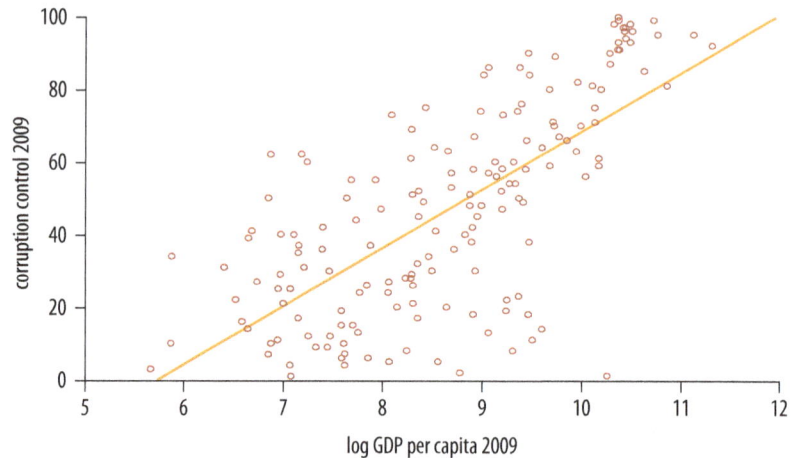

Sources: World Bank, World Development Indicators 2011; World Bank, Worldwide Governance Indicators, http://info.worldbank.org/governance/wgi/index.asp.

Note: Higher scores indicate better control of corruption.

has been estimated at 26 percent in the short run and 40 percent in the long run (Aidt, Dutta, and Sena 2008). Obviously, the causal link and the quantitative estimates need to be viewed with caution. Nonetheless, the Arab awakening illustrates what can happen when political leaders optimize rent extraction under a rigid system of constraints: citizens protect themselves by sheltering in the informal sector but may eventually move to depose the greedy rulers, either through elections or, when that avenue is blocked, through a coup or revolution (Ferejohn 1986).

Excessive administrative discretion in the implementation of rules and regulations has been a hallmark of the MENA region, making it prone to corruption. According to Transparency International, among world regions, only Eastern Europe and Central Asia have a higher perception of corruption than the MENA region (figure 4.9). This perception is confirmed by firm surveys conducted by the World Bank in different regions. They indicate that corruption is indeed a major constraint for firms in MENA countries, which has the highest regional level of corruption after South Asia (figure 4.10). More than half the firms surveyed in MENA countries cite corruption as a major impediment to doing business. Another source of rankings is the WEF's *Global Competitiveness Report*, which contains an executive opinion survey on ethics and corruption. It further confirms the seriousness of corruption in Partnership countries and the

FIGURE 4.9

Transparency International Corruption Perceptions Index for MENA Countries and Selected Comparators, 2011

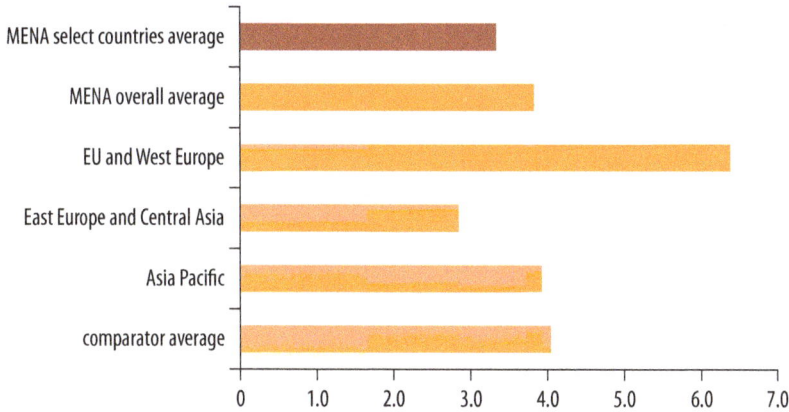

Source: Transparency International, Corruption Perception Index, 2011.

Note: Comparator average represents the combined average of Poland, Georgia, Turkey, the Czech Republic, and Azerbaijan. The scale is from 0 to 10, with lower numbers signifying a higher perception of corruption.

FIGURE 4.10

Perceptions of Corruption in World Bank Enterprise Surveys, by Region

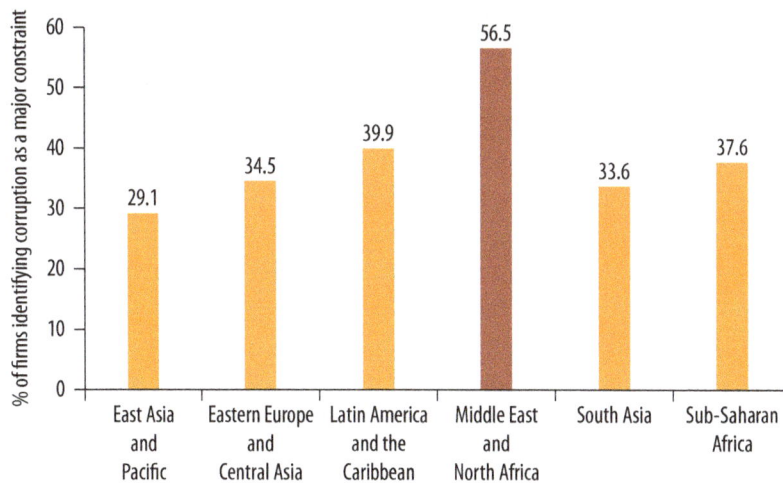

Source: International Finance Corporation, Enterprise Survey Data, http://www.enterprisesurveys.org.

Note: Regional averages are computed by taking a simple average of country-level point estimates. For each economy, only the latest available year of survey data is used in this computation.

diverging trend with comparator countries in recent years. Indeed, the WEF survey shows a negative trend in most Partnership countries over the last five years, despite the fact that all countries have ratified the United Nations Convention against Corruption. This calls into question the effectiveness of past anticorruption strategies, which have essentially focused on high-level international commitments without the necessary enforcement mechanism or on creation of toothless anticorruption institutions.

The Partnership countries are characterized by a considerable gap between the legal frameworks for combating corruption and their actual implementation. Governance indicators of de jure and de facto measures for Morocco, Egypt, and Jordan indicate "very weak" implementation of anticorruption frameworks, illustrating the extent of unequal legal discretion in enforcement within these countries.[6] Tunisia never adopted the implementing regulations for its legal framework and had no anticorruption body. Until the recent constitutional revision, Morocco's anticorruption institution focused on advocacy and lacked autonomy. Recent reforms undertaken in Morocco, Tunisia, and Jordan aim at fully implementing their international commitments and strengthening the effectiveness and transparency of their anticorruption frameworks. Effective cooperation with the police and the judiciary remains a challenge, however, and setting up a collaborative anticorruption chain, from investigation to prosecution to whistleblower protection, is a priority.

Discretion and arbitrariness in policy making represents a serious economic governance issue that extends beyond corruption. The gap between legal frameworks and actual implementation of laws is confirmed by the Global Integrity Scorecards for 2008 and 2009. With the exception of Jordan, all MENA countries assessed received a score of less than 50 percent on the "rule of law" indicator, measuring implementation of legal frameworks. The gap is particularly striking for Egypt, Jordan, and Morocco when their ratings are compared to the average ratings of comparator countries such as Chile, Brazil, Mexico, Hungary, Poland, and Turkey (figure 4.11). Such discretionary power tends to undermine the effectiveness of economic policies and institutions, disrupt competition, and discourage private sector investment and innovation, particularly by SMEs or firms without political connections. Overall, it is detrimental to growth and job creation. The market dominance of a few protected and privileged groups with low productivity and no incentive to innovate eventually stifles economic and job opportunities—which was precisely what fueled the youth resentment and frustration leading to the Arab awakening.

FIGURE 4.11

Ratings for MENA Countries and Comparator Countries on Global Integrity's Rule of Law Indicator

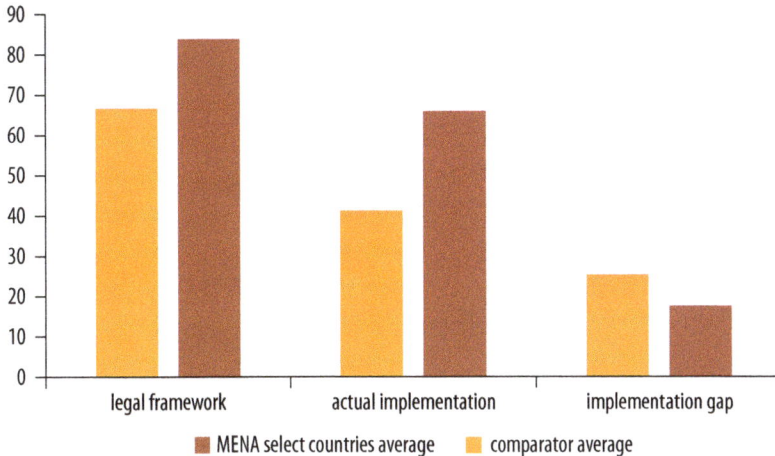

Source: Global Integrity website, www.globalintegrity.org.

Note: "MENA select countries average" represents the combined average of the Arab Republic of Egypt, Jordan, and Morocco. "Comparator average" represents the combined average of Chile, Brazil, Mexico, Hungary, Poland, and Turkey.

Voice and Accountability

The cause of this prevalent corruption and policy implementation uncertainty lies mainly in the structural weaknesses of the countries' governance structures, characterized by a significant lack of voice, participation, and accountability. Until recently, a singular lack of voice and accountability in public decisions and actions allowed the status quo to remain entrenched in all Partnership countries. This speaks to the heart of the credibility problem: exclusivity and discretion serve to undermine state credibility with investors and discourage formal entry and investment. Irregular and exclusive consultations between the public and private sectors left most of the business community out of the policy process, so that entrepreneurs were often blindsided by changes when they came. Decision-making power was concentrated at a very high level, often beyond government. The governance system suffered from limited checks and balances in the absence of strong parliaments and a truly independent judiciary, a deficiency magnified by flawed electoral systems in some countries. These shortcomings significantly reduced citizens' voice and the accountability of ruling elites, fueling widespread sentiments of mis-

FIGURE 4.12

Ratings for MENA Countries and Comparators in Global Integrity's Executive Accountability Rankings, 2010

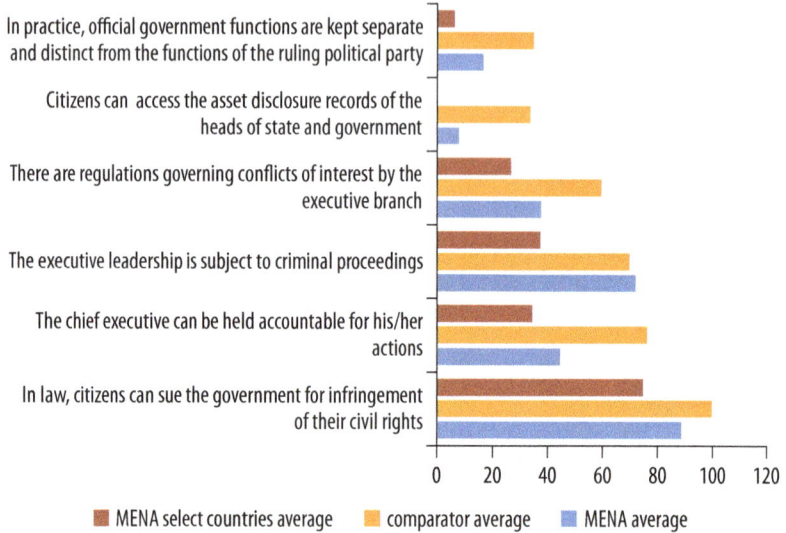

Source: Global Integrity website, www.globalintegrity.org.

Note: "MENA select countries average" represents the combined average of the Arab Republic of Egypt, Jordan, Morocco, and Tunisia (data not available for Libya). "Comparator average" represents the combined average of Poland, Turkey, Georgia, the Czech Republic, and Azerbaijan. "MENA average" represents the overall regional average.

trust and disenfranchisement. This led to the calls in Tunisia and beyond for full civic rights, dignity, and the renegotiation of the social contract based on modern governance principles and inclusion.

International governance indicators such as Global Integrity's rankings or the Economist Intelligence Unit's Democracy Index confirm important weaknesses in the Partnership countries' accountability frameworks. They find unclear separation between official government and political party functions, undefined accountability and undisclosed assets of leaders, and, more broadly, an almost complete lack of legislation and institutions to guard against conflicts of interest (figure 4.12). As a result, the accountability of the executive in Partnership countries is weak. Global Integrity indicators measuring the strength of conflict of interest laws that regulate the executive branch rank Morocco and Jordan at 32 percent in 2010, well below the 74 percent and 75 percent regional averages of the Europe/Central Asia and Latin America/Caribbean regions, respectively). Likewise, the Democracy Index indicates weaker ratings on average for Partnership countries than for five comparator countries in all

FIGURE 4.13

Ratings for Deauville Partnership Countries and Comparators on Economist Intelligence Unit's Democracy Index, 2011

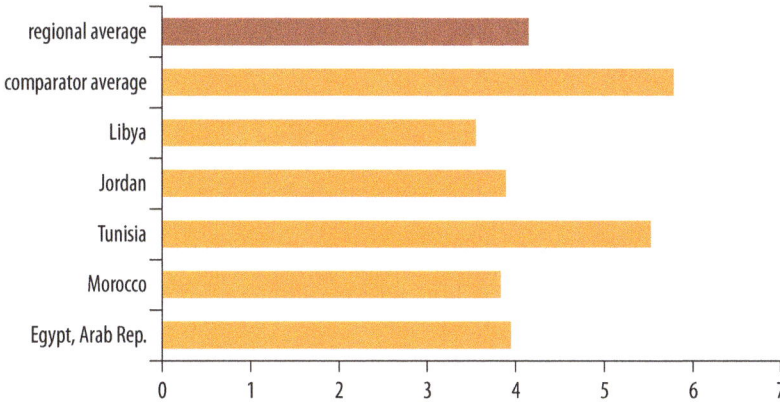

Source: Economist Intelligence Unit Democracy Index 2011.

Note: "Regional average" represents the combined average of select MENA countries including Libya, Jordan, Tunisia, Morocco, and the Arab Republic of Egypt. "Comparator average" represents the combined average of Poland, Turkey, Georgia, the Czech Republic, and Azerbaijan. The Democracy Index ranks countries on a scale of 0 (weakest) to 10 (strongest) in five categories: electoral process and pluralism, functioning of government, political participation, political culture, and civil liberties.

five categories: electoral process and pluralism, functioning of government, political participation, political culture, and civil liberties (figure 4.13).

The lack of voice and accountability translates into poorly informed economic decisions, irrational policy choices, and, ultimately, poor economic competitiveness (figure 4.14). Empirical evidence (Kaufmann and Bellver 2005) shows that countries with strong voice and accountability framework have more effective economic institutions and are more competitive. For instance, Tunisia's dismal governance regime undermined its strategy and efforts to develop a knowledge-based economy. Substantial resources were devoted to promoting innovation and research, with numerous technology parks, important subsidy programs, and tax breaks, but these resources did not yield significant results. Even though 1.3 percent of GDP went to research and development in 2009, only 26 international patents were registered. Likewise, Tunisia had one of the lowest shares of high-tech industries (5.4 percent in 2009, compared to 11.5 percent in Jordan). As documented in the World Bank's (2010b) development policy review on Tunisia, these unsatisfactory outcomes were largely due to governance constraints, such as the very limited access to public information and statistics, the censorship of Internet and foreign

FIGURE 4.14

Voice and Accountability vs. Competitiveness around the World

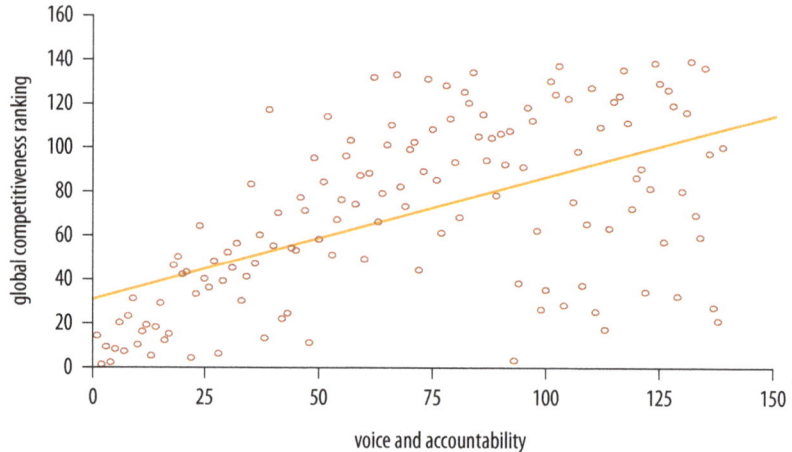

Sources: World Bank, Worldwide Governance Indicators, http://info.worldbank.org/governance/wgi/index. asp; World Economic Forum, http://www.weforum.org.

Note: Lower scores indicate better accountability and higher competitiveness.

publications, the absence of critical debate, and the constrained mobility of researchers. In the absence of voice and contestability, this detrimental status quo lasted until the 2011 revolution.

Most Partnership countries have acknowledged these governance deficiencies and have undertaken major reforms of their political institutions. Morocco has revised its constitution and electoral process with a view to strengthening checks and balances and key accountability institutions such as the parliament, the head of government, and the judiciary. The amended constitution elevates good governance principles and strengthens institutions in charge of their enforcement, such as the anticorruption agency and the competition authority. In Tunisia, parliamentary elections were held in 2011, and the political and democratic transition has been entrusted to representative interim institutions until the constitution is revised and free presidential and legislative elections can be held. Essential democratic rights have been reestablished, such as the freedom of association and of information. In Libya, a national (unity) transitional council is working to stabilize the country and reestablish law and order so that an orderly political transition can begin. Egypt completed its parliamentary elections in January 2012, and a revision of the constitution is also under way.

Beyond the restructuring of the Partnership countries' overall governance frameworks, currently in process, reforms related to conflicts of interest, asset disclosure, and complaint mechanisms would do much to strengthen accountability and transparency. A first priority is to strengthen the legal framework and practices regarding conflicts of interest. In principle, political leaders should divest from existing economic ventures that could create conflicts between their public responsibilities and their private interests. At the very least, they should publicly disclose information on their participation in such ventures and recuse themselves from decision making in related areas. In addition, regulations and mechanisms for income and assets disclosure should be revised to make them more comprehensive and more available to the public. This would build trust, facilitate public scrutiny, and offer a more effective tool for corruption prevention than the currently limited use of assets declarations in prosecution. Third, the existing complaint and recourse mechanisms should be overhauled to provide citizens with an effective instrument of dispute resolution. This would require the establishment of effective monitoring and evaluation systems within the administration, among other reforms. Witness and whistleblower protection is another key means of encouraging citizen feedback and strengthening the fight against corruption.

Rule of Law and the Quality of Institutions

The most crucial need is not the adoption of new rules but the firm enforcement of existing ones so that institutions function as they should. In general, Partnership countries have on the books all the legal and administrative provisions necessary for good institutions, but effective and credible enforcement is lacking. North (1991) defines institutions not only according to their formal and informal rules and constraints but also based on their enforcement characteristics. Institutions should set rules of behavior and apply sanctions when the rules are breached; this requires instruments for enforcing the rules and applying sanctions, as well as procedures for mediation and resolution of conflicts. Enforcement of rules gives them credibility. This has economic as well as ethical dimensions, leading to various economic gains. It allows reduction in transaction costs, reduction in the risk of undertaking transactions, protection of property rights, and restriction of unjustified interference from politicians and interest groups. Conversely, the lack of commitment to and enforcement of rules depresses growth, contributes to an unfair wealth distribution, and reduces trade and FDI. There is now an extensive academic literature on the importance of different institutional factors as determinants of economic growth and long-term development. This suggests that sound institutions deliver economic prosperity (e.g., Acemoglu 2005; Mauro 1995; Rodrik and Wacziarg 2005) and change the distribution of wealth and income (Chong and Gradstein 2007; Easaw and Savoia 2009).

Lack of citizen voice and weak accountability affect the rule of law and the quality and independence of institutions, including the judiciary. Before the Arab awakening, political interference and capture were witnessed in many countries in the region. Captured institutions advanced the interests of the ruling elite and were sometimes even misused for political or predation purposes, as in Tunisia. Throughout the region, key economic institutions, such as competition authorities and inspectorates, tax and customs authorities, and anticorruption authorities, were particularly exposed and undermined. The capture of these institutions affected the incentive structure for officials. Rather than seeking to ensure effective and fair policy implementation and achieve the intended economic outcomes, officials demanded allegiance in exchange for privileges. This resulted in a lack of credibility and consistency in policy implementation and fostered corruption as firms competed to gain privileges or simply ensure self-preservation. The perceived lack of credibility and fairness also negatively affected firms' compliance with the rules and taxes, as evidenced by the prevalence of informal sector activity and the narrow tax base.

The lack of voice and accountability also has the perverse effect of suppressing all feedback mechanisms that could strengthen the rule of law. Mutual mistrust between government and the private sector has undermined dialogue. The political economy in much of the MENA region limits the willingness and ability of policy makers to reform institutions and strengthen the rule of law. On the demand side, reform is weak because incumbents and beneficiaries of the status quo, seeking to protect their rents, are more vocal and better organized than those who do not benefit from the system. On the supply side, policy-making institutions lack credible commitment to reform, and policy makers lack willingness to limit their own discretion and control of rents. In general, public policy in a wide range of areas has been closed and nontransparent, excluding all but a privileged few (figure 4.15).

The dichotomy between the onshore and offshore sectors in Tunisia and their divergent economic performance illustrates how weaknesses in the accountability framework can affect the quality and performance of economic institutions. Before the change of government, offshore export-oriented firms were exempt from the supervision of key economic institutions, such as the tax and competition authority, and largely sheltered from corruption and predation. This reflected the strong international competition to attract FDI. Export-oriented firms even benefitted from annual high-level consultations to address specific business environment issues. Domestic firms, by contrast, were largely viewed with suspi-

FIGURE 4.15

The Firm and Its Investment Climate: Rules and Policies and the Institutions That Implement Them

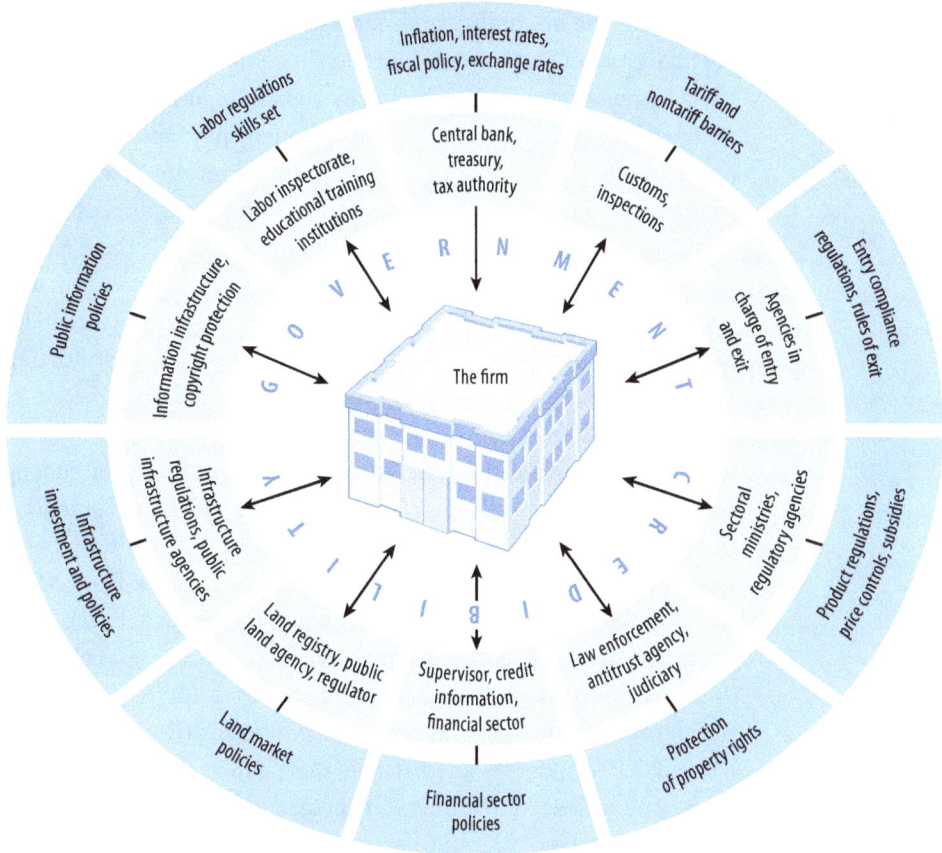

Source: World Bank 2009.

cion and treated as a source of rents. The continuous increase in FDI, including from SMEs, while domestic private investments remained low and stagnant reflects this uneven treatment.

The lack of strong, effective, and credible institutions able to enforce rules and discipline has detrimental effects on trade and FDI. Legal and administrative provisions necessary for good institutions exist in most Partnership countries. However, they are undermined by lack of enforcement. A lack of commitment to enforce rules negatively affects manufactured exports and FDI in MENA countries (Méon and Sekkat 2004). It is likely that a significant improvement in the quality of institutions could multiply the effects of trade opening and also significantly increase the ratio of FDI inflows to GDP. Empirical results indicate that Tunisia and Egypt would be able to raise their FDI ratio by more than 1 percentage point of GDP if they improved the risk associated with the uncertainty of rules to the level of Switzerland (using the International Country Risk Guide indicator). The FDI ratios of Morocco and Jordan would also increase, although to a lesser extent. Reform efforts should therefore aim at improving the credibility and quality of public institutions. The new elected governments should decentralize power and delegate some of their authority and legitimacy to key economic institutions, such as the competition authority, the anticorruption agency, and tax and customs agencies, and provide them a clear mandate for reform. A transparent and merit-based appointment of agency heads and high officials should become the rule so as to provide them legitimacy to shield them from interference. Public performance contracts should bind independent agencies and their managers based on objectively verifiable performance indicators aligned with the intended policy outcomes. Key administrative procedures and authorizations should be standardized and simplified to reduce the potential for discretion and corruption.

Poor or nonexistent democratic processes can thwart the functioning of institutions. Democracy is clearly associated with better functioning of institutions. There are, of course, a few exceptions that have been analyzed in the literature, such as Chile and the Republic of Korea (Giavazzi and Tabellini 2005; Rodrik, Trebbi, and Subramanian 2002). But some intrinsic features of democracy make such an association likely in reality. These include the clear separation of executive and legislative powers, which prevents the abuse of power by politicians (Persson, Roland, and Tabellini 1997); checks and balances that limit rent seeking and massive theft of public wealth (Dethier, Ghanem, and Zoli 1999); and legitimacy, which allows democratically elected governments to implement required institutional reforms (Mishra, Giuliano, and Spilimbergo 2010). Such expectation is confirmed in the empirical literature. Montinola and Jackman (2002) showed a significant (negative) relationship between democracy and corruption, although nonlinear. Bäck and Hadenius (2008) confirm the existence of a significant impact of democracy on administrative capacity. Keefer and Vlaicu (2007) argue that the key element is not the level of democracy, but the time of exposure to democratic institutions. Empirically, Keefer (2007) shows that more years of democracy are correlated with better government performance.

Sound institutions contribute to delivering economic prosperity and change the distribution of wealth and income. Institutions can either directly affect the willingness of agents to trade abroad, or affect economic variables that may in turn lower the propensity of agents to trade. The direct impact of institutions on the propensity to trade runs through the reduction of the return of trading abroad and through the risks associated with international transactions (Anderson and Marcouiller 2002; Rodrik,

Trebbi, and Subramanian 2002). Policies could include measures to improve the regulatory environment, reduce currency and financial risk, and avoid political and social instability.

A truly independent and effective judiciary is a key determinant of a well-functioning accountability framework as it strengthens checks and balances and ensures an even rule of law. Throughout the MENA region, inconsistent and unequal enforcement of laws has eroded public trust in government and has negatively affected business confidence and foreign investment. Global Integrity ratings for the strength of the rule of law in MENA highlight enforcement of judicial decisions and judicial independence as two areas of particular weakness. Furthermore, in many countries in the region, regulations governing conflicts of interest in the national judiciary are weak or nonexistent.

Many judiciaries in the MENA region suffer from a lack of independence and credibility. The problem does not stem from the countries' constitutions, which generally support the principle of judicial independence. In practice, however, the judiciary in many countries is subject to political interference and operates under the thumb of an executive branch that dominates both the judicial and legislative branches. In some countries, judicial independence is further undermined by parallel systems of security—military courts or specialized networks within civil courts—that are entrusted with politically sensitive cases and represent the interests of the ruling elite. The judiciary in Tunisia was the object of serious criticism over its independence, neutrality, and relationship to the executive branch during the protests of 2010/11. Legally, the independence of Tunisian judges was guaranteed by the constitution, and there was, in principle, a higher judicial council to protect the judiciary. In reality, the executive constantly meddled in the judiciary, especially with respect to judicial appointments. Furthermore, in politically motivated cases, courts did not ensure due process and routinely issued convictions, including postprison terms of "administrative control" tantamount to internal exile. Such cases, although limited in number, further damaged the independence and credibility of the judiciary, preventing it from exercising real checks on the executive branch and exposing it to further corruption. The overall situation of the judiciary also had a detrimental impact on legal certainty and contract enforcement, undermining efforts to improve the business environment.

These weaknesses are widely recognized and efforts to reform the justice sector are under way in some countries. Morocco has made justice sector reform a top priority and has taken initial steps to renew and strengthen its judiciary council. Jordan and more recently Morocco have invested heavily in court automation to foster transparency and efficiency. Reforms have not yet started in Tunisia, which has been focused on the political transition and transitional justice. The new governments emerging from recent elections should have the necessary mandate and legitimacy to tackle these sensitive and urgent reforms.

Reform efforts should focus on improving the independence, accountability, and effectiveness of the judiciary. Although issues and priorities vary across countries, recent assessments suggest the need to address both the de jure and de facto independence of judiciaries. Recommended steps include fully separating the high judicial council from the ministry of justice and insulating administrative and human resource regulations for judges from undue interference. A common challenge is to provide courts with the necessary means and management autonomy to perform their functions independently, with the expectation that this will lead to increased effectiveness and accountability for performance. This in turn requires clear performance objectives along with monitoring and evaluation underpinned by integrated and comprehensive information systems. Important past investments in modernization of the courts and their information technology (IT) systems offer the opportunity to substantially improve transparency and performance mergers and acquisitions, provided there is the political will to do so.

Freedom of Information and Transparency

Greater government transparency and access to public information are key levers to improve trust and strengthen the Partnership countries' governance frameworks and development outcomes. When politicians and rulers are not held accountable for their actions, they face enormous temptation to use public funds or public policy for their personal benefit. However, when rulers' actions are monitored, evaluated, and subject to public scrutiny, their incentives change and become more aligned with citizens' interests. Citizens must have access to information in order to monitor the use of public funds, evaluate the effectiveness of the policies adopted by the rulers they have elected, and debate public policy matters based on solid information. Freedom of information leads to better policy decisions and a more efficient delivery of public services, thus improving the lives of all citizens, but especially the poorest, who depend the most on these services. At the same time, more transparent, timely, and reliable economic information helps level the playing field and allows private investors to make better economic and financial decisions.

The Partnership countries are among the worst performers on indicators measuring access to information, negatively affecting their business environment and capacity to attract foreign investment. According to Global Integrity, the MENA region is the weakest on indicators measuring civil society, public information, and media, at 32 percent below the global average. MENA countries are characterized by a general lack of transparency and limited availability of information, even within the governments themselves. A 2011 map of press freedom by Reporters Without Borders shows most countries in the region as very restrictive toward the media. Tunisia was labeled as the region's most repressive regime with respect to civil liberties. The countries' specific challenges stem in part from legal and political restrictions that stifle the media and impose limitations on public involvement in government affairs.

Problems of access to information cannot be tackled effectively without the implementation of legislation and practices aimed improving transparency in government decision making, the judiciary, and other spheres. At present, only Jordan has a specialized freedom of information law, and it needs to be strengthened to meet international standards.[7] Tunisia recently enacted an access to information law and needs to adopt the necessary rules and regulations for implementation. Morocco's new constitution provides the right to access public information, but the enforcement of this right will require specific legislation and an institutional framework. In both countries, massive information, communication, and training efforts are needed across the public sector to promote a widespread change in mindset and practices.

Greater transparency and access to information, which is a public good, offers important economic and social benefits that are largely untapped in the region. Open access to information and data reduces information asymmetry for economic operators, thus reducing uncertainties and transaction costs to mitigate the related risks. Furthermore, public sector information (spatial information, transport and logistics information) has a market value in itself and constitutes a valuable resource for the development of innovative applications, goods, and services, thus contributing directly to the development of a knowledge-based economy. Recent studies in the EU estimate the direct and dynamic gains from the use and reuse of public sector information at up to 1.7 percent of GDP for the EU27 in 2008 (Vickery 2011). In the Partnership countries, this growth, innovation, and employment potential remains largely untapped.

The Open Government Partnership, launched in September 2011 by eight governments to promote transparency and accountability, offers an opportunity to Partnership countries committed to these modern governance principles.[8] As of mid-2012, a total of 55 governments are participating in this multilateral initiative. They have prepared, or are preparing, action plans that document their past and planned efforts to foster open governance. Participants must meet minimum eligibility criteria and demonstrate commitments in four areas: fiscal transparency, access to information through a law that guarantees the public's right to information and access to government data, disclosures related to elected or senior officials, and citizen engagement in policy making and governance. So far, Jordan is the only country in the MENA region that is participating. However, as the above-mentioned areas of reform are high priorities for the newly elected governments in the region, this could soon change. Trust in government and economic institutions, built on openness, accountability, and transparency, remains an overarching goal for fostering sustainable and inclusive growth and thus a key priority of the Deauville Partnership.

Economic governance: Key selected recommendations

Short-term:

- Adopt a policy on transparency and free access to information and ensure that it is effectively implemented through clear and binding legislation, a strong institutional enforcement mechanism, and credible monitoring and evaluation and complaints systems. Conduct communication and training campaigns to inform the public and civil servants of their rights and obligations.

- Strengthen the independence and accountability of those economic institutions and regulators in Partnership countries whose credibility and effectiveness may have been undermined by capture and arbitrary use of discretion, such as the competition and tax authorities, customs, and economic and import control bodies.

- Adopt an effective anticorruption institutional framework and implementation mechanism based on a strong and independent anticorruption body and on a credible and effective anticorruption chain involving dedicated and specialized units in the police and the judiciary.

Medium-term:

- Strengthen the independence, accountability, and effectiveness of the judiciary, especially by fully separating the high judicial council from the ministry of justice, by insulating administrative and human resource management for judges from undue interference, and by establishing robust performance evaluation schemes, underpinned by automated case management systems.

- Improve the accountability framework in Partnership countries by empowering accountability institutions with the necessary mandate and capacity to fully exercise their new role of checks and balances. Enhance the accountability of these institutions themselves by subjecting their actions to public scrutiny and by strengthening the regulatory framework on conflicts of interest and public disclosure of assets for senior officials and parliamentarians.

The Knowledge Economy

Key Issues

The promotion of innovation and human capital is key to the emergence of higher-value, better-paid jobs in Partnership countries. MENA countries tend to lag behind their competitors on measures such as the World Bank Institute's Knowledge Economy Index: while they have made valuable improvements, the pace of reform nonetheless has been slower than the global average. Limited competition, deficiencies in education, and limited linkages between FDI and domestic firms have tended to impede technological spillovers.

There are a number of obstacles to address. In education, elementary and secondary schooling has leapt forward, and the average number of schooling years has doubled since 1990. Yet higher education has lagged. Tertiary enrollment rates are 12.9 and 28.5 percent, respectively, in Morocco and Egypt, while quality as measured by the Programme for International Student Assessment (PISA) and similar measures is limited. Performance incentives for teachers and quality assurance frameworks show scope for improvement.

Technological infrastructure can be expanded, building on promising initiatives such as technology parks, clusters, and networks to facilitate technology transfer. Examples include the Tangiers automotive city and Nouasser Safran aerospace city in Morocco, as well as Tunisia's 10 competitiveness poles. Such policies can be strengthened with a focus on backward linkages to promote SME suppliers. Business incubators and other support services to reinforce innovation can be increased. Deauville partners can support these objectives and help scale up broadband Internet access as well. This is an area where the region lags behind the competitors such as Romania, which has nine times the international bandwidth capacity per capita as Morocco. ICT has been at the forefront of the Arab Spring and can, with appropriate public interventions, help create jobs and raise efficiency.

Knowledge and innovation are drivers of growth through increases in total factor productivity (TFP) and accumulation of human capital. Countries that have successfully promoted a knowledge-based economy have experienced stronger productivity-based growth, benefiting from the increasing returns of technology and its effect on competitiveness of the domestic economy. During the four decades from 1960 to 2000, the MENA region scored second-lowest (after Sub-Saharan Africa) in terms of annual change in TFP, lagging well behind the East Asian tigers on this measure (0.08 percent against 0.60 percent annual TFP change). However, during the past decade the MENA region has witnessed an acceleration of growth explained partly by productivity gains. Partnership countries have started to catch up with respect to TFP—Egypt, Libya, and Tunisia since the 1990s and Jordan and Morocco since 2000. It has been estimated that a one-unit increase in the Knowledge Economy Index[9] adds between 0.6 and 0.9 percentage point to annual GDP growth per worker over five years. In the MENA region the contribution of growth effects linked to a KE has been particularly strong in the last decade, accounting for up to a quarter of annual growth rates (Pipitone 2009).

Knowledge and innovation strategies are key to the emergence of higher-value, better-paid jobs in Partnership countries. By nature, a KE creates new opportunities, especially for highly skilled job seekers. It has been estimated that a one-unit increase in the Knowledge Economy Index between 2001 and 2005 raised employment by 0.8 percent in Egypt, 0.7 percent in Jordan, and 0.5 percent in Morocco and Tunisia (Chen, Diop, and Muller 2012). Innovative approaches like clusters, business services like marketplaces, exports development and technology extension, and support to micro, small, and medium enterprises (MSMEs) and entrepreneurs have shown positive results in terms of job creation. Innovative enterprises, even those specialized in processes, exhibit higher employment growth than noninnovative enterprises. They also tend to create unskilled jobs and jobs for women, and in that sense are well-tailored strategies for job creation and inclusive growth (Dutz et al. 2011). Moreover, a KE has positive effects on the supply of labor by ensuring a match between skills and needs through more relevant education and training. Finally, a KE promotes more efficient labor markets and better intermediation between labor supply and demand, especially through the use of ICTs.

Knowledge and innovation strategies increase export competitiveness, attract FDI and skilled workers, and foster technological spillovers to the domestic economy. A KE-driven strategy is above all based on a sound macroeconomic foundation: macroeconomic stability and external competitiveness, trade liberalization and integration, a friendly business environment, competition, labor market efficiency, financial depth, and good governance. All these policies are geared toward attracting FDI and increasing participation in international trade, two major channels for technology transfers. Since Partnership countries are not on the technology frontier, an effective strategy for innovation is to adopt and adapt existing technologies by channeling them from the frontier to the domestic economy through trade and FDI. A KE-driven strategy aims to harness the spillovers of FDI to the domestic economy. For example, open FDI regimes and competition will increase pressure on domestic firms to innovate. Trade integration will remove the antiexport bias faced by domestic firms and eliminate some of the barriers to economic transformation that have trapped Partnership countries in low-value-added, low-innovation activities. Other elements are increasing the pool of skilled and highly

FIGURE 4.16

Performance of Deauville Partnership Countries and Comparators on the Knowledge Economy Index, by Component, 2011

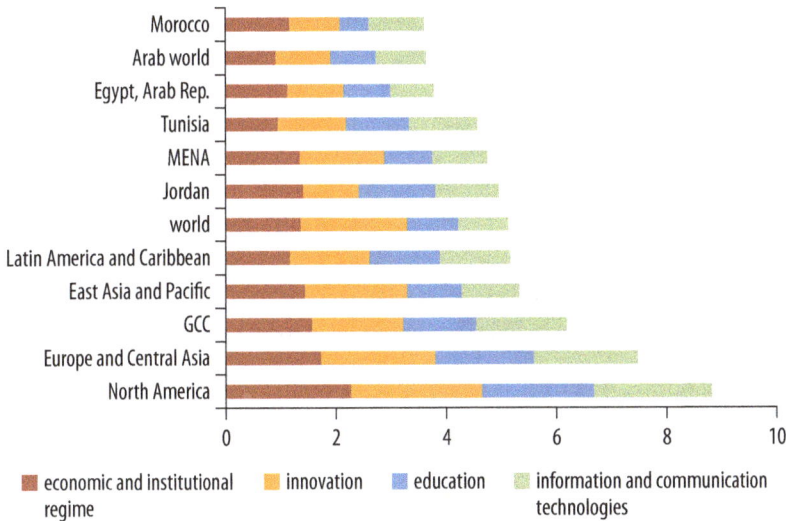

Source: World Bank calculations based on the World Bank Institute's Knowledge Assessment Methodology.
Note: "Arab world" excludes countries without data.

productive workers, upgrading infrastructure and services for innovation, especially ICT infrastructure, and protecting intellectual property rights.

Partnership countries lag behind developed and emerging economies in terms of KE achievements, and their relative rankings on the main KE dimensions have tended to decline in recent years. Partnership countries perform below the world average on the Knowledge Economy Index (figure 4.16). Jordan and Tunisia are slightly ahead of Egypt and Morocco because of their better outcomes in education and ICTs. Morocco is dragged down by its poor performance in education, and Egypt by education and ICTs. Over time, only Tunisia did not lose ground, with its score on the index increasing slightly from 4.3 in 2000 to 4.6 in 2011. Egypt, Jordan, and Morocco, on the other hand, have seen their scores decline (Koivisto 2012). This does not mean that those countries are not moving ahead, but that their progress is slower than the global average. This trend adversely affects their competitiveness and hence their performance in terms of growth and employment.

Economic and institutional regimes are still hindering trade and FDI and impeding technological spillovers because of market rigidities, low vertical linkages with domestic firms, limited competition, and inadequate flow of information with and within business organizations. These weaknesses have prevented Partnership countries from improving the efficiency of resource allocation, increasing investment, and boosting the contribution of net exports to growth. Harnessing FDI and trade spillovers can be done through several key channels:

- *Workforce training and mobility.* People who acquire knowledge and skills through participation in a foreign company could move to domestic firms or set up their own enterprises, as witnessed in the successful special economic zones. Highly skilled workers can also help disseminate knowledge through networking. However, Partnership countries still have cumbersome labor regulations that constrain hiring and firing, in some cases by imposing large redundancy costs; as a result, skilled workers may be stuck in low-productivity jobs.

- *Vertical linkages with domestic firms.* Especially important are technology transfers from FDI firms or imports of intermediate products and capital equipment providers or international suppliers and clients in the context of participation in world supply chains. Ireland, ranked first in FDI technology transfer (WEF 2011), is well known for its successful program of linkages between FDI firms and SMEs. The National Suppliers Development Program in Egypt stands out as a good practice, though it could be improved and expanded to services. Promoting innovation policies would also require the strengthening of intellectual property rights.

- *Competition that brings pressure for innovation.* Partnership countries still lack a competition framework. They have extensive public sector involvement in production and significant economic concentration that interferes with a level playing field, maintains barriers to access in many markets, and discourages price controls.

- *Demonstration effects.* Products and processes could be replicated by domestic firms, and information and communication tools could be used to disseminate knowledge brought in by FDI and trade. Business organizations can play a crucial role if the public sector is open to them, but this potential has not been fully realized in the past.

Human capital accumulation is hindered by the limited quantity and low quality of education. From a quantitative perspective, elementary-secondary education has taken a leap in recent years, contributing to a sharp decrease in youth illiteracy and a doubling of the average number of schooling years since 1990. However, higher education has lagged.

Tertiary enrollment rates are only 12.9 and 28.5 percent, respectively, in Morocco and Egypt, far lower than in most other regions—for example, in the Organisation for Economic Co-operation and Development (OECD) the rate is 72.1 percent. Dropout rates remain significant, especially in Morocco (19.6 percent at the primary level in 2009) and to a lesser extent in Tunisia (7.2 percent in 2008). Educational quality is also a problem. Scores on the Trends in International Mathematics and Science Study (TIMSS) and the Programme for International Student Assessment (PISA) show that the best performer among Partnership countries has a mean score that is 13 percent below the scale average for TIMSS 2007 and 19 percent under the OECD average for PISA 2009. This poor record reflects, among other factors, lack of appropriate performance incentives for teachers and managers and deficiencies in the quality assurance framework.

There is an obvious mismatch between the skills needs of the economy and the outputs of the education and training system. Private sector surveys point to lack of appropriate education and skills, especially soft skills, as one of the most important constraints for business development in the region. In a World Bank survey (2009), 33.4 percent of firms in the MENA region say education is a major constraint. A recent WEF (2011) survey found that 13.4 percent of firms in Egypt see it as the biggest problem; only policy stability was named by more firms. There are high levels of unemployment among the educated: in Egypt, people with a postprimary education represent 42 percent of the labor force but more than 80 percent of the unemployed. The skills gap is especially evident in some of the most promising and tradable sectors, such as electronic and mechanical industries in Tunisia, and tourism and ICTs in Jordan. The missing link between education and employment needs to be addressed through more and better vocational training, yet postsecondary education remains dominated by universities. There is low private sector participation, in particular FDI, in providing both higher education and vocational training, which remain constrained by the underdevelopment of education financing mechanisms. The private sector needs to become more engaged, collaborating with the public sector to address the skills mismatch by reorienting education toward workforce needs. This can be done through internships, reskilling, and work readiness programs, such as the promising Maharat internship program managed by the Business Development Center in Jordan.

Beyond the formal education system, workers need to continue upgrading their knowledge for higher productivity. The region needs a lifelong learning system, especially for workers, but this is underdeveloped.

The private sector reports that relevant government regulations and incentives are complex. On the staff training score developed by the WEF, only Tunisia ranks above the global average (38th out of 142 countries, with a 4.4 score). Other Partnership countries lag far behind, especially Egypt (ranked 131st, with a 3.0 score).

The brain drain is detrimental to domestic absorptive capacity. A significant share of highly educated people migrate from MENA countries to find better opportunities. The outflow is especially significant from Morocco and Tunisia, where corresponding figures were 18.6 and 12.6 percent in 2000. Well-tailored educational and labor policies could help stem this trend. In addition, to turn the brain drain into a brain gain, strategies should be developed to mobilize diaspora communities for engagement that goes beyond the sending of remittances. Emigrants can become involved in transferring technology, financing MSMEs, promoting FDI, and facilitating access to global markets, as has been done successfully in India for the IT industry.

Finally, economic integration requires greater mobility of skilled labor, underpinned by international quality standards. For example, the Bologna Process seeks to establish a Euro-Mediterranean space for higher education. Networks of education and training institutions that share resources efficiently (such as the Euro-Mediterranean University, EMUNI) and programs that promote the mobility of students (such as the European Commission's successful ERASMUS program) should be extended to and replicated within the Arab world.

Innovation policies are embryonic in the region, and outcomes are still modest in terms of both R&D results and growth of innovative businesses. Partnership countries have generally given little priority to R&D, spending on average under 1 percent of GDP. The exception is Tunisia, which has pursued an innovation-driven growth strategy. Tunisia increased its share of R&D spending (from 0.3 percent of GDP in 1996 to 1.1 percent in 2009) and more than doubled the density of researchers (from 708 to 1,863 per million inhabitants). These values are still much lower than the OECD average, however (2.3 percent in 2007 for spending and 3,493 for density). Throughout the region, most R&D is carried out by the public sector, mainly public research organizations and universities, with much scope for greater involvement by the private sector. The outcomes of R&D are largely insignificant. Together, the Partnership countries account for less than 0.01 percent of patents granted by the United States Patent and Trademark Office in 2010, suggesting a low level of research efficiency. The production of technical and scientific articles by researchers is about half the world average. Egypt, Jordan, Morocco, and Tunisia all have laws that are in compliance with the Agreement on Trade-Related

Aspects of Intellectual Property Rights (the TRIPS Agreement) and have witnessed an increase in patent filing by nonresidents.

Hence, the region still falls far short of the technology frontier. Its policies should devote more attention to incremental innovation and support the private sector in tapping into global knowledge. The first imperative is to build technological infrastructure, especially in promising sectors, by setting up specialized technology parks, clusters, and networks to facilitate technology transfer. Morocco has set up 22 integrated industrial platforms, including the Tangiers automotive city and the Nouasser aerospace city, and has been able to attract FDI from big players (Renault in Tangiers, Boeing and Safran in Nouasser). Most importantly, it has made progress on the difficult task of developing backward linkages with MSMEs to supply these centers. Tunisia has also put in place 10 competitiveness poles, although several of them still face obstacles due to highly centralized public management and coordination gaps. Further decentralization is of paramount importance to the effectiveness of local clusters. However, this kind of reform is only in the beginning stages in most of the Partnership countries. According to the WEF survey, only Morocco has a clustering score better than the world average (3.8, ranking 52nd against 3.6) (WEF 2011).

A second imperative is to provide business services to innovators, especially to start-ups and MSMEs. These services could include incubators, coaching and accelerators, promotion and marketing; technology extension, quality management, and information and communication services. Incubators are an essential means to nurture ideas in a conducive environment (World Bank 2010a). There are some success cases in the region, such as the Casablanca Technopark, run by the private sector with support from InfoDev. It is hosting more than 130 companies, most of them start-ups and SMEs, though some multinational corporations are included. In general, however, the MENA region has one of the lowest densities of firm entry (0.63, only ahead of Sub-Saharan Africa). Tunisia has the best record, while Egypt and Jordan are under the regional average. Promotion and marketing are key elements for success, as illustrated by initiatives for exports development in Tunisia. Demand-driven technology extension services are also crucial to increase productivity. These are particularly needed in the agricultural sector and could require setting up centers of technology transfer from abroad, such as the ETTICs (technology transfer and innovation centers) in Egypt. Quality management has experienced some improvements in the region. In Egypt, for example, the share of enterprises certified by the International Organization for Standardization rose from 12 percent in 2004 to 21 percent in 2008. However, these levels are still too low to ensure sufficient access to external markets and to FDI. Moreover, sanitary and phytosanitary standards are becoming one of the most important nontariff barriers to exports from MENA countries. For example, none of the Partnership countries has yet concluded an Agreement on Conformity Assessment and Acceptance for industrial products with Europe.

Third, financing innovation is a central issue in a region where small enterprises are struggling for access to funding. Fewer than 20 percent of SMEs in the Arab world have such access, the worst performance of any region (Radwan and Strauss 2011). The venture capital industry is underdeveloped. However, it is gaining momentum, with 87 and 72 percent of private equity funds raised since 2005 for the Maghreb and Mashreq, respectively (ANIMA 2011). The amounts targeted by the recently launched funds are quite substantial. According to the Emerging Markets Private Equity survey in 2011, the slowdown in most developed economies has increased interest in emerging economies, so the MENA region could conceivably take a larger share of private equity. Among negative factors, 32 percent of SMEs surveyed saw political risk as a deterrent, 39 percent cited the failure to train world-class managers, and 33 percent noted the failure to scale up market opportunities. Moreover, most of these private equity funds are concentrated on upstream investments, while only 15 percent are financing early stages of innovation. There is a need to promote more engagement of business angels and accelerators, make better use of ICT opportunities for crowd funding, and further engage the diaspora. The role of the state is also important—not only to offer the right incentives to the private sector for innovation funding, but also to provide financing through seed money, matching grants, and guarantee schemes, and to use state procurement effectively to promote domestic innovation and technology transfer.

Despite recent progress, there is a need to increase broadband capacity and spread ICT usage more widely in productive sectors. The Partnership countries have made great strides toward catching up in ICT diffusion, especially through mobile telecommunications, often with FDI. This progress has accelerated since the mid-1990s due to liberalization reforms in the region and rapid global technological developments that have driven down costs and made access easier. There has been a dramatic increase in telecommunications penetration, which now ranges from 66 percent in Egypt to 100 percent in Jordan; this is due mostly to mobile penetration, which accounts for 85.5 percent of overall density on average. Internet diffusion, however, has seen less rapid improvement and stands at only at 21.8 percent (Morocco is the best performer, with 33 percent, while Egypt has only 17 percent). This is still hindered by low broadband access (1.4 percent in fixed broadband) and international bandwidth capacity (2.9 kb/s/capita on average, with Tunisia doing better at 4.9 kb/s/capita). This lags well behind the performance of many potential competitors; for example, Romania, which competes with Morocco in offshoring, has nine times the international bandwidth capacity per capita. Obstacles include the lack of competition in some services, such as international long-distance telecommunications in Egypt and Tunisia, and fixed broadband, where Morocco has the worst ranking among the four by the ICT basket price (ITU 2011).

ICT usage has increased dramatically, as witnessed in the important role of social media during the Arab Spring. The public sector could play a greater role in fostering further increases in ICT usage in several ways. First, it can develop e-government services and information (Partnership countries averaged 89th out of 178, according to the United Nations e-government readiness ranking in 2007). Special attention should be paid to measures to facilitate trade, such as electronic data interchange and e-customs, and business, including electronic and online regulation, registration, taxation, procurement, and payment. Second, the government can promote e-education and online learning by ensuring Internet access in public education institutions and developing local content adapted to domestic needs. Third, the state can take advantage of the Internet and mobile technologies in the health sector, especially in rural areas. In all these respects, promotion of wider ICT penetration can contribute to demand for good governance.

ICT has been one of the most important sources of economic growth and job creation in the past decade. The Partnership countries have attracted significant FDI in ICTs, both in telecommunications services (Vivendi in Morocco, Orange in Tunisia and Jordan, Vodafone in Egypt) and in the IT industry. The region has also promoted the development of business process outsourcing to enlarge its ICT exports base. There have been positive achievements during the past decade in Tunisia (share of ICTs in services exports increased from 1.2 to 4.7 percent), Morocco (3.7 to 7.5 percent), and Egypt (3.4 to 4.7 percent). Egypt was ranked in the top 10 destinations by A.T. Kearney, a global management consulting firm, in 2009. Recent data show that call centers, R&D centers in IT, and software services are seen by foreign investors as one of the most important niches for growth and employment, with a job intensity ranging between 103 and 299 jobs per million euros invested (ANIMA 2011). The Partnership countries have attracted a number of large players such as Cisco, Microsoft, IBM, and Yahoo. However, there is still a huge untapped potential for growth, considering that globally the average share of ICTs in overall exports (12 percent) is well ahead of the Partnership country levels.

Knowledge and innovation strategies are essential for harnessing the growth potential of key sectors through FDI and trade, as the Partnership countries have acknowledged. Promising sectors for development include agriculture; industrial sectors such as machinery, electrical, transport, and electronics; chemicals; green energy technologies; tourism, including medical tourism; ICT offshoring; and creative industries. However, few of those sectors are currently meeting their potential (Radwan and Strauss 2012). Knowledge and innovation–based policies are critical for speeding up growth and creating jobs in each sector.

Agribusiness, a promising sector for growth and exports, is impeded by its low level of labor productivity, lack of innovation, and other constraints in the value chain. Agribusiness is an important sector for Morocco (15 percent of GDP), Egypt (14 percent), and to a lesser extent Tunisia (8 percent). It could be one of the drivers of growth, exports diversification, and poverty alleviation if further global, and especially European, market access is provided. Moreover, volatile food prices in the past four years highlight the importance of this sector for food security and poverty alleviation. However, the sector has a high share of workers who are trapped in poverty due to low yields. The wheat yield in Morocco is 27 percent that of Germany, the tomato yield in Egypt is 51 percent that of the United States, and the olive yield in Tunisia is 16 percent that of Spain. The main constraints are shortcomings in skills, R&D, technology extension services, and access to markets.

The machinery, electrical, transport equipment, and electronics industries have shown rapid growth in production and exports, but they are held back by a shortage of skilled workers, insufficient vertical linkages with domestic suppliers, and low, albeit increasing, collaboration between research and industry. The machinery and transport equipment sector is becoming one of the growth drivers in the region, representing a large and growing share of exports (24.5 percent in Tunisia, 17.6 percent in Morocco, and 11.2 percent for Jordan in 2006). The sector could benefit from rising domestic demand, made possible by investments in physical capital, as households catch up in terms of home appliances and cars (the best equipped are Tunisians, with 125 cars per 1,000 inhabitants, still well behind Europe with 586). This sector also offers good possibilities for backward linkages with local parts suppliers and even clustering with research centers, some already established with participation from large FDI players. The capacity for harnessing this growth potential is closely linked to knowledge and innovation policies.

The chemicals industry is becoming a competitive sector in the region, but it continues to suffer from lack of skills, business services, innovation, and access to financing and markets. The chemicals sector has shown rapid growth since the mid-1990s and represents a significant share of manufacturing (22 percent in Egypt, 20 percent in Tunisia, 16 percent in Jordan, and 14 percent in Morocco). Medicines, in which the region now has a comparative advantage, are among the region's top five exports to the world (1.7 percent of exports, of which only 0.9 percent goes to Europe). The chemicals industry in the region has been able to attract multinational corporations, to cover a larger share of domestic needs, and to diversify its regional markets, with Africa presenting a huge potential for growth. Key constraints include those related to skills, quality management, and infrastructure for certification, R&D, property rights enforcement, domestic firm technological capabilities, market size, and funding.

Green energy is still underdeveloped in the region, but it has a huge growth potential that could be spurred by KE-driven strategies. This is both an opportunity and an imperative for the region. Opportunities include energy efficiency in the construction, transport, and waste management sectors, as well as renewable energy, which is expected to show rapid growth consonant with international commitments to increase the green share in energy consumption. The region has a huge solar energy potential for growth, employment, and net exports. Large projects, including Desertec and the Ouarzazate 500-megawatt plant in Morocco, are already in the pipeline. Taking advantage of this sector will require massive investment in skills, R&D, and clustering, including firms and training institutions, business services, and especially technology transfers to local firms.

Tourism has been one of the most important contributors to exports, employment and GDP in the region, though it has been hit hard by the turmoil of the Arab Spring. There is still much undeveloped potential in terms of both quantity—the MENA region receives only 2.5 percent of Europe's outbound tourism, and little from other regions—and value added per tourist. Many of the constraints could be alleviated by well-targeted knowledge and innovation strategies. There is a special need for skills development, which could be supplied by projects such as the Education for Employment (E4E) exercise in Jordan. Communication skills are particularly needed in the Maghreb countries in order to diversify their tourism markets. Also important are ICT infrastructure and e-services, especially marketing but also electronic commerce and payments, and support to start-ups, MSMEs, and the creative industries in particular.

Medical tourism requires a highly skilled workforce and world-class, internationally certified health services. It is clearly a niche with potential, considering the high global demand for medical care, lower costs in the region, and increasing tendency of insurers in the developed world to outsource treatment. A case in point is Singapore, which in 2006 received 410,000 foreign patients, half of them from the Middle East. The availability of affordable care could also provide an additional incentive for the elderly to retire to sunny locales in the MENA region. All the Partnership countries have a large market potential in Europe and the Gulf Cooperation Council: Jordan is well positioned to tap it, and Tunisia has already experienced an impressive growth in its medical workforce. To harness this potential, however, steps must be taken to provide better market access; invest in adequate skills; set up international quality standards, including infrastructure for certification and its full recognition by the patients' home countries; and develop incentives, information, and funding to enable local suppliers to adapt their capabilities to the expected demand.

ICT offshoring has been growing rapidly over the past decade, but its high potential is still hampered by low skills and infrastructure gaps. ICT is one of the most innovative sectors in the region and an enabler for productivity in the overall economy. Some Partnership countries are now well positioned to take up opportunities for more offshoring from the developed world, according to the A.T. Kearney (2011) Global Services Location Index. However, the size of the sector is still under the global average. The industry remains constrained by the lack of skills, as documented by the E4E exercises in Jordan and Tunisia. This sector should be one of the pillars of any KE strategy.

Emerging creative industries are promising but still underdeveloped due to weaknesses in entrepreneurship, business environment, and the overall context for freedom of expression. Globally, creative industries have recently enjoyed unprecedented dynamism; but the MENA region, excluding Lebanon and to a lesser extent Dubai, remains marginalized. The share of copyright income in GDP is almost insignificant in most Partnership countries (Jordan 0.8 percent, Morocco 0.6 percent, and Tunisia 0.6 percent, compared to 11.1 percent for the United States). The creative industries have a huge potential for growth and exports in view of the present underdevelopment of the sector, the number of talented people in the region, the recent surge of audiovisual media, demographic and economic trends (notably the youth bulge and rising incomes), as well as the richness of Arab culture and its growing international importance. This sector is still constrained, however, by lack of skills, especially soft skills, and weak support for innovation through incubators, accelerators, marketing, and above all funding. It also is lacking in property rights protection, ICT infrastructure and services, and regional trade integration. Alleviating those constraints should be a key goal of KE-driven strategies.

The knowledge economy: Key selected recommendations

Short-term:

- Liberalize fully the telecommunications sector in Partnership countries, step up competition, increase broadband capacity, and upgrade mobile technology by moving toward 4G licensing and using it in some cases to obtain full telecommunications licenses for existing operators to foster competition.

- Cooperate on intellectual property rights with G8 countries in support of national innovation policies, possibly in the context of future deep and high-quality trade agreements.

Medium-term:

- Develop an innovation-driven development strategy that steps up investment and trade and encourages their technological spillovers in Partnership countries with effective and well-coordinated institutions, medium-term budgeting, and monitoring and evaluation frameworks. Instruments can include the European Innovation Scoreboard.

- Reform the public R&D system to better align it with national priorities and increase substantially the public resources allocated to innovation in Partnership countries (e.g., seed capital, matching grants). At the same time, grant incentives to the private sector to step in, and reinforce the protection of property rights to attract more foreign-financed research and patenting. Support from Deauville partners can include the establishment of innovation funds.

- Expand innovative sites (special economic zones, technology parks, knowledge clusters, and knowledge cities) in Partnership countries based on comparative advantages and private sector–led approaches that group together businesses, education and training institutions, and R&D centers.

Notes

1. The five Partnership countries have entered into a large number of international investment agreements. The number of agreements ranges from 32 (Libya) to 84 (Egypt) for BITs, and from 12 (Libya) to 48 (Egypt and Morocco) for DTTs. Between 25 percent (Egypt and Morocco) to over half (Libya) of the BITs signed by a Partnership country have yet to enter into force. Jordan and Libya do not have a BIT between them, and only Morocco has DDT with the other four Partnership economies.
2. Bolaky and Freund (2004) also find that once they "control for the effect of trade on growth in heavily regulated economies, the evidence that trade positively affects growth is stronger than has been found in previous studies. Ex-

cessive regulations restrict growth because resources are prevented from moving into the most productive sectors and to the most efficient firms following liberalization. In addition, in highly regulated economies, increased trade is more likely to occur in the wrong goods—that is, goods where comparative advantage does not lie."

3. Walsh and Yu state (2010), "While FDI flows into the primary sector show little dependence on [macroeconomic, developmental, and institutional/ qualitative] variables, secondary and tertiary sector investments are affected in different ways by countries' income levels and exchange rate valuation, as well as development indicators such as financial depth and school enrollment, and institutional factors such as judicial independence and labor market flexibility."

4. The comparison of average wait times across countries should be regarded with caution for some regulatory services. For instance, an operating license might be associated with mandatory complementary registrations or inspections (e.g., safety or health inspections) in some countries, which would bias the mean upward. The comparison of the dispersion of wait times across countries, however, does not suffer from this bias since the coefficient of variation (s.d./mean) corrects for such level differences across each country.

5. We do not include the wait times for import licenses in Morocco, as this information is only available for five firms.

6. Information for Tunisia and Libya is not available. See the Global Integrity website at www.globalintegrity.org.

7. Article 19, *Memorandum on Jordanian Draft Law on Guarantee of Access to Information*, December 2005.

8. The eight founding governments are Brazil, Indonesia, Mexico, Norway, the Philippines, South Africa, the United Kingdom, and the United States. See http://www.opengovpartnership.org/.

9. The Knowledge Assessment Methodology developed by the World Bank Institute has four pillars: economic incentive and institutional regime, education, innovation, and ICTs. Countries and regions are rated on a Knowledge Economy Index (0–10) based on a simple average of indexes for the four pillars, each covering three variables. For more details, see www.worldbank.org/kam.

References

A. T. Kearney. 2011. *Off-Shoring Opportunities amid Economic Turbulence: The A.T. Kearney Global Services Location Index 2011*. Chicago, IL: A.T. Kearney.

Acemoglu, Daron. 2005. "Politics and Economics in Weak and Strong States." *Journal of Monetary Economics* 52 (7): 1199–226.

Acemoglu, Daron, and James Robinson. 2010. "The Role of Institutions in Growth and Development." *Review of Economics and Institutions/Economia, Società e Istituzioni* 1 (2), Article 1.

Aidt, Toke, Jayasri Dutta, and Vania Sena. 2008. "Governance Regimes, Corruption and Growth: Theory and Evidence." *Journal of Comparative Economics* 36 (2): 195–220.

Alvarez, Roberto. 2004. "Sources of Export Success in Small- and Medium-Sized Enterprises: The Impact of Public Programs." *International Business Review* 13 (3): 383–400.

Anderson, James, and Douglas Marcouiller. 2002. "Insecurity and the Pattern of Trade: An Empirical Investigation." *Review of Economics and Statistics* 84 (2): 342–52.

ANIMA. 2011. *MedFunds2011: An Overview of Private Equity in the Mediterranean Region*. Marseilles, France: ANIMA. http://www.animaweb.org/en/etudes. php.

Bäck, Hanna, and Alex Hadenius. 2008. "Democracy and State Capacity: Exploring a J-Shaped Relationship." *Governance* 21 (1): 1–24.

Banga, Rashmi. 2006. "The Export-Diversifying Impact of Japanese and US Foreign Direct Investments in the Indian Manufacturing Sector." *Journal of International Business Studies* 37 (4): 558–68.

Bolaky, Bineswaree, and Caroline Freund. 2004. "Trade, Regulations, and Growth." Policy Research Working Paper 3255, World Bank, Washington, DC.

Borchert, Ingo, Batshur Gootiiz, and Aaditya Mattoo. 2012. "Policy Barriers to International Trade in Services: New Empirical Evidence." World Bank Policy Research Working Paper WPS6109, World Bank, Washington, DC.

Chen, Derek H. C., Ndiame Diop, and Sophie Muller. 2012. "Knowledge, Economic Growth and Employment Creation: The MENA Experience." Unpublished background report, World Bank, Washington, DC.

Chong, Alberto, and Mark Gradstein. 2007. "On the Determinants and Effects of Political Influence." RES Working Paper 4540, Inter-American Development Bank, Washington, DC.

Dasgupta, Dipak, Mustapha Kamel Nabli, Christopher Pissarides, and Aristomene Varoudakis. 2002. "Making Trade Work for Jobs: International Evidence and Lessons for MENA." MENA Region Working Paper 32, World Bank, Washington, DC.

De Meneval, Philippe, and Said Hanafy. 2010. *Commercial Law in MENA: An Opportunity for Regional Economic Integration?* World Bank MNA Knowledge and Learning Fast Brief 73. Washington, DC: World Bank.

Dennis, Allen. 2006. "Trade Liberalization, Factor Market Flexibility, and Growth: The Case of Morocco and Tunisia." Policy Research Working Paper 3857, World Bank, Washington, DC.

Dethier, Jean-Jacques, Hafez Ghanem, and Edda Zoli. 1999. "Does Democracy Facilitate the Economic Transition: An Empirical Study of Central and Eastern Europe and the Former Soviet Union." Policy Research Working Paper 2194, World Bank, Washington, DC.

Dutz, Mark, Ioannis Kessides, Stephen O'Connell, and Robert Willig. 2011. "Competition and Innovation-Driven Inclusive Growth." Policy Research Working Paper 5852, World Bank, Washington, DC.

Easaw, Joshy, and Antonio Savoia. 2009. "Inequality in Developing Economies: The Role of Institutional Development." Working Paper 121, Society for the Study of Economic Inequality (ECINEQ), Palma de Mallorca, Spain.

Farole, Thomas, and Gokhan Akinci, eds. 2011. *Special Economic Zones: Progress, Emerging Challenges, and Future Directions*. Washington, DC: World Bank.

Ferejohn, John. 1986. "Incumbent Performance and Electoral Control." *Public Choice* 50 (1–3): 5–25.

Galal, Ahmed. 2011. "Egypt Post January 2011: An Economic Perspective." Policy Perspective PP_03, Economic Research Forum, Cairo.

Gehlbach, Scott, and Philip Keefer. 2011. "Investment without Democracy: Ruling-Party Institutionalization and Credible Commitment in Autocracies." *Journal of Comparative Economics* 39 (2): 123–39.

Giavazzi, Francesco, and Guido Tabellini. 2005. "Economic and Political Liberalizations." *Journal of Monetary Economics* 52 (7): 1297–330.

Hassani, Z., S. Arvai, and R. Rocha. 2010. "Credit Where Credit Is Due: Partial Credit Guarantee Schemes in the Middle East and North Africa." Background paper prepared for the MENA Financial Sector flagship report, World Bank, Washington, DC.

Hayakawa, Kazunobu, Hyun-Hoon Lee, and Donghyun Park. 2011. "Do Export Promotion Agencies Increase Exports?" IDE Discussion Paper 313, Institute of Developing Economies, Japan External Trade Organization (IDE-JETRO), Chiba, Japan.

Hermes, Niels, and Robert Lensink. 2003. "Foreign Direct Investment, Financial Development and Economic Growth." *Journal of Development Studies* 40 (1): 142–63.

ITU. 2011. http://www.itu.int/net/pressoffice/backgrounders/general/pdf/5.pdf

Kaufmann, Daniel, and Ana Bellver. 2005. "Transparenting Transparency: Initial Empirics and Policy Applications." MPRA Paper 8188, University Library of Munich, Germany.

Keefer, Philip. 2007. "Insurgency and Credible Commitment in Autocracies and Democracies." Post-conflict Transitions Working Paper 1, World Bank, Washington, DC.

Keefer, Philip, and Razvan Vlaicu. 2007. "Democracy, Credibility and Clientelism." *Journal of Law, Economics, and Organization* 24: 371–406.

Khemani, R. Shyam. 1997. "Competition Policy and Economic Development." *Policy Options/Options Politiques*, 18: 23–27.

Klapper, Leora, and Inessa Love. 2010. "The Impact of the Financial Crisis on New Firm Registration." Policy Research Working Paper 5444, World Bank, Washington, DC.

Koivisto, Marjo. 2012. "Knowledge Weak Competition and Growth in the MENA Region." Unpublished background report, World Bank, Washington, DC.

Lederman, Daniel. 2007. "Product Innovation by Incumbent Firms in Developing Economies: The Roles of Research and Development Expenditures, Trade Policy, and the Investment Climate." Policy Research Working Paper 4319, World Bank, Washington, DC.

Macario, Carla. 2000. *Export Growth in Latin America: Policies and Performance.* Boulder, CO: Lynne Reinner.

Marchat, J. M. N. 2011. "Barriers to Trade and FDI for Maghreb Countries: A Firm Level Perspective." Unpublished paper, World Bank, Washington, DC.

Mauro, Paolo. 1995. "Corruption and Growth." *Quarterly Journal of Economics* 110 (3): 681–712.

Méon, Pierre-Guillaume, and Khalid Sekkat. 2004. "Does the Quality of Institutions Limit the MENA's Integration in the World Economy?" *World Economy* 27 (9): 1475–98.

MIGA (Multilateral Investment Guarantee Agency). 2002. *Foreign Direct Investment Survey: A Study Conducted by the Multilateral Investment Guarantee Agency with the Assistance of Deloitte & Touche LLP*. Washington, DC: World Bank.

Mishra, Prachi, Paola Giuliano, and Antonio Spilimbergo. 2010. "Democracy and Reforms: Evidence from a New Dataset." IMF Working Paper 10/173, International Monetary Fund, Washington, DC.

Mohamed, Sufian Eltayeb, and Moise G. Sidiropoulos. 2010. "Another Look at the Determinants of Foreign Direct Investment in MENA Countries: An Empirical Investigation." *Journal of Economic Development* 35 (2): 75–95.

Montinola, Gabriella, and Robert Jackman. 2002. "Sources of Corruption: A Cross-Country Study." *British Journal of Political Science* 32 (1): 147–70.

North, Douglass. 1991. "Institutions." *Journal of Economic Perspectives* 5 (1): 97–112.

North, Douglass, John J. Wallis, and Barry Weingast. 2009. *Violence and Social Orders*. New York: Cambridge University Press.

Omran, Mohammed, and Ali Bolbol. 2003. "Foreign Direct Investment, Financial Development and Economic Growth: Evidence from the Arab Countries." *Review of Middle East Economics and Finance* 1 (3): 231–49.

Pearce, D. 2010. "Financial Inclusion in the Middle East and North Africa: Analysis and Roadmap Recommendations." Background paper prepared for the MENA Financial Sector flagship report, World Bank, Washington, DC.

Persson, Torsten, Gerard Roland, and Guido Tabellini. 1997. "Separation of Powers and Political Accountability." *Quarterly Journal of Economics* 112 (4): 1163–202.

Pipitone, Vito. 2009. "The Role of Total Factor Productivity in the Mediterranean Countries." *International Journal of Euro-Mediterranean Studies* 2 (1): 27–52.

Radwan, Ismail, and Pierre Strauss. 2011. "Knowledge-Based Sectors for Growth in MENA." Unpublished paper, Centre for Mediterranean Integration, Marseille, France.

———. 2012. "Knowledge Economy for Growth and Employment in MENA." Unpublished background report, World Bank, Washington, DC.

Rajan, Raghuram, and Luigi Zingales. 1998. "Financial Dependence and Growth." *American Economic Review* 88 (3): 559–86.

Rocha, Roberto, Subika Farazi, Rania Khouri, and Douglas Pearce. 2010. "The Status of Bank Lending to SMEs in the Middle East and North Africa Region." Background paper prepared for the MENA Financial Sector flagship report, World Bank, Washington, DC.

Rodrik, Dani, Francesco Trebbi, and Arvind Subramanian. 2002. "Institutions Rule: The Primacy of Institutions over Integration and Geography in Economic Development." IMF Working Paper 02/189, International Monetary Fund, Washington, DC.

Rodrik, Dani, and Romain Wacziarg. 2005. "Do Democratic Transitions Produce Bad Economic Outcomes?" *American Economic Review* 95 (2): 50–55.

Rose, Andrew. 2007. "The Foreign Service and Foreign Trade: Embassies as Export Promotion." *World Economy* 30 (1): 22–38.

Sengupta, Rijit, and Udai S. Mehta. 2011. *Understanding the State of Domestic Competition and Consumer Policies in Select MENA Countries.* Jaipur, India: CUTS International.

UNCTAD (United Nations Conference on Trade and Development). 2011. *World Investment Report 2011.* Geneva: UNCTAD.

Vickery, Graham. 2011. "Review of Recent Studies on PSI Re-Use and Related Market Developments for the European Commission." Paper prepared for the European Commission, Brussels.

Volpe Martincus, Christian, and Jerónimo Carballo. 2010. "Beyond the Average Effects: The Distributional Impacts of Export Promotion Programs in Developing Countries." *Journal of Development Economics* 92 (2): 201–14.

Walsh, James, and Jiangyan Yu. 2010. "Determinants of Foreign Direct Investment: A Sectoral and Institutional Approach." IMF Working Paper 10/187, International Monetary Fund, Washington, DC.

WEF (World Economic Forum). 2011. *Global Competitiveness Report 2011–2012.* Geneva: WEF.

World Bank. 2008. *The Road Not Travelled: Education Reform in the Middle East and North Africa.* Washington, DC: World Bank.

———. 2009. *From Privilege to Competition: Unlocking Private-Led Growth in the Middle East and North Africa.* MENA Development Report, World Bank, Washington, DC.

———. 2010a. *Innovation Policy: A Guide for Developing Countries.* World Bank: Washington, DC.

———. 2010b. *Republic of Tunisia: Development Policy Review: Towards Innovation-Driven Growth.* Report 50847-TN, World Bank, Washington, DC.

———. 2011a. *Doing Business 2012: Doing Business in a More Transparent World.* Washington, DC: World Bank.

———. 2011b. *Financial Access and Stability: A Road Map for the Middle East and North Africa.* Washington, DC: World Bank.

———. 2011c. *Middle East and North Africa: Investing for Growth and Jobs: A Regional Development and Prospects Report.* Washington, DC: World Bank.

CHAPTER 5

Facilitating Trade, Access to Trade Finance, and Remittances

Tackling costs associated with inefficient trade facilitation and logistics and weak access to trade finance and remittances is central to further integration of Partnership countries, both regionally and globally. The costs of "connectivity" are often fixed, and as a result they disproportionately affect small firms, farmers, and the poor, severely limiting their participation in trade and investment. Reducing the costs associated with moving goods along international supply chains, whether these costs are measured in terms of time, money, or reliability, is a core element of a trade and foreign direct investment (FDI) agenda. Such costs are also partly determined by access to and pricing of trade finance and associated export credit insurance products. This factor has become more important for Partnership countries' exporters, especially small and medium enterprises (SMEs), since the recent financial crisis, as higher financing costs are expected to prevail in the medium term. There are three Deauville Partnership priorities in this area:

- Modernize *trade facilitation* services by enhancing the performance of trade corridors, whether air, sea, or land; by improving markets for logistics services; by increasing the efficiency of border management, including customs; and by facilitating the cross-border movement of service suppliers.

- Improve access to affordable *trade finance* and related insurance and guarantee products for SMEs, including Islamic finance; build the technical capacity of both SMEs and financial institutions in the management of trade finance at all transaction stages; and develop new interfirm finance products, such as factoring.

- Harness the remittances, technology and skills transfer, and investments of workers abroad by strengthening engagement with the *diasporas*, using government institutions such as embassies and consulates;

by reducing the transaction costs of transferring remittances; by mobilizing diaspora savings through the issuance of targeted financial instruments, such as diaspora bonds; and by establishing more dedicated diaspora programs to promote development in countries of origin.

Trade Facilitation

Key issues

Logistics data show that firms in Partnership countries face significant hurdles in getting their goods from point of production to market. Proximity to the European Union's (EU) 500 million consumers provides Partnership countries with a geographic advantage, but bottlenecks in trade facilitation offset this. Container dwell times in Morocco or Tunisia are about a week, compared to four days in Malaysia or two and a half days in Shanghai. Logistics services such as trucking are fragmented by country, with small providers and few incentives for efficiency gains. There are relatively few priority transport corridors, and border crossings entail an above-average level of physical inspections.

These logistics and trade facilitation costs make up a high and increasing share of overall trade costs for Middle East and North Africa (MENA) firms. Such costs are often fixed, and hence affect small firms disproportionately. Trade facilitation reforms can bring costs down by addressing three pillars: quality of ports, airports, roads, and railways; procedures of customs and other border control agencies; and quality of logistics services such as trucking, warehousing, freight, and forwarding.

Most Partnership countries have invested in road, port, and airport infrastructure serving areas of economic activity in coastal and metropolitan areas. Such "hard" infrastructure offers scope for incremental improvements, but the main bottlenecks are in soft infrastructure. In customs, further computerization and investment in human capital can improve performance. Other border management agencies such as health, agriculture, quarantine, police, and standards can be modernized through a single-window approach and greater information sharing, thereby expediting cargo and reducing physical inspections.

Deauville Partnership technical assistance can help broaden border management reform beyond customs modernization. It can also support the creation of effective subregional trade corridor projects in the Mashreq and Maghreb regions, linking infrastructure upgrades with the institutional and policy changes needed to maximize their effects. The agenda can be strengthened by building on successful recent experience in transport sector reform, and by harnessing Gulf countries' expertise in trade facilitation and logistics.

To be successful, an export-oriented trade and investment policy must be in harmony with and facilitated by modern trade logistics. This is an additional condition for the development of an intra-regional trade and FDI network that can lead to the emergence of an Arab Factory within Partnership countries. No cross-border value-added chain can develop, thrive, and foster a regional competitive advantage unless there is a high degree of fluidity in the movement of goods and services. The trade facilitation and logistics agenda is broad. It includes addressing the links between investments in hard infrastructure and the policy actions that are needed to facilitate trade flows and improve the efficiency of supply chains linking domestic producers and buyers to their international partners, whether in the same or distant regions. The concept of logistics performance helps capture the different dimensions of supply efficiency and the ways in which efficiency is influenced by national endowments and policies. There are three main pillars of logistics performance: the availability and quality of trade-related infrastructure (ports, airports, roads, railroads); the friendliness and transparency of procedures implemented by customs and other border control agencies; and the development and quality of logistics services such as trucking, warehousing, freight, forwarding, shipping and customs, and value-added logistics services.

Trade facilitation reforms aim to reduce the costs of trade-related transport and logistics and increase their timeliness and reliability. Research demonstrates that high trade transaction costs are among the most important obstacles that developing countries face in exploiting the opportunities presented by the world trading system (Hoekman and Nicita 2010; Wilson, Mann, and Otsuki 2003). The MENA region is no exception. These costs are often fixed and disproportionately affect small firms, farmers, and the poor, sharply reducing their participation in trade. Priorities for trade facilitation and logistics have been evolving in the last few years and vary across countries.

At the aggregate level, the MENA region is characterized by relatively high trade costs. Trade costs between two trading partners depend in part on geography, especially the distance between partners, and other exogenous factors. But they also hinge on controllable factors such as logistics performance (price, time, reliability); facilitation bottlenecks at origin and destination; the international connectivity of the countries (e.g., existence of regular maritime or ground services, which is affected by the hub-and-spoke organization of international transportation routes); customs and other border procedures for contiguous countries; and finally, tariffs, nontariff barriers, and other restrictions on trade. A computation of bilateral trade costs around the Mediterranean countries indicates that, as compared to the EU, trade costs are typically twice as high in the MENA region, especially for regional trade (Shepherd 2011). Maghreb countries have lower trade costs with Europe than between themselves (table 5.1).

The size difference between MENA and European markets is not the only explanation for MENA's relatively small share of regional trade:

TABLE 5.1

Costs of Bilateral Trade in Industrial Products between Selected Trade Partners in the Mediterranean Region, 2007

% ad valorem equivalent

Trade partner	Maghreb	Mashreq	GCC	Egypt, Arab Rep.	France/ Italy/Spain	Greece
Maghreb	95	152	167	126	75	151
Egypt, Arab Rep.	126	112	111		119	163
Mashreq	152	77	96	112	149	185
France/Italy/Spain	75	149	132	119	50	96
Greece	151	185	169	163	96	
GCC	167	96	69	111	132	169

Source: Arvis and Shepherd 2012.

internal supply side constraints and inefficiencies also matter greatly. Since trade in the Mediterranean region mainly takes place within single markets, such as the EU or Gulf Cooperation Council (GCC), or through preferential arrangements, such as the Euro-Med Association Agreements, Pan Arab Free Trade Area (PAFTA), and Agadir Agreement, the cost differentials relate mainly to distance, trade logistics, facilitation issues, and the existence of nontariff measures. Trade costs are consistently higher for agricultural products (figure 5.1). This reflects the higher transportation costs (per unit value) and time sensitivity of perishables, but also potentially the impact of more control at the borders and more

FIGURE 5.1

Trade Costs for Industrial vs. Agricultural Goods Traded between Selected Maghreb and European Countries, 2007

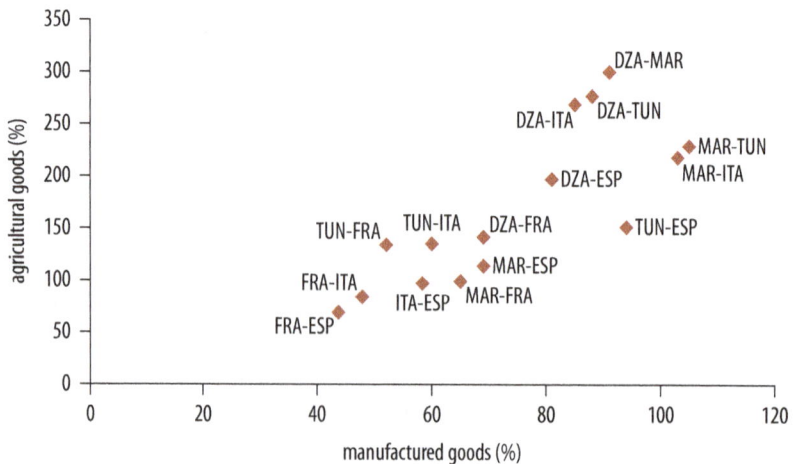

Source: Arvis, Shepherd, and Ghzala 2011.

nontariff measures. In short, MENA fares better in terms of connectivity than in terms of facilitation and logistics; its geographic advantage is offset by weak logistics performance and facilitation bottlenecks.

Data on the performance of logistics services and on the internal costs associated with shipping goods from factory gate to port, and from port to retail outlets, suggest that traders in Partnership countries confront significant hurdles in the region. This can be measured using three different indicators: (a) the Logistics Performance Index (LPI) developed by the World Bank from a survey of logistics professionals, who scored countries on several dimensions including infrastructure, services, and procedures (box 5.1); (b) the Liner Shipping Connectivity Index (LSCI) of the United Nations Conference on Trade and Development (UNCTAD), which assesses how well a country is served by container shipping (countries hosting shipping hubs score high); and (c) the cost of trading across borders in the World Bank's Doing Business index. Although the overall picture that emerges is mixed, it is clear that significant performance bottlenecks exist in many Arab countries.

According to the LPI, the MENA region performs better than Sub-Saharan Africa and South Asia but lags slightly behind East Asia and Pacific, Latin America and Caribbean, and Europe and Central Asia (figure

---

BOX 5.1

The Logistics Performance Index

The LPI has two parts, international and domestic. Each part uses a numerical scale of 1 (weakest) to 5 (strongest) to assess logistics performance.

International LPI is based on assessments by logistics professionals of the environment in the major trading partners of the country where they work. It is a weighted average of six components:

1. Efficiency of the border clearance process
2. Quality of trade- and transport-related infrastructure
3. Ease of arranging competitively priced shipments

4. and quality of logistics services
5. Ability to track and trace consignments
6. Frequency with which shipments reach the consignee within the scheduled or expected time

Domestic LPI is based on assessments by logistics professionals of the environment in the country where they work. It contains detailed information on individual aspects of logistics performance, such as:

1. Quality of trade-related infrastructure
2. Competence of service providers
3. Efficiency of border procedures
4. Data on the time and cost of moving goods across borders

5.2). Within the MENA region, the gap between the Gulf states and the rest of the region is stark in areas such as infrastructure quality and efficiency of border clearance. In these areas, the Gulf countries can provide regional leadership on trade facilitation by helping to spread best practices. The standout performer is the United Arab Emirates, ranked 24th in the world in the 2010 LPI, with a score comparable to that of Korea. The Mashreq countries' score is in line with the middle-income average, but performance lags in the Maghreb. Among Partnership countries, Tunisia posts the best overall performance, followed by Jordan, the Arab Republic of Egypt, and Libya.[1] Except in the Gulf countries, areas that need further attention include infrastructure quality, efficiency of border clearance, and the quality and competence of service providers. Figures 5.3 and 5.4 compare the logistics performance of each individual Partnership country to the average of the MENA region and to the best performer in the region—the United Arab Emirates.

The LSCI also suggests that the region and the Partnership countries in particular could expand trade by addressing their trade logistics and facilitation bottlenecks (table 5.2). For instance, a 5 percentage point reduction in trade costs between the Maghreb and Western Europe would potentially increase North–South trade by 22 percent for industrial goods. A reduction of intra-Maghreb trade costs by the same 5 percentage points would similarly increase trade by some 20 percent. If the intra-Maghreb trade cost could be reduced to the current trade cost level within Europe (France-Italy-Spain), one could expect an increase of some 134 percent in intra-Maghreb trade (Shepherd 2011).

FIGURE 5.2

LPI Scores for MENA Compared to Other Regions

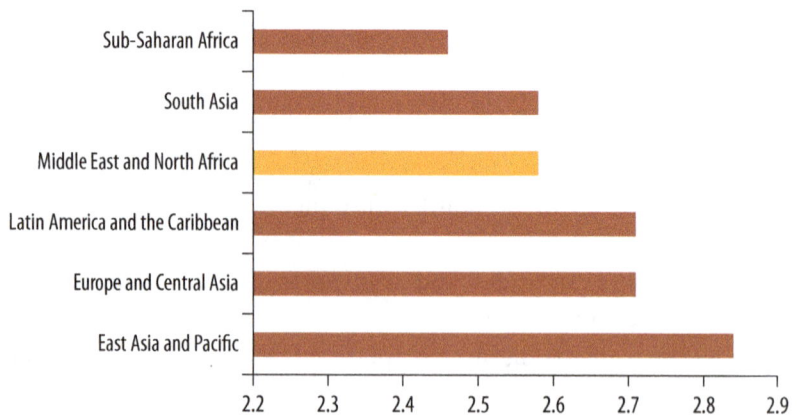

Source: World Bank, Logistics Performance Index 2012.

FIGURE 5.3

LPI Scores for Deauville Partnership Countries Compared to MENA and the United Arab Emirates

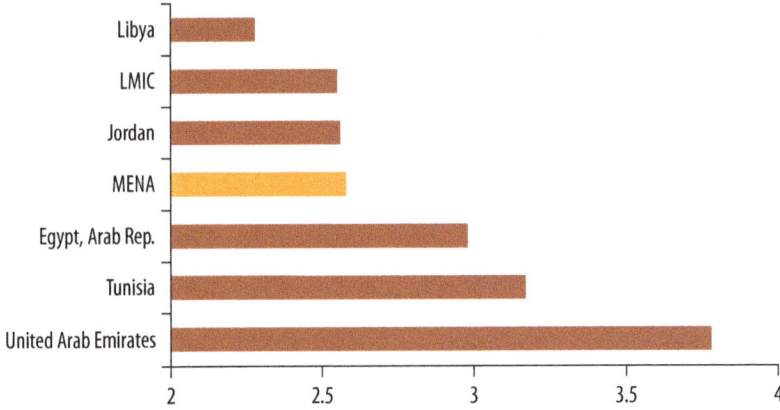

Source: World Bank, Logistics Performance Index 2012.

Note: LMIC = lower-middle-income countries.

FIGURE 5.4

LPI Component Scores for Deauville Partnership Countries Compared to MENA and the United Arab Emirates

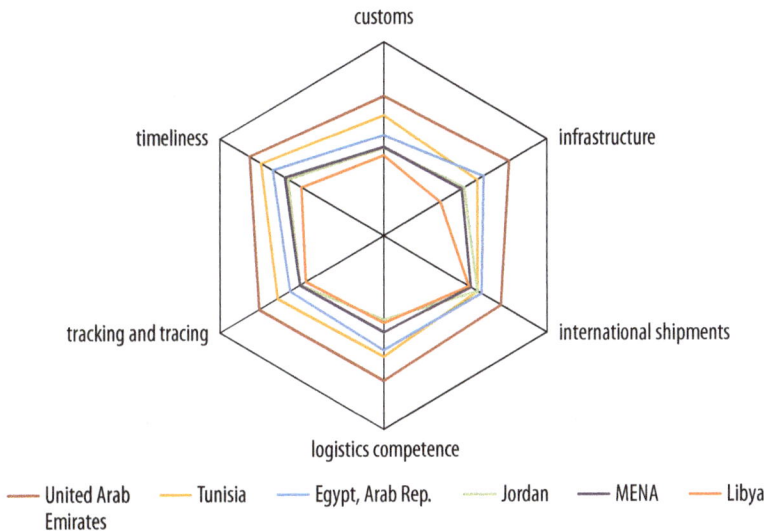

Source: World Bank, Logistics Performance Index 2012.

The Doing Business data on trading across borders indicate that the costs associated with completing the procedures to export or import a 20-foot container (document and administrative fees for customs clearance and technical control, terminal handling charges, and inland trans-

TABLE 5.2

Shipping Connectivity (LSCI) and Logistics Performance (LPI) in Selected MENA and European Countries, 2010 and 2012

Country	LSCI (0–100)	Rank LSCI/183	LPI (1–5)	Rank LPI/155
France	75	11	3.9	12
Spain	74	12	3.7	20
Italy	60	16	3.7	24
Greece	34	30	2.8	69
Turkey	36	29	3.5	27
Cyprus	16	64	3.2	35
Morocco	49	18	3.0	50
Algeria	31	35	2.4	125
Tunisia	6	105	3.2	41
Egypt, Arab Rep.	48	20	3.0	57
Lebanon	30	39	2.6	96
United Arab Emirates	63	15	3.8	17
Saudi Arabia	50	17	3.2	37

Sources: UNCTAD, Liner Shipping Connectivity Index 2010; World Bank, Logistics Performance Index 2012.

port) remain high in the region[2] (table 5.3). None of the Partnership countries was among the 30 top performers in 2012, and they all ranked behind Saudi Arabia and the United Arab Emirates, the best MENA performers (World Bank 2011a).

While modernizing and upgrading trade-related infrastructure remains a priority, hard infrastructure does not appear to be the main trade logistics bottleneck in Partnership countries. Most countries have invested in road, port, and airport capacity. Providing key trade infrastructure is made easier by the fact that most trading activity is concentrated in relatively narrow corridors, such as the coastal area in the Mediterranean countries (box 5.2). However, port constraints do exist, notably in

TABLE 5.3

Ease of Trading across Borders, MENA Countries, 2012

Country	Rank	Country	Rank	Country	Rank
Bahrain	49	Algeria	127	Djibouti	37
Kuwait	112	Egypt, Arab Rep.	64	Jordan	58
Oman	47	Iran, Islamic Rep.	138	Lebanon	93
Qatar	57	Iraq	180	Morocco	43
Saudi Arabia	18	Syrian Arab Republic	122	Tunisia	32
United Arab Emirates	5	Yemen, Rep.	118		

Source: World Bank Doing Business database, http://www.doingbusiness.org/rankings.
Note: The ranking is out of 183 countries.

the Maghreb. Except in Morocco, there is significant potential for upgrading the rail networks and providing missing links (in the eastern Maghreb, for instance). A focus on identifying incremental improvements with a strong return on investment, rather than major projects, would probably be the best approach. Coordinating regional investment initiatives, perhaps through a dedicated corridor agency, could facilitate development and efficient management of trade corridors.

The main trade logistics bottlenecks are to be found instead in soft infrastructure constraints, such as customs and other border agencies, trade and transport facilitation frameworks, and trade logistics services

---

BOX 5.2

Trade Infrastructure in Partnership Countries

Morocco has had the most consistent program to develop trade-related infrastructure for all modes of transportation. Port capacities have increased over a decade, thanks to the successful investment in Tanger Med (mostly but not only for transshipment) and capacity investment and reorganization in Casablanca. Port management was modernized with the separation of landlord and operational activities, and participation of the private sector in Tangier and Casablanca. Railroads and the toll road network have been expanded and modernized and will be soon continuous from Agadir to the Algerian border (a connection already exists from Marrakesh).

Tunisia implemented a number of reforms early on, such as unbundling port operations, but has somewhat neglected its trade-related infrastructure. The port capacity (mostly in Radès-Tunis) is limited, and government has not yet decided between expansion and a new port. The highway system is not yet complete, and the railroad is in need of upgrading (for instance, one-meter gauge south of Tunis).

Egypt has become a major transshipment hub and hosts several efficient, state-of-the-art port facilities. It has also invested in the modernization of air transport infrastructure. Given the density and congestion in the major economic centers, there are serious concerns about inland trade logistics. These have to do in part with services like trucking but also concern the availability of infrastructure for logistics and multimodal transport operations.

Jordan has invested in road infrastructure in its major corridors linking the Amman region to neighboring countries and the Red Sea through the port of Aqaba. Objectives include relieving urban congestion through a ring road and easing the flow of truck traffic in Aqaba. Jordan is also undertaking major development of its railroad network.

providers. These are best illustrated by anecdotal evidence. For instance:

- Container dwell times in Morocco or Tunisia are about a week, which is substantially more than the Organisation for Economic Co-operation and Development (OECD) average (three days) and also exceeds those of emerging economies in Asia (Malaysia has four days, and transit time in Shanghai is two and a half days).

- Markets for logistics services, including trucking, are fragmented by country, with many small providers and few incentives for consolidation and efficiency gains.

- There are relatively few active corridors between MENA countries. Prior to the Arab Spring, the most active corridors were Tunisia-Libya, Turkey-Syria-Jordan, and Jordan-Iraq, as well as corridors within the GCC. Apart from the Tunisian-Libyan experiment at Raz Jair, there is no cross-border coordination between countries (a joint border post, for instance), and there is often a wide no man's land between posts. There are typically many controls on each side of a border, including for security purposes: a 2009 World Bank mission counted about 10 controls in crossing from Damascus to Amman, equally distributed on either side of the border.

- Last but not least, the physical movement of goods and people is sometimes restricted or discouraged in the region for purely political reasons linked to ongoing disputes.

Customs

All Partnership countries have implemented significant customs reforms (box 5.3), but not necessarily in a coordinated and coherent way; this complicates any path toward harmonization. In the case of Morocco and Tunisia, reforms have been driven by the imperative of the Association Agreements with the EU and convergence with EU customs code and processes. Some inputs and technical assistance were received from EU countries, reinforcing substantial own capacity development. Morocco has developed its own customs information technology (IT) solution, while Tunisia has opted for a blend solution with ASYCUDA World (ASYCUDA is UNCTAD's Automated Systems for Customs Data). Customs reform in Egypt and Jordan has been supported by U.S.-funded technical assistance and is also considered successful. Jordan is regarded as a showcase of implementation of ASYCUDA World. While all the reforms are consistent with World Customs Organization (WCO) principles, different customs arrangements and management in Partnership

BOX 5.3

Status of Customs Reforms in Partnership Countries

All the Partnership countries have participated in the WCO's Columbus Programme to determine the strengths and weaknesses of their customs administration through a diagnostic accompanied by recommendations. Findings include the following:

The structure of customs should be adjusted to meet the speed and flexibility demands of a modern customs administration. Specific issues include transparency in personnel management; a review of salary structures to promote integrity; modernization of staff training, including competence in IT; and availability of skilled specialists, such as marine experts and operators of scanners. Customs modernization is hampered by delayed reforms by partner services at the border, such as security, health, port, and transit services. Procedures partly comply with international conventions, including World Trade Organization (WTO) customs valuation and the WCO Harmonized System (HS). As elsewhere in the region, security is the primary concern. The new administration understands this and plans to take measures, in particular at the Egyptian border, to curb imports of spoiled food, counterfeit medicines, and the like. Bilateral agreements will be drafted on information exchange and enforcement, with joint control offices at the Tunisian and Egyptian borders. The customs computer system (ASYCUDA World) is being modernized, but too many procedures are still based on manual processing and registers.

Tunisian customs is advanced in its reform process. The ratio of the cost of customs administration to revenue collected was 2.75 percent in 2006. Customs computerization is being updated (ASYCUDA World). However, the international codification standards (HS, International Organization for Standardization, UNCTAD, WCO, WTO) have not been fully introduced. Operators' computer systems are not interlinked. This limits the effectiveness of customs controls and extends clearance times, and it does not promote dialogue between the different operators, which may lack real-time knowledge of vessel or aircraft movements and access to vessel and aircraft manifests. Customs feels that it lacks operational resources. Risk analysis needs to be further developed to allow implementation of a posteriori controls and reduce clearance times. There are no memoranda of understanding with the main border services, which hampers cooperation. Lack of integrity on the part of some officials is a problem recognized by the government and customs management. Finally, Tunisian customs would like to see enhanced application, including by neighboring states, of the bilateral protocols for exchange of information on rules of origin.

Moroccan customs has undertaken a process of in-depth modernization. Middle management and officers have understood the need to change their working methods, as have private sector operators and other state services. Reform is focused on modernization of clearance procedures and the fight to curb the counterfeiting of highly taxed goods. A particular issue of concern is con-

(continued on next page)

BOX 5.3   *Continued*

trolling the export of prohibited goods, such as counterfeit drugs. Nonintrusive control systems are widely used, but their assimilation in the clearance chain has not yet been optimized. Information and risk analysis should be used more in selecting goods for control. Integrity issues are handled by a customs–private sector integrity observatory, a pilot project launched in 2010 in partnership with the WCO; however, more staff and resources are needed.

Egyptian customs reform is well advanced, with legislation that approaches international standards. It is hampered by lack of staff training, however. Customs structures outside the major ports of entry need modernization, and the regulatory and tariff regime does not yet meet global standards. There is a need to further improve transparency, including the establishment of a dispute settlement body. The application of customs valuation legislation remains a source of contention between customs and importers. The port of Alexandria, which is the main port of entry, benefits from greater efforts in terms of clearance time (less than two days), computerization, nonintrusive controls, and risk management. However,

this progress is not equally distributed across all clearance points, and use of paper registers remains widespread. In some places, control materials are still poorly maintained by untrained staff working in unsecured areas. Customs IT, which is not fully developed, does not completely fulfill its purpose of securing revenue and statistics.

Jordan is engaged in a customs reform process. There is a need to upgrade the legal rules governing the performance of customs activity and increase staff training. The computerized clearance system (ASYCUDA World) is being disseminated across the country; however, it still needs to fully integrate all the useful databases to optimize its contribution to securing revenue and statistics. This results in risk management that does not always allow satisfactory targeting and exchange of information. The existing partnership with the private sector (Golden List Program) does not fully incorporate arbitration and conflict resolution rules. The statistical picture of business activity requires attention to enable the establishment of reliable performance indicators. Technical control resources also need to be evenly distributed across the different posts.

Source: World Customs Organization.

countries (e.g., Jordan's special regimes and higher emphasis on security) may complicate any future plan for harmonization.

The security context in the MENA region clearly obliges the customs administrations to prioritize rigorous border surveillance procedures. the MENA region is therefore at the bottom of the list as regards accessibility of cross-border documents, according to Doing Business 2012. This explains why the World Bank's Logistic Performance Index 2010 ranks Tunisia 61st in overall logistics performance but 73rd in terms of the

customs indicator; Jordan 81st, but 93rd for customs; Egypt 92nd, but 122nd for customs. A substantial informal sector remains, and the industrial fabric is still not up to the standards of international competition. Finally, the key clearance points are the major ports and a small number of land border posts on coastal routes, but there are many other land border crossings in remote, semidesert areas, exposing technical resources and installations to the climate and to insecurity.

Most customs control structures are in need of modernization. Customs staff are often not trained to go into companies to exert technical controls, and they do not necessarily have the resources to travel. The search for fraud is focused on prohibitions linked to the public order, with less attention to commercial prohibitions such as counterfeiting or infringements of rules of origin. Here again, insufficiently developed computerization hinders the creation of up-to-date databases that use data mining (extraction and analysis of data), cover the entire territory, and allow effective targeting. Access to useful private and public databases of port container parks, airplane and vessel movements, and airplane and vessel manifests is still limited. Internal and external consultation structures often function poorly: there is a climate of mutual distrust with the private sector, which means that operators hesitate to signal their difficulties, conciliation structures are often formal, and customs officials retain a culture of disputes and control.

Progress in bilateral and multilateral customs cooperation is slow. Bilateral agreements are being introduced to resolve specific issues between neighboring countries, but the mutual administrative assistance agreements are being implemented only slowly. The reason often cited is the preference given to more important trading partners (the United States, the European Union) rather than to neighboring countries, which are also competitors for direct investments and international aid. Under these conditions, computer networks are not interlinked, there are few exchanges of experience, and joint training or resource-sharing actions are difficult to implement in practice beyond the reiterated statements of intent.

Other Border Agencies

Customs is not the only agency involved in border management. Partnership countries need to pay more attention to modernizing other control agencies at the border, including health, agriculture, quarantine, police, immigration, and standards. Recent analytical work makes clear that improving trade facilitation at the border involves reforming and modernizing a wide range of border management agencies (McLinden et al. 2011). In Partnership countries, one-third to nearly one-half of goods are subject to physical inspection, and customs reforms alone will not address the performance concerns. Improving border management entails a coordinated approach involving all agencies involved in the clearance process. Partnership countries are already working on making these processes part of a single window and better integrating the various controls to avoid redundant inspections. This modernization agenda is also tied to the reduction of nontariff measures. Port transit time (or dwell time of containers) depends not only on the efficiency of customs and other border control agencies but also on other agents in the supply chain: port operators, shipping and forwarding agents, consignees, trucking companies, and so on. It also reflects coordination issues between those operators and agents, and the incentive for speed. In Morocco, for instance, until recently much of the transit time took place before customs intervention, as regulations did not reward timely submission of manifests by shipping agents. Broader automation in the form of a port community system or automated single window typically helps coordination and speeds the communication of documentation and information about the clearance process. Information sharing between trading communities (e.g., freight forwarders) and trade-related agencies, whether in the same country or between countries, is also important.

Trade Corridors

Partnership countries have much to gain from improving subregional trade corridors and regional trade facilitation frameworks. In most trade corridors, existing or projected investment in infrastructure will not deliver benefits without effective transit systems. The efficient movement of goods and vehicles across borders and overland for long distances relies on having in place a seamless transit system at the regional level, or at the very least between neighboring countries. While various formal regional and bilateral agreements are in place, implementation is often jeopardized by poor cross-country cooperation. In larger countries such as Egypt, the performance of internal corridors is also a key priority for reducing poverty in lagging areas and addressing rising concerns about development disparities within the country (Kunaka 2011). While the focus to date has largely been on international trade facilitation reforms, recent empirical evidence suggests that measures to improve internal logistics performance in order to facilitate connections to international trade corridors and supply chains is just as important, if not more so.

With the Arab Maghreb Union, there is little communication between technical agencies (customs, transportation) aimed at reaching agreement on a common trade and transport facilitation framework. This is an area where Partnership countries could learn from the GCC. For instance, there is no agreement on a transit regime to facilitate movement from origin to destination along several borders, although several countries are already parties to the International Road Transport (TIR) convention.[3] In fact, many forums where MENA policy makers meet also involve Europe. The Transport Group of the Western Mediterranean (GTMO 5+5), supported by the Centre for Transportation Studies for the Western Mediterranean (CETMO) in Barcelona, played an important role in mapping needs and fostering dialogue across countries in the Western Mediterranean and beyond, with a primary focus on transport networks. The WCO is the current platform for exchange between customs experts in the region.

Partnership countries would benefit from coordinating their policies and regulatory changes, as well as transport and border crossing infrastructure investments in key transport corridors. A recent World Bank study examines two trade corridors in the Mashreq region: the north-south corridor linking Europe to Saudi Arabia and the Gulf States via Turkey, the Syrian Arab Republic, and Jordan, and the east-west corridor linking Mediterranean Mashreq ports to Iraq and Jordan to Iraq (Ghzala 2011). It identified the main regional trade facilitation, logistics, and transport issues:

- Lack of coordination in implementation of national projects and policies.

- No integration of cross-border facilities or procedures between countries.

- Lack of confidence in application of rules of origin within PAFTA.

- Low quality of trucking fleets, low usage of TIR, and long delays at borders with third countries.

- Missing or inadequate transport infrastructure and lack of properly equipped border crossing facilities.

- No regional trade hub to serve the northern Mashreq region.

- Lack of subregional economic and corridor management arrangements.

The Deauville Partnership could support the creation of effective subregional trade corridor projects in the Mashreq and Maghreb regions. A number of development partners including the World Bank are already supporting a 15-year (2013–27) regional Cross-Border Trade Facilitation and Infrastructure action plan for the Mashreq countries.[4]

The plan will provide funds for infrastructure improvements such as roads, railways, and border facilities, as well as support for institutional and policy improvements such as customs modernization/harmonization, transport logistics regulation, and regional coordination. It will also finance the design and implementation of sustainable Mashreq trade corridor management arrangements. The Deauville Partnership could support a similar initiative for a subregional trade corridor in the Maghreb region.

Trade Logistics Services

Despite progress in upgrading the competence and quality of service providers in air and maritime transport and freight forwarding, Partnership countries are still struggling with the modernization of logistics services. Regulations often reduce the efficiency of trucking markets, while prevailing business and operating practices may interfere with the integration of domestic supply chains into the networks of global logistics providers. Rationalizing and simplifying regulations and increasing the competitiveness of a range of service providers can make trade faster and more cost-effective, thus helping attract FDI to export industries and infrastructure, as well as to logistics and ancillary services (Teravaninthorn and Raballand 2009). In Partnership countries, increasingly, major bottlenecks and steep trade costs are often due to the inefficiency of private sector service providers and to ineffective and anticompetitive regulation. Priorities are shifting to a range of new issues: broadening border management reform beyond customs modernization, making transit systems work, improving the quality of services, and facilitating the cross-border movement of service suppliers.

Trucking reform is a priority in Morocco, Tunisia, and Egypt. Informality and relatively short distances prevent the emergence of a network of high-quality medium-size transport operators, which has implications not only for logistics but also for road safety and urban management. Intermediary professions (e.g., brokers, agents) also tend to be very fragmented, with insufficient quality control, while nationality requirements for brokers (except in Morocco) favor a small number of well-connected domestic operators. Yet reforms are possible. In 2007 Jordan implemented an innovative loading-by-appointment system at the port of Aqaba, which forced truckers to operate in formal companies. This transformed the market structure of trucking operations in the corridor serving Amman and Iraq. Morocco has also promoted the development of new logistics services for the manufacturing industry, operating in parallel to the "old" fragmented trucking and brokerage sector. The reform involved developing logistics zones (e.g., Tangier, Casablanca), opening up the sector to FDI, and installing new customs regimes suitable for logistics activities.

The Gulf countries could assist Partnership countries and transfer their expertise and know-how in the areas of trade facilitation, infrastructure, and services logistics. Within MENA, the GCC countries stand out in terms of their performance in these areas, which comes close to that of other high-income economies. The United Arab Emirates has developed a world-class logistics hub in Dubai. Furthermore, the GCC is the most advanced case of subregional integration in the broader MENA region. For the GCC countries, regional security threats, the proliferation of regional trading agreements worldwide, and the rising forces of globalization have contributed to the momentum toward integration in recent years.

Trade facilitation: Key selected recommendations

Short-term:

- Pursue the modernization of customs in Partnership countries, including through computerization and by training staff in techniques for efficiently controlling violations.

- Upgrade the quality of logistics service providers in air and maritime transport and freight forwarding in Partnership countries, including by rationalizing and simplifying regulations and increasing competition in a range of service providers (e.g., truckers, brokers, agents).

Medium-term:

- Automate the operations of all other border agencies in Partnership countries through single windows to better coordinate and accelerate communication among agencies.

- Improve subregional trade corridors and regional trade facilitation frameworks in Partnership countries, including agreement on transit regimes to facilitate movements from origin to destination along several borders (building on the TIR convention), and coordinate policies and regulatory changes as well as transport and border crossing infrastructure in key transport corridors.

Trade Finance

Key issues

Exporters in MENA countries depend on a steady supply of trade finance to mitigate the risks that arise between shipping and final receipt of funds. When trade credit availability tightens, SMEs are particularly vulnerable due to their weaker capital base and limited bargaining power in relation to global buyers and banks. Protecting and expanding trade credit in the MENA region means addressing the share of the market intermediated by banks and the share provided directly in the course of interfirm transactions.

Partnership countries perform relatively well in extending trade credit to large firms, but its availability to SMEs constitutes an important bottleneck. The challenge is exacerbated by more stringent due diligence requirements by international banks. Several regulatory approaches can help ease access. Reviewing national laws on bankruptcy and commercial disputes could increase confidence; the credit reporting industry can be reinforced; and Islamic trade finance instruments can be expanded. Deauville partners and international institutions could increase their support for trade finance and assist with strengthening Partnership countries' export credit agencies.

> With more than 90 percent of international trade transactions involving some kind of credit, insurance, or guarantee, trade finance plays a critical role in facilitating the international trading system. The global trade finance market, worth about $16 trillion before the 2008 crisis (figure 5.5), provides capital to firms engaged in international trade transactions, reduces the risks related to these transactions, and provides payment mechanisms. Trade finance refers to a wide range of instruments that are offered by banks or companies to cover the short-term capital requirements that arise between production and shipment of goods and final payment by customers. Typical trade-related financial services include letters of credit, import bills for collection, import financing, shipping guarantees, checking and negotiation of documents, preshipment export financing, invoice financing, and receivables purchase. Trade finance instruments can be structured to include export credit guarantees or insurance. Several factors, from the specific features of the economy to the nature of the goods exchanged, influence usage of the various instruments. In the MENA region, while the majority of trade transactions have been open account, the Islamic trade finance sector has recently evolved rapidly.[5]

FIGURE 5.5

Global Trade Finance Arrangements by Market Share, 2008

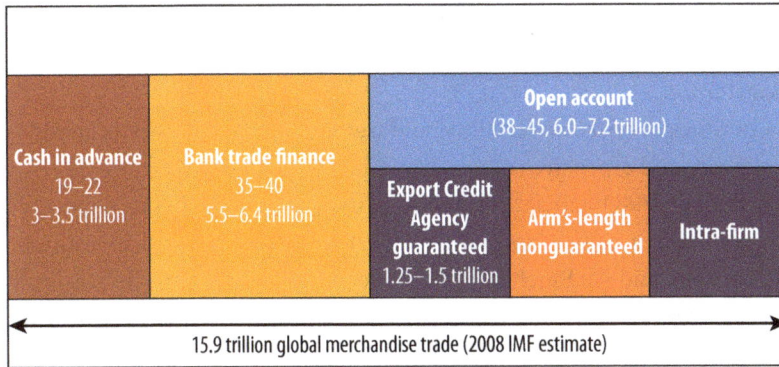

| Cash in advance 19–22 3–3.5 trillion | Bank trade finance 35–40 5.5–6.4 trillion | Open account (38–45, 6.0–7.2 trillion) | | |
| | | Export Credit Agency guaranteed 1.25–1.5 trillion | Arm's-length nonguaranteed | Intra-firm |

15.9 trillion global merchandise trade (2008 IMF estimate)

Sources: IMF estimates; IMF/BAFT surveys of commercial banks; Berne Union data.

With the emergence of regional and global value chains, trade finance activities have also evolved. They now go beyond providing traditional bank-intermediated financial solutions for import and export operations to develop more advanced interfirm modes of financing. International supply chain arrangements have globalized not only production but also finance, mainly in the form of interfirm trade credit involving contracts between buyers and suppliers. At the global level, supply chain finance and structured trade finance solutions now account for more than a third of the revenue pool, up from less than 20 percent in 2000. Sophisticated supply chain financing operations, including those for SMEs, rely on a high level of trust and confidence in global suppliers that they will deliver their share of the value added and have the necessary financial means to produce and export in a timely manner. Any disruption to the financial sector's ability to provide working capital or preshipment export finance, issue or endorse letters of credit, or deliver export credit insurance could create a gap in complex, outward-processing assembly operations and lead to a contraction in trade and output.

Trade finance, whether through banks or interfirm credits, is the lifeblood of exporters and importers, especially SMEs. Trade finance allows producers to access short-term capital to finance their export transactions and import raw materials and semifinished goods. Increasingly, governments also use trade finance facilities to finance imports of petroleum and other national necessities, or to secure supply and regulate prices. But it is for SMEs and new exporters that access to affordable trade finance is especially critical. SMEs are vulnerable to a tightening of trade finance conditions, especially when they operate in countries with underdeveloped financial systems and weak contractual enforcement systems. Small enterprises are usually more affected than large firms by the lack of access to trade finance because of their weaker capital base and bargaining power in relation to global buyers and banks. Also, SMEs are often provided with higher-cost trade finance instruments than larger firms, as banks are generally risk averse and prefer to work with large, established multinational firms.

In times of crisis, uncertainty, and transition, trade finance is an especially rare and expensive commodity. The 2008/09 global economic crisis and the 1997/98 financial crisis showed the critical role that trade finance plays during a crisis, especially in its effects on trade and investment (Chauffour and Malouche 2011). At such times banks are increasingly cautious with real sector customers and counterparty banks, and pricing margins are often increased. These stricter risk management practices are in response to higher risks. In the context of the Arab Spring, for instance, an example is the recent decision by Indian credit insurance to stop covering exports to Tunisia, Egypt, and the Republic of Yemen. As noted above, trade finance shortages adversely affect SMEs more than large firms, and in times of crisis and uncertainty SMEs often experience higher increases than other firms in the cost of trade finance instruments. They may find themselves constrained both by the banking system and by the drop in export revenues and buyer liquidity.

Given the importance of trade finance for export development, especially of SMEs and new exporters, and the importance of SMEs in stimulating growth and employment, trade finance is an indispensable element of any private sector–led growth strategy. Partnership countries already have an extensive web of SMEs. According to the International Finance Corporation (IFC), the MENA region has the highest SME density (number of SMEs per 1,000 population) of any developing region. SME density is about 22 in the MENA region, compared to only four in Sub-Saharan Africa. Egypt, Morocco, and Jordan are among the MENA countries with the highest SME densities, while Tunisia has one of the lowest. Partnership countries perform reasonably well when it comes to the provision of competitive trade finance facilities to large firms. When companies have access to trade finance, trade finance requirements are met at a competitive price (pricing as low as 30 basis points are reported for all four countries). Yet access to trade finance—and for that matter, access to finance in general—remains a key bottleneck for SME development in Partnership countries and in the region more broadly. The pre-shipment export finance guarantees facility given to Tunisia under the World Bank–supported Export Development Project in 2000 attempts to mitigate this bottleneck and ensure the benefits of trade finance. The present value of net social benefits during five years was estimated at $277 million, with the assumption that 100 jobs would be created for each $1 million of additional exports.

Deauville partners, especially the international and regional financial institutions, could scale up their trade finance liquidity programs for SMEs along the lines of the World Bank's Global Trade Liquidity Program. Trade finance and export credit institutions in Partnership countries have not been immune to the liquidity crunch that has hit financial institutions all over the world. Banks are deflating asset prices and consolidating balance sheet positions, thereby limiting the amount of money available to be lent against a reduced capital base. Notwithstanding large injections of liquidity by central banks or low mandatory reserve requirements, the banking systems in Partnership countries continue to face difficulty in meeting trade requirements, notably from SMEs, while international banks continue to limit trade lines to counterpart banks.

Bankers and some international institutions consider Basel II regulations to have further constrained the supply of trade finance since the 2008 global crisis, especially from banks based in low-income countries and from second- and third-tier banks in middle-income countries such as Egypt, Jordan, Morocco, and Tunisia. Concerns have also been expressed about the potential unforeseen impacts on trade finance of proposed Basel III changes. In particular, banks argue that the increase in new liquidity and capital prudential requirements and the nonrecognition of trade assets as highly liquid and safe will lead to a significant increase in the cost of bank-provided trade finance, which in turn will lead to lower supply, higher prices, or both. Egypt continues to face a serious trade finance liquidity constraint, according to recent surveys (Malouche 2009). This is consistent with an overall credit crunch (figure 5.6). The World Bank Group, through the IFC, launched the Global Trade Liquidity Program in 2009 to rapidly mobilize and channel funding to support underserved developing-country markets by providing trade credit lines and refinancing portfolios of trade assets held by selected banks.

In this period of heightened economic uncertainty, Deauville partners could also strengthen their trade finance insurance and guarantee programs by focusing on SMEs that have little access to international markets and no or low international ratings. The recent consolidation of the banking sector in Egypt, Jordan, Morocco, and Tunisia has helped strengthen the position of larger banks that generally meet the requirements of confirming banks without the need for trade support in the form of insurance or guarantees. However, the adverse political and economic situation has significantly affected the macro risk of the four countries, with Egypt, Jordan, and Morocco all falling into junk status since 2007, according Moody's ratings, while prospects are again negative by the end

FIGURE 5.6

Constraints on Bank-Intermediated Trade Finance, by Country, 2010

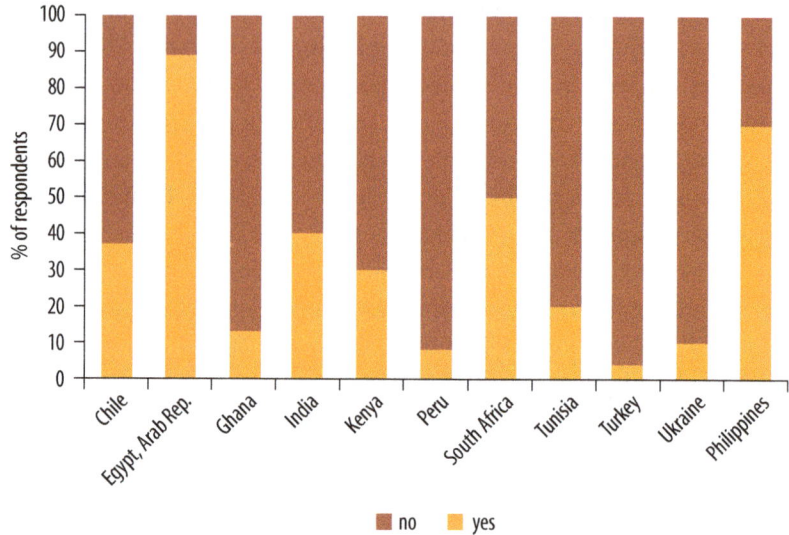

Source: Malouche 2009.

Note: Respondents were asked: "Is your bank still imposing more stringent credit eligibility criteria for trade finance transactions?"

of 2011 for Egypt, Jordan, and Tunisia (table 5.4). Trading activities will therefore be exposed to increased country and foreign exchange risks, and traders will have to face more stringent requirements from banks in terms of lending securities. In addition to heightened risk exposure, traders

TABLE 5.4

Moody's Credit Ratings for Deauville Partnership Countries, 2007, 2010, and 2011

Country	Moody's rating			Moody's outlook
	December 2007	April 2010	December 2011	
Egypt, Arab Rep.	Baa2	Ba2	B1	Negative
Jordan	Baa3	Ba2	Ba2	Negative
Morocco	Baa2	Ba1	Ba1	Stable
Tunisia	A3	Baa3	Baa3	Negative

Source: Moody's website.

Note: Gradations of creditworthiness are indicated by rating symbols, with each symbol representing a group in which the credit characteristics are broadly the same. There are nine symbols, ranging from **Aaa**, which indicates least credit risk, to **C**, which indicates greatest credit risk: **Aaa Aa A Baa Ba B Caa Ca C.** Moody's appends numerical modifiers 1, 2, and 3 to each generic rating classification from **Aa** through **Caa**. The modifier 1 indicates that the obligation ranks in the higher end of its generic rating category; 2 indicates a mid-range ranking; and 3 indicates a ranking in the lower end of that generic rating category.

suffer from banks' lack of confidence in trade securities. The development of structured trade finance and Islamic trade finance has increased the demand for trade finance transactions, but lack of credit information, trade dispute settlement mechanisms, and local hedging instruments makes banks wary of higher exposure.

Group of Eight (G8) countries and other Deauville partners could increase their trade insurance and guarantee support along the lines of the IFC's Global Trade Finance Program. This program doubled its revolving ceiling to $3 billion in late 2008 to offer confirming banks partial or full guarantees covering payment risk on banks in emerging markets for trade-related transactions. The African Development Bank established a $1 billion Trade Finance Initiative in January 2009 as part of its broader package of crisis response initiatives; this could be usefully directed to the Partnership countries to accompany their economic transition. The Islamic Development Bank Group offers Shariah-compliant trade financing. Once the European Bank for Reconstruction and Development secures its new operational mandate to operate in the Partnership countries, its Trade Facilitation Program could be extended to these countries.

To deal with the high regional political risks associated with the Arab Spring and democratic transitions, international financial institutions could scale up their efforts to provide nonsovereign guarantees to investors in Partnership countries. A foreign investor survey undertaken jointly in 2011 by the World Bank's Multilateral Investment Guarantee Agency (MIGA) and the Economist Intelligence Unit (EIU) found that the turmoil in the region had a significant impact on the investment intentions of corporate investors worldwide. About a quarter of investors had put their plans for further investment in the MENA region on hold, while others were reconsidering, cancelling, or withdrawing existing investments (figure 5.7). Political violence, especially civil disturbance and to a lesser extent war and terrorism, ranked as the risk of greatest concern to foreign investors (figure 5.8). Investors were also concerned about governments' ability to honor their sovereign financial obligations in light of increased sovereign risk, rising sovereign credit default risk spreads, and foreign currency sovereign debt rating downgrades. Going forward, just over half the firms surveyed appeared ready to invest in the MENA region, assuming that there is at least a year of stability under a democratic government. International financial institutions could thus usefully scale up their efforts to provide nonsovereign guarantees to investors in Partnership countries. For instance, the World Bank's MIGA has developed a MENA Initiative to mitigate the costs associated with heightened risks for investors in the region (box 5.4).

In addition, Partnership countries' export credit agencies would benefit from support from Deauville partners to expand their insurance and

FIGURE 5.7

Effect of the Recent Turmoil in MENA on Investment Plans in the Region, 2011

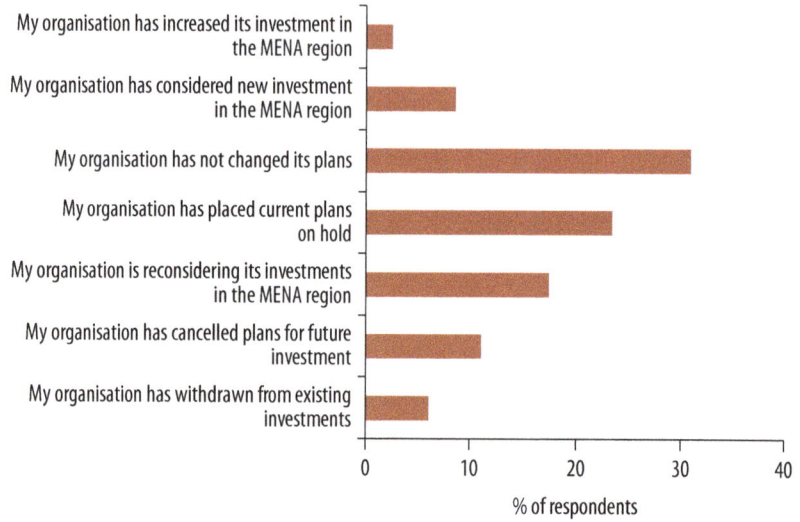

Source: MIGA 2011.

FIGURE 5.8

Effect of the Recent Turmoil in MENA on Perceptions of Political Risk in the Region, by Type of Risk, 2011

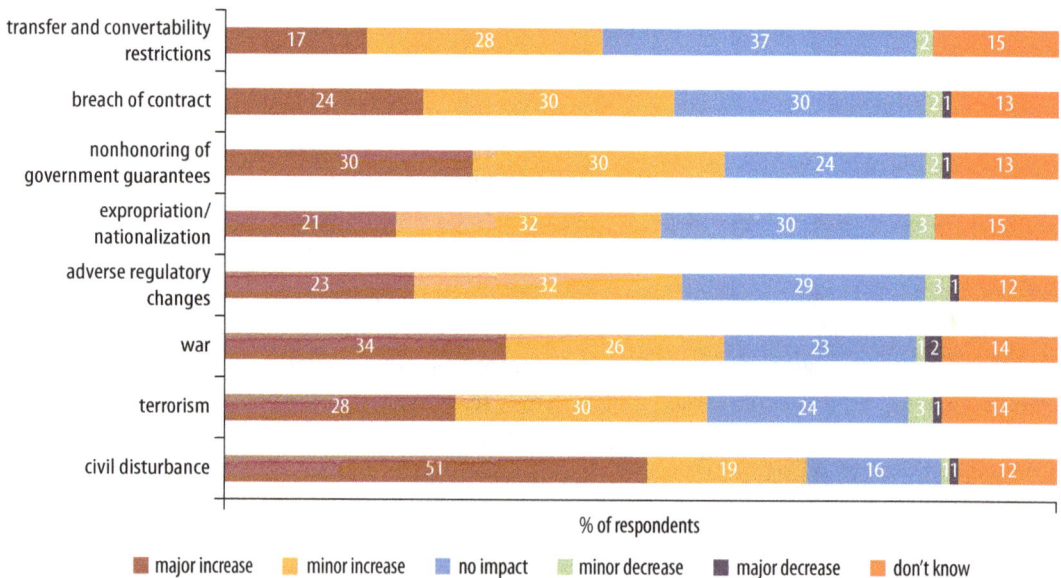

Source: MIGA 2011.

BOX 5.4

Dealing with Increased Political Risks: MIGA's MENA Initiative

The events of the Arab Spring have drastically increased the risk perceptions of foreign investors and tourists in the MENA region. This has led to a shrinkage of FDI flows and plummeting tourism in the countries directly affected, which has negatively affected economic growth. Following the G8 Summit in Deauville in May 2011, the World Bank Group's MIGA was appointed to take the lead in coordinating the response of international financial institutions for nonsovereign guarantees in the region. MIGA has developed a specific "MENA Initiative" to scale up new business development efforts in the region, including the development of a strong pipeline of possible projects in Egypt, Jordan, Morocco, and Tunisia. The initiative has two principal components:

- *Guarantees.* MIGA has allocated up to $1 billion for new guarantees for cross-border investments in the region, $500 million of which will be MIGA's internal capacity alongside a similar amount of reinsurance capacity. The program will be particularly useful for private financing of infrastructure as well as potentially for food processing/production, pharmaceu-

ticals, and other manufacturing and services. MIGA will prioritize investments that create employment. In addition to providing coverage for new investments, this program can be used to guarantee existing investments that might otherwise withdraw because of risk concerns.

- *Knowledge sharing.* MIGA is drawing on its extensive global experience with political risk and transitions in emerging markets to help attract FDI to MENA countries. MIGA is undertaking a series of knowledge-sharing events focusing on regional opportunities and on effective ways to manage risk. These events are reinforced by dedicated media campaigns and targeted communications efforts.

As an example, in July 2011 MIGA provided $225 million in coverage to BNP Paribas for a nonshareholder loan to a Tunisia ferry project. The project involves financing the acquisition of a ferry for a state-owned company. MIGA was engaged at very short notice to replace an insurer that pulled out due to increased political risks. Without insurance, the financing would not have been possible.

guarantee schemes for SMEs and new exporters. Strengthening the role of the credit agencies in Partnership countries could help enhance the participation of private banks in financing trade and investment activities and SMEs. Currently, the volume of business insured by the four export credit agencies is marginal. Partnership countries could benefit from the Organisation of Islamic Cooperation's (OIC) Executive Program for Enhancing Intra-OIC Trade to promote the development of credit and political risk insurance among OIC member countries (box 5.5). Also, establishing a one-stop shop for exporters could facilitate access to trade insurance and guarantees. The International Islamic Trade Finance Corporation (ITFC), secured by the Islamic Corporation for the Insurance of Investment and Export Credit (ICIEC) of the Islamic Development Bank Group, could offer its expertise in this matter.

When it comes to the technical capacity of SMEs in Partnership countries to raise trade finance, three main challenges arise: (a) producing bankable proposals supported by sound financial figures and business plans, (b) receiving adequate support from national institutions and sector associations, and (c) bridging the knowledge gap that impedes credit assessment by lending institutions. Initiatives are under way in Partnership countries to build capacity of both beneficiaries and financial institutions in the management of trade finance at all transaction stages. These include the preapplication stage, where the client seeks the right instrument and lender; the application stage, where the client applies for financing and negotiates with banks; the disbursement stage, where the bank and the beneficiaries process the transaction; and finally the repayment stage, where the transaction is closed.[6] But structural issues such as skill mismatch, information asymmetries (e.g., absence of audited financial statements or credit histories), and adverse selection still pose great challenges to the provision of efficient and competitive trade finance facilities to SMEs. Credit information and creditor rights remain relatively strong in Egypt, Jordan, Morocco, and Tunisia, but an information and knowledge gap exists when it comes to access to credit by SMEs. In the current uncertain context, development of hedging strategies is also very necessary. There is a general lack of capacity in that regard, and the financial industry or local exchanges fail to provide adapted hedging instruments. Due diligence policies of international banks have also become more stringent, requiring provision of standard due diligence information by correspondent banks, which is sometimes lacking.

Finally, the regulatory environment governing trade finance could be strengthened with the modernization of a series of related laws dealing with bankruptcy, commercial disputes, and other business matters. Private sector operators in Partnership countries often mention bankruptcy laws as cumbersome legal processes that fail to secure full realization of the value of assets in case of default. This and other regulatory deficiencies could be addressed as part of the regulatory convergence negotiated in free trade agreements. The proposed EU Deep and Comprehensive Free Trade Areas (DCFTAs) could offer an opportunity to support this process of regulatory convergence with international standards. In the

BOX 5.5

Islamic Development Bank Recommendations to Improve the Executive Program for Enhancing Intra-OIC Trade

The Organisation of Islamic Cooperation's (OIC) Executive Program for Enhancing Intra-OIC Trade promotes the development of credit and political risk insurance among OIC member countries. At its 2010 annual meeting, the Islamic Development Bank made the following recommendations:

- Design OIC-specific trade information tools such as an OIC market access map, OIC trade map, and OIC product map.

- Enhance networking and cooperation among trade promotion organizations of member countries and support the establishment of an export federation or network of OIC trade promotion organizations.

- Support accession and negotiation process of member countries to the WTO in order to have a common trade policy framework among OIC member countries under the umbrella of WTO membership.

- Urge member countries to simplify and harmonize customs and cross-border procedures and utilize international conventions and instruments developed by the WCO in order to facilitate intra-OIC trade.

- Focus on development of trade corridors and logistical services in OIC countries, particularly for the benefit of the landlocked countries in Africa and in the Commonwealth of Independent States. Organize a specific expert group meeting on transportation and trade facilitation.

- Develop a mechanism by which governments of member countries can support the objective of the Executive Program and integrate their local efforts within the framework of the program.

- Organize a meeting for the private sector to review the Executive Program and a meeting for trade ministers to determine the roles of governments in implementation of the program.

- Increase the budget allocated to trade promotion within the International Islamic Trade Finance Corporation and the Islamic Centre for Development of Trade. Establish an export diversification fund and seek potential donors who can contribute to financing the activities of the Executive Program.

- Prepare investment plans for the sectors with high trade potential. Develop sector-specific national exports strategies, which may help member countries diversify their market and export products.

Source: 35th Islamic Development Bank Group Annual Meeting, Baku, Azerbaijan 2010

same vein, alternative mechanisms for dispute settlement could be developed to bypass current delays and inefficiencies in the legal system.[7] In each country, there is scope to expand the credit reporting industry, which is often a monopoly of the public credit registries. Adverse business practices (e.g., red tape, lenders' reluctance to share data due to low awareness about information-sharing benefits) are also impeding the development of trade transactions into a transparent and openly competitive sector.

In the medium term, SMEs in Partnership countries would benefit from reforms aimed at expanding access to conventional financing and developing alternative sources of financing such as Islamic finance. Addressing the problem of restricted access to finance requires implementation of a comprehensive financial development agenda that includes improvements in financial infrastructure (credit information and credit rights); measures to enhance banking competition and address the historical connections between large banks and large industrial groups; and measures to diversify the financial system through the development of nonbanking institutions, instruments, and markets (World Bank 2011b). Partnership countries may want to consider expanding Islamic finance under a suitable regulatory environment (box 5.6). Access to Islamic finance for SMEs appears to be easier and more resilient. Moreover, it appears that Islamic banks have also weathered the recent global economic crisis better than conventional banks. The financing activities of Islamic banks are tied more closely to real economic activities, Islamic banks have largely avoided direct exposure to exotic and toxic financial derivative products, and Islamic banks in general have kept a larger proportion of their assets in liquid form.

In the context of interfirm finance, Partnership countries should explore means to develop both factoring and reverse factoring to provide alternative financing sources for SMEs. Factoring penetration is very low in the region, with very few exceptions such as the United Arab Emirates, Tunisia, and Kuwait. Partnership countries have technological, regulatory, and judicial barriers to the expansion of factoring, as well as a shortage of information on SMEs that may be involved in such transactions. Tunisia is a positive regional example of growth from a low base, with $352 million of invoices purchased in 2008 (up 10 percent from 2007), involving 511 firms and 24,156 buyers. Egypt has recently implemented reforms to foster the factoring industry, including the amendment of regulations to the investment law, setting rules governing factoring activities, licensing, registration requirements, and procedures. No MENA country has yet developed reverse factoring, which can be an important source of working capital financing for SMEs, especially in

---

BOX 5.6

The Scope for Developing Islamic Trade Finance Instruments

Islamic finance has harnessed sizeable savings in Partnership countries that would otherwise have been kept outside the financial systems for religious reasons. Islamic modes of financing are largely based on trade contracts. For example, Murabaha (installment sale, i.e., cost-plus financing) and Salam (advance payments for future delivery of goods) are efficient financing facilities through which the bank becomes a trade partner. These instruments are well suited to trade finance development. Hence, the development of Islamic finance institutions in Partnership countries is an avenue for resource mobilization and trade development.

Islamic finance has shown solid growth in the global finance system in terms of both volume and innovation. For example, Sukuk—the Islamic equivalent of financial certificates or bonds—have been successfully used to mobilize resources for sovereign needs to finance budget deficits, as well as for corporate project finance facilities. The GCC, Turkey, and Islamic financial institutions such as the Islamic Development Bank are well placed to support the development of Islamic finance regulations and institutions in Partnership countries.

---

countries with poor credit information (Klapper 2006). The Mexican experience in this area could be particularly relevant for Partnership countries (box 5.7).

In addition to trade finance, SMEs in Partnership countries need access to long-term financing instruments for their investments, including well-designed guarantee schemes. While state support to investment finance may be still be needed for some time in Partnership countries, this support could take the form of well-designed guarantees in support of greater private bank participation in long-term lending. Governments may consider the introduction of liquidity/rollover guarantees on medium-term corporate or bank bond issues to finance investment, as this could help jump-start the bond market and generate better outcomes than direct investment lending by state banks. MENA countries that have larger credit guarantee schemes, such as Lebanon, Morocco, and Tunisia, also have larger shares of loans to SMEs in total loans and larger shares of investment lending to SMEs. However, while the average size of guarantee schemes, 0.3 percent of gross domestic product (GDP), is in line with the international average, the number of guarantees issued per year (scaled by population) is low by international comparison, and the average value of guarantees (scaled by per capita income) is high. These re-

BOX 5.7

Reverse Factoring: The Case of NAFIN, Mexico's Development Bank

Nacional Financiera (NAFIN), Mexico's state-owned development bank, has succeeded in expanding finance to SMEs since the program's inception in September 2001. As of mid-2004, it had established productive chains with 190 large buyers (about 45 percent in the private sector) and more than 70,000 SMEs (out of a total of 150,000 participating suppliers). About 20 domestic lenders, including banks and finance companies, participate. As of mid-2004, NAFIN had brokered more than 11 million transactions—98 percent by SMEs—at a rate of about 4,000 operations per day.

NAFIN uses an electronic platform that provides online factoring services, which further reduces costs and improves security; more than 98 percent of all services are provided electronically. Many small suppliers that participate in the NAFIN program have no other source of financing. Many had no access to external financing before receiving financing from NAFIN and depended on internal funds and credit from their own suppliers. Suppliers prefer NAFIN financing to bank financing, because banks are slower to make credit decisions and charge higher rates.

The NAFIN program depends on the existence of electronic signature and security laws. Its platform helps prevent fraud, which can occur even in developed countries. As only large buyers are able to enter new receivables, sellers cannot submit fraudulent receivables. Moreover, as the bank is paid directly by the buyer, suppliers cannot embezzle the proceeds.

Source: Klapper 2006.

sults suggest that guarantees may still be concentrated in a relatively limited segment of firms (perhaps medium-size firms) and do not yet reach a significant number of smaller and more constrained firms.

An assessment of the design of these schemes suggests that there is scope for calibrating their rules and achieving gains in outreach and additionality. Some schemes should consider tightening their eligibility criteria to improve targeting, reducing the ceiling on firm and loan size. Most schemes should consider slightly reducing their coverage ratios to levels closer to international standards and linking both coverage ratios and fees more closely to risk. In some countries, guarantee schemes could play a more proactive role in capacity building, including training of banks in SME lending and risk management, and training of SMEs in the development of project proposals, loan applications, and financial reporting (World Bank 2011b).

The GCC financial centers provide another option for deepening long-term finance. GCC banks are liquid and well-capitalized. The centers in Bahrain, Dubai, and Qatar have already gained significant investment finance capacity. Bahrain leads in syndicated lending and cross-border banking; Dubai has created a corporate bond market. The flexibility offered by financial centers also provides a platform for cross-border banking within the region, which would facilitate links between the pools of wealth in the GCC and the significant investment needs of the rest of the region. There are already examples of outward-looking GCC banks which with the right enabling environment would be willing to expand in Partnership countries. One example is Ahli United Bank of Bahrain, which has a subsidiary in Egypt and plans to expand in the wider MENA region. The IFC has invested in this company (through equity and subordinated debt) to support its expansion plans and in particular its ability to draw on market skills developed in its sophisticated markets for the benefit of its newer areas of operation. Similarly, Qatar National Bank has a subsidiary in Tunisia.

Trade finance: Key selected recommendations

Short-term:

- Improve access to trade finance in Partnership countries by developing credit bureaus and credit information exchanges, expanding credit insurance facilities (e.g., hedging instruments, political risk guarantee facilities), easing regulations (e.g., foreign exchange controls for international traders, requirements for SME lending), and promoting SME capacity to access modern trade finance mechanisms.

Medium-term:

- Promote two-step Murabaha financing by Islamic finance institutions and provide venture capital in the form of Murabaha financing to local banks for SME development.

- Scale up support to trade finance liquidity as well as trade finance insurance and guarantee programs for SMEs in Partnership countries, including financial institutions such as the African Development Bank, the Islamic Development Bank, and the World Bank.

Diaspora Engagement

Key issues

A more active engagement with diaspora communities can produce significant benefits for Partnership countries. First-generation diaspora members number at least 8 million, while remittance income exceeded $20 million in 2010. The Arab diaspora includes a significant share of skilled workers, and patterns of destination are complex and differentiated.

Global experience points to many channels through which diaspora populations can influence the origin country. Households receiving remittances may invest more in education and productive assets, while income distribution and power relations may shift to the benefit of women and children. Diaspora links are a conduit for technology transfer and can stimulate exports by establishing sales contacts and filling information gaps on market conditions.

These positive effects can be strengthened by measures that promote emigrants' engagement with their country of origin. These range from providing dual citizenship and voting rights to founding diaspora networks and hometown associations. Countries have successfully used their embassy networks for systematic programs of diaspora outreach. In addition, Partnership countries can consider use of diaspora bonds to harness a key sources of savings. Deauville partners could offer assistance by partially guaranteeing such transactions.

The MENA region offers one of the most complex migration patterns of any part of the developing world.[8] It is both a labor-sending and labor-receiving region and has recently become a transit destination for migrants from Sub-Saharan Africa. It is characterized by outflows to Europe and North America and inflows into the oil-exporting economies of the GCC. The diaspora from Egypt, Jordan, Libya, Morocco, and Tunisia was estimated at 8.2 million in 2010, if only persons born in those countries and recorded as living abroad are counted (World Bank 2010). The actual size of the diaspora, including unrecorded migrants and second- and third-generation descendents, is certainly significantly larger (box 5.8). France is the main destination for Morocco and Tunisia; Saudi Arabia for Egypt; West Bank and Gaza for Jordan; and Israel for Libya (table 5.5). Spain has attracted an increasing number of Moroccan migrants, and Italy has become a new destination for both Moroccans and Tunisians. Due to labor migration agreements and family reunification, there are also substantial Moroccan communities in Belgium, the Netherlands, and the Federal Republic of Germany. The importance of colonial ties has weakened over time as new destinations for migrants have emerged.

BOX 5.8

Defining Diasporas

A diaspora can be defined as people who have migrated and their descendents who maintain a connection to their homeland. The U.S. State Department defines diasporas as those migrant groups who share the following features: (a) dispersion, whether voluntary or involuntary, across sociocultural boundaries and at least one political border; (b) a collective memory and myth about the homeland; (c) a commitment to keeping the homeland alive through symbolic and direct action; (d) the presence of the issue of return, though not necessarily a commitment to do so; and (e) a diasporic consciousness and associated identity expressed in diaspora community media, creation of diaspora associations or organizations, and online participation. This is different from the definition used by the African Union, which defines the African diaspora as "consisting of people of African origin living outside the continent, irrespective of their citizenship and nationality and who are willing to contribute to the development of the continent and the building of the African Union."[a]

Estimating the size of a diaspora is complicated by several factors, such as place of birth, time of emigration, citizenship, and questions of identity. For example, estimates of U.S.-based diasporas are constructed using the "place of birth for the foreign-born population" available from the U.S. census. Most European OECD countries, Japan, and the Republic of Korea classify immigrants based on the ethnicity of the parent, which results in higher estimates of the stock of immigrants compared with a classification based on the place of birth. Temporary immigrants may be considered part of a diaspora but may not be captured in immigration statistics. Origin countries also use different definitions of diasporas. For example, India uses three categories: nonresident Indian, person of Indian origin, and overseas citizenship of India.

In this section we use a narrow but convenient definition of the diaspora as "foreign-born population." Such data capture only first-generation migrants, thus excluding children and grandchildren who may have ties to the origin country. Yet the conclusions of this section should hold, irrespective of the definition of diaspora.

Source: Plaza and Ratha 2011.

a. See African Union (2005). The African Union considers its diaspora as the sixth Regional Economic Community; see "Statement at the African Union Consultation with the African Diaspora in the US: Building Bridges across the Atlantic," http://www.unohrlls.org/en/orphan/791/.

The Arab diaspora includes a significant share of skilled workers. More than 50 percent of all emigrants from Egypt and Jordan hold a tertiary education degree, while the share is around 20 percent for Morocco and Tunisia. As a share of the comparable population of the origin country (i.e., people holding a similar degree), high-skilled migration is always greater than low-skilled migration (Docquier and Marchiori 2012). The

TABLE 5.5

Top Destinations of Migrants from Deauville Partnership Countries, 2010

Morocco			Tunisia		
Destination	Migrant stock 2010 (thousands)	%	Destination	Migrant stock 2010 (thousands)	%
France	841.0	28	France	302.4	46
Spain	778.5	26	Italy	121.7	19
Italy	475.8	16	Libya	84.6	13
Israel	245.6	8	Germany	37.0	6
Belgium	172.7	6	Israel	14.8	2
Netherlands	167.4	6	Saudi Arabia	12.4	2
Germany	108.4	4	Other South	11.4	2
United States	84.5	3	Belgium	11.1	2
Canada	45.5	2	Canada	8.6	1
Saudi Arabia	20.6	1	United States	8.5	1
Other	76.8	3	Other	39.2	6
Total	**3,016.6**	100	Total	**651.7**	100

Egypt, Arab Rep.			Jordan			Libya		
Destination	Migrant stock 2010 (thousands)	%	Destination	Migrant stock 2010 (thousands)	%	Destination	Migrant stock 2010 (thousands)	%
Saudi Arabia	1,005.9	27	West Bank and Gaza	369.1	50	Israel	28.5	26
Jordan	851.8	23	Saudi Arabia	172.3	23	United Kingdom	12.1	11
Libya	397.1	11	United States	72.3	10	Chad	11.1	10
Kuwait	319.5	9	Other South	46.3	6	United States	10.8	10
Other South	176.1	5	Germany	15.7	2	Jordan	8.0	7
United Arab Emirates	140.9	4	Oman	11.6	2	Egypt, Arab Rep.	7.3	7
United States	132.5	4	Canada	8.7	1	Germany	4.5	4
West Bank and Gaza	119.6	3	Egypt, Arab Rep.	7.1	1	Other South	3.9	4
Italy	90.5	2	Australia	4.8	1	Turkey	3.4	3
Qatar	87.7	2	United Kingdom	4.1	1	Canada	3.0	3
Other	419.6	11	Other	22.2	3	Other	17.4	16
Total	3,741.1	100	Total	734.1	100	Total	110.1	100

Source: World Bank 2010.

Note: Percentages may not sum to 100% because of rounding.

Arab country most affected by the former is Morocco, where skilled migrants account for around 16.5 percent of the total skilled population. Tunisia follows closely, at around 12 percent. More than 70 percent of skilled migrants from the Maghreb go to Europe, while skilled migration from Egypt and Jordan goes mainly to North America and Europe.

The diaspora, and especially its skilled members, can be an important and resilient source of benefits for countries. The recent literature dealing with the effects of diasporas on origin countries points to positive impacts in terms of remittances, return migration, business and trade networks, human capital, and quality of institutions. Remittances, discussed in more detail below, can have a strong impact on poverty and on households' decisions about work, investment, and education (Edwards and Ureta 2003; Hanson and Woodruff 2003). Although little is known about the magnitude of return migration, the fact that some migrants accumulate knowledge and financial capital in rich countries before returning to spend the rest of their lives in their origin country is potentially important. The prospect of migration can also induce more people to invest in education at home. The creation of migrants' networks can facilitate the movement of goods, factors, and ideas between the migrants' host and home countries. Ethnic networks help overcome information problems linked to the nature of the goods exchanged. Rauch and Trindade (2002) found that ethnic Chinese networks affect trade in differentiated goods. In the same vein, Docquier and Lodigiani (2010) found that skilled migration has a stimulating effect on FDI. Finally, a very recent strand of the literature focuses on the positive noneconomic impacts on the origin country. Such impacts may be felt in a wide range of areas related to ethnic discrimination (Docquier and Rapoport 2003b), fertility (Beine, Docquier, and Schiff 2009), corruption (Mariani 2007), and democracy (Spilimbergo 2009).

Remittances have traditionally been an important and resilient source of income for Partnership countries. Total remittances to the five Partnership countries amounted to about $20 billion in 2010 (table 5.6). In Jordan, remittance inflows exceed export income and are the most important source of foreign exchange, representing about 16 percent of GDP. In Morocco and Tunisia, remittances account for 9.5 and 5 percent of GDP, respectively (Mohapatra, Ratha, and Silwal 2011). Remittances are

TABLE 5.6

Total Remittances to Deauville Partnership Countries, 2010

Country	Remittance inflows in 2010 (US$, millions)
Egypt, Arab Rep.	7,725.2
Jordan	3,640.6
Libya	17.3
Morocco	6,422.5
Tunisia	1,970.2
Total	**19,775.8**

Source: World Bank 2010.

one of the most tangible and resilient links between migration and development. They tend to be relatively stable and may even behave countercyclically because relatives and friends often send more when the recipient country is in an economic downturn or experiences a disaster (Ratha 2007). In the aftermath of the Arab Spring, remittances held up relatively well in Egypt, Morocco, and Tunisia. While the crisis has spurred hundreds of thousands of Egyptians to return to their native land, data suggest that the dollar value of remittance inflows increased by $500 million in Egypt in 2011. However, in the case of Jordan, remittances dropped 5.2 percent in 2011 (Tayseer 2012). In 2012, Morocco and Tunisia could be affected by the economic crisis in Europe, since these countries are more dependent on the EU for their remittance flows (table 5.7).

Transfers of migrant remittances, as well as the other important contributions of the diaspora, expand opportunities for growth, employment, and poverty reduction. Remittances play an important role in reducing the incidence and severity of poverty in recipient countries. They help households diversify their sources of income while providing a much-needed infusion of savings and capital for investment. In Morocco, for example, remittances account for more than 50 percent of the household budget of the lowest income quintile and reduce by half the probability of being poor (World Bank 2010). Remittances are also associated with increased household investments in education, entrepreneurship, and health, all of which have a high social return in most circumstances (box 5.9). But the diaspora's role goes well beyond the sending of remittances. Emigrants help their countries of origin by stimulating FDI, improving access to foreign capital markets through investment funds and diaspora bonds, providing grants for development, establishing contacts to promote trade and investment, increasing demand for exports (the "nostalgic" trade), and transferring technology and know-how through, for example, professional associations, temporary assignments of skilled expatriates in origin countries, and the return of emigrants with enhanced skills.

Diasporas and country networks abroad are an especially important reservoir of knowledge about trade and investment opportunities. Migrants can help origin-country exporters find appropriate distributors and buyers, improve their knowledge of the market, and comply with government requirements and market standards. Sharing the same language or a similar cultural background eases communication and facilitates better understanding of transport documents, procedures, and regulations. In other words, migrants help overcome information asymmetries and other market imperfections. A growing body of empirical evidence suggests that trade and migration are complements rather than substitutes.[9] Some governmental agencies, such as the Office for Tunisians

TABLE 5.7

Top Sources of Remittances to Deauville Partnership Countries, 2010

Libya		Morocco		Tunisia		Egypt, Arab Rep.		Jordan	
Source	Remittance inflows in 2010 (US$, millions)	Source	Remittance inflows in 2010 (US$, millions)	Source	Remittance inflows in 2010 (US$, millions)	Source	Remittance inflows in 2010 (US$, millions)	Source	Remittance inflows in 2010 (US$, millions)
Israel	4.5	France	1,804.4	France	935.8	Saudi Arabia	2,177.1	West Bank and Gaza	1,605.1
United Kingdom	2.0	Spain	1,631.0	Italy	369.4	Jordan	1,492.7	Saudi Arabia	938.8
United States	1.8	Italy	992.4	Libya	231.7	Libya	813.7	United States	471.1
Chad	1.6	Israel	496.2	Germany	117.1	Kuwait	711.0	Germany	96.5
Jordan	1.2	Netherlands	382.6	Israel	43.9	United States	340.8	Oman	64.8
Egypt, Arab Rep.	1.1	Belgium	380.7	Saudi Arabia	35.6	United Arab Emirates	339.1	Canada	53
Germany	0.7	Germany	239.7	Belgium	35.1	Italy	209.7	Egypt, Arab Rep.	31.2
Turkey	0.5	United States	199.5	West Bank and Gaza	28.1	West Bank and Gaza	209.5	Australia	29.8
Canada	0.5	Canada	99.8	United States	27.1	Qatar	186.8	United Kingdom	25.1
Italy	0.3	Saudi Arabia	39.5	Canada	21.4	Canada	114.3	Italy	21.8
Other	3.0	Other	156.5	Switzerland	125.1	Other	1,130.6	Other	303.3
Total	17.3	Total	6,422.5	Total	1,970.2	Total	7,725.2	Total	3,640.6

Source: Mohapatra, Ratha, and Silwal 2011.

BOX 5.9

Evidence on the Poverty Reduction Effects of the Diaspora in Partnership Countries

Data from household surveys in Morocco and Egypt show that re-mittances have reduced the level of poverty in these countries. Many migrants transfer funds to households in their origin countries for the purpose of investment in health and education. In both Egypt and Morocco, migration and remittances have led to greater investment in the welfare of children. Remittances also apparently trigger a more equal intra-household allocation of education and food between boys and girls, offsetting a gendered bias and favoring gender parity in children's human capital accumulation, especially in rural areas where girls are marginalized (Binzel and Assad 2009). In Jordan, the household expenditure and income survey of 2006 shows that receiving remittances increases the probability of attending school and university for males. Males and females in households receiving remittances attain higher levels of education than their counterparts in nonreceiving households (Mansour, Chaaban, and Litchfield 2011).

Abroad (Office des Tunisiens à l'Étranger), as well as private firms in these countries are asking their diasporas to provide market information in the countries where they now live. Activities include the establishment of diaspora trade councils and participation in trade missions, business networks, and business forums. For example, the U.S. Department of State convened a one-day Tunisia Partnerships Forum to link investors to the Tunisian diaspora.[10] Members of a diaspora may be more willing than other investors to take risks in their country of origin because they are better placed to evaluate investment opportunities and have contacts to facilitate this process (Lucas 2001). Emotion, a sense of duty, social networks, the strength of diaspora organizations, and visits to the origin country may also be important determinants of diaspora investment (Nielsen and Riddle 2007).

To leverage remittances for development, it is important to reduce the transaction cost of transferring remittances and to facilitate diaspora access to investment opportunities at home. Sending money to Partnership countries remains costly, up to 10 percent of the principal or even more, especially from France and Germany to Morocco and Tunisia (table 5.8). Remittance fees can be reduced by introducing modern, cheaper transfer technology, such as the Internet and mobile phones, and by improving competition in remittance transfer markets. Discouraging exclusive partnerships, such as those between banks and international money transfer agencies, would reduce remittance costs, benefitting both migrants and remittance recipients. Policies designed to increase financial sector development—for example, by encouraging greater competition among banks and promoting alternative providers, such as microfinance institutions, credit cooperatives, and postal savings banks—would also have a beneficial impact on the market for remittances. Increasing the role of postal savings banks deserves emphasis given their strong networks in both urban and rural areas.

Although regulations aimed at anti-money-laundering and combating the financing of terrorism (AML/CFT) are necessary for security reasons, they should not make it difficult for money service businesses to operate accounts with correspondent banks. Developing transparent compliance guidelines on AML/CFT regulations should be a policy priority. While financial intermediaries such as banks, microfinance institutions, and credit unions can help transfer remittances, they can also benefit by offering remittance services that may attract new customers and then encourage them to save and invest. Besides encouraging consumers to save a portion of their remittances, these financial intermediaries can develop remittance procedures linked to consumer or housing loans and insurance products. They can also use the history of remittance receipts in the evaluation of a recipient's creditworthiness (figure 5.9).

To mobilize diaspora savings, there is space for facilitating diaspora access to investment opportunities in the origin country. Some governments are providing incentives to attract investment from the diaspora. For example, Egypt provides diaspora members the same benefits and

TABLE 5.8

Costs of Sending Remittances to Deauville Partnership Countries, Third Quarter 2011

Source	Destination	Cost to send $200		Cost to send $500	
		%	US$	%	US$
France	Morocco	10.8	21.60	5.9	29.61
France	Tunisia	12.3	24.64	6.5	32.45
Germany	Morocco	13.8	26.40	7.8	38.90
Italy	Morocco	7.2	14.44	4.6	22.84
Netherlands	Morocco	7.1	14.26	4.1	20.59
Saudi Arabia	Egypt, Arab Rep.	4.9	9.71	2.7	13.31
Saudi Arabia	Jordan	5.3	10.62	3.1	15.66
Spain	Morocco	7.1	14.17	5.1	25.47

Source: World Bank, Remittance Prices Worldwide database, http://remittanceprices.worldbank.org/.

FIGURE 5.9

FIGURE 5.9

The International Remittances Agenda

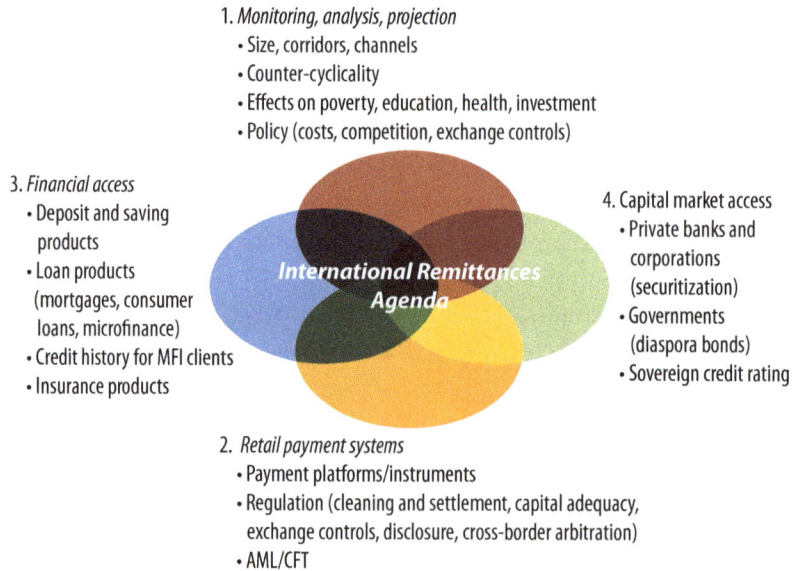

1. *Monitoring, analysis, projection*
   - Size, corridors, channels
   - Counter-cyclicality
   - Effects on poverty, education, health, investment
   - Policy (costs, competition, exchange controls)

3. *Financial access*
   - Deposit and saving products
   - Loan products (mortgages, consumer loans, microfinance)
   - Credit history for MFI clients
   - Insurance products

International Remittances Agenda

4. Capital market access
   - Private banks and corporations (securitization)
   - Governments (diaspora bonds)
   - Sovereign credit rating

2. *Retail payment systems*
   - Payment platforms/instruments
   - Regulation (cleaning and settlement, capital adequacy, exchange controls, disclosure, cross-border arbitration)
   - AML/CFT

Source: Ratha 2007.

rights as domestic investors. Some countries are considering having one window at a government institution for diaspora members where all the paperwork for the different administrative levels can be handled. This could facilitate diaspora access to investment opportunities at home. Egypt has recently established such a one-stop shop for new business and investment transactions by the diaspora at the Ministry of Investment. The Tunisian Agency for Industrial Promotion and the Agency for the Promotion of Agro-Industry operate one-stop shops for Tunisians living abroad. Egypt provides a series of incentives to its diaspora, including exemptions from all taxes and fees on returns to deposits in Egyptian banks. Morocco and Tunisia have established government agencies to encourage diaspora members to invest, assist local communities, and provide policy advice. Such agencies are also involved in the collection of data on diasporas, provision of information and counseling services, provision of consular services, and, at times, facilitation of diaspora participation in social security, housing, and insurance programs at home.

More broadly, Partnership countries need to better engage with their diasporas and organize at home to harness the diaspora potential. Government institutions abroad, especially embassies and consulates, can play a key role in reaching out to the diaspora. A recent survey of embassies found that several have little information on the number of diaspora members, that coordination between the embassies and government ministries needs to improve, and that embassy staff need training on how to work with diaspora members. Steps that could improve embassies' engagement with diasporas include outreach programs to gain more information, the training of embassy staff in contacting diaspora members and facilitating investment and trade contacts, and the use of embassies as a vehicle for marketing investment and financial mechanisms such as diaspora bonds. At home, government initiatives have taken various forms, from the creation of dedicated ministries that deal with migrant communities to the addition of specific functions to such ministries as foreign affairs, interior, finance, trade, social affairs, and youth. In addition, some governments have set up institutions such as councils or decentralized institutions that deal with migrant community issues, with varying degrees of success. Morocco and Tunisia have dedicated agencies to deal with their migrants abroad, but these agencies have not adapted their services to keep up with demographic shifts in the new diaspora.

Partnership countries could more systematically survey the human resources available in their diasporas and create active networks, activities, and programs to tap this potential. One immediate step would be to direct their embassies abroad to more systematically engage with the diasporas. Some government agencies in Egypt, Morocco, and Tunisia have begun to improve their contacts with diasporas to generate investment opportunities for origin-country firms. For example, since 2002 Morocco has set up 16 regional investment centers that offer advice and assistance to Moroccans abroad in relation to specific investment projects. The Office for Tunisians Abroad, in collaboration with Tunisian embassies and consulates, the Ministry of Higher Education and Scientific Research, and the Ministry of Public Health has established a database of high-skilled individuals in the Tunisian diaspora. Egypt targets its diaspora, mainly in the United States, through the General Authority for Investment and Free Zones (GAFI), and Tunisia has been using the Tunisian Agency for Industrial Promotion (API) and the Agency for the Promotion of Agro-Industry (APIA).

Partnership countries should consider mobilizing diaspora savings by issuing innovative financial instruments such as diaspora bonds. Diasporas can act as catalysts for the development of capital markets in their countries of origin by diversifying the investor base, introducing new financial products, and providing reliable sources of funding. Origin countries could take advantage of the fact that diasporas tend to be a more stable source of funds than other foreign investors because their familiarity with the home country often gives them a lower perception of risk. Diaspora members are less concerned with devaluation risk because they are more likely to have a use for local currency (Ketkar and Ratha 2010).

Diaspora bonds are an innovative instrument that can tap into emotional ties—the desire to give back—and potentially help lower the cost of financing for development projects back home.

Deauville partners, including international financial institutions, could support the issuance of diaspora bonds by partially guaranteeing and enhancing their creditworthiness. The issuance of diaspora bonds in Partnership countries suffers from the same constraints that all investors are facing: high political risks, weak legal systems, absence of global banking networks, and limited financial expertise. Government bonds would become more attractive to diasporas if they were partially guaranteed by highly rated borrowers. Since diaspora savings are mostly held as cash under the mattress or in low-yielding bank accounts in the destination countries, offering an interest rate of 4 or 5 percent per year on diaspora bonds could be attractive to diaspora investors. Diaspora bonds can be sold globally to diaspora members through national banks with banking licenses abroad, international banks, money transfer companies, and post offices. They can be marketed through embassies and consulates overseas, but also through civil society networks including churches, community groups, ethnic newspapers, stores, and business associations in places with large migrant communities. The bonds could be sold in various denominations to tap both poor and wealthier migrants, diaspora groups, and institutional investors. Diaspora bonds do not even have to be issued separately; a portion of an ongoing domestic bond issuance could be marketed to the diaspora (Okonjo-Iweala and Ratha 2011). The money raised through diaspora issuances could be used to finance projects that interest migrants—typically housing, schooling, hospitals, and infrastructure projects that have a concrete benefit to their families or local communities back home.

Partnership countries could also mobilize resources from diasporas by encouraging their participation in social security, housing, and microfinance programs. The Philippines, for example, allows its citizens to enroll in or continue their social security coverage while abroad. Workers from the Philippines can also continue contributing to the Home Development Mutual Fund, accessing the fund through diplomatic offices abroad (ADB 2004). Tunisia implemented some similar initiatives to generate savings such as bilateral agreements on social security. Tunisians abroad can have foreign currency accounts and convertible dinar accounts. They receive higher interest on bank deposits and are exempt from paying taxes on interest received in order to avoid double taxation.

The diaspora can be an important source and facilitator of research and innovation, technology transfer, and skills development. Japan, Korea, and Taiwan China are examples of economies that have relied on their diasporas as knowledge sources. Diaspora skills can be tapped by establishing networks of research and innovation with initiatives such as mentor-sponsor programs in certain sectors or industries, joint research projects, peer review mechanisms, and short-term visits and assignments. For example, diaspora members have been invited to teach courses in Tunisian universities through small pilot initiatives. Morocco and Egypt have some experiences in involving their emigrant scientists in promotion of science and research at home. Diasporas may also provide origin-country firms access to technology and skills through professional associations, chambers of commerce, temporary assignments of skilled expatriates working in origin countries, distance teaching, and the return (mainly short-term) of emigrants with enhanced skills. In the aftermath of the Arab Spring, several diaspora groups have initiated support to science, innovation, education, and entrepreneurship programs in their countries of origin.[11]

The diaspora facilitates the diffusion of knowledge and tends to broadly improve the quality of institutions. The role of the Indian diaspora in developing the Indian IT sector is well known (box 5.10). Kerr (2008) used patent citation data to examine the transfer of knowledge between the United States and the home countries of U.S.-based migrants and found strong evidence of knowledge diffusion through ethnic diaspora channels. Moreover, such transfers have a direct positive effect on manufacturing productivity in the home countries, especially in the high-tech sector. Other recent studies examine the link between the diaspora and the quality of institutions in the origin country. Beine, Docquier, and Schiff (2009) investigated the impact of emigration on democracy and civil liberties in the origin country, finding that the total emigration rate has a positive effect. Spilimbergo (2009) examined the impact of foreign-educated individuals on democracy in their home countries. The study found that the foreign-educated promote democracy in their home countries, but only if the foreign education is acquired in democratic countries. Beine and Sekkat (2011) investigated the impact of emigration on the quality of "market-friendly" institutions in the origin country, using the indicators developed by Kaufmann, Kraay, and Zoido-Lobaton (1999): voice and accountability, government effectiveness, regulatory quality, and control of corruption. They found a positive impact for all indicators except voice and accountability. In that case, the effect of emigration is negative and significant, suggesting that emigration reduces the voicing capacity at home, which in turn weakens pressures for institutional improvement. Similar results hold for skilled migration (positive impact for all indicators except voice and accountability), but its impact is much higher.

Allowing dual citizenship and granting voting rights to the diaspora are important means of encouraging greater engagement with origin

BOX 5.10

The Indian Diaspora and Development of the Indian IT Industry

The Indian diaspora has been singled out as a primary factor propelling India's emergence onto the global IT scene (Kapur 2010). As such, it provides an interesting illustration of diaspora feedback to the development of the origin country. Docquier and Rapoport (2011) review recent literature on the community of Indian high-tech professionals and entrepreneurs in California's Silicon Valley and their role in the rise of the IT sector in India. Saxenian (2002) noted the large numbers of Indian (and Chinese) entrepreneurs in Silicon Valley. Indians were shown to run 9 percent of Silicon Valley start-ups in the period (1995–98), with a majority (70 percent) of these start-ups in the software sector. Saxenian (2002) also documented the diaspora's strong business links with India: 52 percent of the Indian entrepreneurs travelled to India for business purposes at least once a year; 27 percent regularly exchanged information on jobs, business opportunities, and technology with people back home; 46 percent had been a contact for a domestic Indian business; 23 percent had invested their own money into Indian start-ups; and 45 percent said it was likely that they would eventually return to live in India.

countries. Dual citizenship can encourage migrants to maintain ties with their origin countries by facilitating travel. Dual nationals also avoid the constraints foreigners face on some transactions, such as temporary work and land ownership, and retain access to public services and social benefits. Beyond that, dual citizenship can help sustain migrants' emotional ties with their homelands, encouraging their continued contact and investment. Egypt, Morocco, and Tunisia allow dual citizenship. This allows Tunisian nationals living abroad to purchase land and property, enabling investments. Origin countries can also strengthen diaspora ties by allowing their citizens who reside abroad to vote without returning. Some countries give nationals abroad voting rights, and some also reserve a specific number of seats in parliament for diaspora representatives. After the Arab Spring, Egypt, Morocco, and Tunisia allowed their citizens abroad to vote. For example, Tunisians living abroad voted for the Constituent Assembly in October 2011, and Moroccans living abroad registered to vote in the referendum on the new constitution. Egypt has changed its constitution to give voting rights to Egyptians in the diaspora.

Deauville partners could further assist Partnership countries in establishing more dedicated diaspora programs with a view to promoting development in origin countries. G8 countries have yet to develop well-defined comprehensive programs to facilitate diaspora trade, investment, and technology transfer. Existing programs have consisted of small grants or matching grants initiatives, such as the Development Marketplace for African Diaspora in Europe, the African Diaspora Marketplace, and the European Commission–United Nations Joint Migration and Development Initiative. The Fonds Sindibad has, together with the French Development Agency, provided additional funds for innovative projects run by Moroccans living in France. France and Tunisia established in 2008 a Framework Agreement on Migration and Development to support initiatives by Tunisians living in France for the transfer of remittances and investments in manufacturing, agricultural, and service activities. However, little evaluation of these programs has been conducted. New programs have also been established.[12]

Diaspora engagement: Key selected recommendations

Short-term:

- Strengthen engagement of Partnership countries' embassies with their diasporas with a view to identifying the diaspora and facilitating investment and trade contacts. Steps include outreach programs to gain more information, coordination with ministerial departments, and training of embassy staff in contacting diaspora members.

Medium-term:

- Establish dedicated diaspora programs in Deauville partners to facilitate diaspora trade, investment, and technology and skill transfers, and promote development in origin countries, in consultation with Partnership countries.

- Harness diaspora savings through the possible issuance by Partnership countries of targeted financial instruments, such as diaspora bonds and housing and microfinance programs.

Notes

1. Morocco is not included in the International LPI ranking due to limited data availability.
2. The cost measure does not include tariffs or trade taxes. Only official costs are recorded. Inland transport costs are based on distance to the shipping port. The methodology, surveys, and data are available at http://www.doingbusiness.org.
3. Morocco, Tunisia, Syria, and Jordan are members of TIR, but it is used exclusively for trade with third countries (Europe or Turkey).

4. In addition to the World Bank, the plan has support from the European Investment Bank, EU, French Development Agency, Islamic Development Bank, Arab Fund, Kuwait Fund, Saudi Fund, Japan International Cooperation Agency, and the United States Agency for International Development.

5. According to the Accounting and Auditing Organization for Islamic Financial Institutions, trade among members of the OIC is expected to reach $4 trillion in 2012, of which 20 percent would be financed through Islamic finance instruments.

6. Among these initiatives are the Global Credit Bureau Program of IFC, which is developing credit assessment capacities in member countries; the development of credit ratings by financial institutions; the capacity-building programs of national and international trade support organizations; the liberalization of auxiliary financial services, etc.

7. For example, the Rabat International Center for Mediation and Arbitration (CIMAR) reports only a few cases per year.

8. Data in this section were obtained from the World Bank's Migration and Remittances Factbook 2011 (World Bank 2010). Migration data come from the United Nations Population Division, national censuses, labor force surveys, population registers, and other national sources. Data on remittances come from the International Monetary Fund Balance of Payments database as well as from central banks, national statistical agencies, and World Bank country desks. However, currently available migration and remittance data should be viewed with caution. Remittance flows may be underestimated due to the use of informal remittance channels, and estimates of the stock of migrants are affected by irregular migration and by ambiguity in the definition of migrants (foreign-born versus foreigner, seasonal versus permanent, etc.).

9. See Gould (1994); Rauch and Trindade (2002); and Bandyopadhyay, Coughlin, and Wall (2008).

10. See the Tunisia Partnerships Forum page on the US Department of State website, http://www.state.gov/s/partnerships/tunisia/.

11. Several organizations in the United States and Europe are developing new initiatives in the transfer of technology and skills. For example, the Tunisia American Young Professionals and the North American Tunisian Engineers Group are organizing an entrepreneurship program aimed at graduating and graduate students in Tunisia's top engineering schools, to be held in July 2012. The Society for Advancement of Science and Technology in the Arab World (SASTA) is working on some initiatives to transfer skills and technology.

12. The U.S.-North Africa Partnership for Economic Opportunity (NAPEO), launched in 2010, offers U.S.-Maghreb networking and investor platforms; innovation and technology incubation; access to finance (e.g., diaspora angel networks and diaspora direct investment); skills training for youth and entrepreneurs; entrepreneurship training for regional artists; and better linkages with business schools, think thanks, and researchers in the United States.

References

ADB (Asian Development Bank). 2004. "Enhancing the Efficiency of Overseas Filipino Workers' Remittances." Unpublished paper, Asian Development Bank, Manila.

African Union. 2005. "Report of the Meeting of Experts from Member States on the Definition of the African Diaspora." Addis Ababa, April 11–12.

Arvis, Jean-François, and Ben Shepherd. 2012. "Trade Costs and Facilitation in the Maghreb 2000–2009." Unpublished paper, World Bank, Washington, DC.

Arvis, Jean-François, Ben Shepherd, and Abdelmoula Ghzala. 2011. "Trade and Transport Facilitation in the MENA Region." Unpublished paper, World Bank, Washington, DC.

Bandyopadhyay, Subhayu, Cletus C. Coughlin, and Howard J. Wall. 2008. "Ethnic Networks and U.S. Exports." *Review of International Economics* 16 (1): 199–213.

Beine, Michel, Frederic Docquier, and Maurice Schiff. 2009. "International Migration, Transfers of Norms and Home Country Fertility." Policy Research Working Paper 4925, World Bank, Washington, DC.

Beine, Michel, and Khalid Sekkat. 2011. "Emigration and Origin Country's Institutions: Does the Destination Country Matter?" FEMISE Discussion Paper, Forum Euroméditerranéen des Instituts de Sciences Économiques, Marseille, France. http://www.femise.org/PDF/wks-migration-2011/4_Beine_Migation_and_institutions.pdf.

Binzel, Christine, and Ragui Assad. 2009. "The Impact of International Migration and Remittances on the Labor Supply Behavior of those Left Behind: Evidence from Egypt." Discussion Paper 954, DIW Berlin (German Institute for Economic Research), Berlin.

Chauffour, Jean-Pierre, and Mariem Malouche, eds. 2011. *Trade Finance during the Great Trade Collapse*. Washington, DC: World Bank.

Docquier, Frédéric, and Elisabetta Lodigiani. 2010. "Skilled Migration and Business Networks." *Open Economies Review* 21 (4): 565–88.

Docquier, Frédéric, and Luca Marchiori. 2012. "The Impact of MENA-to-EU Migration in the Context of Demographic Change." *Journal of Pension Economics and Finance* 11 (2): 243–84.

Docquier, Frédéric, and Hillel Rapoport. 2003a. "Remittances and Inequality: A Dynamic Migration Model." Working Paper 2003-05, Department of Economics, Bar-Ilan University, Israel.

———. 2003b. "Ethnic Discrimination and the Migration of Skilled Labor." *Journal of Development Economics* 70: 159–72.

———. 2011. "Globalization, Brain Drain and Development." IZA Discussion Paper 5590, Institute for the Study of Labor, Bonn.

Edwards, Alejandra Cox, and Manuelita Ureta. 2003. "International Migration, Remittances, and Schooling: Evidence from El Salvador." *Journal of Development Economics* 72 (2): 429–61.

Ghzala, Abdelmoula. 2011. "Regional Cross-Border Trade Facilitation and Infrastructure Study for Mashreq Countries." Unpublished paper, World Bank, Washington, DC.

Gould, David. 1994. "Immigrants' Links to the Home Country: Empirical Implications for U.S. Bilateral Trade Flows." *Review of Economics and Statistics* 76 (2): 302–16.

Hanson, Gordon, and Christopher Woodruff. 2003. "Emigration and Educational Attainment in Mexico." Working paper, University of California, San Diego, CA.

Hoekman, Bernard, and Alessandro Nicita. 2010. "Assessing the Doha Round: Market Access, Transactions Costs and Aid for Trade Facilitation." *Journal of International Trade and Economic Development* 19 (1): 65–80.

Kapur, Devesh. 2010. *Diaspora, Development, and Democracy: The Domestic Impact of International Migration from India*. Princeton, NJ: Princeton University Press.

Kaufmann, Daniel, Aart Kraay, and Pablo Zoido-Lobaton. 1999. "Aggregating Governance Indicators." Policy Research Working Paper 2195, World Bank, Washington, DC.

Kerr, William. 2008. "Ethnic Scientific Communities and International Technology Diffusion." *Review of Economics and Statistics* 90 (3): 518–37.

Ketkar, Suhas, and Dilip Ratha. 2010. "Diaspora Bonds: Tapping the Diaspora during Difficult Times." *Journal of International Commerce, Economics and Policy* 1 (2): 251–63.

Klapper, Leora. 2006. "The Role of Factoring for Financing Small and Medium Enterprises." Policy Research Working Paper 3593, World Bank, Washington, DC.

Kunaka, Charles. 2011. *Logistics in Lagging Regions: Overcoming Local Barriers to Global Connectivity*. Washington, DC: World Bank.

Lucas, Robert. 2001. "Diaspora and Development: Highly Skilled Migrants from East Asia." Institute for Economic Development Working Paper DP-120, Department of Economics, Boston University, Boston, MA.

Malouche, Mariem. 2009. *Trade and Trade Finance Developments in 14 Developing Countries Post September 2008: A World Bank Survey*. Washington, DC: World Bank.

Mansour, Wael, Jad Chaaban, and Julie Litchfield. 2011. "The Impact of Migrant Remittances on School Attendance and Education Attainment: Evidence from Jordan." *International Migration Review* 45 (4): 812–51.

Mariani, Fabio. 2007. "Migration as an Antidote to Rent-Seeking?" *Journal of Development Economics* 84 (2): 609–30.

McLinden, Gerard, Enrique Fanta, David Widdowson, and Tom Doyle, eds. 2011. *Border Management Modernization*. Washington, DC: World Bank.

MIGA (Multilateral Investment Guarantee Agency). 2011. *World Investment and Political Risk 2011*. Washington, DC: World Bank.

Mohapatra, S., D. Ratha, and A. Silwal. 2011. *Migration and Remittances Brief 17: Outlook for Remittances Flows 2012–14*. Washington, DC: World Bank.

Nielsen, Tjai, and Liesl Riddle. 2007. "Why Diasporas Invest in the Homeland: A Conceptual Model of Motivation." Working Paper Series, George Washington University, Washington, DC.

Okonjo-Iweala, Ngozi, and Dilip Ratha. 2011. "A Bond for the Homeland." *Foreign Policy*, May 24.

Plaza, Sonia, and Dilip Ratha, eds. 2011. *Diaspora for Development in Africa*. Washington, DC: World Bank.

Ratha, Dilip. 2007. *Leveraging Remittances for Development*. MPI Policy Brief. Washington, DC: Migration Policy Institute.

Rauch, Jams, and Vitor Trindade. 2002. "Ethnic Chinese Networks in International Trade." *Review of Economics and Statistics* 84 (1): 116–30.

Saxenian, AnnaLee. 2002. "Silicon Valley's New Immigrant High-Growth Entrepreneurs." *Economic Development Quarterly* 16 (1): 20–31.

Shepherd, B. 2011. "Trade Costs in the Maghreb." Unpublished paper, MNA Region, World Bank, Washington, DC.

Spilimbergo, Antonio. 2009. "Democracy and Foreign Education." *American Economic Review* 99 (1): 528–43.

Tayseer, M. 2012. "Jordan's Reserves, Remittances Drop on Unrest, Al Arab Says." Bloomberg.com, January 22. http://www.bloomberg.com/news/2012-01-22/jordan-s-reserves-remittances-drop-on-unrest-al-arab-says.html.

Teravaninthorn, Supee, and Gaël Raballand. 2009. *Transport Prices and Cost in Africa: A Review of the Main International Corridors*. Washington, DC: World Bank.

Wilson, John, C. Mann, and T. Otsuki. 2003. "Assessing the Potential Benefit of Trade Facilitation: A Global Perspective." Policy Research Working Paper 3224, World Bank, Washington, DC.

World Bank. 2010. *Migration and Remittances Factbook 2011*. Washington, DC: World Bank.

———. 2011a. *Doing Business 2012: Doing Business in a More Transparent World*. Washington, DC: World Bank.

———. 2011b. *Financial Access and Stability: A Road Map for the Middle East and North Africa*. Washington, DC: World Bank.

CHAPTER 6

Promoting Inclusiveness, Equity, and Sustainability

The process of integration—like the process of change brought about by technological progress—benefits society at large, but it also generates winners and losers. To be sustainable, the political economy of trade and foreign direct investment (FDI) requires that the benefits of integration, which are often concentrated in the large cities and among the more privileged sectors of the population, be shared as widely as possible across regions and people. Addressing and dealing with the short-run distribution effects of opening up and technological upgrading will probably be the most critical social challenge facing Partnership countries in the coming years. Trade and FDI are more than simple exchanges of material goods and services: they have to do with people and their norms and values. Trade partners need to recognize the possible tensions between those societal policies, as they relate for instance to women's rights, labor rights, or other human rights, and find ways to ease these tensions over time. There are three priorities for the Deauville Partnership in this area:

- Target *social policies* to help the most vulnerable people manage trade- and FDI-related shocks, address the needs of the unemployed during transition periods, and retrain workers in sectors that lose as a result of integration.

- Develop *regional policies* to connect lagging and remote areas to urban centers, promote internal trade, and help poor people in these areas connect to the places where opportunities are concentrated.

- Promote common *societal policies* in trade and investment rules, including in the areas of women's rights, labor rights, and other human rights.

Social Policies

Key issues

Trade and FDI integration leads to a reallocation of resources between and within firms and sectors in a process that creates winners and losers. To ensure support for the reform process, it is necessary to compensate the negatively affected groups through active government interventions. The productivity and output gains from a successful integration process provide the additional resources to do so.

Partnership countries have a wide range of social protection programs that can be scaled up in response to adjustment needs, including innovative use of mechanisms such as social funds. However, a significant part of the relevant expenditure is on nontargeted subsidies that are inefficient and favor rich households. Well-targeted social safety nets protect against risk and offer incentives to invest in human capital. Deauville partners can bolster their support for expanding the best-performing instruments in the context of transition to a more open economy. Expansion of training and retraining schemes can help by addressing equity concerns while facilitating a stronger supply-side response to new market opportunities.

The vision of a greater economic integration of Partnership countries into the global economy needs to include complementary social policies to enhance economic efficiency, promote equity of opportunities to the extent possible, and provide the necessary social safety nets. Simply removing economic barriers between countries may not be sufficient to produce economically desirable outcomes, either because the presence of market imperfections prevents efficient outcomes or because such outcomes have distributional consequences (between and within countries) that make them politically unfeasible. As is well known, there has been a significant increase in the wage premium for skilled labor around the world, a rise in the ratio of skilled-to-unskilled employment in all sectors, and rising relative inequality between the skilled and unskilled. Legitimate concerns exist about certain effects of globalization on jobs, wages, and job insecurity. One concern is that globalization may not have provided the same opportunities to all and may even have contributed to greater inequalities within and between societies. There may also be situations where liberalization produces undesirable macroeconomic results or, conversely, where poor macroeconomic policies have a negative impact on market integration. Hence, economic integration is likely to require some complementary social policies to be inclusive, equitable, and sustainable. Market integration will require some degree of policy integration, and the greater the extent of market integration, the greater the need for policy integration is likely to be.

Empirically, technological upgrading and skills availability seem to be two important factors needed to reconcile economic liberalization and equity objectives. Meschi and Vivarelli (2007) found that total aggregate trade flows are not significantly related to within-country income inequality in developing countries. Disaggregating total trade flows according to their areas of origin/destination, they found that trade with high-income countries worsens income distribution in developing countries. However, this effect does not hold for countries that have greater potential for technological upgrading in terms of both their higher "absorptive capacity" and their superior ability to serve the differentiated and high-quality markets of the developed world. In this framework, the domestic level of economic and human development does matter in shaping the direction and the impact of globalization on within-country income inequality. Bottlenecks in the supply of educated and skilled labor may condemn a developing country to economic marginalization and to high levels of domestic income inequality.

At the same time, greater economic integration can only explain a small fraction of the general increase in wage inequality observed in both developed and developing countries. Adjustment costs associated with trade liberalization were a major issue in the 1980s and 1990s, but they have become less important with the liberalization of tariffs. Analyses of the poverty implications of changes in trade policy and, more generally, the linkages between trade and poverty reduction tend to conclude that changes in trade policies do not often generate large effects for the poor, whether positive or negative, because changes in prices due to these policy changes are mostly small. Much more important are the economic transformation and changes in prices brought about by the related technological progress and technology diffusion. As far as trade is concerned, there has not been a large decline in the relative price of goods that use low-skilled labor relatively intensively.

One implication of the finding that large-scale reallocation of workers across sectors is not the norm following a trade liberalization episode is that the direct effects of trade reform on aggregate employment tend to be limited. Policy makers are often very concerned about the effects of trade on overall employment. It is important to recognize that in principle, trade opening or trade shocks should not have an effect on overall employment levels in the long run—rather, these levels will be determined by macroeconomic variables and labor market institutions. Trade may affect the quality of jobs, by increasing the demand for workers with higher skills or by providing workers with greater access to productivity-enhancing equipment and tools, but it does not, generally speaking, affect the quantity of jobs. This observation may not hold, however, for countries with significant preexisting underemployment. Accordingly, in the case of the Partnership countries, new trade opportunities should translate into investment in tradable sectors and increase formal employment.

An integration agenda nevertheless needs to deal with the possible adverse short-term effects of trade- and FDI-related shocks and ensure that the greatest number benefit from economic integration. Making integration more beneficial to the poorest households is critical for the sustainability of the reform process. Trade and FDI integration will result in a reallocation of factors of production within and between firms and sectors. This is the source of the efficiency improvements that underpin the gains from trade and investment, but it also brings adjustment costs. There are, therefore, winners and losers. Attenuating the negative effects of integration for disadvantaged groups is an important task for governments, and in principle, the gains from trade generate the resources that governments can use to accomplish this.

The design of public policies to facilitate the transition and smooth the adjustment process needs to be informed by an understanding of the impacts of trade reforms and the responses by firms, workers, and households (Porto and Hoekman 2010). For instance, in Partnership countries, given the structure of the economy and the relatively sluggish process of creative destruction, governments should promote entry by new firms and remove barriers to exit, including restrictive labor market regulation. Given that managers of firms confront incentives to improve performance as trade openness increases, measures to promote innovation through research and development and assist in upgrading existing firms would also make sense (Motohashi 2002; Pakes and Ericson 1998). This can include policies that facilitate learning about managerial performance and measures that encourage the use of new technology to improve performance (Hoekman and Javorcik 2004). More generally, all the actions discussed in this report to reduce transaction costs, improve access to credit, and improve access to information through trade support services can be very beneficial from a poverty reduction and trade expansion perspective. Much of this agenda could usefully be supported by the Group of Eight (G8) countries and other Deauville partners in the context of their various aid for trade programs.

Notwithstanding the labor market efforts to facilitate the reallocation of factors during periods of increased economic integration, unemployment may rise in the short run, calling for targeted social policies. To be effective and efficient, such policies need to be well designed and targeted. In developed countries, there has been a long history of direct assistance for the restructuring of firms and industries. This includes subsidies, bailouts, and government involvement in downsizing industry, or managing supply through "crisis cartels" and forced consolidation through mergers. Such policies are often very costly, in part because they prolong the adjustment period and distort competition (Noland and Pack 2003). Policies are better directed at facilitating adjustment through proactive labor market policies, retraining programs, and financing for skills enhancement. Some have suggested a policy package combining (a) income maintenance programs, that is, cash transfers to low-paid poor workers; (b) interventions that facilitate flexible-hours arrangements; and (c) policies that compensate workers for temporary reductions in standard working hours—for example, by granting partial compensation from the unemployment benefits system or by providing paid training opportunities (Khanna, Newhouse, and Paci 2011).

Partnership countries would gain social cohesion by strengthening existing mechanisms to assist those adversely affected by structural reforms, targeted toward poor and vulnerable households (box 6.1). Complementary or transitional policies as well as compensation mechanisms and targeted programs are also needed to ensure that firms and workers can benefit from the new opportunities generated by trade openness. Policies and actions to achieve these objectives require coherence and coordination in policy making, as they typically involve labor and finance ministries in addition to trade and industry or planning ministries.

Taking advantage of the opportunities created by trade and investment liberalization often requires substantial effort and investment in upgrading the production process. However, at a general level, neither theory nor experience provides unambiguous guidance regarding the design of policies to support such investments. Much depends on whether there are spillovers, on whether these are international or domestic, and on the capacities of firms and workers to absorb and adapt new technologies (Iacovone and Javorcik 2010). In the case of East Asia, it was found that social policies in tandem with export-oriented policies were key to the process of economic transformation. For example, Korea provided an extensive system of health and pension entitlements and high educational spending, alongside export promotion. During the 1997/98 crisis, countries in East Asia launched large public works programs to deal with growing unemployment. In addition, most of these countries' development strategies featured heavy public investment in infrastructure.

One essential element of a successful and inclusive liberalization strategy is the extent to which complementary mechanisms are in place to offer training and retraining to workers. An expansion of training provided to workers by firms would help in addressing unemployment among graduates, attracting high-spillover FDI, and upgrading the composition

BOX 6.1

An Overview of Social Policies in Partnership Countries

Partnership countries already have in place comprehensive social programs covering a wide range of policies aimed at preventing, mitigating, and coping with economic hazards.

Preventive policies seek to promote employment by reducing segmentation in the labor market through labor market reform, including specific measures to reduce informality, promote school-to-work transition, increase the efficiency of active labor market policies, and improve migration outcomes. One of the main goals of a trade and FDI strategy in Partnership countries is to improve employment creation and job quality through labor market reforms, including efficient intermediation of labor demand and supply. In addition to employment in national markets, an integration strategy also seeks to promote employability in global and regional labor markets through improved migration management.

Mitigation policies include social insurance coverage such as pensions, unemployment insurance, and disability benefits. All countries in the Middle East and North Africa (MENA) region have implemented defined-benefit pay-as-you-go pension systems, and a number of them have health insurance. However, social security coverage is limited (only 33 percent of the population in MENA countries is covered by a mandatory pension). Benefits for the affiliated are usually large, often redistributing from poorer to richer beneficiaries, and the existing rules often give incentives to game the system. Additionally, the increasing economic integration of MENA countries with the global economy has imposed important reallocations of resources across sectors and led to restructuring of public firms. Such changes have made unemployment insurance an increasingly relevant feature of social security, and having such insurance in place can open the way for a domestic dialogue on reform of labor market regulations. Efficient pension systems and well-functioning unemployment insurance systems are important enablers for dynamic labor markets and, ultimately, growth.

Coping policies provide the necessary social safety nets, including conditional and unconditional cash transfers, specific youth programs, child protection, and social care. Social safety nets are a crucial component of a well-functioning economy, serving as an instrument to enable investment in human capital, manage household risk, and promote equity. Partnership countries spend significant amounts on social safety nets, but mostly on nontargeted subsidies that are inefficient, favor the rich, and can result in significant fiscal liabilities in times of crisis. When well targeted, social safety nets not only protect against risk, but can also offer incentives to invest in human capital through health and education of children and training of young entrants in the labor market. A number of MENA countries have launched innovative approaches, such as social funds, to allow communities to allocate social spending according to their own priorities.

of exports to a higher technological level. The high share of jobless graduates reveals both the mismatch between the demand and supply of skills and the inability of the economy to offer jobs to skilled people. There is a clear missing link between education and employability that needs to be strongly addressed through more vocational training. Postsecondary education remains university-dominated, with low private sector participation in providing both higher education and vocational training. Beyond the formal education system, the system of lifelong learning, which allows workers to continue upgrading their knowledge for higher productivity, is still underdeveloped. Figures suggest that firms in Arab countries are not taking an active part in such training programs (figure 6.1).

Empirically, it has been found that training not only improves productivity (which improves competitiveness) but also increases employment. A number of empirical studies investigated the impact of firm-sponsored training in developing countries. Revenga, Riboud, and Tan (1994) found that in Mexico, training reduces the mean duration of unemployment and increases the monthly earnings of men. Attanasio, Kugler, and Meghir (2008) showed that training raises earnings and employment in Colombia. Aedo and Núñez (2001), focusing on Argentina, concluded that training positively affects earnings and employment. Rosholm, Nielsen, and Dabalen (2007) focused on the impact of training on workers' earnings in Kenyan and Zambian manufacturing firms and found weak support for a positive return on training. Achy and Sekkat (2011), using a large sample

FIGURE 6.1

Share of Firms Offering Formal Training in Egypt, Morocco, and Selected Comparators

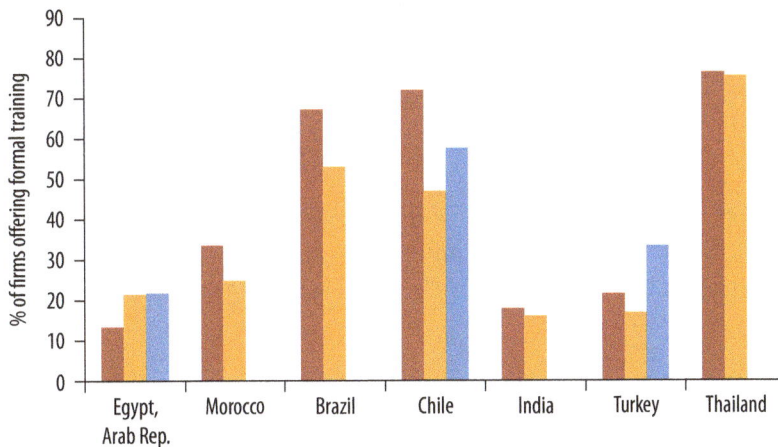

Source: World Bank, World Development Indicators 2011.

Note: The period of observation is the 2000s. Bars are in chronological order, from older to recent. The dates of observation differ between countries due to data availability.

of big and small firms covering seven industries in Morocco, found that firms' investment in human capital (i.e., training) allows them to create jobs. Sekkat (2011), using a similar sample but focusing on productivity, showed that the intensity of training has a significant and positive impact on productivity in small and medium enterprises.

Whether the impacts of trade opening operate more or less through wages as opposed to employment depends significantly on labor market institutions, the efficiency of capital markets, and social policies. In developing countries, wage responses seem to be greater than impacts on employment. There is substantial evidence that trade liberalization has decreased industry wage premiums in those sectors that experienced the largest tariff reductions. The recent global crisis has generated additional evidence that wages bear the brunt of adjustment to external shocks. Based on a sample of 41 middle-income developing countries, Khanna, Newhouse, and Paci (2011) concluded that the impact of the economic downturn during 2008/09 fell disproportionately on the quality of employment rather than on the number of jobs. Slower growth in earnings accounts for nearly three quarters of the total adjustment for the average country, driven by a reduction in working hours, as well as a shift away from the better-paid industrial sector and toward informal or rural employment.

Social policies: Key selected recommendations

Short-term:

- Improve the targeting of social safety nets in Partnership countries, such as conditional and unconditional cash transfers, youth programs, child protection, and other social benefits, including through innovative approaches to allow communities to allocate social spending according to their own priorities (such as social funds).

Medium-term:

- Reduce segmentation in Partnership countries' labor markets through labor market reforms, including specific measures to reduce informality, promote school-to-work transition, increase the efficiency of active labor market policies, and improve migration outcomes.

- Strengthen social insurance coverage in Partnership countries, including unemployment insurance.

Regional Policies

Key issues

The transition to a more open economy has consequences for regional disparities. Trade openness can increase the returns to technology- and skill-intensive activities, adding to agglomeration effects that can promote the concentration of activity. Industry spillovers, labor market pooling, and proximity to consumer markets tend to increase productivity in the long run, but the resulting geographic disparities risk being a source of political grievance.

Partnership countries should focus on ensuring that the benefits from trade integration are broadly shared, without leaving lagging regions behind, by formulating region-specific strategies. These should connect remote areas to the poles of growth, including through better transport infrastructure, trade facilitation, and rural penetration of information and communication technologies (ICTs). Farmers should be connected to urban markets and rural labor should be connected to employment sites.

Extending the benefits of trade and FDI to lagging regions within Partnership countries is another key dimension of an inclusive and sustainable integration strategy. In Partnership countries, metropolitan areas (Amman, Cairo, Casablanca, and Tunis) and coastal areas (Aqaba, Alexandria, and Tangier) have captured most of the gains from past reforms and episodes of growth acceleration. Peripheral geographic areas, particularly those that are remote and sparsely populated, have lagged behind. Unless strategies are developed to improve competitiveness and the quality of logistics infrastructure and services at the subnational level, large numbers of people may not benefit from globalization. This does not mean that economic activity in Partnership countries should necessarily be balanced or symmetric, but rather that people in remote areas should have more opportunities to connect to those places where agglomeration (e.g., markets, employment) occurs.

Partnership countries therefore need to steer a careful course between fostering concentration, which encourages long-term productivity gains, growth, and jobs, and encouraging dispersion, which leads to more balanced regional development. Concentration forces, in the form of industry spillovers, labor market pooling, access to intermediate inputs, and proximity to a large market, serve to increase productivity and income in the long run (World Bank 2008). However, such concentration might induce a widening of income inequality between regions of a country and also a worsening of the situation of urban dwellers through the formation of slums and an increase in crime and unrest (Glaeser, Resseger, and Tobio 2008). From a sociopolitical perspective, spatial disparities can have worrisome effects. They can become a source of political grievance for residents of low-income areas. The relationship between concentration of economic activities and sustainable and inclusive economic growth is therefore complex and depends on several factors, such as the initial level of development and the relative influences of concentration and dispersion forces over time. Moreover, the empirical literature suggests that such a relationship is neither unidirectional nor linear (Brülhart and Sbergami 2009; Davis and Henderson 2008). While the severity of poverty in Partnership countries is generally lower than in other developing countries, it is increasing more rapidly in extent. As in other world regions, poverty is more severe in rural areas but is increasing more rapidly in urban areas.

The risk of a core–periphery divide in the pursuit of further economic integration may also occur at the regional level between Partnership countries and their main trade partners. Partnership countries, which tend to be at the periphery of the Euro-Mediterranean area, may understandably be concerned that their nascent industries could migrate to the European Union (EU) core or other advanced markets in order to benefit from agglomeration economies, thereby dashing the hope of income convergence with more advanced countries. In that case, the spatial concentration of economic activity would create circular forces that encourage further spatial concentration, such as with the emergence of industrial clusters. On the other hand, EU countries, especially those already plagued by high unemployment and deindustrialization, may fear the risk of "social dumping" due to lower wages and social conditions in Partnership countries and other dispersion forces that favor the geographic spreading out of economic activity. The classic example is the price of land, which affects the price of housing, office space, and so on, making built-up areas less competitive and attractive (Puga and Venables 1998).

Partnership countries may raise legitimate concerns about the type and quality of economic development. Integration may have different effects on different categories of products. With the removal of trade barriers, countries, especially on the periphery, may find themselves locked into the "wrong" type of specialization, that is, production of low-valued-added products requiring low skills and knowledge. Again, evidence from economic integration around the world suggests that liberalization generally leads to increases in both interindustry specialization (i.e., specialization between different sectors or categories of products, as in the case of standardized industrial products) and intra-industry specialization (i.e., specialization within sectors through the emergence of clusters, value chains, and other trade organized around networks). The dynamic effects of economic integration arise through economies of scale, gains in productivity, and higher savings and investment rates (Baldwin 1989). Importantly, in view of the objective to develop knowledge-based economies, economic integration facilitates the exploitation of increasing returns to scale in the production of knowledge (Grossman and Helpman 1991).

These concerns are not new and have been expressed in all cases of accelerated regional integration, including in the early days of the EU's own enlargement to include the Southern Mediterranean countries. A question asked by many people at the time was whether the new, geographically peripheral southern EU countries could withstand the combined effects of accession and completion of the single market. A related question was whether incomes in the south would converge with those in the north, or whether the south instead would remain relatively poor—and if so, whether this would generate large flows of labor from the south to the north. There were also concerns that the reverse might occur, with industrial jobs moving from the high-wage north to the low-wage south. In the end, the successive EU enlargements, coupled with EU assistance, played a critical role in facilitating the income convergence of the new members.

The same cause should produce the same effects in the new context of a broader Euro-Mediterranean economic integration. On balance, when accompanied by appropriate domestic policies, the effect of trade liberalization should increase the attractiveness of less-developed areas. The reason is that lower trade costs between two nations or groups of nations would tend to weaken both agglomeration and dispersion forces, but on balance would spark some industrialization in the periphery, especially when trade barriers are already reduced and market size becomes less relevant than factor costs of production (Baldwin 2001; Krugman and Venables 1990). While trade integration is likely to reduce differences in factor prices among countries, trade alone cannot produce complete equalization. The mobility of labor and capital, while often more politically sensitive, would be just as important as a means to achieve a more efficient use of resources in the Deauville Partnership.

A well-designed policy package focusing on a region-specific growth strategy along with transport and ICTs infrastructure could help reduce concentration. There is no doubt that the best way to address these issues is to make the lagging regions attractive to producers, investors, traders, and consumers. This includes better access to social services and an improved business climate to enhance private sector interest in these areas. One needs to match the policy package to the place, taking into account the unique characteristics and distinctive assets of each lagging area (OECD 2011). Examples include cross-border trade facilitation in lagging regions, city-level partnership arrangements between migrant-sending and destination countries, and integrated service delivery strategies matched to local inward FDI projects. Of prime importance is to break the isolation of remote areas by improving their connections to the poles of development, in particular by connecting farmers to markets in urban centers and by facilitating the movement of rural labor to employment sites. Transport infrastructure on rural roads and trade facilitation can thus play a crucial role in mitigating the effects of concentration. Besides transport, Partnership countries should focus on supporting the rural penetration of ICTs in the form of mobile phones, Internet access, and other communication technologies. By enabling people to perform some tasks remotely, ICTs can ease the isolation of rural areas and reduce pressures for urban migration.

Regional policies: Key selected recommendations

Short-term:

- Support the rural penetration of ICTs in Partnership countries in the form of mobile phones, Internet access, and other communication technologies.

Medium-term:

- Develop a regional development strategy in Partnership countries to make the lagging regions attractive to producers, investors, traders, and consumers, by means of better access to social services and an improved business climate to enhance private sector interest in these areas.

- Improve transport infrastructure on rural roads and trade facilitation in lagging regions to break the isolation of remote areas and connect them to poles of development, in particular by connecting farmers to markets in urban centers and by facilitating the movement of rural labor to employment sites.

Societal Policies

Key issues

The MENA region has a growing demographic of young, educated women who want to work. However, although women have on average more years of education than men in Partnership countries, female unemployment is especially high. A range of social and legal barriers constrain women's access to the labor market: social norms constrain participation in male-dominated sectors; maternity and child care policies raise the cost of hiring women; and legal restrictions exclude women from sectors that involve working at night or in nominally hazardous occupations.

Major changes to the status of women will take time. However, the Deauville Partnership offers an opportunity for dialogue on the best ways to defend and enhance women's roles, and on the economic gains from doing so. Productivity growth and expansion of export industries will occur more rapidly if labor and managerial constraints are relaxed through female participation. Similarly, labor and human rights standards can usefully be debated through the Partnership. Inclusion of such provisions in trade agreements can bolster domestic reform agendas and expand technical assistance and civil society dialogue.

Women's Rights

Since the beginning of the Arab Spring, women have been at the forefront of calls for change in the political and economic spheres. This showcases their desire to be equal participants in these aspects of national life. There is wide variation across countries in the region in the degree of women's involvement in economic and political affairs, yet rates of political and labor force participation remain on average much lower in the MENA region than in most other regions. In all Partnership countries there is a growing demographic of young, educated women who want to work. These women could be direct beneficiaries of a trade and FDI integration strategy that creates more jobs. Indeed, the most direct positive impact of economic integration on women's welfare is through increased female employment. This leads to further indirect benefits over time, as women who earn their own income typically acquire greater bargaining power and agency in the household and the society (Duflo 2000; Duflo and Udry 2004). Thus the first-round impact of trade and FDI on women's welfare through employment would translate, in the long run, into enhanced political and social status as well.

There remain considerable rigidities and constraints in the labor markets of the Partnership countries that could limit women's access to new jobs. In other regions, growth in agricultural and manufacturing employment has substantially, if not predominantly, gone to women. Given the presently large shares of women in Partnership countries who remain outside the paid labor force (figure 6.2), the scope for progress is large—but it is not clear that the experience in other regions can be replicated in the MENA region. While MENA governments have often made it their policy to expand the public sector in order to absorb surplus labor, this is no longer feasible, given the sheer number of new jobs that would need to be created for the "demographic bulge" of young jobseekers. The jobs sought by these young people must therefore come from the private sector. The growth of trade-oriented, labor-intensive sectors such as manufacturing and services is one of the best options open to Partnership countries looking to reduce levels of unemployment.

Whether trade translates into female employment depends to a large extent on the relaxation of constraints that presently hamper women from taking jobs in the private sector. Public-private pay gaps tend to be greater for women than for men. This is due primarily to the lower rates of pay

FIGURE 6.2

Labor Force Participation Rates by Gender in the MENA Region, 2010 or Latest Data

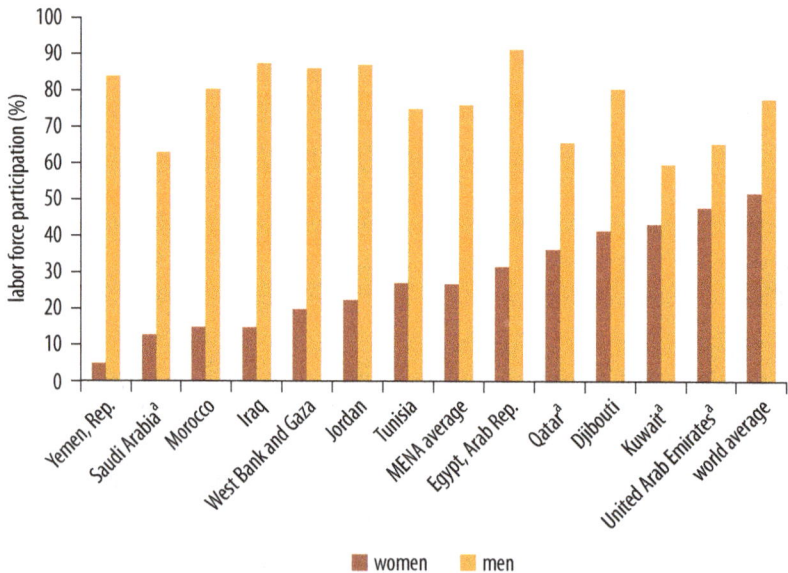

Source: World Bank calculations from national households and labor force surveys.

a. Excludes nonnationals.

women receive for private sector jobs, while public pay rates are less gen-
der-differentiated. As a result, some women may reject private sector job
offers in the hope of finding a well-paid public sector job. Women are
more likely than men to be employed in the public sector in Partnership
countries (figure 6.3).

Women's educational choices may steer them away from the private
sector and contribute to high unemployment rates among women.
Women in Partnership countries are, on average, better educated than
men: they are staying in school longer and attain more years of education
than their male counterparts. Despite their investments in education,
however, finding a job can be difficult. Long-term unemployment rates
for women in MENA countries are considerably higher than those for
men (table 6.1). Since unemployment in the region is most pronounced
among highly educated workers, women's educational attainment is one
reason they tend to experience higher unemployment rates than men. In
some regions, and for certain subjects, more than half of female graduates
from tertiary education remain unemployed for over a year after graduating. Moreover, women tend to specialize in fields more suited to the public sector, such as teaching, health care, and the humanities—required

FIGURE 6.3

Public Sector Employment as a Share of Total Employment, by Gender, in the MENA Region

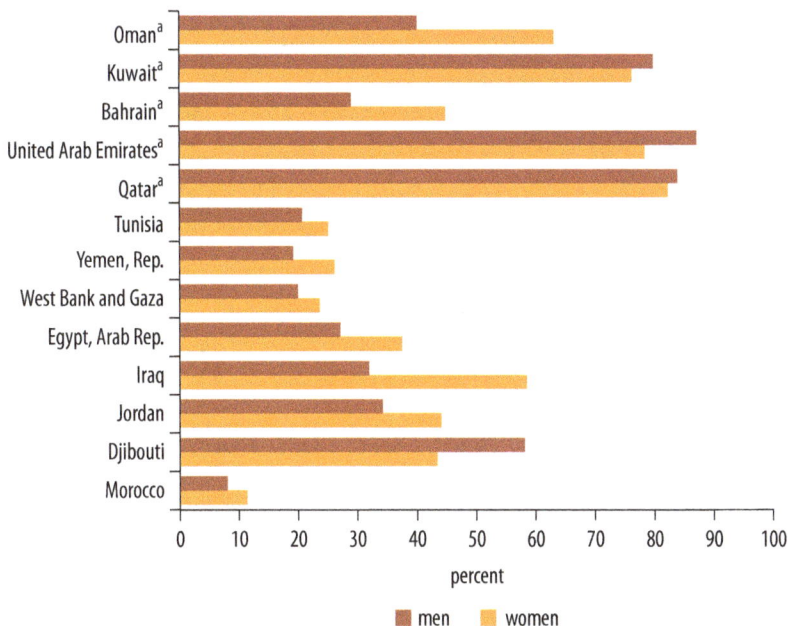

Source: World Bank calculations from national households surveys and official statistics.
a. excludes nonnationals

TABLE 6.1

Rate of Long-Term Unemployment among the Unemployed, by Education and Gender, in Jordan, the Arab Republic of Egypt, and Tunisia (%)

Education level	Jordan		Egypt, Arab Rep.		Tunisia	
	Women	Men	Women	Men	Women	Men
Less than primary[a]	—	22.2	43.5	21.6	25.5	30.3
Primary	48.5	36.2	57.5	31.0	26.5	34.2
Secondary	40.2	24.2	78.7	56.0	31.8	33.3
Postsecondary	37.9	29.3	66.8	57.4	41.1	46.3

Source: World Bank calculations from national household and labor market surveys, 2005–10.

Note: Long-term unemployment is defined as being unemployed for more than 12 months.

a. Data not available for Jordanian women with less than primary education.

qualifications for many public sector jobs, but not highly valued by the private sector (World Bank 2011). Thus their educational path may limit their ability to find private sector employment. Furthermore, to the extent that export-driven demand for workers focuses on women with lower levels of education or more technical skills, its impact on the high rates of unemployment among well-educated women may be limited. Growth in service industry jobs is more likely to suit the skills and earnings expectations of these women. Data from the Tunisia Labor Force Survey suggest that discouragement is a serious problem for women, especially those with only some postsecondary education (World Bank 2011). This implies that the female unemployment rate greatly understates the number of potential female workers available.

Social and legal barriers continue to make it difficult for women to work, even when jobs are available. Traditionally, women in the region did not participate in the labor force, especially those who were married and had children. Today, many young women are eager to work, but entrenched social norms, reinforced by gender-based laws, still make many firms reluctant to hire women and families reluctant to allow women to work. Social norms and legal restrictions also discourage or prevent women from accepting certain types of jobs. Several constraints can be noted:

- *Traditional social norms and attitudes portray women as less capable and reliable employees than men.* While attitudes in the region are slowly changing, lingering stigmas about women's abilities remain a challenge for women seeking to work in the private sector or in male-dominated fields.

- *Restrictive guardianship laws limit women's employment options.* In the Arab Republic of Egypt and Jordan, as in most MENA countries, women's status, rights, and obligations within the household and society are defined by family codes. In many countries, these laws restrict a woman's freedom by requiring her to obtain a male guardian's permission in order to accept a job, apply for a passport or driver's license, take out a loan, travel, or even leave the house (table 6.2). By setting strict limits on women's freedom of movement and autonomy, guardianship laws make it difficult or impossible for women to work, look for work, or run a business.

- *Safety concerns further limit women's options.* In addition to social norms, concerns about safety prevent women from traveling or living alone. This limits their ability to migrate for work, a constraint that disproportionately affects women in rural or less prosperous areas. The geographic inflexibility of the female labor force contributes to the higher female unemployment rates in remote areas. This may be a significant factor in determining whether trade-oriented jobs are taken by men or women, since the location of factories or offices implicitly determines the size of the local female labor pool.

TABLE 6.2

Legal Restrictions on Women in MENA Countries

	Unmarried women	Married women
Women are not permitted to do the following in the same way as men		
Apply for a passport	Saudi Arabia	Egypt, Arab Rep.; Iran, Islamic Rep.; Jordan; Kuwait; Oman; Saudi Arabia; United Arab Emirates; Yemen, Rep.
Travel internationally	Saudi Arabia	Iran, Islamic Rep.; Saudi Arabia; Syrian Arab Republic
Travel domestically		Iran. Islamic Rep.; Saudi Arabia; Yemen, Rep.
Get a job or pursue a trade	Kuwait, Oman	Iran, Islamic Rep.; Jordan; Oman; United Arab Emirates
Women must obey their husbands	n.a.	Egypt, Arab Rep.; Jordan; Lebanon; Saudi Arabia; Syrian Arab Republic; United Arab Emirates; West Bank and Gaza; Yemen, Rep.
The constitution		
Bans gender discrimination	Algeria; Oman; West Bank and Gaza	
Guarantees gender equality	Algeria; Egypt, Arab Rep.; Iran, Islamic Rep.; Jordan; Kuwait; Lebanon; Morocco; Oman; Syrian Arab Republic; Tunisia; United Arab Emirates; West Bank and Gaza; Yemen, Rep.	

Source: Women, Business and the Law database, 2012, http://wbl.worldbank.org.
Note: n.a. = not applicable.

- *Harassment in the workplace remains a serious problem in some countries.* Only four countries in the MENA region (Algeria, Iraq, Morocco, and Tunisia) have legislation that criminalizes sexual harassment in the workplace and allows women to take legal action against such offences. These laws are a start, but their implementation remains a challenge. Legal and policing systems may not be strong enough to create an effective deterrent against such crimes, and many women are reluctant to report harassment. Even though attitudes toward women are gradually changing and laws are slowly extending real protections to working women, people still express concern about the risk of harassment at work or while traveling to work.

- *Laws guaranteeing maternity leave and child care benefits impose additional costs on firms that hire women.* All countries in the MENA region mandate some form of maternity leave, and some also have provisions for child care. But these policies have the unintended consequence of raising the cost of hiring women, since firms are usually expected to pay for the cost of leave and replace women workers while they are on leave.

- *Laws restrict women from working at night and limit the industries in which women can work.* All countries in the world have some forms of restriction on the jobs women can do. However, these restrictions cover more industries in the MENA region than elsewhere, including not only jobs that might be strenuous or physically harmful, but also those considered morally harmful. MENA countries are also unusual in banning women from working at night. Such restrictions are intended to protect women, but end up limiting their flexibility and choice of work.

To ensure that women gain directly from the employment opportunities created by trade and FDI, Partnership countries should address the factors constraining women's access to employment. The legal and regulatory environment needs to be reformed with a view to not only fostering job creation and a competitive labor market, but also making these new jobs available to women. Governments should work to reduce the distortionary effect of the public sector on the private labor market and reform education to better equip young women with the skills required by industry. Certain laws must change because they discourage firms from hiring women; these include requirements for employer-funded maternity leave and restrictions on women working in certain industries or at night. Clearly, women will benefit little from new manufacturing jobs if they cannot work night shifts. Governments need to ensure that laws and the judicial system protect women from harassment in the workplace and on their way to work; only visible enforcement of these protections will begin to change attitudes. Finally, as illustrated by the history of development in East Asia, women need mobility and flexibility of choice in order to benefit from new jobs in the tradable sector. Governments should consider how the current legal and social environment, including certain gender-based laws, might hamper this, and seek to address such constraints.

Major changes to the status of women in the region will take time. There is, moreover, a concern that efforts to advance women's rights may be halted or even reversed as new governments come to power. This is particularly the case in Tunisia and Egypt, where reforms to women's rights were a dimension of the previous regimes' modernizing agendas. These reforms could be targeted by parties looking to signal a break with the past. Short-run volatility associated with economic reform and opening of markets may well exacerbate the political pressures in this regard. The Deauville Partnership is an opportunity for dialogue on the best ways not only to defend the rights of women in Partnership countries, but to enhance them.

Labor Rights

Pursuing core labor standards simultaneously with trade and FDI could help spread the benefits of globalization more broadly, discourage the worst abuses of workers, and increase public support for trade agreements and economic integration.[1] The policy debate and the accompanying literature on whether trade and labor standards should be linked, and if so, how, reflect two main schools of thought. On the one hand, free market advocates argue that trade and FDI encourage growth, which in turn will bring about higher productivity, wages, and better working conditions. In this view, no special attention to labor standards in trade or investment agreements is needed. Some argue that pushing developing countries to adopt higher standards would make them uncompetitive in export markets and lead to fewer jobs and worse conditions. On the other hand, labor standards advocates, led by unions and many human rights groups, maintain that competition to attract FDI or to capture a larger export market share causes countries to suppress labor standards, or at least not to raise them, leading to a "race to the bottom." There is, however, little compelling evidence in the empirical literature either of a race to the bottom in labor standards or of protectionist abuse of trade-labor linkages where they exist. The effect of higher standards on competitiveness is more complicated than is usually assumed, and any higher costs of compliance that do materialize are often offset by higher productivity (Freeman and Medoff 1984). A meta-survey of the literature published by the World Bank in 2002 found "little systematic difference in performance between countries that enforce [union rights] and countries that do not" (Aidt and Tzannatos 2002, 4). Nor does the experience of nearly two decades offer support for the concern that trade sanctions to enforce labor standards are simply protectionism in disguise.

One key to realizing the complementarities between open trade and labor rights and avoiding potential negative effects is to distinguish "core" labor standards from others. Some labor standards—for example, wages and health/safety regulations—clearly will have to vary with countries' levels of development and local standards of living. However, the core labor standards set forth in the Declaration on Fundamental Principles and Rights at Work that was issued by the International Labour Organization (ILO) in 1998 are meant to be upheld by all countries, regardless of their level of development. The ILO document lists four core labor standards as deserving of universal application, which may be summarized briefly as:

- Freedom of association and "effective recognition" of the right to collective bargaining.

- Elimination of forced labor.

- Effective abolition of child labor.

- Elimination of discrimination in employment.

These standards are part of the framework rules that govern labor market transactions; they do not specify particular outcomes, such as wages. They are comparable to the rules that protect property rights and freedom of transactions in product markets, which most economists view as necessary if market economies are to operate efficiently. The core labor standards are also fundamental elements of well-functioning democracies. And, just as the universality of property rights and freedom of market transactions does not imply identical laws or institutions in all countries, universality of these core labor standards does not imply uniformity in the details of protection or in the institutions that implement it.

Demands to include labor rights in trade agreements began with the United States and the negotiation of the North American Free Trade Agreement with Mexico and Canada in the early 1990s. Every U.S. preferential trade agreement (PTA) since then has incorporated legally binding and enforceable provisions on labor rights in the text of the agreement. For instance, the U.S.-Jordan PTA, negotiated in 2000, includes a section on labor in the main text of the agreement and makes it subject to the same dispute settlement procedures and remedies as the rest of the agreement. Thus, if consultations, a dispute settlement panel, and the joint committee created to implement the agreement as a whole do not resolve a dispute, the complaining party is authorized "to take any appropriate and commensurate measure." The U.S.-Jordan labor text is also the first to reference the 1998 ILO declaration defining core labor standards—although achieving compliance with the ILO standards is stated as an aspiration rather than an obligation. The agreement with Jordan, like those that followed up to 2007, continues to use the previous U.S. definition of "internationally recognized labor rights," which excludes nondiscrimination and includes "acceptable conditions of work" with respect to minimum wages, hours of work, and occupational safety and health. Each of the other U.S. PTAs negotiated with Arab countries during the period—those with Bahrain, Morocco, and Oman—retained the Jordan practices of incorporating the labor chapter into the main text and using the same general dispute settlement process for labor as for other parts of the agreement.

While members of the Partnership are committed to those core labor standards, the Deauville Partnership could support their effective implementation. In its trade agreements with developing countries, Canada has followed a path regarding labor standards that is adapted to its constitutional structure and political needs, but with language on labor standards that is similar to that in the U.S. PTAs. The key differences are not so much in the legal obligations that each country seeks to promote as in the enforcement measures and the relative role of cooperation in protecting worker rights. Traditionally, agreements to which the EU is a party often have language addressing human rights, not worker rights specifically (see next section). However, the economic partnership agreement between the EU and the Caribbean region contains provisions on worker rights. The relevant section in the CARIFORUM agreement reaffirms the parties' commitment to internationally recognized labor standards, as defined in the ILO Declaration, but it also recognizes the right of the parties to "establish their own social regulations and labor standards in line with their own social development priorities." The parties then agree that they should not "encourage trade or FDI to enhance or maintain a competitive advantage" by weakening labor laws.

Whatever the details of the language on labor standards in trade agreements, and in line with the aspirations of the Arab Spring, the Deauville Partnership could also provide a framework for financial and technical capacity-building assistance to improve implementation of core labor standards in Partnership countries. Precedents do exist. A 2009 investigation by the U.S. Government Accountability Office looked at the implementation of four U.S. PTAs, with Chile, Jordan, Morocco, and Singapore. It concluded that free trade agreement negotiations spurred some labor reforms in each of the selected partners, but that progress has been uneven and U.S. engagement limited. An example cited was Morocco's enactment of a long-stalled overhaul of its labor code. However, partners reported that enforcement of labor laws continues to be a challenge, and some significant labor abuses have emerged (USGAO 2009). Another example is the 2008 Better Work Jordan project, supported by the ILO and the International Finance Corporation (IFC) and jointly funded by the Jordanian government and the U.S. Agency for International Development (USAID). The project independently monitors factory conditions in the Jordanian garment industry to encourage improvements in labor standards compliance and boost the industry's performance in global supply chains (box 6.2).

Human Rights

A shared understanding among partners of the human values embodied in the goods or services being exchanged would also improve the chances of success of the integration strategy.[2] Respect for fundamental freedoms can no longer be disentangled from the pursuit of sustainable and inclusive trade and investment relationships. Contrary to what used to be conventional wisdom, trade and human rights go hand in hand (Lamy 2010). Open trade and human rights are based on the same values: individual freedom and responsibility, nondiscrimination, transparency, welfare. Both are aimed at advancing human liberties and opportunities. International obligations undertaken by countries must therefore be respected, whether in trade or human rights. If designed carefully, human rights provisions in trade and investment relations can work both to improve governance and to empower people to claim their rights (Aaronson 2011).

Freedom of exchange is not merely a means to spur economic growth, create jobs, and reduce poverty; it is also a way to advance human liberties (Chauffour 2009). Trade policy delineates the freedom of exchange across national boundaries, which in turn directly affects people's freedom and development. Provided that the exchange between two parties does not have adverse impact on a third party, any restriction on the ability of individuals to enter into a mutually beneficial exchange, whether domestic or international, should be regarded as a danger to individual freedom and economic growth. Trade liberalization is often presented as a threat to human rights—accused of being unfair, of exacerbating inequality, both within and between countries, and of inciting a race to the bottom on social welfare standards, environmental standards, worker protection legislation, and so on. Ironically, it is the very restrictions and discrimination that liberalization seeks to remove that constitute the true threat to human rights.

BOX 6.2

Jordan: Responding to a Sweatshop Scandal through Capacity Building and Monitoring

In early 2006, the National Labor Committee, a New York–based nongovernmental organization that investigates labor abuses around the world, released a report alleging serious violations of worker rights in Jordanian garment factories employing mainly migrant workers from South Asia and China and exporting to the United States. The AFL-CIO, the main U.S. union federation, took up the case, filing a petition under the U.S. PTA with Jordan and pointing out a major gap in Jordanian labor laws, which require workers to be citizens in order to be eligible to join unions.

The Jordanian government responded immediately and, in coordination with USAID, ordered an independent investigation, which confirmed many of the labor committee's allegations. The government also took a number of immediate steps between May 2006 and the end of the year, which included raising the minimum wage, increasing the Ministry of Labor budget by 80 percent, beefing up inspections and closing some factories, creating a multilingual hotline for worker complaints, launching a review of its labor laws with the aim of bringing them

closer to international standards, and reaching agreement with the ILO on developing a Decent Work country program.

In February 2008, Jordan, the ILO, and the IFC launched the Better Work Jordan project, jointly funded by the Jordanian government and USAID. In addition to independent monitoring and transparent reporting on factory conditions to encourage improvements in labor standards compliance, the project also has an explicit objective of improving "enterprise performance in global supply chains in developing countries." The factory assessments will be entered in a database that can be made available to buyers or others as desired by participating factories. Public reports will be issued containing aggregated data on trends and the key issues uncovered, as well as documents naming individual factories and providing indicators of performance in key areas. It is hoped that the system will be credible enough that international buyers will forgo their own factory audits, as Walmart and Sears/Kmart have agreed to do, thereby lowering costs for both factory and consumer.

Source: Elliott 2011.

Freedom of exchange is also a means to promote other dimensions of freedom. Trade and FDI restrictions in the form of tariff and nontariff barriers (e.g., quotas, licenses, marketing restrictions, exchange rate controls) have the effect of limiting, reducing, or delaying the ability of individuals to pursue their economic goals. As a result, they constitute a threat to the principle of freedom of exchange and nondiscrimination. Openness to trade likely leads to a higher rate of interchange of ideas and information among countries (Sykes 2003). As trade expands, individuals exchange ideas, technologies, processes, and cultural norms and goods. In turn, as people in nations with fewer rights and freedoms become aware of conditions elsewhere, internal pressures for greater rights may grow. Isolated societies, by contrast, may be more prone to human rights abuses (van Hees 2004). Empirical evidence tends to confirm the positive link between openness of trade, the level of civil liberties and political rights, and democracy (Hamilton 2002). Looking at the spatial dependence in economic freedom between geographic neighbors and trade partners, Sobel and Leeson (2007) found evidence that economic freedom does indeed spread through both geography and trade, though modestly. By fighting protectionism and liberalizing their trade with foreign nations, economically free countries maximize the odds of exerting a positive impact on economic freedom in less-free nations.

International agreements linking trade and human rights have the potential to support homegrown change as they set up mechanisms for dialogue, allowing civil society in multiple countries to foster effective commitment to international norms. To be sure, many economists conclude that policy makers need not include human rights provisions in trade agreements, even though trade can have positive human rights spillovers (Bhagwati 1996, 1; Sykes 2003, 2–4). Yet whether or not human rights is considered a trade issue, the fact of the matter is that trade agreements are a means to promote governance, transparency, and participation. Recent research suggests that these agreements empower domestic as well as foreign actors, who gain benefits from increased transparency, greater evenhandedness, and the due process rules promoted in these agreements.

Many of the world's most important trading partners, from the United States, Canada, and the EU to Brazil and Chile, include human rights language in their PTAs (table 6.3). It has been estimated that over 75 percent of the world's governments now participate in PTAs with human rights provisions (Aaronson 2011). These nations have adopted various strategies for embedding human rights provisions in trade agreements. The EU has been the most enthusiastic proponent of the inclusion of human rights provisions in PTAs and has included human rights clauses in all its Association Agreements with Partnership countries. Until recently, the United States sought to promote certain specific human rights in its trade agreements. As noted in the preceding section, the United States was initially most concerned about using these agreements to advance labor rights among U.S. PTA partners. More recently, the United States has broadened its PTA chapters to encourage transparency (access to information), public participation, and due process. Although the lan-

TABLE 6.3

Examples of Human Rights in Preferential Trade Agreements: Comparing the European Free Trade Association, the European Union, the United States, and Canada

Feature of agreement	European Free Trade Association	European Union	United States	Canada
Strategy	Universal human rights	Universal human rights and specific human rights	Specific human rights	Specific human rights
Which rights?		Labor rights, transparency, due process, political participation, privacy rights	Transparency, due process, political participation, access to affordable medicines, labor rights	Transparency, due process, political participation, labor rights, privacy rights, cultural and indigenous rights
How enforced?	No enforcement.	Human rights violations lead to dialogue and possible suspension, depending on nature of violation.	In newest agreements, labor rights can be disputed under dispute settlement body affiliated with the agreement. Process begins with bilateral dialogue to resolve issues.	Monetary penalties, but only for labor rights. Use dialogue first.

Source: Aaronson 2011.

guage in these chapters varies from agreement to agreement, in general the passages are framed in the language of human rights. They require governments to publish, in advance, laws, rules, procedures, and regulations affecting trade, thereby giving "persons of the other party that are directly affected by an agency's process . . . a reasonable opportunity to present facts and arguments in support of their positions prior to any final administrative action." These agreements also contain a section on review and appeal, designed to give the parties a reasonable opportunity to support or defend their respective positions.

Drawing on international experience, Partnership countries may see the introduction of human rights provisions in trade agreements as a way to secure democratic change for the long haul. Those normative provisions may encourage future partner governments to allow public participation and continue to encourage citizens to engage and challenge policy makers. For instance, since signing free trade agreements with the United States, PTA partners Chile, the Dominican Republic, Jordan, Mexico, and Morocco have established channels through which organized civil society can comment on trade policies (Aaronson and Zimmerman 2007). Deauville partners could usefully support Partnership countries in promoting a trade and FDI agenda based on a core set of fundamental freedoms. This would involve enhanced cooperation to monitor and review Partnership countries' obligations and increased support for their effective implementation.

Indeed, the Deauville Partnership is ultimately a vehicle for dialogue, cooperation, and support. Promoting a trade and FDI strategy that is embedded in shared human values, including respect for fundamental freedoms, will be a way to unify the three pillars of the partnership: the trade/commercial pillar would converge with the governance and finance pillars to support the democratic transition and homegrown strategies for sustainable and inclusive growth.

Societal policies: Key selected recommendations

Short-term:

- Reform the legal and regulatory environment in Partnership countries to facilitate women's participation in the labor force and make more jobs available to women by, inter alia, reducing the distortionary effect of the public sector on the private labor market, reforming education to better equip young women with skills required by industry, amending laws that discourage firms from hiring women (e.g., employer-funded maternity leave and restrictions on women working in certain industries or at night), revising limitations on women's mobility (e.g., guardianship laws), and protecting women from harassment in the workplace and on their way to work.

Medium-term:

- Use future deep and high-quality trade agreements with Deauville partners as a framework to coordinate approaches in promoting and implementing core labor and human rights standards.

Notes

1. This section draws on Elliott (2011).
2. This section draws on Aaronson (2011).

References

Aaronson, Susan Ariel. 2011. "Human Rights." In *Preferential Trade Agreement Policies for Development: A Handbook*, ed. Jean-Pierre Chauffour and Jean-Christophe Maur, 443–66. Washington, DC: World Bank.

Aaronson, Susan Ariel, and Jamie Zimmerman. 2007. *Trade Imbalance: The Struggle to Weigh Human Rights in Trade Policymaking*. New York: Cambridge University Press.

Achy, Lahcen, and Khalid Sekkat. 2011. "Training, New Equipment and Job Creation: A Firm-level Analysis Using Moroccan Data." *Journal of Development Research* 23 (4): 615–29.

Aedo, Cristián, and Sergio Núñez. 2001. "The Impact of Training Policies in Latin America and the Caribbean: The Case of Programa Joven." Research Network Working Paper R-483, Inter-American Development Bank, Washington, DC.

Aidt, Toke, and Zafiris Tzannatos. 2002. *Unions and Collective Bargaining: Economic Effects in a Global Environment.* Washington, DC: World Bank.

Attanasio, Orazio, Adriana Kugler, and Costas Meghir. 2008. "Training Disadvantaged Youth in Latin America: Evidence from a Randomized Trial." NBER Working Papers 13931, National Bureau of Economic Research, Cambridge, MA.

Baldwin, Richard. 1989. "Measureable Dynamic Gains from Trade." NBER Working Paper 3147, National Bureau of Economic Research, Cambridge, MA.

———. 2001. "Core-Periphery Model with Forward-Looking Expectations." Regional Science and Urban Economics 31 (1): 21–49.

Bhagwati, Jagdish. 1996. "Introduction to Economic Analysis." Vol. 1 of *Fair Trade and Harmonization: Prerequisites for Free Trade?* ed. Jagdish Bhagwati and Robert Hudec. Cambridge, MA: MIT Press.

Brülhart, Marius, and Federica Sbergami. 2009. "Agglomeration and Growth: Cross-Country Evidence." *Journal of Urban Economics* 65 (1): 48–63.

Chauffour, Jean-Pierre. 2009. *The Power of Freedom: Uniting Human Rights and Development.* Washington, DC: Cato Institute.

Davis, James, and J. Vernon Henderson. 2008. "The Agglomeration of Headquarters." *Regional Science and Urban Economics* 38 (5): 445–60.

Duflo, Esther. 2000. "Child Health and Household Resources in South Africa: Evidence from the Old Age Pension Program." *American Economic Review* 90 (2): 393–98.

Duflo, Esther, and Christopher Udry. 2004. "Intrahousehold Resource Allocation in Côte d'Ivoire: Social Norms, Separate Accounts and Consumption Choices." NBER Working Paper 10498, National Bureau of Economic Research, Cambridge, MA.

Elliott, Kimberly Ann. 2011. "Labor Rights." In *Preferential Trade Agreement Policies for Development: A Handbook*, ed. Jean-Pierre Chauffour and Jean-Christophe Maur, 427–42. Washington, DC: World Bank.

Freeman, Richard B., and James L. Medoff. 1984. *What Do Unions Do?* New York: Basic Books.

Glaeser, Edward L., Matthew G. Resseger, and Kristina Tobio. 2008. "Urban Inequality." NBER Working Paper 14419, National Bureau of Economic Research, Cambridge, MA.

Grossman, Gene M., and Elhanan Helpman. 1991. "Trade, Knowledge Spillovers, and Growth." *European Economic Review* 35 (2–3): 517–26.

Hamilton, Carl B. 2002. "Globalization and Democracy." CEPR Discussion Paper 3653, Centre for Economic Policy Research, London.

Hoekman, Bernard, and Beata Smarzynska Javorcik. 2004. "Policies Facilitating Firm Adjustment to Globalization." Policy Research Working Paper 3441, World Bank, Washington, DC.

Iacovone, Leonardo, and Beata Javorcik. 2010. "Multi-product Exporters: Product Churning, Uncertainty and Export Discoveries." *Economic Journal* 120 (May): 481–99.

Khanna, Gaurav, David Newhouse, and Pierella Paci. 2011. "Fewer Jobs or Smaller Paychecks? Aggregate Crisis Impacts in Selected Middle-Income Countries." Policy Research Working Paper 5791, World Bank, Washington, DC.

Krugman, Paul, and Anthony Venables. 1990. "Integration and the Competitiveness of Peripheral Industry." CEPR Discussion Paper 363, Centre for Economic Policy Research, London.

Lamy, Pascal. 2010. "Trade and Human Rights Go Hand in Hand." Presentation to United Nations Institute for Training and Research, September 26. http://www.wto.org/english/news_e/sppl_e/sppl172_e.htm.

Meschi, Elena, and Marco Vivarelli. 2007. "Globalization and Income Inequality." IZA Discussion Paper 2958, Institute for the Study of Labor, Bonn, Germany.

Motohashi, Kazuyuki. 2002. "Use of Plant-Level Micro-Data for the Evaluation of SME Innovation Policy in Japan," OECD Science, Technology and Industry Working Paper 2002/12, Organisation for Economic Co-operation and Development, Paris.

Noland, Marcus, and Howard Pack. 2003. *Industrial Policy in an Era of Globalization: Lessons from Asia.* Washington, DC: Peterson Institute for International Economics.

OECD (Organisation for Economic Co-operation and Development). 2011. *OECD Regional Outlook 2011: Building Resilient Regions for Stronger Economies.* Paris: OECD.

Pakes, Ariel, and Richard Ericson. 1998. "Empirical Implications of Alternative Models of Firm Dynamics." *Journal of Economic Theory* 79 (1): 1–46.

Porto, Guido, and Bernard M. Hoekman, eds. 2010. *Trade Adjustment Costs in Developing Countries: Impacts, Determinants and Policy Responses.* Washington, DC: Center for Economic and Policy Research and World Bank.

Puga, Diego, and Anthony Venables. 1998. "Trading Arrangements and Industrial Development." *World Bank Economic Review* 12 (2): 221–49.

Revenga, Ana, Michelle Riboud, and Hong Tan. 1994. "The Impact of Mexico's Retraining Program on Employment and Wages." *World Bank Economic Review* 8 (2): 247–77.

Rosholm, Michael, Helena Skyt Nielsen, and Andrew Dabalen. 2007. "Evaluation of Training in African Enterprises." *Journal of Development Economics* 84 (1): 310–29.

Sekkat, Khalid. 2011. "Firm Sponsored Training and Productivity in Morocco." *Journal of Development Studies* 47 (9): 1391–409.

Sobel, Russell, and Peter Leeson. 2007. "The Spread of Global Freedom." In *Economic Freedom in the World: 2007 Annual Report,* ed. James Gwartney, Randall Holcombe, and Robert Lawson, 29–37. Vancouver, Canada: Fraser Institute.

Sykes, Alan O'Neil. 2003. "International Trade and Human Rights: An Economic Perspective." Olin Working Paper 188, University of Chicago Law School, Chicago, IL.

USGAO (U.S. Government Accountability Office). 2009. *International Trade: Four Free Trade Agreements GAO Reviewed Have Resulted in Commercial Benefits, but Challenges on Labor and Environment Remain.* GAO Highlights 09-439. Washington, DC: GAO.

van Hees, Floris. 2004. "Protection v. Protectionism: The Use of Human Rights Arguments in the Debate for and against the Liberalization of Trade." Abo Akademi University, Turku, Finland. http://web.abo.fi/instut/imr/norfa/floris.pdf

World Bank. 2008. *World Development Report 2009: Reshaping Economic Geography.* Washington, DC: World Bank.

————. 2011. *World Development Report 2012: Gender Equality and Development.* Washington, DC: World Bank.

Potential for Diversification into More Sophisticated Products in Partnership Countries

While the Deauville Partnership countries, except for Libya, display some diversification over the years (see box 2.2 in chapter 2), their exports remain concentrated in peripheral clusters such as petroleum, garments, textiles, and agricultural products. This is shown by their revealed comparative advantage (RCA) in tables A.1 through A.5. The Arab Republic of Egypt and Tunisia appear to have acquired more RCA in products closer to the core of world trade during the 2000s, such as electronics, machinery, chemicals, road vehicles, and metal manufacturing.

Figures A.1 through A.5 depict products in which countries have an RCA as "black boxes" in each country's product space. The size of each node (or box) represents the share of that product in total world exports, according to the product space methodology of Hausmann and Klinger (2007). This concept is based on the assumption that the production processes of different products are related. Production processes of two different and seemingly unrelated products might involve similar factor intensities of labor or human capital, similar levels of technological sophistication, or vertically integrated value chains of production, or they might require similar product-specific institutions (e.g., quality standards, research) or infrastructure (e.g., cooling and storage facilities, transportation, information and communication technologies). Thus, countries that are already successful in producing product A (e.g., milk and cream) might also be successful in producing a new but related product B (e.g., cheese and curd). The product space illustrates the existence of a densely connected core of products and several peripheral clusters. Products with high productivity content are typically located in the core of world trade in manufactured products. If a country has an RCA in many products close to the core (or some densely connected cluster), it has a better diversification potential.

Firms in *Egypt* diversified to some extent into core industries during the 2000s. Only a few Egyptian export successes were close to the core of the product space in 2000–02, namely paper and paperboard, pharmaceu-

TABLE A.1

Egypt: RCA for Selected Products with Highest Export Share, 2000–02 and 2007–09

Egypt, Arab Rep. 2000–02		Egypt, Arab Rep. 2007–09	
RCA in 131 products	% of total exports	RCA in 176 products	% of total exports
Cotton (other than linters)	8.08	Petroleum gases	17.96
Sinks, wash basins, bidets, water closets	4.54	Mineral or chemical fertilizers, nitrogenous	2.95
Cotton yarn	4.30	Oranges, mandarins, clementines	1.88
Rice, semi-milled or wholly milled	4.01	Wood- and resin-based chemical products	1.59
Bed linen, table linen	3.90	Building and monumental stone	1.43
Chemical elements	2.26	Carpets, carpeting and rugs	0.81
Building and monumental stone	2.16	Potatoes, fresh or chilled	0.79
Mineral or chemical fertilizers, nitrogenous	1.95	Natural calcium phosphate	0.74
Coke and semi-coke of coal, lignite, or peat	1.69	Petroleum jelly and mineral waxes	0.73
Oranges, mandarins, clementines	1.45	Mineral or chemical fertilizers, phosphatic	0.42
Cotton fabrics, woven, unbleached	1.31	Plants, seeds, fruit used in perfumery	0.33
Potatoes, fresh or chilled	1.13	Molasses	0.19
Building and monumental stone	1.00	Guano	0.17
Sanitary or toilet articles	0.85	Flax and ramie, flax tow, ramie noils	0.08
Molasses	0.79	Copra	0.03

Note: RCA = revealed comparative advantage.

FIGURE A.1

Egypt: Product Space, 2007–09

(Black boxes in the product space depict products in which the country has a revealed comparative advantage)

Source: World Bank calculations from UN Comtrade data.

Note: n.e.s = not elsewhere specified. The numbers in brackets refer to the 4-digit SITC product classification from the United Nations.

TABLE A.2

Jordan: RCA for Selected Products with Highest Export Share, 2000–02 and 2007–09

Jordan 2000–02		Jordan 2007–09	
RCA in 119 products	% of total exports	RCA in 106 products	% of total exports
Medicaments (including veterinary)	9.35	Mineral or chemical fertilizers, potassic	9.95
Natural calcium phosphates, natural aluminum	5.85	Other outer garments and clothing	9.50
Trousers, breeches, etc., of textile fabrics	3.97	Medicaments (including veterinary)	8.68
Mineral or chemical fertilizers, nitrogenous	3.51	Natural calcium phosphates, natural aluminum	6.94
Shirts, men's, of textile fabrics	3.51	Mineral or chemical fertilizers, nitrogenous	5.72
Other fresh or chilled vegetables	3.32	Other fresh or chilled vegetables	3.61
Animal/vegetable oils and fats	3.10	Tomatoes, fresh or chilled	3.43
Inorganic acids and oxygen compound	2.97	Inorganic acids and oxygen compound	2.70
Tomatoes, fresh or chilled	2.84	Insulated electical wire, cable, bars	2.40
Suits, men's, of textile fabrics	2.53	Casks, drums, boxes of iron/steel	2.39
Portland cement	1.95	Jewelry of gold, silver or platinum	2.31
Undergarments, knitted of cotton	1.86	Metallic salts and peroxysalts	1.93
Jackets, blazers of textile fabrics	1.80	Jerseys, pull-overs, twinsets, cardigans	1.90
Cigarettes	1.36	Other outer garments of textile fabrics	1.71
Paper and paperboard, corrugated, crepe	1.28	Under garments, knitted, of synthetics	1.69

Note: RCA = revealed comparative advantage.

FIGURE A.2

Jordan: Product Space, 2007–09

(Black boxes in the product space depict products in which the country has a revealed comparative advantage)

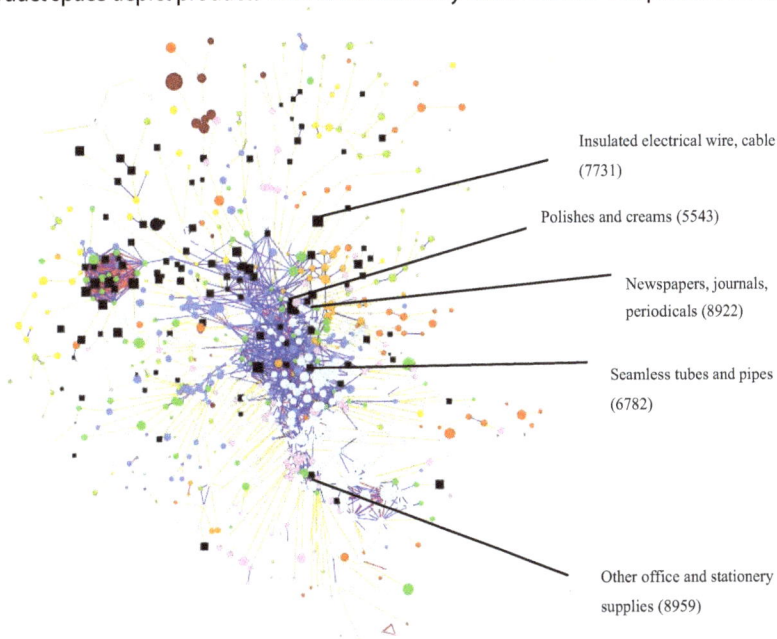

Insulated electrical wire, cable (7731)

Polishes and creams (5543)

Newspapers, journals, periodicals (8922)

Seamless tubes and pipes (6782)

Other office and stationery supplies (8959)

Source: World Bank calculations from UN Comtrade data.

Note: n.e.s = not elsewhere specified. The numbers in brackets refer to the 4-digit SITC product classification from the United Nations.

TABLE A.3

Libya: RCA for Selected Products with Highest Export Share, 2000–02 and 2007–09

Libya 2000–02		Libya 2007–09	
RCA in 14 products	% of total exports	RCA in 12 products	% of total exports
Petroleum oils and crude oils	91.93		
Petroleum gases	2.10	Petroleum oils and crude oils	86.87
Acyclic hydrocarbons	1.14	Petroleum gases	7.16
Mineral or chemical fertilizers, nitrogenous	0.72	Petroleum gases	1.85
Acyclic alcohols	0.92	Gold, nonmonetary	0.95
Iron or steel coils for re-rolling	0.47	Acyclic hydrocarbons	0.67
Mineral tars and products	0.38	Acyclic alcohols	0.40
Iron or steel powders	0.26	Iron or steel coils for re-rolling	0.39
Other inorganic bases and metallic oxides	0.23	Mineral or chemical fertilizers, nitrogenous	0.36
Kerosene and other medium oils	0.18	Mineral tars and products	0.25
Sheep and lamb skins without the wool	0.06	Iron or steel powders	0.18
Groundnuts (peanuts)	0.05	Sulfur of all kinds	0.05
Roasted iron pyrites	0.003	Sheep and lamb skins without the wool	0.01
Goat and kid skins	0.00		

Note: RCA = revealed comparative advantage.

FIGURE A.3

Libya: Product Space, 2007–09
(Black boxes in the product space depict products in which the country has a revealed comparative advantage)

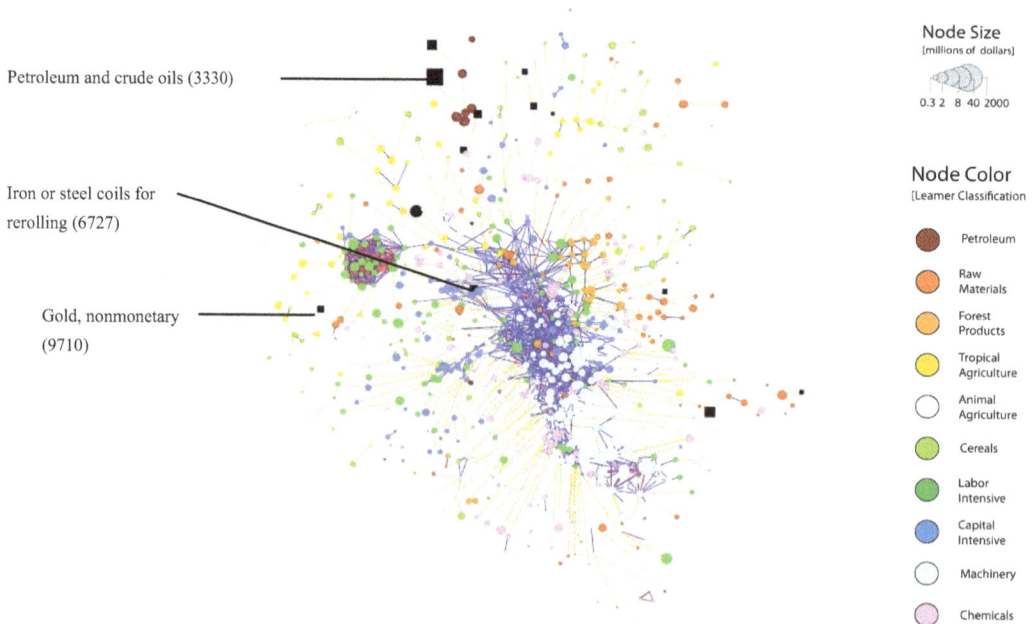

Source: World Bank calculations from UN Comtrade data.

Note: n.e.s = not elsewhere specified. The numbers in brackets refer to the 4-digit SITC product classification from the United Nations.

TABLE A.4

Morocco: RCA for Selected Products with Highest Export Share, 2000–02 and 2007–09

Morocco 2000–02		Morocco 2007–09	
RCA in 115 products	% of total exports	RCA in 130 products	% of total exports
Crustaceans and mollusks	7.54	Inorganic acids and oxygen compound	10.57
Inorganic acids and oxygen compound	6.60	Insulated, elect. wire, cable, bars	7.58
Other outer garments of textile fabric	6.41	Natural calcium phosphates, natural aluminum	7.46
Diodes, transistors	6.12	Fertilizers, n.e.s.	4.43
Trousers, breeches, etc., of textile fabric	5.34	Crustaceans and mollusks	3.90
Natural calcium phosphates, natural aluminum	5.20	Other outer garments of textile fabric	3.83
Fertilizer, n.e.s.	3.74	Diodes, transistors	3.67
Insulated, electrical wire, cable, bars	3.40	Fish, prepared or preserved	3.48
Fish, prepared or preserved	3.16	Trousers, breeches, etc., of textile fabric	2.50
Undergarments, knitted of cotton	2.75	Oranges, mandarins, clementines	2.05
Oranges, mandarins, clementines	2.64	Mineral or chemical fertilizers, phosphatic	1.82
Jerseys, pull-overs, twinsets, cardigans	2.56	Electrical appliances such as switches	1.76
Other outer garments and clothing	2.42	Mineral tars	1.70
Corsets, brassieres, suspenders	1.72	Footwear	1.65
Other outer garments of textile fabric	1.66	Tomatoes, fresh or chilled	1.61

Note: RCA = revealed comparative advantage; n.e.s. = not elsewhere specified.

FIGURE A.4

Morocco: Product Space, 2007–09

(Black boxes in the product space depict products in which the country has a revealed comparative advantage)

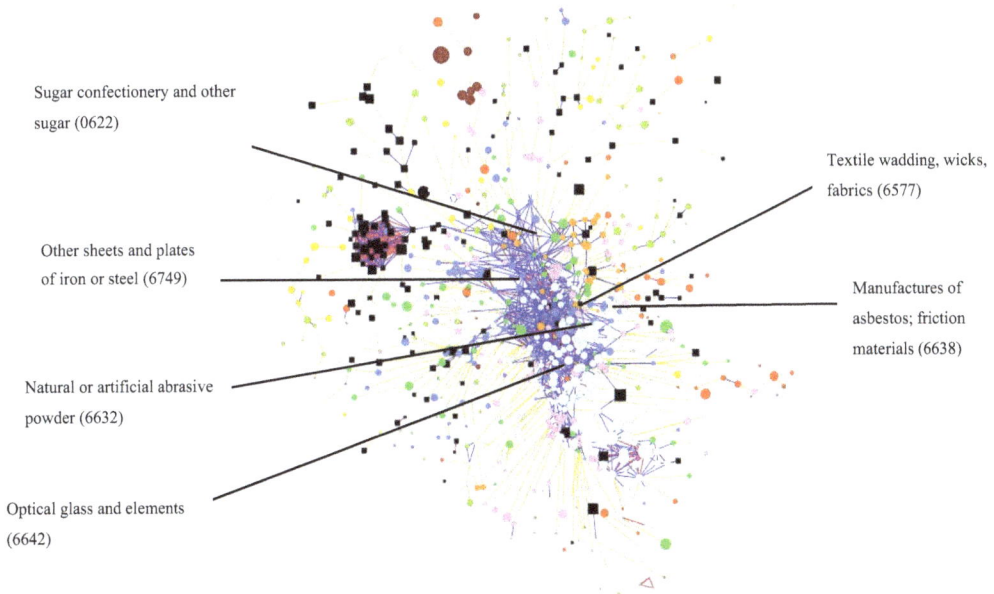

Sugar confectionery and other sugar (0622)

Textile wadding, wicks, fabrics (6577)

Other sheets and plates of iron or steel (6749)

Manufactures of asbestos; friction materials (6638)

Natural or artificial abrasive powder (6632)

Optical glass and elements (6642)

Source: World Bank calculations from UN Comtrade data.
Note: n.e.s = not elsewhere specified. The numbers in brackets refer to the 4-digit SITC product classification from the United Nations.

TABLE A.5

Tunisia: RCA for Selected Products with Highest Export Share, 2000–02 and 2007–09

Tunisia 2000–02		Tunisia 2007–09	
RCA in 131 products	% of total exports	RCA in 140 products	% of total exports
Trousers, breeches, etc., of textile fabric	9.86	Petroleum oils and crude oils	13.35
Petroleum oils and crude oils	8.44	Insulated electrical wire, cable, bars	5.46
Other outer garments of textile fabric	6.96	Electical appliances such as switches, relays.	4.87
Other outer garments of textile fabric	6.34	Trousers, breeches, etc., of textile fabric	4.78
Insulated electrical wire, cable, bars	4.11	Other outer garments of textile fabric	4.73
Electrical appliances such as switches	2.89	Fertilizers, n.e.s.	3.53
Fertilizers, n.e.s.	2.83	Olive oil	3.49
Footwear	2.65	Other outer garments of textile fabric	3.48
Inorganic acids and oxygen compound	2.61	Inorganic acids and oxygen compound	2.79
Jerseys, pull-overs, twinsets, cardigans	2.47	Mineral or chemical fertilizers, phosphatic	2.56
Parts of footwear	2.30	Footwear	2.48
Undergarments, knitted of cotton	2.16	Undergarments, knitted of cotton	2.09
Corsets, brassieres, suspenders	2.14	Jerseys, pull-overs, twinsets, cardigans	1.49
Other outer garments and clothing	1.99	Metallic salts and peroxysalts	1.39
Olive oil	1.99	Fruit, fresh or dried, n.e.s.	1.26

Note: RCA = revealed comparative advantage; n.e.s. = not elsewhere specified.

FIGURE A.5

Tunisia: Product Space, 2007–09

(Black boxes in the product space depict products in which the country has a revealed comparative advantage)

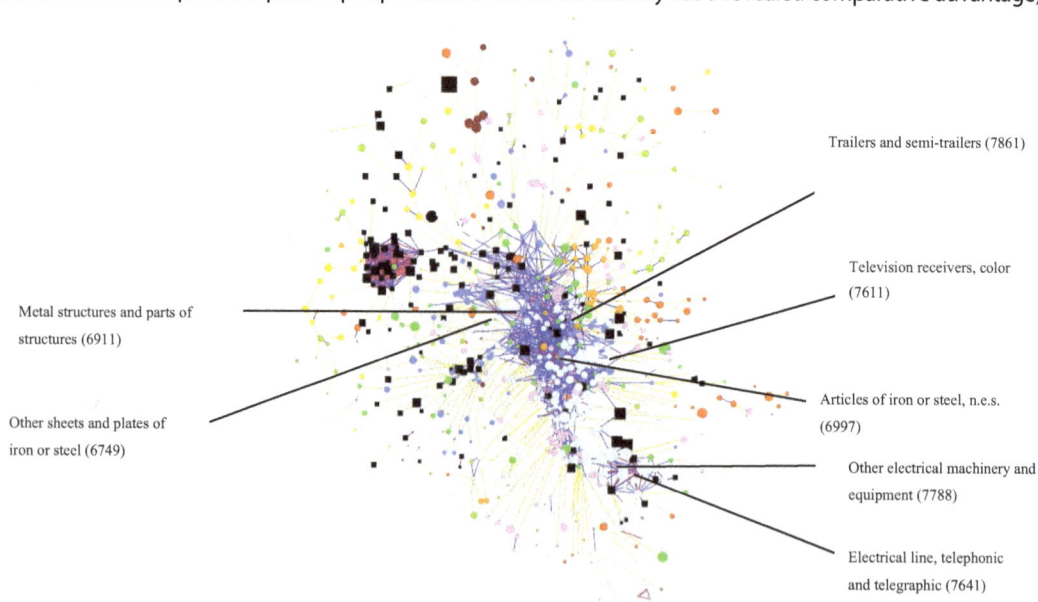

Trailers and semi-trailers (7861)

Television receivers, color (7611)

Metal structures and parts of structures (6911)

Articles of iron or steel, n.e.s. (6997)

Other sheets and plates of iron or steel (6749)

Other electrical machinery and equipment (7788)

Electrical line, telephonic and telegraphic (7641)

Source: World Bank calculations from UN Comtrade data.

Note: n.e.s = not elsewhere specified. The numbers in brackets refer to the 4-digit SITC product classification from the United Nations.

tical goods, and sanitary/toilet parts. Figure A.1 illustrates the product space for Egypt in 2007–09, revealing an increasing number of export successes in products that are more connected to the core. Egypt succeeded in developing RCA in household refrigerators, iron and steel, etc., bringing its product specialization to the core of the product space, which has many related products. Egypt has increased RCA in manufacture of metals, road vehicles, and general industrial machinery.

Jordan appears to have lost RCAs between 2000–02 and 2007–09 (table A.2). While it has gained some RCA in five products close to the core (including printed matter, office and stationary supplies, and soap and cleansing preparations), it has lost RCAs in about 10 products that were closely connected to the dense part of the product space, namely metalworking machinery, general industrial machinery and equipment, nonmetallic mineral manufactures, iron and steel, manufactures of metal, road vehicles, and plastics in nonprimary form (figure A.2).

The product space shows that *Libya* typically has RCAs in weakly connected peripheral clusters (crude oil, gold, and derived petroleum products, etc.) and none at the core (figure A.3). In 2000–02 Libya showed RCAs in iron and steel and derived products (bars and rods of iron and steel). However, all these products show a decrease in the RCA during the 2000s (table A.3). Libya's product space is concentrated around the oil industry.

In 2000–02, *Morocco* had RCAs for only two products in the densely connected core (nonelectrical measurement instruments and manufactures of asbestos). Morocco has gained one additional RCA. Morocco's exports exhibited some diversification away from agriculture and fertilizers to manufacturing with moderate technological content. Such new industries include apparel and parts and components related to automobiles. Morocco appears to have also specialized in mineral manufacture over the years, as well as in sugar confectionery and optical glass and elements.

In 2000–02, *Tunisia* had RCA close to the core in articles of plastics and rotary converters (motors and generators) as well as chemical-related products such as varnishes and lacquers. Firms in Tunisia appear to have gained RCAs in road vehicles (mainly trailers), telecommunication equipment (television receivers), and household-type electrical equipment and electrical parts for line telephony, as well as metal manufacturing.

Additional Sources Consulted

Dadush, Uri, and William Shaw. 2011. *Juggernaut: How Emerging Markets Are Reshaping Globalization*. Washington, DC: Carnegie Endowment for International Peace.

Fernandez-Stark, Karina, Penny Bamber, and Gary Gereffi. 2011. *The Offshore Services Global Value Chain: Economic Upgrading and Workforce Development*. Chapel Hill, NC: Duke Center on Globalization, Governance, and Competitiveness.

Fink, Carsten. 2008. "Services PTAs: Friends or Foes of the Multilateralism?" In *Opening Markets for Trade in Services: Countries and Sectors in Bilateral and WTO Negotiations*, ed. Juan A. Marchetti and Martin Roy. Geneva: World Trade Organization.

Hausmann, Ricardo, and Bailey Klinger. 2007. "The Structure of the Product Space and the Evolution of Comparative Advantage." CID Working Paper 128, Center for International Development, Harvard University, Cambridge, MA.

Hoekman, Bernard, and Aaditya Mattoo. 2011. "Services Trade Liberalization and Regulatory Reform: Re-invigorating International Cooperation." Policy Research Working Paper 5517, World Bank, Washington, DC.

Mattoo, Aaditya, and Lucy Payton, eds. 2007. *Services Trade and Development: The Experience of Zambia*. Washington, DC: World Bank.

Mattoo, Aaditya, and Pierre Sauvé. 2011. "Services." In *Preferential Trade Agreement Policies for Development: A Handbook*, ed. Jean-Pierre Chauffour and Jean-Christophe Maur. Washington, DC: World Bank.

Mattoo, Aaditya, and Robert Stern. 2008. "Overview." In *A Handbook of International Trade in Services*, ed. Aaditya Mattoo, Robert Stern, and Gianni Zanini. New York: Oxford University Press.

Messerlin, Patrick, Michael Emerson, Gia Jandieri, and Alexandre Le Vernoy. 2011. *An Appraisal of the EU's Trade Policy towards Its Eastern Neighbours: The Case of Georgia*. Brussels: Center for European Policy Studies.

Miroudot, Sebastien, and Ben Shepherd. 2012. "Regional Trade Agreements and Trade Costs in Services." Unpublished paper, Groupe d'Économie Mondiale de SciencesPo, Paris.

O'Sullivan, Anthony. 2010. "FDI Trends in the MENA Region and Persisting Policy Challenges." Contribution to the Working Group on Investment Policies and Promotion, MENA-OECD Investment Program.

Stephenson, Sherry, and Gary Hufbauer. 2011. "Labor Mobility." In *Preferential Trade Agreement Policies for Development: A Handbook*, ed. Jean-Pierre Chauffour and Jean-Christophe Maur. Washington, DC: World Bank.

World Bank. 2010. *Economic Integration in the GCC*. Office of the Chief Economist MENA Region. Washington, DC: World Bank.

———. 2010. *Economic Integration in the Maghreb*. Office of the Chief Economist MENA Region. Washington, DC: World Bank.

———. 2010. *Economic Integration in the Mashreq*. Office of the Chief Economist MENA Region, Washington, DC: World Bank.

www.ingramcontent.com/pod-product-compliance
Lightning Source LLC
Chambersburg PA
CBHW080412270326
41929CB00018B/2992